THE FORGOTTEN PALESTINIANS

Born in Haifa, Israel, ILAN PAPPÉ is Professor of History at the University of Exeter. He is the author of numerous books, including *A History of Modern Palestine: One Land, Two Peoples* (2003), *The Ethnic Cleansing of Palestine* (2006) and *Gaza in Crisis* (2010, with Noam Chomsky).

THE FORGOTTEN PALESTINIANS

A History of the Palestinians in Israel

Ilan Pappé

YALE UNIVERSITY PRESS
NEW HAVEN AND LONDON

In memory of the thirteen Palestinian citizens who were shot dead by the Israeli police in October 2000

Copyright © 2011 Ilan Pappé

First published in paperback in 2013

The right of Ilan Pappé to be identified as author of this work has been asserted by him in accordance with the Copyright, Designs and Patents Act 1988.

For information about this and other Yale University Press publications, please contact:
U.S. Office: sales.press@yale.edu   yalebooks.com
Europe Office: sales@yaleup.co.uk   www.yalebooks.co.uk

Library of Congress Cataloging-in-Publication Data

Pappé, Ilan.
Forgotten Palestinians : a history of the Palestinians in Israel / Ilan Pappé.
    p. cm.
  ISBN 978-0-300-13441-4 (cl : alk. paper)
  1. Palestinian Arabs—Israel—History. 2. Arab-Israeli conflict—History.
  3. Israel—Ethnic relations. 4. Minorities—Israel. I. Title.
  DS119.7.P288825 2011
  956.94'0049274—dc22

                                                                                    2010051045

Set in Janson Text by IDSUK (DataConnection) Ltd
Printed and bound by CPI Group (UK) Ltd, Croydon, CR0 4YY

A catalogue record for this book is available from the British Library.

ISBN 978-0-300-18432-7 (pbk)

2016 2015 2014 2013
10 9 8 7 6 5 4 3 2 1

MIX
Paper from
responsible sources
FSC
www.fsc.org   FSC® C013604

CONTENTS

And therefore,
If you wish, I will say I am the man
A Pre-Islamic Poet who spread his wings and flew into the desert
And I was a Jew before Jews floated on the Sea of Galilee,
And I was a sun-stricken Arab in the morrow's shift . . .
And I was a rock, an olive tree that remained.
All the country became home, but I was a stranger in it.
I was a Muslim in Jesus' land and a Catholic in the desert.
Not that any of this altered my way of life; only that I have not
*   forgotten*
That I was born in the sand, and wandered with the light until
*   I landed*
At the shadow of a callous knowledge tree.
I tasted its fruit.
I was eternally excommunicated, unable to return
Like the water that flowed and never returned to the river . . .

Salman Masalha, 'Final answer to the question
"How do you define yourself?" '

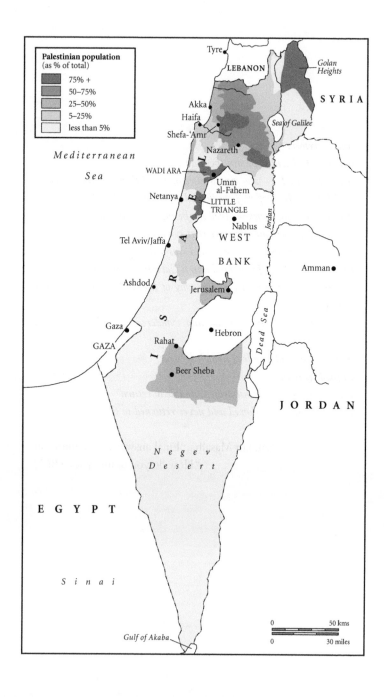

Palestinian population
(as % of total)

75% +
50–75%
25–50%
5–25%
less than 5%

Mediterranean
Sea

LEBANON

Tyre

Golan
Heights

S Y R I A

Akka
Haifa
Shefa-'Amr

Sea of Galilee

Nazareth

WADI ARA

Umm
al-Fahem

Netanya

LITTLE
TRIANGLE

Nablus

Tel Aviv/Jaffa

W E S T

B A N K

Amman

Ashdod

Jerusalem

Gaza

Hebron

Dead Sea

Jordan

I S R A E L

GAZA

Rahat

Beer Sheba

J O R D A N

N e g e v
D e s e r t

E G Y P T

S i n a i

0   50 kms

0   30 miles

Gulf of Akaba

HOSTILE ALIENS IN THEIR
OWN HOMELAND

THE EARLY ZIONIST settlers were compulsory diarists. They left the historians mountains of travelogues, journals and letters, writing from almost the moment they landed in Palestine, at the very beginning of the twentieth century. The land was unfamiliar and their journey from Eastern Europe was quite often harsh and dangerous. But they were well received, first in Jaffa where small boats took them ashore from their ships and where they looked for their first temporary abode or piece of land. The local Palestinians in most cases offered these newcomers some accommodation and advice on how to cultivate the land, something about which the Zionists had little to no knowledge as they had been barred for centuries from being farmers or landowners in their home countries.[1]

The settlers did not reciprocate in kind; at night, when they wrote the early entries in their diaries by candlelight, they referred to the native Palestinians as aliens roaming the land that belonged to the Jewish people. Some came with the notion that the land was empty and assumed that the people they found there were foreign invaders; others, like the founder of the Zionist movement, Theodor Herzl, knew that Palestine was not a land without people but believed that its native inhabitants could be 'spirited away' to make room for the Jewish return to, and redemption of, Eretz Israel.[2] To quote the late Ibrahim Abu Lughod, 'the denial and total disregard of the Palestinians *in situ* by early Zionist settlers shocked well-meaning but rather ineffectual Jewish European thinkers at the time'.[3]

The perception of the Palestinians as unwanted and unwelcome has remained a potent part of Zionist discourse and attitude in what became Israel in 1948. More than a century later, the descendants of some of these Palestinians are citizens of the Jewish state, but this status does not protect them from being regarded and treated as a dangerous threat in their own homeland. This attitude permeates the Israeli establishment, and is expressed in various different ways.

The Israeli College for National Security is the local 'West Point' for the most senior officers in the army and the officials in the security services, both for the domestic secret service, the Shabak, and for the famous (or infamous, as the case may be) Mossad. The future heads of the army and these security apparatuses have to graduate from this college, which works very closely with the University of Haifa's Center for National Security Studies and Geostrategy. Year after year they issue papers warning of the threat of 'Arab' takeover of land in the north and south of Israel. Arab here means the Palestinian citizens of Israel. This is the equivalent of the FBI warning the US government that the Native American citizens of the USA are buying flats and houses in increasing numbers.

The report of 2007 declared, 'the state institutions are terribly worried about the increased attempts by Arab (citizens) to buy land in the Negev and in the Galilee'.[4] This particular report was the most ironic of them all. It pointed out that the main efforts in the south to buy private land are made by Bedouin, and in the Galilee by Bedouin and Druze. These are the two communities within the Palestinian community in Israel that are supposed to receive a better treatment since their members serve in the Israel army, while the rest of the Palestinian citizens do not, an exemption often brought up as a pretext for the discrimination against them (although one should note that only a very small minority among the Bedouin in the south serve in the army; the majority of recruits come from the north). Seemingly if you are an Arab, even one serving in the Israeli army, when you buy land you still become the enemy from within.

Even those rare Palestinian citizens who have succeeded by means of appeals to the Israeli Supreme Court in being allowed to purchase land – quite often land or property which was expropriated from them earlier by the state in the 1950s or 1970s – are not immune from a second takeover. In September 1998 a battle raged around the Palestinian town of Umm al-Fahem in the Wadi Ara area. Tear gas and both rubber and live bullets were used by the army and the police to disperse angry landowners whose plots had been taken from them by the army for the purpose of turning them into weapon-firing training fields for the Israel Defense Forces (IDF). The army would never contemplate confiscating Jewish properties for such a purpose. As one scholar put it: 'Israel is at war with the Palestinian citizens over the question of land ownership.'[5]

Mainstream historians who write nostalgically about Israel's first decade regard the 'takeover of Arab land' as the most important national mission to be executed by early governments.[6] A century-old ideology holds that the land of Israel belongs exclusively to the Jewish people and that Judaizing those parts which are still owned by Arabs, and preventing Arabs from buying more land, is a sacred, national and existential task for the survival of the Jewish people. In 2010 the 'Arabs' own about 2.5 per cent of the land and they have been unable to increase that proportion in all the years of Israel's existence, despite the increase in their numbers – which Israeli newspaper headlines like to describe as the 'demographic time bomb'.

To be a hostile alien in one's own land not only involves facing daily challenges about the right to own land, it also affects whom one may marry and build a family with. In the dead of night between 23 and 24 January 2007, the village of Jaljulia was encircled by military and police forces. The aim of this siege was to capture eight Palestinian women, originally from the West Bank, who had lived with their husbands for years and had raised families at a time when Israelis encouraged Palestinians from the occupied territories to work as cheap labour in the Jewish state when there was relatively free movement in and out of the West Bank. These women were arrested and expelled back to the West Bank on the same night.

Following this incident, Oded Feller, from the Association for Civil Rights in Israel, wrote to Eli Yishai, the Minister of the Interior:

The darkness must have blinded the police and prevented them from seeing the repulsive repercussions of the destructive display of power they performed in the dead of night in the midst of an Arab village. The break into the houses, the terror on the faces of the toddlers, the shock of pulling women out of their beds, the men and children waiting in the freezing night at the local police station and pleading for their mothers and wives, the humiliation of the hurried expulsion, the babies left without their mothers – all this was hidden from the eyes of the police due to the darkness of the night.[7]

As Amany Dayif, a Palestinian Israeli scholar, wrote, 'The new law reflects the Israeli desire for a "quiet transfer" of the Palestinians from Israel or in other words the expulsion of the Palestinians from the state to the enclaved West Bank.'[8]

The policy against the couples with spouses from the occupied territories was initiated by Eli Yishai, the Minister of the Interior, who claimed such marriages constituted 'a demographic existential threat to Israel'.[9] As a result of a long process of legislation beginning in 2003 and ending in 2007, spouses were forced to leave or separate. The government was authorized by the courts to enforce this expulsion.[10]

These laws reflect a wider wave of legislation on related issues, beginning in 2007 and fully endorsed by the Israeli ministers of justice and the intra-ministerial committee for legislation. They include a law of loyalty which requires citizens to express full recognition of Israel as a Jewish and Zionist state; the banning of the commemoration of the *Nakbah* – the 1948 catastrophe – in public events or school curricula and textbooks; the right of communities in Jewish suburbia not to accept Palestinians as residents; the right of the state to discriminate by law against Arabs in the privatization of land (known as the 2007 Jewish National Fund Law) and many similar ones.[11]

Palestinians have also seen other rights denied to them. On 9 May 2010 fifty non-governmental organizations (NGOs) of Palestinians in Israel, practically all the major ones, held an emergency meeting warning against what they saw as a systematic and continuous violation of the basic human and civil rights of the Palestinians in Israel. Their press release stated: 'Arrests at the dead of night, confiscation of mobile phones and computers, banning publicizing these arrests, prohibiting those arrested from seeing their lawyers, remind us of darker ages and regimes.' The meeting, organized partly in response to the arrest of Amir Makhoul (the chair of *Ittijah*, the umbrella organization of the Palestinian NGOs in Israel), was designed to confront what the NGOs saw as the 'orchestrated assault on the freedoms and rights of the Arab citizens in Israel'.

Amongst other restrictions, the right to protest and organize is not a given for Palestinians in Israel. On the eve of Israel's attack against the Gaza Strip in January 2009, codenamed 'Cast Lead', the police arrested eight hundred activists to prevent them from demonstrating and organizing demonstrations the day after. The urgency felt by the civil society was not only due to the wave of legislation and arrests, but also to the worrying increase in the number of Palestinians shot by the police and Jewish citizens, and the attitude of those in power towards killing Palestinians, which is strikingly different from their attitude towards Israeli Jews. In October 2010, the Israeli police simulated a scenario whereby parts of Israel in which Palestinians lived were appended to the West Bank – while the illegal Jewish settlements in the West Bank were incorporated into the Jewish state. For that manoeuvre the army and police were ordered to use excessive force of the kind they had used in October 2000, when the Palestinians in Israel protested against the Israeli policy in the occupied territories; an event that ended with the killing of thirteen Palestinian citizens by the Israeli police.

Since 2000, another forty-one citizens have been killed.[12] The forty-first was Salman al-Atiqa, a petty car thief who was shot after he had been arrested and handcuffed. While some have died in similar circumstances, others have been ordinary citizens with no connection to crime. Most of the resulting lawsuits, apart from two, were closed by the State Attorney General due to lack of evidence and public interest. Attacks by members of the public or police on Palestinian citizens never result in the perpetrators being sent for trial.[13]

On top of all these challenges can be observed the consequences of a sustained policy of discrimination and exclusion which has existed since the creation of the state of Israel. Half of the families considered to be below the poverty line in Israel are Palestinian, while the Palestinian community accounts for nearly 20 per cent of the population. Two-thirds of the children defined as suffering from malnutrition in 2010 in Israel are Palestinians.[14]

This is by no means the full picture. As individuals, some Palestinian citizens have achieved real success in the Jewish state as businessmen, judges, medical professionals, writers, broadcasters, academics and even in football (although Palestinians invited to play for the national team find it difficult to join in the national anthem, traditionally sung before international games, which stresses the yearning of the Jewish people for Eretz Israel). The number of Palestinian students and lecturers is growing, as is the number of Palestinians within the civil service.

These individual successes have made the Palestinians a more self-confident community – and thus in turn an even greater threat in the eyes of the Jewish community, which is still by and large motivated by an ideological infrastructure that negates the right of the Palestinians to live alongside them. Recent surveys show that the majority of the next generation, high-school Jewish children, do not believe full rights should be given to the Palestinian citizens in Israel, nor do they mind their voluntary or forced transfer outside the country. They seem to be great supporters of the 2010 Israeli Minister of Foreign Affairs, Avigdor Lieberman, who has publicly expressed his desire, including in a speech given to the UN General Assembly in October 2010, to transfer the Palestinians in Israel to a Palestinian 'Bantustan' in the West Bank in return for annexation of the Jewish settlements in the West Bank to Israel.[15]

This book tries to trace the roots and growth of this dismal reality. Readers familiar with other historical and current case studies will recognize, I believe, aspects of the conditions in which the Palestinian minority lives in Israel. Some aspects might remind them of colonized people in the nineteenth century, others of immigrants and guest workers in present-day Europe. The difference is that in Israel the state immigrated into the indigenous community and thus Israeli policies towards the Palestinians cannot be compared with anti-immigration policies elsewhere. Some aspects may seem worse than the reality of apartheid South Africa, others better. The petty apartheid of full racial segregation is not in force in Israel. Discrimination is more latent and hidden, although the whole educational system up to university and college level is totally segregated.

Latent apartheid works in the following way. In June 2006 ArCafé – an upmarket coffee chain present in almost every shopping mall and commercial centre in the country – declared it would only employ people who had served in the army – which in Israel means Jews and the two small minorities of Druze and Bedouin. In this way it avoided the law that forbids discrimination on the basis of race or religion. In Israel these declarations are never so explicit, but almost every restaurant and coffee shop describes itself as 'looking for young people after their military service'.[16]

So the first part of any history of the Palestinians in Israel is a chapter about discrimination and dispossession. But it is also a story of self-assertiveness and steadfastness. Arnon Soffer of Haifa University, one of the leading professors in Israel who preaches against the demographic danger of the Arabs in Israel, states, 'According to the predictions the Jews will be only 70 per cent of the population; this is a very awful picture.'[17] In response, one can only say that if this is indeed true, despite his and many of his fellow Israelis' ambition to get rid of the Palestinians in Israel, then it is a tribute to the latter's determination and assertiveness. They live – as their theatre, films, novels, poems and media indicate – as a proud national minority, despite being denied basic collective and individual human and civil rights in the self-declared only democracy in the Middle East.

But the future of this community is insecure and precarious. In 2010, the most powerful people in the government of Israel – the Minister of the Interior, Eli Yishai, the Minister of Foreign Affairs, Avigdor Lieberman, and the Minister of Internal Security, Yitzhak Aharonowitz – all spoke openly, both inside and outside Israel, about transferring the Palestinians, robbing them of their citizenship and Judaizing their towns as the strategy of the Jewish state in the next decade. If politicians in the United Kingdom or in the USA spoke about Jewish citizens in the way Jewish politicians have spoken about Palestinians in Israel, they would be forced to resign immediately. In Israel they can expect even more support from the Jewish electorate as a result. There is still considerable might behind those who would not consent to such policies in Israel but it is decreasing incrementally by the day. This book is written with a sense of both urgency and anxiety about this community's future.

INTRODUCTION

THIS BOOK IS NOT the first attempt to narrate the story of a group that numbered a mere 100,000 people when the story began and is today no more than a million and a half. It is not a very sizeable group of people, but nonetheless one that deserves our attention. It has been and still is the subject of much social science research as a case study – or rather a test case – for a plethora of theories. The excellent work done so far, therefore, has focused on specific aspects of this group's life, whether identified chronologically or thematically. The best way of covering this impressive scholarly harvest would be a well-edited book, which I hope will appear before too long. In the meantime, I have added an appendix to this book, giving a short summary of the scholarly developments in the research on the Palestinians in Israel, to complement this narrative.

What most of these works have failed to do – not due to any fault of their own – is to translate their scholarly interest into a more general and political focus. For the world at large, and for that part of it which is energetically engaged in the Palestine issue, the Palestinians in Israel have been an enigma for a long time. Sammy Smooha and Don Peretz called the Palestinians in Israel 'the invisible man'.[1] This may be changing now; as Nadim Rouhana puts it, 'the Arabs in Israel have grown to the point where they can no longer be ignored by either

Israelis or Palestinians'.[2] According to Rouhana this ends a period during which 'the Arabs in Israel have been an invisible, identity-less and potentially de-Palestinized group' and instead turned into a 'conscious, active and dynamic segment of the Palestinian people'.[3] And yet, it seems that on the global scene they are still ignored.

An important step in publicizing the particular circumstances of the community has been achieved by two noteworthy books that have recently covered the topic: Nadim Rouhana's *Palestinian Citizens in an Ethnic Jewish State: Identities in Conflict* (1997) and As'ad Ghanem's *The Palestinian-Arab Minority in Israel* (2001) are both still very valuable sources for anyone wishing to understand the development of the political identity and orientations of this group in a historical perspective.[4]

Rouhana's book focused on the development of the Palestinian identity within the state of Israel, demolishing along the way the prevalent academic assumption that saw the Arabs in Israel as being torn between 'Israelization' and 'Palestinization'. His book showed how the two communities developed in Israel with very little sharing in terms of collective identity. And thus both Jews and Palestinians grew up in Israel possessing incomplete national identities – a situation only reinforced and perpetuated by developments inside and outside the state of Israel, leading to inevitable clashes unless the ethnic state of Israel is replaced by a civil, bi-national state.

As'ad Ghanem's book, published four years later, added a new dimension for understanding the political streams that developed within the Palestinian community and drew our attention to the fact that the world of the Palestinians in Israel should not only be seen in constant reference to the Jewish state and its policies. There were issues of religion, modernity and individuality that also divided the community, and he agreed with Rouhana about the existence of a certain Palestinian consensus within the state of Israel. Ghanem's research in 2001 enabled him to detect the strength of the secular element in the Palestinian society, during a period of global and local Israeli Islamophobia; he also noted, with concern, the return of the clan as a retrograde powerbase for politics. Both books also offer a prescription for the future: a bi-national state instead of the existing Jewish state. In this book I do not provide my own idea of a solution;

I am more concerned about the lessons of history than the perils of the future.

What I would like to add to the existing excellent literature is the historical perspective (and expand on the historical background provided in the two books mentioned above). In the ten years that have passed since these valuable publications have appeared, Zionism and Palestinian nationalism have matured in a way that allows us to locate more clearly the Palestinians in Israel as victims of Zionism and an integral part of the Palestinian movement. As such, this book continues my research on Palestine and Israel, which I began in *The Ethnic Cleansing of Palestine* (2006).[5] It is only through a history of the Palestinian minority in Israel that one can examine the extent to which the long-lived Zionist and Israeli desire for ethnic supremacy and exclusivity has brought about the current reality on the ground.

This book wishes to free the Palestinians of Israel from their role as a case study and tell their history. Only now is this possible, as the group has a history of more than sixty years of existence as a non-Jewish minority in a Jewish state. The reason that a coherent historical narrative of the group has not been attempted before has to do first with this short history – historians need perspective and the passage of time. But there is an additional reason: it is a very difficult group to define, lacking as it does clear ethnic, cultural, national, geographical or even political borders. The Palestinians in Israel themselves, through their leaders, activists, politicians, poets, writers, academics and journalists, are still searching for an adequate definition.

And yet there are good reasons for telling their story. The Palestinians in Israel form a very important section of the Palestinian people, and of the Palestinian question. Their past struggles, present-day situation, and hopes and fears for the future are intimately linked with those of the wider Palestinian population. They have played a marginal role on both the Palestinian and Israeli political scenes, yet any resolution of the present deadlock must take them into account.

There is a second reason for providing a people's history of this particular group. Israel claims to be the only democracy in the Middle East; as its chief minority population, the situation of its Palestinian citizens forms the litmus test for the validity of this claim. Their story is also that of multiculturalism and intraculturalism, issues fundamentally relevant to societies beyond Israel and Palestine and which affect the fate of the East–West relationship in the Middle East as a whole.

This minority is a heterogeneous community in which Christians live side by side with Muslims, Islamists and secularists who compete for political domination, and refugees struggle to make their presence felt in a community the majority of whose members are living in the same villages their ancestors built hundreds years ago.

It is a group that has been dubbed traitors both by the Palestinian movement in the 1950s and by current Israeli political forces. Theirs is an amazing story of almost impossible navigation in a sea of colonialism, chauvinist nationalism, fanatic religiosity and international indifference. It is a narrative of a group to which I do not belong, but in whose midst I lived most of my adult life. As I have outlined in a recent book, *Out of the Frame: The Struggle for Academic Freedom in Israel*,[6] due to my scholarly and intellectual critique of Jewish society I was ostracized by my own community, to the point where I decided to work abroad; I have been involved in public and political life within the Palestinian community since the 1990s. I think it is fair to say that my social connections, and even more so my ideological associations, are uncommon in the Jewish community in Israel. Although not unique, I am one of very few Israeli Jews who feel such a close affinity with the Palestinian minority in Israel. This has led to me undertaking intensive learning of Arabic, with constant reading of Arab literature and listening to Arab media, but more importantly to developing intimate relationships with many members of the community, and sensing a strong affinity and solidarity to the point of becoming a pariah in my own Jewish community. I have never regretted this, even when in October 2009 a small group of young Islamic activists tried to shout me down at a commemoration ceremony for the thirteen Palestinian citizens killed in October 2000 in the village of Arabeh, at which I was the only Jewish speaker tolerated after fierce opposition from the Islamic movement to any others. I am not saying this as a complaint, or because I feel I was unjustly treated; these activists were a small minority within an otherwise very receptive public, and I can understand why they might view me with suspicion. No, the reason is that when you are part of the privileged oppressive majority, you do what you do not in anticipation of a standing ovation, nor indeed in any expectation of gratitude, but rather for your own peace of mind and moral satisfaction. This is the particular angle from which this book is written.

Let me add a word on methodology. On the face of it, this is an old-fashioned narrative history. The appendix to the book covers the theoretical paradigms offered by others as much as possible; these, in the main, lack a historical perspective, but are very useful in terms of analysing the group's present conditions. In its conclusion the book attempts to offer its own paradigm, that of the Jewish *Mukhabarat* (secret service in Arabic) state (a model explained in the epilogue to the book) in view of its major findings from the historical research.

Our narrative moves between two principal perspectives: that of the Israeli regime, in particular its relevant decision makers, and that of the Israeli Palestinian community at large, via its political and educated elite and the writings of or interviews with various members. The analysis is more nuanced in the case of the Israeli Palestinian community for two reasons. First, the state, or rather the decision makers and those operating the policies on the ground, have been informed by the same ideological perspective – Zionism – and therefore more often than not have acted in unison. Second, this book aims to present a people's history as far as possible and therefore the magnifying glass is cast more on the Palestinians than on those who formulated and executed the policies towards them.

The book has a constant variable and a number of dynamic factors. The historical periods are the only concrete foundations of the book, hence the chronological rather than the thematic structure of the book. Within each period the narrative moves from one perspective to the other – not, I hope, in a schematic, artificial way, but rather by the power of association that sometimes blurs the historical picture, but which I believe presents a more authentic image of past reality. The story is not interrupted by theoretical inputs, only by explanations and elaborations of certain events and personalities. Theory comes back into the picture when academia begins to play a role in the relationship between the Israeli Palestinian community and the Jewish state, and therefore alternative scholarly understandings of this history appear twice: in the theoretical appendix and at the various junctures of history where theories introduced by academics became tools either in the hands of the government – such as the theories of modernization – or for those who challenged the governmental policy – such as the theories of internal colonialism and ethnocracy.

Veteran readers of scholarly works will appreciate the unbearable gap between the clean and structured representation of reality and its murky, fractured and chaotic existence as an experience. When the research is too neat, the smells are gone and the sterile pictures fail to illuminate, especially in this history of an almost impossible navigation between conflicting demands, the hardship of daily life and the struggles for survival. This book does not seek to idealize the Palestinians of Israel, or as they are called in the Arab world, the 1948 Arabs; it wishes to humanize them in places where they are either forgotten, marginalized or demonized.

This book is also a modest attempt to understand the reality from the minority's point of view, seeing them not just as a community of suffering, but as a natural and organic part of the Palestinian people and history. You cannot begin to understand what this community has undergone if you do not begin the story at the latest in 1947, when the area that became Israel was still Palestine. This is where our story begins.

CHAPTER ONE

OUT OF THE ASHES OF
THE *NAKBAH*

THE LAND THAT WAS PALESTINE, 1947

The files about Palestinian villages compiled by the intelligence service of the Haganah, the Jewish underground during the British Mandate for Palestine, make a fascinating read. The intelligence officers prepared a file on every Palestinian village, all one thousand of them. The process of registering these villages began in 1940 and lasted for seven years. Every such file contained the most detailed information possible, from the names of the big families, through to the occupation of most of the villagers and their political affiliations, from their history to the quality of the land, the public buildings and even what grew on each of the trees in the orchards that traditionally encircled the villages.[1]

They are an important source first and foremost since they expose the level and depth of the Zionist preparation for the takeover of Palestine. The files included aerial photographs of each village and its environs and indicated the access and entry points to each village, as well as assessing its wealth, and the number of weapons its men and youths held in their homes.

No less important however is the value of these files as a historical source for the social and economic conditions in rural Palestine during the British Mandate. Since the files were updated for the last time in 1947, they also provide a dynamic picture of change and transformation. When the information included in them is matched with other sources, such as the press from that period, including the official *Palestine Gazette* of the British Mandate government, rural Palestine, very much like urban Palestine, appears to be a society on the move, showing signs of economic expansion and social stabilization after years of economic depression and social upheavals.

Almost each village had a school, running water and proper sewage systems for the first time, while the fields were plentiful and old blood feuds – as the village files tell us – had been settled. In the cities and towns prosperity was also budding. The first graduates of the universities around the Arab world, including the American universities of Beirut and Cairo, began their professional careers in Palestine, forming a new middle class, which was so necessary for societies during the transition into the new capitalist world built by European colonialism and imperialism. Quite a few chose a public career in the British Mandate government as senior or junior officials – the latter even joining their Jewish colleagues in a strike for a better pay and conditions as late as 1946. The affluence was visible in the architectural expansion. New neighbourhoods, streets and modern infrastructure were also evident everywhere.

The urban as well as the rural landscape was still very Arab and Palestinian on the eve of the *Nakbah* – the 1948 catastrophe. Politically, however, there was a different balance of power. The international community was about to debate the future identity of the country as if there were two equal contenders for it. The United Nations accepted the mandate for deciding Palestine's future after British rule in the land ended in 1948. Already in February 1947, the British cabinet announced it would transfer the issue of Palestine to the UN, which in its turn appointed a special commission, United Nations Special Committee on Palestine (UNSCOP), to deliberate upon the fate of the Holy Land.

'It is not fair,' complained David Ben-Gurion, the leader of the Jewish community and later on Israel's first prime minister, in front of UNSCOP: 'The Jews are only one-third of the overall population and only have a very small share of the land.'[2] Indeed there were 600,000

Jews and 1.3 million Palestinians; the Jews owned less than 7 per cent of the land, while most and, in some areas, all of the cultivated land was owned by Palestinians.

Ben-Gurion's complaint bewildered the Palestinians, and still enrages them today. Precisely because of this demographic and geographical balance, they deemed that any future plan which did not allow the vast majority of the people in Palestine to decide its future was unacceptable and immoral. Moreover, the majority of the Jews were newcomers and settlers – most of whom had arrived only three years before this, while the Palestinians were the indigenous and native population.[3] But their views were ignored. It did not help that the Palestinian leadership decided to boycott UNSCOP and that the politics of Palestine were run mainly by the Arab League, which did not always have the Palestinian interest in mind.

The UN decided to appease Ben-Gurion: it opened the gates for an unlimited immigration of Jews and granted 55 per cent of the land to the Jewish state.

The principled Palestinian and Arab rejection of, and objection to, the partition plan was well known to the Jewish leadership, even before it was asked to respond to the UN plan. Therefore, when the Jewish community sent its agreement for the plan, it already knew that there was little danger of the plan being implemented due to the Arab and Palestinian resistance. Nonetheless, Israeli propaganda has ever since quoted Israel's acceptance of the plan and the Palestinian rejection as an indication of its peaceful intentions towards the intransigent Palestinians. More importantly, this Palestinian rejection was later used as an explanation by the Israeli government for its decision to occupy parts of the land accorded to the Palestinians in the UN partition plan.

The Arab world declared its intention to go to war against the implementation of this plan, but did not have the means or the will to stop it. Three months before the Arab armies entered Palestine in May 1948, the military forces of the Jewish community began to ethnically cleanse the Palestinians from their houses, fields and land. In the process the Jewish forces added another 23 per cent to that granted to them by the UN. By January 1950, Israel as a state covered almost

80 per cent of Palestine. In it those who were left became the 'Arabs in Israel', slowly building their life out of the ashes of their catastrophe.

THE ZIONIST DREAM AND THE BI-NATIONAL REALITY, 1949

The photographs from the early days of 1949 tell it all. Palestinians appear in them looking frightened, confused, disorientated and more than anything else traumatized. They woke up to a new geopolitical reality. Palestine as they knew it was gone and replaced by a new state. The visible changes were too clear for anyone to ignore. Many of their fellow countrymen, about 750,000 of them, were expelled in 1948 and not allowed to return. They became refugees or citizens of the Hashemite Kingdom of Jordan, or lived under military rule in the Egyptian Gaza Strip. Out of the one million Palestinians who used to live within what became the state of Israel (78 per cent of the British Mandate for Palestine), 160,000 remained in 1949.

Photographs still remain of the small areas in the midst of urban centres, cordoned off with wires and fences, in which for days and sometimes weeks those who remained in the destroyed and deserted towns and cities were forced to dwell. These initial attempts to concentrate Palestinians who had lost their homes but remained within the boundaries of the hometown were supervised by Israeli officers, who called these confinement areas 'ghettos'. They disappeared by 1950 as a more humane geopolitical landscape emerged, but in the meantime they symbolized, more than any other image, the plight in which these Palestinians found themselves.[4] No less dramatic was the picture of those expelled for trying to return back home once the fighting had subsided.

The new sights were augmented by the noise of the tractors and bulldozers operating on behalf of the Jewish National Fund (JNF) and other Israeli governmental agencies ordered by the government to Judaize, as quickly as possible, the previously Palestinian rural and urban areas. The aim was not only to de-Arabize Israel but also to provide land and housing for the influx of new Jewish immigrants from Europe and the Arab world. The operation of demolition and destruction was designed and supervised by Yosef Weitz, the director of the JNF's Land Department. This body had attempted to purchase land during the British Mandate, and its basic failure to acquire more than 7 per cent of the cultivable land is one of the reasons the Jewish leadership opted to employ force to take over large parts of Palestine for its future state. On 19 July 1948, Weitz's boss, the first Prime Minister of Israel, David Ben-Gurion, wrote in his diary: 'abandoned Arab villages had to be removed'.[5] Within two years, two million dunams (1 dunam is 3.8 acres) of Palestinian land would belong to the Jewish Agency, which meant they were exclusively for the benefit of Jewish citizens.

How individual Palestinians experienced the trauma depended on where they lived. Those dwelling in the major cities of Palestine where they had been the indigenous majority now became a tiny minority in them, living under a harsh military regime. All around them the familiar face of an Arab city was transformed dramatically: either demolished or taken over by Jewish immigrants. Most of the urban Palestinians were expelled and those remaining were quite often pushed into small ghettos in the poorer parts of Haifa, Jaffa, Ramleh and Lydda. If they lived in the rural areas, they belonged to a hundred and so villages left intact out of more than five hundred whose inhabitants were evicted and in 1949 were wiped out by the Israeli tractors, turning them into either recreation parks or Jewish settlements. Particularly devastating was the experience of those Palestinians who lived on the Mediterranean coast: scores of villages disappeared from the earth in 1948 and only two remained. And if they were nomads or semi-nomads, the Bedouin of the south, they found themselves standing in long queues to be registered as Israeli citizens, signing an oath of allegiance to a Jewish state.[6]

The scenes in the cities of Haifa and Jaffa in those early days of statehood convey the enormity of the transformation and traumatization, felt especially by those who had belonged to the urban population, some of whom were expelled to nearby villages. When listening to the memories and reading the memoirs of these Palestinian citizens of how they fared in the early hours of Jewish statehood one can hear mostly tales of loss, panic and despair.

Some of those expelled to the countryside were later allowed to return, but by no means all. So one trauma was to leave, come back and see that your house was taken. A different one was to dwell for a year or so in your own house and then be evicted and forcibly moved to the countryside (at least as long as the military regime lasted, which was until 1966). 'My mother became hysterical, "Don't you know we are never going back? Not your book [I was reading a book in the midst of the chaos], not us, nothing," ' recalled Umm Muhammad, who was a third-grade pupil when they were evicted from the Halisa neighbourhood in Haifa to a nearby village.[7] Many, like this mother, found out when they attempted to return in the 1960s that others had taken over their houses and their businesses – such as bookshops, law firms or grocery shops – in which they lived and worked for generations. No wonder that many of those who tried to return gave up the idea and had to reconcile themselves to living in the countryside in villages that could hardly sustain themselves, now that their fields had been confiscated by the Israeli authorities.

Worst was watching the loss at close hand in the cities, where properties and business were either turned into rubble or taken over by someone else. Some eyewitnesses still prefer not to be named. Hannan, not her real name, is today a retired citizen of Haifa. Her family lived in an apartment in a building they owned and her father ran a small factory for building materials nearby. The remnants of these two buildings can still be seen. Her family left in January 1948, as did some of the wealthier people of Haifa who had the means to travel and stay in Beirut or Cairo. This upper class did not wish to be in the midst of the impending fighting and hoped to come back later on; they left all they had in their homes. The vast majority of the people of Haifa of course could not afford such an exodus and stayed until they were expelled by the Jewish forces in April 1948. Upon return, Hannan's family found that both their home and their factory had been confiscated and that Jewish dwellers had taken over. Like so many others, the family was never compensated and, according to Hannan's recollection, they lived in constant fear of a new eviction and dispossession from their new abode in the city.[8]

There were many others like Hannan who were the original inhabitants of Haifa but could not live in their own homes. They lived next to them, painfully watching them being occupied by invaders. Under strong international pressure, in particular from the United States, about 25,000 expelled Palestinians returned in the first year of statehood under the framework of family reunions. This took place throughout 1949 when the international community, and in particular the UN, wanted Israel to allow the unconditional return of the refuges to their homes (as articulated in UN General Assembly Resolution No. 194, from 11 December 1948). Israel refused adamantly to adhere to this resolution and as a compromise the government obliged the American administration by facilitating the return of a small number of refugees who were willing to swear an oath of allegiance to the Jewish state.[9]

They came back, mainly from Lebanon, and found that in the short period of their absence their houses had been taken by Jewish immigrants, and thus notable families who had lived in relative luxury on Mount Carmel during the Mandatory Palestine years had to be content with shabby rooms in the dense, poor neighbourhoods of inner Haifa. The Haifa-born writer and later political leader Emil Habibi has recorded this particular aspect of the tragedy. When he came back after the fighting subsided he witnessed his furniture being thrown out from his flat on Abbas Street on the mountain's slopes.[10] He asked the new dwellers why they were throwing out his belongings and they answered, 'This house is now our home.' With great effort he rented a house on the street. Many among the returnees had similar stories to tell.

Habibi lost more than his furniture. In an interview with Shimon Balas, one of the few Iraqi Jewish intellectuals in Israel who remained loyal to their Arab heritage and culture, he remembered: 'After 1948 I moved to Nazareth and there I was frightened to learn that my two daughters were afraid of talking to a boy in the street. We lived in Abbas Street before 1948, Christian and Muslim boys and girls, and we were all friendly with each other, going to the same parties, we had a different life then; we were not afraid of socializing and befriending others.'[11]

For some it was not private property lost and confiscated that marked the new epoch, it was the desecration of everything that was holy and dear to their hearts, such as the churches and mosques in the cities and in the countryside. Father Deleque, a Catholic priest in Jaffa in 1948, recalled: 'Jewish soldiers broke down the doors to my church and robbed many precious and sacred objects. Then they threw the statues of Christ down into a nearby garden.' He was aware of the repeated promises by the government and the local military governors to respect the sanctity of mosques and churches but noted 'their deeds did not correspond to their words'.[12] Churches as a rule were more respected than mosques, which disappeared in huge numbers from the Palestinian landscape in the new Jewish state of Israel.

The destructive transformation of the past into the new reality was particularly difficult to comprehend for the elite in the urban centres. In Haifa the leading Palestinians were called to a meeting with the city's Jewish military governor on the evening of 1 July 1948. These notables represented the few thousand Palestinians left after more than 70,000 other citizens had been expelled. The purpose of the meeting was to order them to facilitate the transfer of the Arabs in the city into one neighbourhood, in Wadi Nisnas, the poorest section of the city. Some of those ordered to move had lived for a long time on the upper slopes of Mount Carmel, or on the mount itself.

The citizens were ordered to complete the move by 5 July 1948. Their leaders were shocked. Many of them belonged to the Communist Party, which had supported partition, and hoped that now that the fighting was over they could begin normal life again. 'I do not understand: is this a military command?' protested Tawfiq Tubi, later a member of the Knesset for the Communist Party. 'Let us look on the condition of these people. I cannot see any reason, even a military one that justifies such a move.' He ended his speech with the words: 'We demand that the people will stay in their homes.' Another participant, Bulus Farah, cried, 'This is racism' and called the move 'ghettoizing the Palestinians in Haifa'.[13]

Even the dry document cannot hide the reaction of the Israeli military commander: frosty and metallic.

> 'I can see that you are sitting here and advising me, while you were invited to hear the orders of the High Command and assist it! I am not involved in politics and do not deal with it. *I am just obeying orders* . . . I am just fulfilling orders and I have to make sure

this order is executed until the fifth . . . If this is not done, I will do it myself. I am a soldier.'

After the commander's long monologue ended, Shehada Shalah asked: 'And if a person owns a house, does he have to leave?'

The commander: 'Everyone has to leave.'

Then came the question of expenses. The notables learned that the expellees would have to pay for the cost of their enforced removal themselves. Victor Hayat tried to reason with the commander that it would take more than a day for people to be notified, and that that would not leave them much time. The commander replied that four days was plenty of time. The person who transcribed the meeting recorded: 'All the Arab representatives cried out, "But it is a very short time", and the commander replied, "I cannot change it." '[14]

Not everyone complied with the order. Wadi Bustani, a lawyer, poet and writer living in the beautiful avenue leading to the sea from the mountain (today Ben-Gurion Avenue connecting the Bahai Temple to the port) could not bear the thought of leaving. He was arrested and detained but, since he did not give in, he was eventually allowed to stay in his home. Less fortunate was the spiritual head of the Orthodox Church, a member of the sizeable Greek community that also left in 1948, who was ordered to forsake his church and monastery and move to Wadi Nisnas. He was obliged to celebrate liturgies in an 'inconvenient hall, facing north to south instead of east to west, contrary to the Church's rites and traditions'.[15]

Other just left, as did Emil Habibi's mother. As the famous writer and poet recollected, his mother's generation could not bear staying in Haifa under such circumstances:

Umm Wadie [Habibi's mother] was unable to overcome the shock of those days [1948; she was in East Jerusalem when Haifa was occupied by the Jewish forces in April]. By then her life was behind her, and most of her sons and grandchildren were scattered in the Diaspora. Once she came down to the premises of our old political club in Wadi Al-Nisnass to participate in a joint Arab-Jewish women's meeting. Those were days of a raging general election campaign. The Jewish speaker was emphasising our struggle for the rights of the Palestinian refugees to return to their homes. Umm Wadie interrupted her saying: 'Will my sons and daughters return?'

Taken aback, the Jewish-Hungarian speaker replied: 'They will return when peace is achieved.' 'Lies,' shouted Umm Wadie, 'my son Emile never lies to me. He told me that their return – if ever they return – will take a long time. By then I won't be here to see them: I'll be in my grave.'

Ever since that meeting, and without me knowing, it became her custom to go secretly to a corner of Abbas Garden near our house. She would lean against a stone shaded by an olive tree and bemoan her destiny – lonely and separated from children, especially her youngest son Naim.

At the end of 1949, those who stayed officially became the 'Arab minority of Israel'. On their ID cards, under the rubric of nationality appeared their religious affiliation and not their national one. According to these documents there were no Palestinians or atheists among these citizens of the Jewish state. In the legal and official jargon of the state they appeared as *beni miutim*, members of the minorities – note 'minorities' in plural, as if there were other minorities apart from the Palestinians. But for all intents and purposes they were Arabs; their identity was the clearest signifier of the identity of the Jew in Israel. In Europe Jews were those who were not Christians, and in the Arab world Jews were those who were not Christians or Muslims. It was a religious definition. In the new Jewish state a Jew became an ethnic identity and a Jew was, apparently, someone who was not an 'Arab' – not any Arab but someone who was not a Palestinian. Without such a definition the question of who was a Jew, a permanent source of trouble in the history of Israeli law-making and administration, would have remained an insoluble issue between religious and national definitions. There were of course Arab Jews, or Jews who came from Arab countries, but they were de-Arabized, voluntarily and by a policy from above: coached to Hebraicize their Arabic names, distance themselves from their Arabic language, history and roots, and adopt strong anti-Arab positions as the best means of integrating into the veteran Ashkenazi, namely European, society.[16]

GEOGRAPHICAL DISTRIBUTION

The new minority lived in six geographical areas in the state. The first was a scattered existence in Israel's urban centres. These metropoles were transformed dramatically during 1948. Covered markets that had existed for centuries were demolished, whole quarters were removed with the intent of de-Arabizing the urban scene and only the houses of the upper class remained intact as they were coveted by the new Jewish dwellers. The skyline that used to be dominated by church spires and minarets was now taken over by cubic high-rise monstrosities built for the many immigrants with little care for the landscape or the humans living in them.

Very small groups were left in the urban spaces that had been cleansed in the operations of the spring and summer of 1948: a few hundred in Haifa and Jaffa, a few thousand in Shefa-'Amr in the western Galilee, who were nearly expelled as well but eventually allowed to stay, and ten thousand or so in Nazareth, again a population that was doomed at first to be cleansed but was allowed to stay after the Israeli political leadership retracted its early decision and left the people there intact. The commander of the Brigade, Brigade 7, that occupied the town telegraphed on 17 July 1948: 'Should we expel the people from the town of Nazareth? I think we should expel everyone apart from the clergymen'; Ben-Gurion replied: 'Don't expel people from Nazareth.'[17]

Many of those who were 'allowed' to stay by Ben-Gurion were internal refugees from the villages around Nazareth. In other places too, those who became the 'Arabs' of Haifa and Shefa-'Amr were internal refugees from villages nearby who arrived there in 1948 after the expulsion and flight, or later on in a process of internal immigration. Very few were the original city dwellers. The houses they moved into, usually rented as most houses were not for sale to Arabs, had quite often previously been owned by Palestinians. This was the troubled beginning of life for the urban Palestinians in Israel.

The second group was the rural population in the lower and upper Galilee who survived the ethnic cleansing operations, for reasons that still have to be properly researched. We presume, in the absence of a better explanation, that it was due to their own resistance and because of the fatigue of the Israeli army that tens of thousands of Palestinians still inhabited the Galilee in 1949. Today, despite governmental efforts in the 1970s and 1980s to Judaize these areas, the scenery is still 'Arab', as are more than 60 per cent of the people living in the region. When you drive through these areas you see mostly large Arab villages, in their traditional locations on the mountain slopes, with minarets and churches being the highest buildings piercing the skyline. And although, unlike in 1948, there are now new Jewish settlements on the top of mountains, these have not yet (for the most part) transformed this more pastoral Middle Eastern view.[18]

The third group were the people living in Wadi Ara, the valley connecting the Mediterranean Jewish town of Hadera with the inner eastern valleys of the land, south of Nazareth and west of Jenin. Those who know the area recognize its peculiarity. In the past the villages were comfortably scattered at a fair distance from each other on the hills overlooking this major and ancient route from the sea to the inner plains and further into the Jordan and Syria of yesteryear. This is where the crusaders' army marched before they were crushed by Salah al-Din's troops in medieval times. Now it is enclaved by Jewish settlements around it, with the villages almost fusing one into the other, seeking space to grow in a state that does not allow any spatial growth for the Arab municipal and rural localities.

This area was originally occupied by the Jordanian Arab Legion in the 1948 war. There was a tacit understanding between this army and the Jewish forces that parts of the state which the UN accorded to the Palestinians in the 1947 partition resolution would be annexed to Jordan in return for the Jordanians limiting their role in the all-Arab operations against the Jewish state. Whether this part was included in that tacit understanding was not clear and hence the Israelis threatened the Jordanians with an additional war if that valley was not given to them. Intimidated by this threat, the Hashemite negotiators decided to allow Israel to take over Wadi Ara as part of an overall armistice agreement between the two states, which was signed in April 1949 and executed in June of that same year. About 15,000 Palestinians became Israeli citizens as a result. The segregation wall and fences which Israel built in 2001 are today the only barriers that separate these villages from those with which they shared land up until 1948. In several cases, such as that of the village of Barta, the village was divided into two by the armistice line and was not, for political reasons, reunited after 1967, although both parts of the village came under Israeli rule.[19]

Similar cases are to be found in the fourth location, the southern Triangle, which consists of a number of Palestinian villages bordering the West Bank, located between the northern part of the Tel Aviv metropolis and the Green Line of 1967. Baqa al-Sharqiyya, the eastern Baqa and Baqa al-Gharbiyya, the western one, is the most famous divided village, with a similar experience to Barta.

This is a more flatland area, closer to the sea, which gradually, due to its proximity to the Tel Aviv metropolis, became the main provider of unskilled labour in the 1960s and 1970s. Economically it is worse off and, apart from one new high-rise complex built in one of the towns in 2010, it is dense and overpopulated due to Israel's spatial policy that prevents the geographical expansion of the villages, thus offering very little hope of economic development and socio-economic prosperity in the near future. It is now bisected by a new highway, Road No. 6, but not connected – apart from one spot – directly to that road (the highway passes within the fields of the villages and towns, but its various exits do not allow these residents to enjoy a better or speedy access to it).

The fifth location is in the south, in the Negev, or *al-Naqb* in Arabic, where mostly the semi-nomadic Palestinians, the Bedouin, live. They dwell mostly in villages which were not recognized as legal settlements by the state for the duration of the period covered by this book. In 1948, not all of the Bedouin were leading a semi-sedentary life; some of them were inhabitants of the ancient town of Bir Saba (today Beer Sheva) and other villages; but they were expelled with tens of thousands of other Bedouin between the years 1948 and 1950.[20]

Finally, there is a group of several villages on the western slopes of the Jerusalem mountain which survived one of the early Israeli operations of ethnic cleansing, the *Harel* operation of April 1948 which dispossessed thirty or more villages in that area in a few days.[21] The best-known today is Abu Gosh – the seat of a famous mountain strongman who controlled the Jaffa to Jerusalem road in the early part of the nineteenth century. Today it is where the Jewish secular Jerusalemites escape to on Saturdays and holidays, when life comes to a standstill in the increasingly religious West Jerusalem and less secure East Jerusalem.

Here too there are divided villages due to the demarcation of the Israeli–Jordanian armistice line. The village of Beit Safafa, in a valley to the south-west of Jerusalem, was cynically divided by Jordanian and Israeli negotiators in the 1949 armistice negotiations. A ruthless hand drew the border in the middle of the village and it was divided by barbed wire. In 1956, a correspondent of *Time* magazine reported an emotional wedding of a bride and groom from the two sides of the divide. The bride, Fatma Bint from the Jordanian side, married Moussa Ayasha from the Israeli side. The bride, as was traditional, left for the groom's house; namely, to the fence and beyond.

> Sisters and brothers and cousins and uncles stretched out their arms across the wire to embrace, to bless and be blessed. The wedding party, silent now, turned toward the bridegroom's home, and the Arabs on the Jordan side watched until Fatma and her bridegroom were over the hill.
>
> Then the border guards straightened up the wire barricade, and, guns ever ready, resumed their patrolling beside the barbed wire that since 1949 divided Beit Safafa.[22]

Israel is thus a matrix of intertwined ethnic communities and there are no coherent homogenous areas; this accentuates the tension between attempts from above to create physical segregation (as has been done with the West Bank and the Gaza Strip) and the reality on the ground.

JEWISH REACTIONS

For the Jewish side the new reality was less traumatic, definitely not as painful, but nonetheless similarly hard to digest. The presence of a Palestinian minority inside the Jewish state was not envisaged by the leaders of the Zionist movement. Conventional historiography would be quick to disagree: such historians would point out that Israel's Declaration of Independence, issued on 14 May 1948, promised equal rights to all its citizens, regardless of their religion or race. But, while these noble aspirations were expressed, the Israeli army was deeply engaged in the ethnic cleansing of these very future citizens of the Jewish state. From oral testimonies given by Palestinian villagers living near the coast, who had no connections with Palestinian paramilitary groups, we know that some were ready to become citizens of the Jewish state on the basis of this declaration, and were surprised when they were ordered to leave.[23]

The gap between the promises and the actual policies on the ground was obfuscated by the war that raged at the time between the nascent Jewish state and the Arab armies that entered Palestine in an attempt to prevent the establishment of the state and to stop the ongoing Israeli expulsion of the indigenous people. The military power of the new state was sufficient, we know in hindsight, to repel the general Arab attack while at the same time conducting a systematic ethnic-cleansing operation on the ground. Before the military operations during the months of October and November 1948, when the north and south of Palestine were still free from Israeli occupation, there were hardly any Palestinians within the space taken over by the Jewish army. Eretz Israel was, or so it seemed at first sight, cleansed of any 'strangers' (*Zarim* in Hebrew, in the language of Ben-Gurion) or 'invaders', as the Palestinians appeared in the final triumphant declarations of the various commanders of the army when the fighting was over.[24]

Given the expulsion plans devised before May 1948 and the constant preoccupation with the possibility of transferring the Palestinians still remaining after the war of 1948, it is clear that the leaders of the Jewish state were not prepared for the possibility of a bi-national state. It was only in the 1960s that the Israeli political elite began to accept the presence of such a minority and began seriously strategizing a possible modus vivendi with the Palestinians inside the state.[25]

Thus, not much thought had been given to the nature of the Arab–Jewish relationship in the new state; however, there were very clear ideas about the nature of the state itself. It was to be a liberal-democratic nation-state based on Western European models. But was it possible to maintain such a state with a national minority in it?

The strategists of the policy towards the Palestinian minority in 1949 were probably aware that their decisions could have a significant impact on the nature of the state and on the orientation of the Zionist project. However, despite the enormity of the issue, or maybe because of it, they preferred not to mention this predicament in their decisions and to keep it very much in the background. Their opinions on the subject can be mostly inferred from their policies rather from their writings or speeches; however, this material is extensive enough to enable us to reconstruct their vision and overall strategy.

Let us first see who were the people making these crucial decisions. The official policy in the first years of statehood was formulated by a small group of leaders who represented what today we would call the more 'hawkish' side of the Israeli mainstream political elite. There were more liberal-minded members of that elite who wished to have an input into the policy, but they were marginalized and their input was inconsequential. This debate was within the Zionist framework and the best way of describing it is to see the ideological spectrum of the time as stretching between democracy and ethnicity. The liberal ones, now known as 'doves', were willing to 'sacrifice', albeit in a limited way, the ethnicity of the state for the sake of its democracy. The 'hawks' deemed the ethnic purity of the state to be a supreme value which superseded any other.

The group depicted here as the 'hawks' were mainly the official advisors on Arab affairs in the Prime Minister's Office. The first person to hold this position, Yehoshua Palmon, epitomized the 'hawkish' point of view in his career and his attitudes. In the very few photos from that period, he appears as an angry, square-built person with a piercing gaze. A former member of the Arabic unit of the Haganah, which comprised Jews who were fluent in Arabic and spied on the Palestinian side, he later became the head of the Arab Section of the Jewish Agency before becoming the first prime-ministerial advisor on the subject. He was born in Palestine to two Jewish settlers who came from Russia and he grew up with Palestinians; it was only in 1948, and even more so in the early 1950s, that he became an ardent advocate of a harsh and inflexible policy towards the Palestinian indigenous population, first by taking part in their ethnic cleansing in 1948, then by regarding almost all the Palestinians left in Israel as a hostile and undesirable group of people.[26] Palmon was behind the expulsion of the people of Majdal in the southern plains (today Askhelon) in 1949; they had been Israeli citizens, according to the UN charter, for almost a year. With his prodding, David Ben-Gurion, the first Prime Minister, authorized the enforced eviction of the people of this town and made them refugees in the Gaza Strip. It was only in 1958 that he conceded in an official document that the option for transfer was not applicable any more.[27] In the official daily of the ruling party, *Davar*, he recommended constantly that the Palestinians should not be given equal rights, which included not being given the right to vote or to be elected, due to their cultural backwardness.[28]

Palmon's successor in the office in 1955 was Shemuel Divon, a former official of the Israeli Ministry of Foreign Affairs. Divon's first official paper was very clear:

> There is no way the Arabs of Israel will be loyal to the state. It would have been advantageous if the state could either expel them or convert them to Judaism, but these are now not realistic options . . . [we should therefore] limit this sore evil [*r'aah hola* in Hebrew] by uprooting their [the Arabs'] bitterness and at the same time be most painstaking about security considerations.[29]

The most famous among the more liberal Israeli politicians who did not share these views included two who, like Palmon, had been born in Palestine. The first was Moshe Sharett, the Foreign Minister, who grew up in a Palestinian village and, although he was not particularly interested in the fate of the Palestinians who were still left in the state, he supported granting them equal rights and rejected the idea of imposing military rule on them. This view was shared by Bechor Shitrit, who, although he was born in Tiberias in Palestine, was regarded as the only Mizrahi Jew (namely one who came from an Arab country) and the token Sephardic Jew in an Ashkenazi government, because his parents came from Morocco, whereas Sharett's parents came from Russia. He served as a judge under Mandatory Palestine rule and believed in the possibility of joint Arab–Jewish life from very early on, suggesting that a bi-national council be the main venue for discussing the relationship between the state and the Palestinian minority, but his ideas remained on paper.[30]

Other voices of dissent were Yitzhak Grinboym, the Minister of the Interior, Yitzhak Ben-Zvi, soon to become Israel's second president, and Pinchas Lavon, the Secretary General of the Histadrut (Israel's general trade union) and the Minister of Defense in Sharett's short-lived government from 1953 to 1954.[31] The strongest voice among them was that of Grinboym, once a leader of the Zionist movement in Poland, and relatively older than the other ministers; he allowed himself every now and then, as a declared atheist and liberal, to compare the treatment of the Jews in his homeland to that of the Arabs in his new country.

But even with such backing, Shitrit had no impact on policy. He was first appointed as Minister of Minority Affairs, but was very soon ousted by pressure from Palmon, who suggested to Ben-Gurion that it would be better to have an advisor on Arab affairs in the Prime Minister's Office than to have a special minister for them. Palmon won the day, and the Ministry for Minority Affairs was dissolved in July 1949. It was to be replaced by the Office of the Advisor on Arab Affairs in the Prime Minister's Office, and the position was given to Palmon.[32]

The Prime Minister, David Ben-Gurion, shared Palmon's uncompromising view on the Palestinian minority: he regarded them as inherently hostile, a 'fifth column'. 'Our policy should be guided,' he said, 'by the potential catastrophe that they can bring on us' (they being the Palestinian minority in Israel).[33] The presence of Palestinians in any number was an anathema for David Ben-Gurion, who had planned and supervised the ethnic cleansing of as many as possible. He now wanted to enclave the Palestinians within security zones and impose military rule upon them.

Some of his colleagues, even those who were privy to that policy back in 1948, were now willing to 'tolerate' the presence of Palestinians in the Jewish state and did not see the necessity of Ben-Gurion's harsh measures. The Prime Minister, however, regarded military rule as the only means of taming a population he conceived as constituting an existential threat to the state's security and Jewish identity. At times, he wished for more, including the total expulsion of that minority or their conversion to Judaism.[34]

The idea of reducing the Palestinian population in the early days of the state was more than wishful thinking, it was in some cases an active policy. Small villages near the border with Syria, in the Triangle on the border with the newly formed West Bank (such as Wadi Fuquin, which was the most famous case as it reached the UN) were threatened with mass expulsion. In more than thirty cases parts of these villages, and in some cases whole villages, were ethnically cleansed between 1948 and 1950.[35] The final expulsion of the people of Majdal on the southern plain to Gaza, mentioned earlier on as Palmon's initiative, has already been recorded and told in many sources; thousands of people were driven out, after being ghettoized behind barbed-wire in sections of their hometown for several months.[36] They were shot at to impel the reluctant Egyptian forces to accept them into the already densely packed and refugee-swollen Gaza Strip.

But some of those who were expelled at that time clung to the land and lived nearby until, after a very long, legal struggle, their settlements were recognized as new villages. This was the case for one clan from the village of Ayn Hawd, whose beautiful village was kept intact so that the Tel Avivian Bohemian artists could settle in it. The expellees rebuilt their life in what became the recognized village of Ayn Hawd in 1998, while the original one was called Ein Hod.

No less beautiful was the village of Ghabsiyyeh, north of Haifa, located on a hill which in those days received the fresh breeze from the Mediterranean but is now a hill of rubble surrounded by a fence. It was famous due to a creek nearby called '*al-magnuna*', 'the crazy one', which gushed forcefully on the rainy wintry days and strongly enough to cool the whole village during the hot summer nights. Like so many of Palestine's water sources, wells and streams, it is dry today and gone. On 24 January 1950, the evicted people of Ghabsiyyeh settled on the nearby hill of Sheikh Danun.

Some tried to fight eviction by going to the court. One of two things then happened: either the Supreme Court would accept the appeal to stop an eviction, as happened in the cases of Ghabsiyyeh, Kafr Bir'im and Iqrit, and the army ignored the Court's ruling, or, more commonly, the Court would reject the appeal, as happened to the people of Khirbet Jalami, who were evicted following a demand by the newly founded left-wing *kibbutz* of Lehavot Haviva in March 1950. They were offered alternative land, but refused to take it at first and went to the Supreme Court, which rejected their request.[37]

One of the tragic sites in this saga was the Jerusalemite village of Abu Gosh. The heads of the village preserved it from enforced eviction in April 1948 thanks to their long collaboration with Jewish underground movements, such as the Stern Gang, during the Mandatory Palestine period. However, hundreds of people were evicted before a leader of the Gang convinced Yitzhak Rabin, the commander of the Jerusalem Brigade (later Israel's General Chief of Staff in the June 1967 war and its prime minister twice before he was assassinated for his role in pushing forward the Oslo Peace process in November 1995), to stop the expulsion. In July 1950, many of those hundreds tried to return *en masse* and were prevented from doing so by the army.[38]

The intriguing aspect of this story is that, despite their dangerous existence and these incidents, those who led, or aspired to lead, the fragmented and traumatized community of Palestinians in Israel operated on the assumption that they were living in a democracy rather than an ethnocracy. Their strategic decision was to work by and large within, and not against, the system the Israeli political leadership built in 1949.

THE STRUGGLE FOR CITIZENSHIP IN THE NEW 'DEMOCRACY'

Therefore, the first and principal struggle of the Palestinian citizens in Israel was not directed against the pillage of land and the overall dispossession, but focused on the question of citizenship. In many ways, this struggle that began in 1949 has not ended. It is a campaign that united the community beyond its religious, ideological and social cleavages.

The Palestinian activists in 1949 demanded full citizenship of Israel on the basis of their natural rights as the indigenous population of the country. They insisted on it unreservedly and unconditionally. From 1949 onwards, the political leaders of the community employed every possible agency and available medium for advocating their case, be it the Knesset, the Supreme Court or the Hebrew press, and even resorted to the old ways, dating back to the Ottoman period, of petitions and demonstrations.

None of the means employed succeeded in influencing the new legal and constitutional realities. Given the inner logic of Zionism and the ideal of a Jewish state, the battle was lost from the start. Non-Jewish citizens could be tolerated as long as they did not endanger a Jewish supremacy in the state and therefore, from its foundation, the state distinguished between Jewish and non-Jewish citizens. This was the background for the governmental discussion of Israel's law of citizenship that lasted for two years between 1950 and 1952. It was part of the overall attempt to build a constitutional infrastructure for the young state that ended with a decision not to promulgate a constitution but to be content with several basic laws that could be amended only with an overall majority in the Knesset.

THE LOST BATTLE AGAINST DISCRIMINATORY LAWS

On the face of it, the most crucial and constitutional basic law that defined the status of the Palestinians in Israel does not look like a discriminatory one. Finalized in 1953, all it did was to declare that only those inhabitants of former Mandatory Palestine who were registered as citizens in the November 1948 census would be automatically recognized as full citizens (the census actually took place on 21 October 1948). However, a cursory knowledge of history reveals two facts that turn this law into a grave act of discrimination. First – and fundamentally – another law, the Law of Return, granted (and still grants) automatic citizenship to all Jews coming to live in Israel; their rights are not connected to their presence or absence in the November 1948 census.

Second, in November 1948, most of those Palestinians who became citizens of Israel lived in areas not yet occupied by Israel and hence could not be visited by the surveyors. Out of 160,000 Palestinians, 100,000 were not registered by November 1948. These were the Palestinians who lived in areas the Israeli army occupied after that date:

certain regions of the Galilee, the Negev and Wadi Ara (the last region was annexed to Israel in June 1949 as a result of the armistice agreement with Jordan signed in April that year). This figure also included those Palestinians who had been expelled during the war and were still in Israel, but who were not living in their original houses when the surveyors came around because their houses had been either demolished or taken over by the army. All these were not automatically Israeli citizens but had to go through a process of being admitted to the state.

The Minister of the Interior, Moshe Haim Shapira, did not regard this differentiation as discriminatory. The leader of the national religious movement, who emigrated from Belarus to Palestine in 1925, he was a very moderate person, despite his religious affiliation and his leadership of a movement that begot the extreme settler movement in the 1967 occupied territories. However, as is very typical of a left-wing Zionist, whether religious or secular, his moderation was lost when it came to the Palestinian minority in Israel. He declared in July 1950:

> if the Arabs really have wanted to be citizens of the state of Israel they would find the way ... It is not such an unreasonable demand for those who forsook their country while it was in flames to make the effort and acquire citizenship in the normal way without expecting the privilege of automatic citizenship.[39]

The Minister of Justice, Pinchas Rosen, notable as one of the leading liberals of the state, went even further two years later, stating, 'those who registered in November 1948 had showed allegiance to the Jews and their state by staying at home; all the rest were enemies who had to prove their loyalty (and repentance)'.[40] In this matter the minister reflected the views of Yehoshua Palmon, the Advisor on Arab Affairs.[41]

This association between a Palestinian's fate during the 1948 ethnic cleansing and his or her right to citizenship had already been made before the May 1948 war. It was a cornerstone of Plan *Dalet* (Plan D) from 10 March 1948, which (at least according to the interpretation of this writer) was a master plan for the ethnic cleansing of Palestine. Conceived by the high command of the main Jewish underground, the Haganah, under the instruction of David Ben-Gurion, it was the blueprint for all the military operations from March 1948 until hostilities ceased at the beginning of 1949. According to Plan D, Palestinian villages that surrendered would not be expelled and those that resisted would be punished by expulsion. The irony was that for a large group of Palestinians in Israel, those living in the Wadi Ara, this was entirely irrelevant as they were not occupied by Israeli forces, and thus could not choose one of the options. They were annexed from the West Bank to Israel in June 1949. Nonetheless they were regarded as disloyal as they were not visited by the census surveyors in November 1948.[42]

So quite a few of the Palestinians had to be naturalized, while all the Jews coming as immigrants were automatically admitted as full citizens. The process of naturalization was detailed in Article 6 of the citizenship law of Israel, which was finalized in 1953. The most important condition was an oath of allegiance to the Jewish state. The article, furthermore, gave the Minister of the Interior the right to decide who was eligible for citizenship and who was not. Thus, for the Palestinians living in Israel, unlike their Jewish neighbours, citizenship was not a legal right but a privilege, granted by the government to those who were the original and indigenous inhabitants of the country. An applicant also had to possess a 'reasonable' knowledge of the Hebrew language (a condition not imposed on new Jewish immigrants, who automatically became citizens upon arrival in Israel).

But even possessing the language was not enough. Hanna Nakkarah had a perfect command of Hebrew but when he applied for citizenship he did not receive it. He had been forced to leave with his family in April 1948, and while in Lebanon tried to convince fellow Palestinians to return to their homes – an activity that enraged the Israeli authorities. When he eventually returned on a plane from Cyprus to Haifa, he was arrested upon arrival, 'disqualified' from being admitted as a citizen and ordered to leave. He refused and was jailed for three months but insisted on his right of citizenship and was eventually released without receiving it.

A leading public figure in the community throughout the years of the military occupation, Nakkarah led most of the legal struggles on matters of citizenship and represented individual pleas by those who were denied citizenship. In 1953, he went to be registered as an election candidate for the municipality of Haifa and upon registration it was discovered he had no citizenship. He then appealed to the local court, which gave him citizenship, because the Supreme Court had already ruled several times in his favour as a litigator and did not want to admit that he had had no citizenship.

Members of another famous Haifa family, the Sahayuns, were not so fortunate. They had a joint business with some Jews who promised to facilitate their 'naturalization' should they return from Lebanon, where they had already fled in January 1948. Upon arrival the former partners were nowhere to be seen and the Sahayuns were arrested and sent back to Lebanon.[43]

Even before the law was passed, the military governors had the power to decide who could stay and who had to leave. The power was vested in them through the military Emergency Rules, already put into effect in 1948. The law of citizenship in many ways legitimized these local decisions in hindsight. The policy of expelling Palestinians who were deemed not fit to be citizens was formulated by David Ben-Gurion, the Prime Minister, who regarded anyone trying to return after the end of the 1948 war as an illegal infiltrator who had to be expelled and (as Benny Morris has shown in his book *Israel's Border Wars, 1949–1956*) could be shot.[44] 'We have to expel infiltrators and exert pressure on the Ministry of Interior to stop giving people permits to stay,' he told his ministers.[45]

Most of those denied citizenship or entry were expelled. In January 1949, the Greek Catholic bishop of Jordan reported to the Vatican that even after the end of the fighting in Palestine, refugees continued to arrive in Amman. These were Palestinians who had attempted to return but were captured by the Israeli army, put on trucks and sent to the other side of the River Jordan – not before their Mandatory Palestine certificates had been confiscated and their jewellery stolen.[46] David Ben-Gurion's diary is full of references to such evictions: for the first half of 1949 alone he reported the expulsion of five hundred villagers from the Safad area and seven hundred from Kafr Yassif.[47] In all cases, people who failed to be 'naturalized' were put on trucks, driven to the River Jordan and forced to cross to the opposite bank.

Others were naturalized, but the price they paid was far more than taking the oath of allegiance to the new state. They were provided with a quid pro quo: instead of being expelled outside the boundaries of the state, they were allowed to stay but not to return to their original homes; their lands and properties were expropriated and they were told to look for new dwellings.

The legal apparatus of the new state was very thorough and even a cursory look at the mountains of documents it left behind shows that these experts were very careful to make sure that everything the Palestinians owned had to be left behind or was pillaged by the state. Hence, officials of a new governmental agency, the Custodian of Absentee Property, wrote lengthy memoranda about the scope and nature of the property left behind by the Palestinians (only very recently was the Palestinian legal NGO, Adalah, of which more is said later in this book, allowed access in principle by the Israeli Supreme Court to this documentation). But even before one could see the documents in full, it was clear from the public statements of the Custodian that every piece of immovable and movable property which the Palestinians left behind them was taken by the state.[48]

The Absentees' Property Law was amended several times over the years, in particular between 1950 and 1956. The gist of most of the changes was to expand the authority of the Custodian of Absentee Property to sell the properties and the lands of the absentees to the state and to individual Jewish citizens. The majority of the original owners have never regained their assets. In 1973, Israel used a new law in the same vein to expropriate the land of absentees in East Jerusalem; when it occupied East Jerusalem it came across property that had belonged to 1948 refugees and the new refugees who had left Jerusalem during the 1967 war or who were expelled by Israel at its end. Since Jerusalem now became a de jure part of Israel, the abandoned Palestinian property was taken over by the Custodian of Absentee Property.

The legal battle against this state robbery of Palestinian property was lost and the relevant laws institutionalizing it were passed. The struggle, however, in hindsight, seemed to be less against the expropriation itself and more against its legitimization. And here the struggle in a way is still not over, as long as the Palestinians in Israel, at least in principle, do not give up the Right of Return of refugees to their homes and properties – even when it was absolutely clear that any Palestinian wishing to return would be denied entry and that any Jew wishing to immigrate would be most welcome in Israel. Moreover, it was clear that even internal refugees, after a successful naturalization, would not be able to win access to their former properties since the Absentees' Property Law of March 1950 cemented governmental control over the expropriated land and property, and prevented these new citizens from having any access to their original assets.

The struggle against these laws ended in defeat not only because of the ideological intransigence of the Israeli Jewish political elite but also due to the disorganization of the Palestinian leaders of the community, who were still traumatized at the time by the 1948 *Nakbah*. Several recognized figures objected publicly to this process of naturalization and property expropriation, some of whom chose a direct confrontation with the new Jewish state as part of the struggle for national liberation. However, anyone pursuing such a mode of resistance had to join other Palestinian groups outside Israel; any such activity from the inside ended in either imprisonment or exile, as is seen clearly from the case of the al-Ard movement discussed in the next chapter or the famous case of the poet Mahmoud Darwish, who in a way exiled himself in order to join the Palestinian national movement's struggle from the outside.

There were also those among the politicians who decided to learn and adapt to the rules of the Israeli system and try to protect the community from further erosion in its status and rights. These activists continued their public struggle throughout the early years of the military rule and I will name them in the next chapter to avoid overburdening the reader with too many details; here I just want to note that whoever decided to represent the community politically did so very early on. The political elite we refer to are those who opted for a middle course, believing that their legal position enabled them to protest within the state organs such as the Knesset or the local press – and this despite the fact that they lived under military rule.

The main arena for voicing opposition to the policies and laws of naturalization was the Knesset. The permission to vote and to be elected stands in stark contrast to the imposition of a harsh military rule. We have no record of any debate on it among the Jewish policy makers and one can only assume that the power struggle between the security-minded Arabists and the liberal-minded politicians within the Israeli political elite produced at least this one achievement for the Palestinian community in the genuine, or cynical, attempt to present Israel as a liberal democracy. The dominant party, Mapai, also wanted to use Arab voters to boost its performance at election time, assuming that the oppressed minority would go with the hegemomic party. In any case, this gesture or decision explains the relative optimism with which the Palestinian politicians approached the struggle for equality before the law.

Palestinian members of the Knesset who chose to join Zionist parties were enraged by the naturalization policy as much as were the members of the Communist Party, the main political vehicle in those days for Palestinians who refused to be incorporated into Zionist political institutions.

'These 100,000 [namely those needing to be re-naturalized] would look upon themselves as the Jewish citizens would look at them, as underprivileged strangers,' complained Saif al-Din al-Zu'abi, in 1950, who was the leading Palestinian member of the Knesset for the ruling Mapai party.[49] Rustum Bastuni, who was a member of another Zionist party, Mapam, said:

> This is a law of clear national discrimination, but it cannot deprive us of our right to be citizens in our own country, in which we were born, on which land we lived for ages and continue to live. I want to remind the Knesset that Article 6 in theory applies to strangers, can you see the Arabs as strangers in this country? . . . their natural right should be safeguarded.[50]

Tawfiq Tubi, a Knesset representative for the Communist Party, echoed these sentiments, arguing, 'Citizenship is given first of all to the population that was born in the country.'[51]

The fact that politicians who joined Zionist parties and those who refused the temptation of being co-opted in such a way were equally opposed to being branded legally as a second-class citizens sheds light on why Mapai could recruit so many Palestinians to its ranks in the early years of statehood: Palestinians could, so to speak, collaborate with the new rulers and yet feel that they had not given up their basic rights and identity.

There were two basic motives for joining Mapai. First, it was the establishment and joining it was like joining any state or governmental organ; second, Mapai personally targeted those who were known to be leaders or organizers in the Mandatory Palestine period and pressured them to join – either by offering them benefits or threatening them with harassment.

Bulus Farah, a Communist activist and writer, recalls an emissary from the Haifa mayor, Aba Hushi, offering him heaven and earth if he would found an 'Arab Workers Union' affiliated with Mapai. 'You will have your own car,' the emissary told him, and made flattering comments on his ability as a union leader.

Bulus Farah refused; he writes in his memoirs that the main reason for this request was a wish to organize as many Palestinians as possible as an ad hoc, unskilled outfit for picking the olives left behind by the expellees and refugees. The Communist Party had already begun such an operation in Ramleh and the Zionist trade unions wished to collect this valuable trophy themselves.

It was not easy for Farah to decline the offer of a car and a job in 1948. He used to have a bookshop, which was looted and destroyed during the fighting. And then one day, after refusing the comfort of a Mapai activist, a woman came asking for a book which he had and he sold it to her and 'the blood gushed in my veins and sweat poured profusely on the forehead. My happiness was complete. Now my mothers and sisters would not feel deprivation. The road opened for me to live a decent life.' But she was the only client, it turned out, and he could not reopen his bookshop. So this union leader and writer of the British Mandate era opened a barber shop instead. In 1952 he became the secretary of the 'Society for the Defence of the Arab Minority Rights in Israel', combining political activism with a new professional career.[52]

Those who were co-opted and those who still resisted developed a similar complex attitude towards the wave of legislation that, in hindsight, determined the Palestinian community's inferior position within the Jewish state. The responses detailed above and the general political behaviour of the political activists in the community showed a resentment of such inferiority, whether they were members of Mapai or the Communist Party. At the same time this attitude indicated a certain trust in the Israeli democracy, or at least a strategic decision not to employ national resistance tactics such as those which other Palestinian groups would adopt later in the struggle against Israel. This is also why this political group of activists decided to take part in the first 1949 Israeli general elections, although there was nothing to celebrate in these elections for them. The Palestinians in Israel did not yet possess the Israeli identity cards that allowed every citizen to vote – in their case it was a far more complex process. On top of that, they needed special permits to travel to the areas where the polling stations were located; and yet they still went and voted.

The swiftness with which the political activists decided to test the validity of the new democracy that was claimed to be in place is quite amazing in hindsight. Without the emergence as yet of a legal cadre to assist them, the Palestinian politicians decided to take their case to the Supreme Court of Israel; this was the first appeal case it had ever presided over. Hanna Naqara took forward the legal part of the struggle almost single-handedly, studying the law and finding its early loopholes to the point that the military rulers became enraged and occasionally put him in jail.[53]

In the event, the Supreme Court's judgment was as harsh as that of the politicians:

> The court asserts that a man who wanders freely and without permit within the defence lines of the state and within the offensive lines of the enemy does not deserve the court's help and assistance.[54]

This was a cruel and cynical reference to the Palestinians who were forced to wander in those places because they were expelled by the Israeli army; some of the 'offensive lines of the enemy' were their homes and fields. Pro-Zionist scholars, such as Amnon Rubinstein, tried to defend this harsh attitude as 'motivated by emotional and irrational grounds', as it totally contradicted the Declaration of Independence.[55] But the truth is the Court's decision did not contradict the ideological position of the state's political elite and hence was neither 'emotional' nor 'irrational'. Moreover, in the coming years the Supreme Court would endorse similar practices, although it would also oppose them in other instances. In a recent article, the Israeli legal historian Ilan Saban has shown that the matrix of legal and constitutional policies initiated in those early years disabled the Supreme Court from serving as the last buffer against state discrimination against the Palestinians either as individuals and or as a collective. The edifice which had been built was such that only direct legal challenge to Israel's ethical and ideological *raison d'être* would have attained such a role for the legal system, and this would have been suicidal for most of its practitioners.[56]

The activist core within the Palestinian minority did not confine its opposition to speeches in the Knesset and appeals to the Supreme Court, but attempted to galvanize their public with a series of demonstrations (in fact, the first recorded demonstrations by Palestinians in Israel were not against the law of citizenship but against the policy of land expropriation). These demonstrations were brutally dispersed by the army, and the local military governors imposed severe punishments on the demonstrators who were arrested. Pre-emptive measures were also common: whole villages were declared a 'closed military area' whenever the Shin Beit (the general security service, which we will refer to from here onwards by its Hebrew acronym as was done by the people themselves, the Shabak) had early knowledge of the intention to hold a meeting or a demonstration. Hence the army could act against the demonstrations behind a veil of secrecy and silence, without anyone in the outside world knowing or reacting.

Palestinians have continued to demonstrate until this very day, but this has always involved clashing with the full might of the Jewish state. Already then, more often than not, in the case of a Palestinian demonstration, the army was appended to the anti-demonstration forces. That usually meant more large-scale arrests, and a greater likelihood of wounded and even dead demonstrators.

The demonstrations against the law of citizenship included a half-day strike, another mode of protest that would be used often by the Palestinians as a collective national group, even before they were recognized as such by others. As one of the first Western political scientists to be interested in the Palestinians in Israel, Joel Migdal, noted, the modes of protest of the Palestinians in Israel were similar to those adopted by other Palestinian groups. In his view they were a mixture of *realpolitik* and self-assertion, namely ones that could be tolerated by the powers that be to a certain extent but at the same time solidified the collective identity.[57] We will come back to this assertion when we discuss the junctures, such as in 1976, 2000, 2006 and 2009, when demonstrations were perceived by the authorities as transcending the lines of tolerated activity.

The struggle against exclusion through the law of citizenship very early on distinguished the Palestinian struggle inside Israel from that of other Palestinian groups. The former wanted to be recognized within the Jewish state, while other Palestinian forces were struggling against the very idea of a Jewish state. In general we can conclude by saying that until 1966, the state responded to these political and national impulses with a mixture of alienation and oppression through the imposition of harsh military rule. The community as a whole was suspected of being a strategic threat to the state. The Israeli political elite's plan for the future included contemplating further ethnic cleansing and conversion to Judaism, while little attention was given to Palestinians' welfare and well-being. The trauma of 1948 was in no way over by the end of 1949.

CHAPTER TWO

THE OPEN WOUND

MILITARY RULE AND ITS LASTING IMPACT

THE MILITARY RULE imposed on the Palestinians in Israel deserves a book of its own, but almost like the *Nakbah* itself, it is still repressed by the traumatized victims and the guilt-stricken victimizers. The rule was imposed on every area that had a large Palestinian population and was based on the British Mandate's Emergency Regulations. It lasted until 1966 and it affected every walk and aspect of life. '*Hamimishar Ha-Zevai*' in Hebrew means 'military rule'. But it was not only a noun describing a legal reality, it was also the name of a unit within the Israeli army that supervised a group of governors ruling under the regional commanders of the army in the south, north and centre of the country. These officers had executive, legislative and juridical powers that only a very dictatorial state possesses in modern times. Military rule scarred the Palestinians in Israel for life, as much as the *Nakbah* tormented the Palestinians as a whole.

Recollections of military rule are bitter and unpleasant – not only for the Palestinian citizens themselves, but for the more conscious Jews who were in powerful positions at the time. One governor-general recalled how poor villagers felt obliged to give a royal reception, comprising a sumptuous meal and very generous hospitality, every time he or other governors visited, always accompanied by a large entourage, as their livelihood totally depended on these guests' goodwill.[1] The late Emil Habibi brought all these bitter memories to the fore in the adventures of his fictional hero, Saeed Abu al-Nahs, in his most famous novel, *The Secret Life of Saeed, the Pessoptimist*, in which Saeed succeeds in surviving the humiliation and degradation of his daily encounters with governors and officials, who have absolute power over his life, by pretending to be the village's clown and idiot.[2] Real life for many was even worse. This harsh reality lasted for nineteen years, but was not at all reported in the world at large, nor were most Israeli Jews aware of it. In 2009, my son's teacher told me that only through the BA studies he undertook in his sabbatical year did he learn that the Palestinians in Israel had lived under military rule. This ignorance is still typical among many educated and professional Israeli Jews today.

But it would be wrong to view the period as static; people's lives did improve as the years went by. Therefore it is useful to divide the military rule period into two rough phases. During the first, up to 1957, the very existence of the community was in question. Their presence was regarded by important figures in the Israeli regime as 'unfinished business', and quite a few of the politicians and heads of the security services still contemplated the removal of the Palestinian citizens from the Jewish state. The second phase saw a relaxation in this expulsionist impulse and a general reconciliation with the bi-national nature of the newly founded Jewish state.

ETHNIC CLEANSING BY DIFFERENT MEANS, 1948–1957

In general the first period was one during which the authorities, under the guidance of the first Prime Minister of Israel, were looking for ways of downsizing the number of Palestinians in the Jewish state. Although in 1955 some members of the bureaucracy that dealt with the Palestinian minority had already abandoned this strategy and begun to get used to the idea of a Jewish state that would include a sizeable number of Palestinians, others, even after 1957, wished they could find a way of keeping the number of Palestinians in the Jewish state to a minimum in every possible way.

During the first period, military rule was intended as the principal tool for alienating the Palestinians from the state.[3] The negative message came across, as we shall see, not only through a series of plans for actual expulsion, but also through a policy designed to encourage people to leave 'voluntarily'. In years to come, a younger generation of Palestinians would look with disdain at their elders and accuse them of succumbing too easily to Israeli humiliation, of surrendering their dignity and national pride without a fight.[4] In fact, those saying this had no understanding of how precarious their elders' existence had been in a state that was contemplating a future without them. Their steadfastness and stubborn determination not to fall prey to the Israeli policies is a chapter of heroism not defeatism, and one of the two main reasons for the failure of this policy; the other was the existence of Jewish policy makers who refused to be part of such a discourse and strategy. Fortunately, some of these were senior enough to make a difference.

The Palestinians faced quite an elaborate system of control and oppression. Military rule was imposed mainly on the rural areas, while the urban centres were put under tight civilian monitoring and control. The military rule areas were administered, as mentioned, by the *Ha-Mimshal Ha-Zvai* (military rule) unit within the Israel Defense Forces, which had its own command. The members of this unit did not have a direct presence in the towns and the cities where Palestinians lived but their counterparts in the 'civilian' authority there emulated their mode of control and enjoyed similar wide powers; hence these areas for all intents and purposes came under military rule as well.

Politically, the military rule unit came under the Ministry of Defense on the one hand and the Israeli secret service, the Shabak, on the other. A special committee met every now and then to coordinate strategy; at its first meeting this committee defined the Palestinian community in Israel as a 'hostile community' which needed to be constantly monitored and supervised. The Palestinians were described there as 'a fifth column' that at any given moment could join the enemies of the state. Senior members of the Shabak, the Prime Minister's Advisors on Arab Affairs, a representative of the trade union, Histadrut, and officials from the 'military rule' unit were all members of this committee, which 'managed' the Palestinian community in Israel until 1966.[5]

It is important to stress that initially there was no dissent inside the Israeli political and military elite about the necessity of military rule. It was imposed on 21 October 1948 by David Ben-Gurion and was based on the Defence (Emergency) Regulations established by the British Mandate in 1945, which gave unlimited control to the military governors over the Palestinian community. According to these regulations the governor had the right to arrest people without a warrant and detain them without trial for long periods; he could ban their entrance to a place or expel them from their homes; he could also confine them under house arrest. He could close schools, businesses, newspapers and journals, and prohibit demonstrations or protests. This is a formative chapter in the history of the state; these regulations are still intact today, although in a less direct way, and have been the basis for Israel's policy in the West Bank and the Gaza Strip during the long years of their occupation.

SETTING THE LEGAL INFRASTRUCTURE

The legal instruments of the military rule imposed on the Palestinian minority in Israel in October 1948 were issued without reference to these Mandatory Regulations. They appeared in two forms. Officially they were declared only after the inauguration of the first Knesset in April 1949. But even before that, the provisional council ruling Israel until the first elections published them in its *Official Gazette* – the governmental ordinances which were based on these regulations. The first ordinance to be announced in such a manner was called the Laws and Administrative Ordinance No. 1. It granted unlimited power to the Minister of Defense to use any of the Mandatory Regulations deemed useful for governance. The first to be used by David Ben-Gurion, who was both the provisional Prime Minister and Minister of Defense, were those allowing the state to take over abandoned property and land left behind by those who were forced out. This was issued on 23 June 1948, even before much of Palestine had been taken over by the Israeli military, when there were already more than 350,000 refugees. This is the clearest indication of the anti-repatriation policy of Israel, which both prevented the original owners from coming back and also barred the access of other Palestinians to their houses, fields and businesses.

The first ordinance was very detailed, specifying movable and immovable property as the objects of the confiscation. During April 1948 whole towns were emptied of their Palestinian population, who more or less had to leave all they ever possessed behind; the government was then already facing a wave of private looting by Jewish soldiers and civilians, and wanted to take control not only of the Palestinians' homes in the towns, but also of their factories full of machinery, warehouses filled with food and banks full of money.

The regulations and ordinances were recognized by many in the new state as a necessary tool for a smooth takeover. But the nature of these regulations, and especially the fact that had been used in the past against the Jewish paramilitary forces, created a more profound and ethical problem for some of the jurists of the new state, especially among the senior officials of the Israeli Ministry of Justice. They were aware of their positions vis-à-vis the regulations when they had been first presented by the British in 1945. Yaakov Shimshon Shapira, the legal advisor to the government and later a Minister of Justice himself, had in 1946 used the following harsh words to describe the very same regulations he was now exercising against the Palestinians in Israel:

> The regime that was established in accordance with the emergency regulations has no parallel in any enlightened country. Even in Nazi Germany there were no such rules, and the actions of Maydanek and its like had been done out of violation of the written law. Only one form of regime resembles these conditions – the status of an occupied country.[6]

At that meeting in 1946 in Tel Aviv other well-known figures in the ministry and some of the prominent lawyers of the Jewish community at the time raised similar objections, even if they phrased them somewhat differently.[7]

Many of the Mapai Knesset members did strive to abolish the regulations as early as 1949. They suggested replacing them with new military regulations that would suit the situation in the new state. But no one took it upon himself to carry such a legislative initiative to an effective end. Two years later, in May 1951, no one in Mapai voted against the following Mapam proposal in the Knesset:

> The Emergency regulations of 1945 that are still intact in the state since the Mandatory period stand in stark contradiction to the fundamentals of a democratic state. The Knesset instructs its committee for constitutional affairs to bring to the Knesset in no less than two weeks a draft law abolishing these regulations.[8]

The government deemed it useful to maintain the regulations for as long as it could, and only in the next century would this legislative process be completed.

THE EMERGENCY REGULATIONS AS A REALITY

The legal system found it difficult to cope with such a regime, and one judge in Tel Aviv, Shalom Qassam, refused to rule on the basis of these regulations since they stood in direct contradiction to his conscience.[9] The two most notorious regulations were No. 109, allowing the governor to expel the population, and No. 110, which gave him the right to summon any citizen to the police station whenever he saw fit. Another famous regulation was No. 111, which sanctioned administrative arrest – arrest for an unlimited period without explanation or trial.[10]

However, the most important was Regulation No. 125, which became an Israeli law in 1949, allowing the Israeli government to impose military rule on any territory within the state. Officially, Regulation No. 125 focused on the prevention of movement into and out of the designated area and sometimes movement within that area. But the prevention of movement was used by the Israeli government to expropriate land without being interrupted by protest or by legal action taken by the victims of this policy. Without the right to move freely the Palestinians had very little hope of finding work outside the restricted area (and work was only to be found in the forbidden Jewish areas), of socializing with other people or of organizing any kind of political action. During election time the government, without any hesitation, used the ban on movement to disrupt the ability of oppositional political parties to convene, campaign or organize their electorates. So the prevention of movement robbed the Palestinians in Israel of their basic civil rights, even if officially the regulation did not relate to every sphere of life.

This regulation and later on other regulations that allowed direct bans on the freedom of press, expression and the ability to lead a normal life became a pernicious tool in the hands of callous and sometimes sadistic military rulers, who were generally drawn from non-combatant units just before their retirement, or who were released from combat duties due to their health or ineptitude. Their cruel behaviour consisted mainly of harassing the population with a range of abuses not unlike those to which new army recruits were subjected. They became absolute monarchs in their little kingdoms.[11]

In July 1953 one such 'little king' imposed a curfew on the village of Tira and began mass arrests for no apparent reason. After a house-to-house search, in which children and women were beaten as the soldiers dragged the men out to the streets, the village elders were caged in a pen – a procedure often used during the 1948 ethnic cleansing – while soldiers were shooting in the air and damaging property. Israeli radio later reported that shots were heard aimed at a low-flying airplane on descent to Lod Airport (later named Ben-Gurion Airport); a day later the story changed and it was alleged that a military officer had been attacked in the village. The shots, by the way, came from the West Bank.[12]

There were other aspects to Israeli military rule. Under its umbrella, the official land confiscation policy was able to continue in the name of 'security' and 'public interest'. Political activists even vaguely suspected of identifying with Palestinian nationalism were expelled or imprisoned. Ben-Gurion's diary reveals that the first head of the military rule apparatus, General Elimelech Avner, was quite worried by this absolutism. Avner complained several times about the absence of a guiding hand and a lack of general guidelines for the governors who were running the Arab areas.[13] His dismay was echoed by other civil servants in the 1950s.

A frequent issue was abuses at the checkpoints at the entrances to villages, where labourers could be stopped from going to work or where villagers could be denied access to a nearby hospital by whimsical guards. In July 1956, the Israeli press noted that in Wadi Ara in particular, workers with permits were prevented for hours from reaching their destinations, and in one case a sick baby died after being refused access to a hospital for more than a week.[14]

Out of all the regulations three restrictions stand out in the collective memory of the people themselves: the bans on movement, the prohibition on political organization and the limitations on job opportunities. One could never know whether a trip to see a relative would be completed under such a regime and, needless to say, there was no incentive to seek jobs or education which involved daily commuting through the military checkpoints – a reality only too familiar to the people living in the occupied territories since 1967.

CONTEMPLATING FURTHER ETHNIC CLEANSING

Had the Palestinians in Israel been aware of the deliberations about their fate during the first eight years of statehood, their lives would probably have been even more anxious and restless. Some could not afford to ignore the existential danger: Palestinians from more than thirty villages, most of them small ones, were expelled either in total or in part to the other side of the Lebanese, Syrian or Jordanian border. This included large sections of Bedouin tribes who lost their traditional *dira* (space) in which they had roamed and on which they had lived semi-settled for more than two centuries.[15]

There were however things that were concealed from the public eye – such as Operation *Hafarferet* (mole), which contemplated, but never implemented, a mass expulsion of Palestinians during a possible war. As we shall see, it nearly materialized in October 1956 during the Sinai campaign. The plan reflected the mindset of the head of the Shabak, Isar Harel, who wanted the 'Arabs to feel that any given moment we can destroy them'.[16]

David Ben-Gurion was particularly inventive when it came to direct and indirect means of limiting the living possibilities for the

Palestinian community in Israel. Verging on the absurd was his idea of turning the Palestinians into an Arab *millet* in Israel (the old status of Christians and Jews under Ottoman rule), which would have turned the Palestinians into a religious community with even fewer rights and privileges than they had held under military rule. In practice, we can assume he never developed the idea beyond this vague reference, but it did reflect the attitude of the man standing at the top of the political pyramid in Israel. Another more plausible idea was to drive a wedge between Christians and Muslims by presenting and treating the Christians as more loyal to the Jewish state. The latter was sometimes attempted locally but always failed.[17] This general attitude to Palestinian citizens probably remains in official circles to this very day, but the actual planning of ethnic cleansing petered out, before it appeared again as a public discourse at the end of our story, at the beginning of the twenty-first century.

The policy towards the Palestinian minority was determined by a security-minded group of decision makers and executed by Ben-Gurion's unfailingly ruthless advisors on Arab affairs, who were in favour of expelling as many Palestinians as possible and confining the rest within well-guarded enclaves.

The expulsionists marked the 'present absentees', Palestinian refugees who were wandering within the state of Israel, homeless and stateless, as the group to be deported. Communist Party activists, supported by Moshe Sharett, the Foreign Minister, came to their rescue and at the end of the day only a few were actually expelled.[18] Sharett was a key figure in the movement for the abolition of the military regime, but it took more than fifteen years for the Zionist liberals to bring an end to it. An important figure was the pompous and otherwise quite nationalist leader of the right-wing opposition party Herut, Menachem Begin. Always a man of contradictions, he had a liberal streak in him and seemed appalled by the use of the British Emergency Regulations against the Palestinian minority as he remembered too well how they had been used against himself and his friends (he compared them to the Nuremberg Laws of the Nazis at the time). However, as Prime Minister in the early 1980s, and for a while also the Minister of Defense, he reissued these regulations without hesitation.[19] Others came from the socialist party, Mapam, and there were a few independent thinkers such as Martin Buber, who used the publications he edited, *Beterm* ('Before it is too late') and *Ner* ('Candle'), to write public letters to Ben-Gurion demanding the abolition of military rule (and occasionally the return of the Palestinian refugees).[20]

It was not easy to counter the Prime Minister and his policies. On this question, Jewish 'public opinion' was on Ben-Gurion's side, and the local Hebrew press was unanimous in its support for the government's policy. But by the early 1960s, the expulsionist activism died out, partly because of a wave of internal criticism by people from left to right who wished Israel to be seen at least from the outside as a democracy – and some probably genuinely wished it to be one. It was a powerful opposition because it included such opposite personalities such as Menachem Begin and Martin Buber, who joined forces both in the Knesset and out of it to exert pressure on the government to abolish military rule. Typically for Israeli society, these criticisms reflected not so much sympathy for the plight of the Palestinians as apprehensions about the moral image and international standing of the Jewish. But when joined by brave public figures in the Palestinian community, organized in the main by the Communist Party, such attitudes had an impact on the policy.

Pressure and protest are never enough though, to bring about change in Israel. A catastrophe of a sort is always needed for things to be transformed significantly. In this particular case it was the massacre in Kafr Qassem on 29 October 1956.

THE KAFR QASSEM MASSACRE

On 29 October 1956, on the eve of the Israeli military invasion of the Sinai Peninsula, as part of its joint campaign with Britain and France to topple the Egyptian leader, Gamal Abdul Nasser, the IDF completed its preparations for controlling the Palestinian areas that were deemed the most problematic in case of a war with Arab neighbours: the villages of the Triangle, the *Muthalath*.

Colonel Issachar Shadmi, a former commander of a POW labour camp of Palestinian prisoners in the 1948 war, and now commanding a brigade, asked and received permission to impose a curfew at 5 p.m. rather than 9 p.m., the time previously announced to the villagers under his command. In a meeting with his soldiers he repeated the general instruction for an Israeli curfew: shoot on sight without warning its violators. Soldiers noted the time difference and asked what they should do with those who were late in returning from the fields or their work. According to their evidence at the trial later, Shadmi retorted, '*Allahu Irhmaum*', 'May they rest in peace'; the Arab blessing for the dead.[21]

Major Shmuel Melinki was the battalion commander of the border police in Kafr Qassem. He too, according to evidence given in court, was asked by his subordinates what to do with the men, women and children labouring in the fields, unaware that the time of the curfew was brought forward. 'Act without any sentimental hesitations. Do as the commander of the Brigade told us.' It seems soldiers wanted clear instructions. Melinki reread the brigade commander's orders which said, 'the rule [of shooting violators] applies to everyone'.[22]

The change of timing did not only occur in Kafr Qassem, it applied to all the villages which were under Shadmi's command and quite a few others all over Israel. But in Qalanswa, Taybeh, Ibtin, Bir al-Saqi, Jaljulya and Kafr Qara, the local commanders allowed latecomers to return until 9 p.m. The court records have a curious but not untypical remark by the commander in Kafr Qara: 'I was somewhat ashamed the next day that nobody in my village was killed.'[23]

Shalom Offer was commanding the main checkpoint at the entrance to Kafr Qassem. Just a few minutes before 5 p.m., two villagers appeared in front of him. Ahmad Farig and Ali Taha alighted from their bicycles and were greeted sarcastically by the officer with the question, 'Are you happy (*mabsustin*)?' [Presumably meaning, 'Are you happy with your-selves for being late?'] 'Yes,' they replied. They were ordered to stand and were shot. 'Enough,' said the officer to his soldiers after a while, 'They are already dead. We have to spare the bullets.' This account was given by Mahmoud Farij and Abdullah Samir Badir who witnessed the event and managed to escape, although they were shot and wounded.[24]

Other villagers who came later were shot in a similar way. Among them was Fatma Sarsur, eight months pregnant, who had just finished picking olives nearby. For an hour the shooting continued, according to the evidence given by Hannan Suleyman Aamer, the only woman who survived from the group that was massacred. Forty-eight villagers met their deaths in that hour, including twelve young women, ten male teenagers and seven boys. Thirteen others were badly wounded.[25]

It took time before the authorities reacted. Two weeks after the massacre the first official Israeli acknowledgement was published. In hindsight it seems to be less an admission of the facts, and much more a pre-emptive attempt to provide immunity to the perpetrators of the crime. On 11 November, the government message to the press blamed it all on the Palestinian *Fidayi* (literally 'volunteer') forces. These were Palestinian refugees who came secretly into Israel, first in an attempt to retrieve lost property or herds, but soon to carry out more sustained acts of sabotage and guerrilla warfare against the Israeli army and civilians; they were supported by the Egyptian army in the Gaza Strip and to a lesser extent by the Syrian and Jordanian military establishments. The government statement read as follows: 'Increased *Fidayi* action on 29 October 1956 led to the imposition of military rule on the villages adjacent to Jordan in order to protect them.' This cynical and insincere double-talk would accompany the Palestinians in Israel for years to come.

Three weeks passed before outsiders could come to the village and see what had happened with their own eyes. The first visitors were the Communist members of the Knesset, Tawfiq Tubi and Meir Vilner, and Latif Dori, a member of Mapam, who managed to bypass the police roadblocks that barred any approach from all the village's entrances. They started collecting evidence from the traumatized and grief-stricken people and tried later to publicize their statements in the local press. This was prevented by the military censor, but Tawfiq Tubi did not give up and wrote a memo which he distributed among hundreds of well-known public figures in Israel.

This created some sort of public pressure, which resulted in the establishment of an inquiry commission. That commission concluded that Melinki, the commander of the battalion, and some of his subordinates should be brought to justice for enforcing an illegal command and it recommended compensating the families of the victims with 1,000 Israeli pounds each.

The committee's recommendations were described by Tawfiq Tubi as a whitewash and cover-up exercise. He blamed the government for producing the atmosphere which encouraged the border police to perpetrate the massacre. In language that tells us something about the assertiveness and sense of injustice Palestinians displayed, notwithstanding the trauma and the oppression, he compared the massacre with that of the Czech village Lidice, all of whose inhabitants were slaughtered by the Nazis in 1942.[26]

The trial validated his apprehensions. None of the accused received any significant punishment, leaving an impression that future atrocities would be treated in a similar way. The Palestinians' sense of fear was augmented by the other, lesser-known killings that took place on that day. In Kafr Tira, in the Triangle, a labourer who worked as a night watchman in the fields, Nimr Abd al-Jaber, sixty years old, was shot by the border police for being late. In the village of Taybeh, also in the Triangle, a fourteen-year-old, Mahmoud Aqab Sultan was shot by the troops on his way home, running an errand for this father that evening. Another fourteen-year-old boy disappeared in the nearby village of Baqa al-Gharbiyya and has never been found. The failure of the state to protect its own citizens incurred little or no public indignation, and was further compounded by the light sentences meted out to the perpetrators.

During the trial for the first time Operation *Hafarferet* or, as it was named in official code, Blueprint S-59, was exposed. Some of the defendants justified the massacre as the implementation of the Blueprint, which, as they understood it, meant them to deal harshly with the Palestinian population. But when their lawyers tried to push forward this argument, they were silenced by the judges. The plan was top secret and its publication would have embarrassed the government. Shalom Offer's lawyer, David Rotloy, managed to say that the Blueprint envisaged imprisoning the Arabs in pens and then forcing them to flee east – towards Jordan – in the chaos of war.[27]

As mentioned, the plan, which has been fully researched by the Palestinian historian Nur Masalha, was indeed a contingency scheme for the expulsion of the Palestinians in the Triangle in the case of a war with Jordan.[28] Most researchers think that Shadmi gave the orders under the assumption that he was beginning to fulfil the plan.[29] This was also the opinion of the late David Horowitz, Israel's leading political scientist for many years and a reporter for the Mapai daily at the time, *Davar*. He thought the operation was based on the assumption that one could provoke the Palestinians to violate the law, and then retaliate by expulsion (this was the logic of the first stage of the ethnic cleansing in 1948).[30]

But in the long run, the Kafr Qassem massacre did have an impact. It highlighted the immorality of the military regime and sent shock waves across the country; it led the government to change its position eventually and abolish military rule in 1966. Public criticism was not aimed at the decision-making apparatus itself as much as at the leniency shown to the murderers. Moreover, the inability of the secret service to expose collaboration with the Egyptian army during the Sinai operation – a ludicrous allegation anyway – convinced many that the military regime was useless and even harmful. It was sold to the public at large as a pre-emptive means to prevent the Palestinians from joining the enemy at a time of war. The 1956 war, the first round of fighting since the creation of the state, passed without any desire or attempt on the part of the Palestinians to 'join forces with the enemy' and the only visible result of the imposition of military rule was the massacre.

Even the head of the Israeli secret service, Isar Harel, tried to convince Ben-Gurion that, from a security point of view, abolishing military rule would be much more constructive than retaining it.[31] In this he was fully supported by the director-general of the Defense Ministry, Shimon Peres. However, nothing was to happen until Ben-Gurion lost his premiership in 1963.

THE 'SOFTER' FACE OF THE RULE: THE PERILS OF THE STICK AND THE TEMPTATIONS OF THE CARROT POLICY, 1957–1967

After the massacre, the coalition of forces and individuals who were calling for the abolition of military rule became stronger and louder. The first 'national' protest against military rule took place in 1957 and the Palestinian demonstrators were joined by Jewish activists. The latter came mainly from the Jewish cadre of the Communist Party, alongside former members of the Brit Shalom movement, a marginal group that had been active in the 1920s and the last days of the British Mandate (acting under a different name) in promulgating the idea of a bi-national state in Palestine. Partly as a result, in that same year the system was transmuted into a more nuanced policy of control. A new element was introduced into the matrix of power: co-optation. The 'sticks' of the military rule were still there, but now a few 'carrots' were thrown in.

The Prime Minister's advisors on Arab affairs devised an elaborate web of inducements. In return for wealth and prestige for themselves and better living conditions for their own communities, notables in the Palestinian community were easily tempted to mute their identification with nationalism. They would go out of their way to host government officials or commemorate Jewish national and religious holidays, and some went as far as collaborating with the Israeli secret service as is detailed, with names and places included, in a recent book published on the topic.[32] They were further encouraged to show their society the benefits that could be accrued by anyone willing to comply with Israel's policy of co-optation. This was a strategy that worked well through the patriarchal and hierarchical structures still in place in rural as well as in nomadic areas. However, the heads of villages (*mukhtars*) and the heads of tribes (*sheikhs*) who agreed to become agents of government policy soon found themselves largely ostracized by their communities, who called them *adhnab al-hukuma* (the government's tails). In the long run, this method of co-optation proved ineffective and counter-productive as it strengthened the resentment and the disgust in the community with this kind of behaviour. When the military regime was abolished in 1966, most of these notables lost their positions.

THE PERILS OF COLLABORATION

It is difficult to be judgemental in hindsight about the issue of collaboration as it came in all kinds of forms and affected all walks of life. We now have the files on actual collaboration in the service of the Shabak

open to us and I am unwilling to delve too deeply into this phenomenon, which was expansive and invasive on levels familiar from the
kind of nets cast by the Stasi in East Germany.

What is clear is that at one point or another under military rule, the
lack of open resistance made it easier for the rule to continue; and yet
since the imposition of that rule was meant to make people leave, the
very fact that they stayed was a form of resistance and success. Apart
from people who were directly employed as informers or agents, I
think it is improper and also historically incorrect to define willingness
to work within the state system as collaboration of any kind. This was
a necessity for survival within a system that, at least in those years, did
not care much if you survived or not.

Muhammad Bakri is a Palestinian actor born in the Galilee who
became one of Israel's best-known performers in recent years. His
career has however been hampered by his occasional clashes with the
Israeli establishment due to his outspoken views about the occupation
of the Palestinian territories and the persecution of the Palestinian
minority in Israel. Bakri is one of the few Palestinian artists today who
engage boldly with the issue of collaboration in the period covered by
this book – the years of the Israeli military rule. He recalls that in his
elementary school days, in his village B'ina, the most pleasant time of
the year was the Day of Independence. No proper schooling, a lot of
good food and plenty of music provided the background for his first
ever performance when he was chosen, being the best orator in the
class, to recite the speech in praise of the state of Israel and its benevolent policy towards its 'Arab' citizens, written by the vice-principal in
the school. The principal did not attend the ceremony and soon after
his deputy replaced him, as Bakri put it, 'with the help of the speech,
Allah and the Israeli Secret Service'.[33] Even today one is not sure who
in the segregated Arab educational system owes his or her job and
career to the Shabak – quite a few, one suspects.

It was in the educational system that these dilemmas were displayed
most forcefully, particularly when schools were asked to celebrate
Israel's Independence Day, which for the Palestinians in Israel was the
day of the *Nakbah*, the catastrophe – an event to commemorate rather
than celebrate. These celebrations were not confined to the schools

but were imposed on the whole community. Many people remember vividly the Israeli flags flying everywhere and young Palestinians marching to the beat of scouts' drums celebrating the catastrophe of 1948. Schoolchildren everywhere were asked to write essays, and, if they were so inclined, poems, celebrating the Jewish state and its achievements. All over the Arab villages the celebration was both enforced and highly visible. Members of Jewish kibbutzim in Wadi Ara recall that their teachers thought that the celebrations in the kibbutzim were not enthusiastic enough, so they were dispatched to Umm al-Fahem to watch the parade of Arab scouts saluting the Jewish state.

The poet and Druze writer Salman Natour recalls how he was forced to celebrate Independence Day in Daliyat al-Karmil. His story is worth dwelling on as it illustrates the complex reality of living as a Palestinian in Israel.[34] Natour still lives today in the Druze village of Daliyat al-Karmil on the top of Mount Carmel. The Druze are a religious sect, an offshoot of Shiite Islam. In Israel, this is considered to be a separate religion, and its communal conduct differs somewhat from similar communities in other Middle Eastern countries (there are Druze in Lebanon, Syria and Jordan, as well as in Israel). During the 1948 war, the elders of the Druze community, sensing where the balance of power was moving, signed a pact of allegiance with the Jewish state. This should have made them first-class citizens as far as full rights and state privileges were concerned. However, they were confined to special units in the army and were not socio-economically equal to most Jewish citizens. Nevertheless, most of their leaders wished to continue the co-optation by and cooperation with Israel.[35]

And yet individual memories from the period of the military rule transcend ethnic or religious affiliations. Years later, members of the Druze community would look back at the 'blood pact' which their elders had signed on their behalf and doubt its wisdom; in particular, young Druze serving in the army in return for preferential treatment by the Jewish state soon realized that in practice they were just as likely to be unemployed and marginalized as their Muslim or Christian brothers. The Druze fulfilled their part of the deal, but the preferential treatment promised did not seem to materialize. The result was their alienation from the wider Palestinian community with no visible advantages.[36]

Some among the Druze saw this frustration coming very early on. Salman Natour, a long-time activist in the Israeli Communist Party, was one of them. His perspective and his memoirs correspond to those of his activist friends in the Muslim and Christian communities.

On Israeli Independence Day, the teacher entered Natour's classroom and asked which of the pupils would write a poem for the celebratory occasion. This was, Natour recalled, a very happy day for the children: no lessons, only rehearsals for a dance and song show in preparation for the principal's speech commending Israel for being the only democracy in the Middle East and thanking the government for its benevolence and kindness.

A third-generation poet, the young Salman confidently raised his hand and proposed to write the poem. The result, however, was not celebratory enough, and the teacher wrote something which Salman was asked to read in his own name as part of a show of deference and respect to Israeli officials. Many years later, that principal was suspected of collaborating with elements 'hostile' to Israel. He urged Natour to come forward and reveal that it was the teacher who wrote this patriotic poem, so that his loyalty to the state could be proved. The poem proved a valuable asset.

THE ILLUSION OF INCLUSION: MILITARY SERVICE

From very early on the Palestinians in Israel realized that the key to being a full citizen in Israel was serving in the Israeli army. Serving in the Israel Defense Forces (IDF) was compulsory for men and women alike, and this was the ticket for full benefits from the state and indeed for a place in the community of citizens of the nation. The elders of the Druze community and some heads of clans in the Bedouin community argued that serving in the army would separate their members of the community from the rest of the Palestinians in Israel and, more importantly, give them preferential treatment, even the status of equal citizenship – as already noted, they were wrong.

But during the period covered in this chapter their experience was somewhat different from that of the other members of the minority.

Just as for everyone else, for them politicization meant a safe navigation between the temptations of co-optation and the perils of resistance. Bedouin life and culture had changed very little in the nineteenth
century and the first half of the twentieth century. The main event in
their history had been the Egyptian rule of Palestine between 1831 and
1840, which allowed them to frequent Palestine from bases in the Sinai
Peninsula, and they continued to make their presence felt, particularly
after the Ottomans returned to power in 1840. They maintained their
nomadic way of life in the east and north of Palestine during the rest
of the Ottoman rule, but after 1900 the main concentration of
nomadic and semi-nomadic Bedouin was in the south, in al-Naqab or
the Negev.

At the turn of the twentieth century, eighty tribes were registered in
seven different locations, which were marked as bases. This elementary structure remained intact until 1948. In 1947, there were 80,000
Bedouin in the south of Palestine, but the Israeli expulsion policy did
not spare them and, when the winds of war subsided, only 13,000 were
left. They regrouped into twenty tribes in three locations, spread
throughout the Negev.

The Bedouin in the south, as mentioned, did not join the army
in great numbers. It was mainly from the northern Bedouin communities that a large number of youngsters joined the army. Scattered from
the western valleys to the eastern border with Syria, these Bedouin are
descendants of tribes who arrived earlier in history from Iraq and Syria.
As a political community they adopted the same strategy as those in
the south, but their way of life was more sedentary than that of the
Palestinians who lived nomadic lives in the south. All in all, those in
the north enjoyed a better standard of living than those in the south, but
not better than the average Palestinian citizen.

It was because of the Bedouin that the Negev remained the only
geographical area in Israel relatively untouched by the fervour for
modernization. Camels and herds of sheep and goats were still an
important part of Bedouin life. However, agriculture and semi-
proletarianization, similar to that which affected the rest of the
Palestinian community in Israel, were beginning to influence Bedouin
life by the end of the 1950s, leading to the abandonment of their

nomadic life. The second half of the decade was particularly dry, and five successive years of drought drove many of the Bedouin north, where the government eventually allowed them to settle in a few villages. Those in the south forsook their pastoral life for unskilled work in agriculture, construction and maintenance, while others opted for a career in the army and the police force.

Similar policies of preferential treatment in return for army service were pursued towards the Circassians, who were a group of a few thousand living mainly in two villages in the Galilee. In the early 1950s, the government was divided on the question of conscription to the IDF. The secret service predicted that the Palestinian minority in Israel would reject conscription, and suggested that all that was needed was to call up one year's intake. Should they refuse, the government would be able to declare that the Palestinian community as a whole refused to serve in the army. When the experiment took place in 1954, to the surprise and bewilderment of the secret service, every conscript responded to the call-up. In addition, the Communist Party supported potential recruits and the call-up day turned into a festive event. No one was actually conscripted; the policy makers simply ignored those people's readiness to serve.[37]

What is more, the government's policy on this issue gave it another tool in its discriminatory policy against the Palestinian minority, which is still being applied today: only people who have served in the army are eligible for state benefits such as loans, mortgages and reduced university fees. There is also a close link between industry and security in the Jewish state, and many employers insist that potential employees have done army service, which means that significant sections (almost 70 per cent) of industry are closed to Palestinian citizens.[38]

The whole question of tempting Palestinians with military service in return for a higher level of citizenship thus had a very strong religious aspect; Christians and Muslims were not even offered such an option. The Israeli authorities' intense interest in, and manipulation of, the religious affiliations of the country's Palestinian citizens continues to this day. Like the British before them, the Israelis thought it would prove easier to control different religious communities than face a national minority. But, contrary to their plans and predictions, religious identity never became an influential factor in the pro- or anti-Israeli attitude of the Palestinians.

CHRISTIANITY AND COMMUNISM IN EARLY ISRAEL

There was however a difference between being a Muslim or a Christian. Being a Christian Palestinian in Israel added another sphere of identity through which a person had to navigate. But for the vast majority of the Christians in Israel, a more pronounced Christian identity coexisted easily with the crystallization of a national identity; in fact, Christians often played leading roles in the nascent Palestinian national movement.[39] The Christian ascendancy within Palestinian politics in Israel was also facilitated by the total collapse of the Muslim structure and hierarchy in Palestine in the catastrophe of 1948. The senior *ulamma* left the country, and it was many years before political Islam reappeared as a significant force. Meanwhile the Israeli government replaced the former Muslim structure with one better suited to helping it to impose its authority on the Palestinian minority. It abolished the Mandatory Palestine bodies and replaced them with *Waqf* (religious endowment) Boards and Court Councils, which were directly supervised by the Ministry of Religions. However, these bodies did not and still do not play a crucial role in the politics of the people, although they governs the religious courts that have a final say on personal matters such as marriage, divorce and inheritance.

The disappearance of the old Muslim structure of yesteryear not only left a leadership vacuum but also left many financial and real-estate assets behind. The public endowments, which had been run by the British Mandate's Supreme Muslim Council until it was expropriated by the British government during the 1936 Arab revolt, became 'absentee property' in 1948, as did private endowments whose supervisors were 'absentees'. In 1965, the Knesset instructed the Custodian of Absentee Property to return the non-absentee endowments to their lawful benefactors and ordered the transfer of the public endowments to an Islamic committee – loyal to the government, of course. Not surprisingly, the former private endowments thrived due to the stamina of the individuals while the latter public ones stagnated.[40]

The destruction of the Islamic structures – in particular the vanishing of the notable families that were the backbone of social and political life from the seventeenth century until the end of the British Mandate and the loss of their financial infrastructures – opened the way for Christians to play a more central role in the Palestinian community in Israel. Christian politicians took on leading positions in the Communist Party, the only organized group expressing the national aspirations of the Palestinian minority; they were also strong in the collaborationist Arab sections of the Zionist parties. The Greek Catholic (Melkite) Church, under the guidance of the charismatic *Mutran* (Bishop) Hakim, was conspicuously active on both sides of the political spectrum. In retrospect his role is still considered to be suspect by professional as well as more popular historians. Hakim was favoured by the ruling party Mapai due to his fiery public attacks on Communism in general and on the Israeli Communist Party in particular. He was enraged when the Communist Party discovered that he was willing to sell church land near Tabor Mountain for the building of new Jewish settlements that disrupted the Palestinian continuity in that area, on the eastern valley of the country. People today also recall his public call to join the Histadrut, which many eventually did as it was impossible to build a Palestinian national trade union.[41] But there was another side to his activity. He worked relentlessly to convince the government of Israel, the Vatican and governments around the Arab world to facilitate the return of his flock, members of the Greek Catholic Church, to Haifa after the 1948 *Nakbah* – with some success. And for this activity some Israeli officials, and even historians today, have regarded him with hostility.[42]

Communism was important for the Orthodox Church because it was Russian; for some members of the Orthodox community it merely replaced their past loyalty to the Russian Tsar with a new allegiance to the USSR. This was the largest denomination among nine recognized churches in Israel, the remainder being the Armenian, the Roman Catholic, the Greek Catholic, the Maronites, the Gregorian-Armenian, the Syriac Catholic, the Chaldean (uniate) and the Syriac Orthodox (some individuals also belong to the Anglican Church). But more than anything else, the Communist Party was a forum where urban Christian intelligentsia could meet Muslim workers (the lower socio-economic stratum was predominantly Muslim), and together try to shape an agenda for action and combat their common social and economic hardships. Significantly, despite its allegiance to an a-national ideology, the Communist Party emerged as the only national party; that is, it enabled people to express their national aspirations without risking arrest, as long as they did so in the form of a Marxist discourse. Thus, if they chose to wave a Palestinian flag or any other symbol they risked imprisonment, but if they chanted a Communist slogan about the right of self-determination, they would be relatively immune from the authorities' wrath. There was still a huge Jewish community in the Soviet Union, and this, together with the obvious importance of the USSR in world politics, explained the pragmatic and tolerant attitude of the Israeli government towards Israel's Communist Party.[43]

Communism, or whatever was understood as Communism in the very peculiar circumstances the community lived in, was therefore the preferred political choice of the Palestinians in Israel. In May 1953, the first elections to the city council of Nazareth took place. The Communists won 38 per cent of the vote and no coalition of the Zionist parties was possible without them. In the first meeting conducted that month, the speeches of Tawfiq Zayyad and Fuad Khoury, the leading members of the party, were interrupted by the temporary chairman, who called the police to disperse the meeting after he failed to silence them himself.[44]

The Israeli government's attitude towards any form of Palestinian nationalism, including that expressed via Communism, indicates that although transfer and expulsion strategies disappeared from the governmental decision-making desks after 1956, the pattern of discrimination against the Palestinian minority in Israel remained the same. The co-optation policy, the military regime and the basic predicament of being a Palestinian citizen within the Jewish state generated several political responses from within the community, all of which pointed to a strong wish to remain part of the Palestinian people while at the same time becoming citizens of Israel with equal rights. Some believed that Communism would lead to a social revolution, rendering nationalism secondary and bringing equality to all. Others joined the Communist Party for less altruistic reasons. They used its internationalist discourse to disguise their more authentic national aspirations, the expression of which would have indubitably led them into trouble with the Israeli authorities. Affiliation to Communism ensured career support via the party or, even better, a ticket to higher education in the Eastern bloc, which could then open the door to professions such as law and medicine, which the Palestinians in Israel were in practice, though always unofficially, barred from pursuing.[45] Others tied their political future to Zionist parties, creating their own satellite parties or joining as members. This may have furthered their own interests, but did very little, compared with the Communists, to improve the collective lot. Thus, by 1967, the Communist Party had become the most significant political force within the Palestinian minority. But inside and outside the party, individuals and small groups adopted other modes of activism as unionists, individual fighters and cultural producers.

UNION ACTIVISM UNDER THE MILITARY BOOT

There was room for activism because, despite the repression, one basic right was never taken away: the right to vote and to be elected. The inner debates on these two rights by the Mapai, the ruling party throughout the period of military rule, make interesting reading. It is impossible to miss the irony of the fact that the new instinct for vote gathering was allowed to overshadow the principal issue of full apartheid. In particular, the Histadrut, the general trade union, could not resist the power the Palestinian electorate might supply, and fought, as though they were genuine humanitarians, for the right of the Palestinians to vote. Even Ben-Gurion, who wrongly predicted that all the Palestinians would vote *en bloc* for the Communist Party, reluctantly recognized that they could be a useful tool for keeping Mapai in power.

This is probably why the Histadrut executive committee decided to accept 'Arab' members at the beginning of May 1953, after previous attempts had been rejected. The urge to unionize was acute and appeared very early on. It was the most natural response to the transformation of the Palestinian villagers from peasants into a daily skilled and unskilled workforce in the Jewish Israeli market. The rapidly growing industrialized Israeli economy and the modern-day taxation policy of a capitalist society triggered a process sociologists call semi-proletarianization within the Palestinian community in the first twenty years of statehood.[46] While certain aspects of the Israeli economy in those years were still centralized and monopolized, the market was already affected by the capitalist forces of supply and demand. The agricultural produce from the villages had no real market in the Jewish urban centre, first because of preferential policy from above pushing Jewish agricultural products at the expense of Palestinian ones, and second because the general demand for agriculture decreased. This forced a considerable number of farmers in the Palestinian countryside to seek work as day labourers in the Jewish city, mostly in unskilled jobs. They still cultivated the land for domestic consumption but could no longer live off the land as they had in the past.[47]

This predicament was part of a wider economic picture. The capitalist system that had begun to thrive at the end of the British Mandate collapsed and disappeared, while the new one erected by Israel excluded the Palestinian community left after 1948 from any role in it or benefits from it. There were vast investments in the Jewish sector, during the years in which military rule barred the Palestinians from any share in this development (the only exception was the introduction by the government of new species and updated technologies that enriched rural agricultural products, but this was not enough to allow people to live off the land).[48]

Palestinians were directed into the market of unskilled work by the government policies of investment and military rule, mostly in construction, services or Jewish agriculture, where the pay was low, the status inferior and where there was no guarantee of any tenure in the job. For construction work the military rulers would allow ad hoc groups of builders to move into a Jewish project and work there, under unfavourable conditions, and only for the duration of the projects. All over the Palestinian areas, villagers who became unskilled workers asked to be accepted as members of the Histradrut or to be allowed to form their own union. Palestinians urgently needed some union protection, not just in the traditional realm of pay, rights and so on, but also because for most of them employment entailed passing through the military checkpoints, which were very stingy with permits on such occasions. In the villages of Umm al-Fahem and Taybeh, unskilled workers asked to join the Histadrut or to be allowed to form their own union as early as March 1950, when the trauma was still fresh and the future not clear at all, but they were not allowed to do either.[49] In September 1950, following the attempts in the villages, the smaller urban communities also tried to organize unionism under the leadership of the Communist Party, but their activists, who began distributing pamphlets in the name of the old British Mandate's Arab Workers' Congress, were arrested in Wadi Nisnas in central Haifa.[50]

Moved by their plight, the Communist member of the Knesset Tawfiq Tubi submitted a motion demanding that the government allow the workers of Umm al-Fahem and Taybeh to establish a workers' union. The military governor refused to grant such a permit and the people of these two villages, like so many others in their area, Wadi Ara, spent hours at dawn hoping to be allowed to pass into the Jewish areas and look for a job. These same sights would reappear not far away from there, on the checkpoints between the West Bank and Israel after 1967, when the Palestinian workers from nearby villages would wait for hours at the same time each day to be allowed to work inside Israel.[51]

Even if one made it to the city or nearby town, there was the question of sleeping over and finding a temporary abode. In the 1950s there was plenty of space one could squat in, as the evicted and deserted Arab houses and buildings stood empty. By the end of the decade most of this property had been given to Jews to settle in, and any Palestinian work seeker staying in one was chased out by the police or the army. The Custodian of Absentee Property pressed those in control of military rule not to allow such squatting.[52]

The new policy of admitting Palestinians into the Histadrut was accompanied by an unsuccessful attempt by the leaders of this Jewish trade union to bar Arab Communists from registering as members. These small victories kindled the fire of hope among activists that tangible successes were possible, albeit on a small and limited scale, even though the superstructure in which they were operating did not allow any fundamental revision in the constitutional and political reality around them.

The struggle against the Arab Workers' Congress was not only about workers' rights and privileges but also about collaboration. The presence of a Communist union troubled the experts on Arab affairs in Ben-Gurion's government. After consultation among them, it was decided not to ban it but to cause it to disintegrate by creating a special union for 'Arab' workers (there was one already in existence from the British Mandate times, when it had collapsed and proved to be a total failure). The new outfit was called Brit Poalei Eretz Israel (Union for the Workers of Eretz Israel) or Brit for short. Heads of councils and towns, such as the mayor of Nazareth, who cooperated with the Brit – and most of the breadwinners in those days were workers – received benefits from the government in terms of budgets, infrastructure and so on, while those who seemed loyal to the Arab Workers' Congress received none. This battle between the Brit and the Congress ended when the Histadrut agreed to accept Palestinian members. The Brit was disbanded and the Communist Party became a faction within the Histadrut fighting for the rights of Arab workers from within the establishment.[53]

As far one can judge from the Palestinians workers' point of view, joining the Brit was understandable but a very negative manifestation of collaboration. The Brit was run as a closed Zionist outfit. At first, its Jewish organizer, Amnon Linn, considered offering Palestinians the chance of being elected to it, but then decided to appoint people. They were not just appointed to a 'trade union', they were also selected to informal and anonymous 'consultancies' – *veadot meyazot* – that advised the powers that be how best to control the Palestinian community. With the help of these consultancies it was decided which local council would receive the best the state could offer and which should be punished for its lack of cooperation. Amnon Linn wrote in his memoirs:

> The composition of the committees was decided with my friend . . . [here he gives a name of his main collaborator]. I am afraid the members of these consultancies are doomed to remain anonymous. I will always be grateful to them, but it would not benefit those who live and those who passed away if I mention their names.[54]

He then laments that most of their children became 'extreme nationalists'.

Those who succumbed to the temptation would later, in the 1970s, be condemned by their communities and in some cases would lose their power base – although in many villages the power base was and still is the clan, the *hammula*, and hence one branch with collaborationist tendencies can be replaced by a more assertive one.[55]

OTHER FORMS OF ACTIVISM

Outside the Knesset and the Histadrut, very few opted for a direct confrontation with the Israelis by declaring open allegiance to Palestinian nationalism, as represented by the Palestinian guerrilla movement that began to emerge at that time in the refugee camps of Gaza, Jordan and Lebanon. After 1959, the popularity of the Palestinian resistance movement soared among the Palestinians in Israel. This was the year when the Fatah movement appeared on the regional map, established in 1954 by Palestinian refugee students in the Arab world as the first national liberation movement after 1948. It pursued guerrilla warfare against Israel from 1965 onwards and took over the Arab League's championed Palestine Liberation Organization (the PLO) after 1967.

But the struggle during the period covered in this chapter was not yet for the right to be a Palestinian or to identify openly with the Palestinian national movement. This would undoubtedly be the agenda in the next decades. The struggle at this point was more existential, and while the decade began with the attempt to be recognized as full citizens in the new state before it completed its initial constitutional legislation, by the end of the decade the most urgent issue seemed to be the protection of the limited habitat allowed to the Palestinians in a state that declared the Judaization of the land – namely, not allowing Arabs to live on it – a prime national strategy.

Hence activism of a more confrontational nature evolved around the question of land expropriation and the building of new Jewish settlements on Palestinian land in the country. This kind of activity peaked in 1961 after the government expropriated more than 5,000 dunams from several Palestinian villages for the construction of Carmiel, a new Jewish town in the Galilee.

This new city, as well as that of Upper Nazareth, was built under the orders of David Ben-Gurion and Shimon Peres in the 1950s. Ben-Gurion was outraged by the presence of so many 'Arabs' in the Galilee when he toured the region in 1953, a few days before he retired for a year and half from his premiership (he returned in 1955). Already in November 1948 he warned: 'We have liberated the Galilee and the Negev. It is not enough to expel the foreign invader – we have to replace him with the Hebrew settler.'[56]

He appointed the then general director of the Ministry of Defense, Shimon Peres, to 'Judaize' the Galilee by using Emergency Regulations that allowed the army to confiscate land from the Palestinians and to commandeer the national resources needed for such a project. Three 'Jews only' cities were built to satisfy him: Carmiel, Migdal Ha-Emek and Upper Nazareth. An IDF document from 1953 spelled out the motivation behind the building of a new city: the final aim of Upper Nazareth was to swallow up the Arab city and transfer the centre of gravity of life from Nazareth to the new Jewish town.[57]

The army ordered its senior officers to live in the latter when it opened in 1957, with the result that the old city of Nazareth, exclusively Palestinian, was surrounded not only by new Jewish settlers overlooking them from the eastern mountains but also by a heavy presence of senior military personnel.[58] While the Palestinian community reluctantly accepted this new landscape by and large, it symbolized the oppressive nature of the Israeli spatial policies and some of these places were targeted in 2000 by angry protestors in events that are described later in this book.

But active struggle against the Judaization policy emerged in force later on in the 1970s. Activism was limited to a very few proponents in the days of the military rule. Most of the nearly 200,000 Palestinians were not politically active and, as always in such situations, were struggling to survive as the poorest section of the society, able to think about tomorrow, or maybe the day after, but not about a more distant future.

As in the new Palestinian refugee communities all over the Arab world, here too inside Israel the *Nakbah* obfuscated previously clear social structures and hierarchies. The advent of Communism as a political ideal, if not a practical experience, added to the dismemberment of the previous social stratification. However, the politics of the

Palestinian community in Israel during the days of military rule remained elitist and largely male-dominated. Even the debates between the collaborationists and the Communists took place within elite politics, while the rank and file had to survive the brutality of the military regime and the growing economic hardship. The Palestinian minority had the highest level of unemployment and underemployment in Israel, caused by the accelerated proletarianization of a society that was traditionally mostly agrarian. Peasants employed in unskilled and poorly paid jobs had to return home every day to the families they were struggling to support, as they were not allowed to stay overnight in the Jewish areas.

For women, this meant a relative improvement. As they too were needed to work outside the home, women could in return demand more education and a larger say in the community's affairs. However, it would be wrong to describe this as a feminist revolution among the Palestinians in Israel or a fundamental change in gender relations in the community. This is a very measured dialectical process in which tradition is not always a negative factor and modernity is not necessarily the salvation. The transformation of women's position is not over yet, either in Israel and Palestine or in the Middle East. The role of Israel or Zionism in this case is no different from that played by Western colonialism or capitalism in the area as a whole. A complex impact of feminist ideas, national and economic oppression, and supremacist ideologies have left researchers still bewildered about how best to assess its effect.[59]

CULTURAL ACTIVISM

Away from direct political activism the survival instinct, and again this was not unique to this particular oppressed minority, propelled cultural activity. The results paled in comparison with the richness of cultural life up until 1948, but it was the beginning of getting up from the ashes of destruction and providing the society with something no government or regime could easily either prevent or provide.

Among the cultural elite, one group stands out as united and aloof from the tension between collaboration with the Jewish state and opposition to it. These were the poets. Poetry was the one area in which national identity survived the catastrophe of 1948 unscathed. What political activists did not dare to express, poets sang out with force. Poetry was the one medium through which the daily events of love and hate, birth and death, marriage and family could be intertwined with the political issues of land confiscation and state oppression, and aired in public at special poetry festivals, such as the one that took place periodically in Kafr Yassif in the Galilee. The Israeli secret service was unable to decide whether this phenomenon was a subversive act or a cultural event.[60] The security apparatus would be similarly puzzled in the early 1980s, when it began monitoring festivals organized by the Islamic movement.

These poets were not opposed to the Hebrew culture that developed around them. While Jewish poets and writers, to this very day, do not bother to learn Arabic, let alone take any interest in Arab or Palestinian heritage, their counterparts among the Palestinians in Israel were keen connoisseurs of the hegemonic culture. Thus, for instance, Rashed Husayn, from Musmus in Wadi Ara, translated the works of the celebrated Zionist poet, Haim Bialik into Arabic without in any way abdicating his commitment to the Palestinian national struggle. Such knowledge of Hebrew, however, failed to impress the vast majority of the Jewish public. A poem by Tawfiq Zayyad titled 'The prayer of an Arab Israeli worker', which vividly describes life under military rule, was published in the daily *Maariv*, but otherwise went unnoticed.

As a poet, Rashed Husayn was also aware of the complicated matrix of culture and politics in which Palestinians in Israel were asked to exist. In 1959, he participated in the conference of the non-aligned states in Belgrade. These were the days when the leader of Yugoslavia, Marshal Tito, and President Nehru of India, together with Gamal Abdul Nasser of Egypt, sought to create a third force to counter the two superpowers of the day. Needless to say, the Palestinians in Israel were even more enchanted by this scenario than the one offered by Moscow. But the main disenchantment for Husayn was the cold reception he received from his fellow intellectuals from the Arab world whom he met there. He asked afterwards:

Who are we, the Arabs of Israel? Here they see us as a fifth column, there as traitors. We live in two worlds and belong to none. I did not expect them to embrace me but was unwilling to hear the same allegations I hear in Israel. Only in Belgrade did I fully comprehend the tragedy of the Palestinians in Israel. I decided we suffered the result of the *Nakbah* even more than the refugees. In Belgrade I did not know who I was, a national Arab loyal to his people or a suspect Israeli citizen.[61]

Husayn's experience brings to the fore once more the organic connection of the Palestinian community in Israel with the history of the Palestinian people in general. For him there was the country Palestine and the state Israel, whereas his Jewish peers, poets and writers, did not have this distinction in mind; moreover, to this very day Jewish intellectuals regard such a distinction as a subversive act against their own existence. Husayn's dilemma, a double pressure from the state to be loyal and from the Arab world to be truthful, would be less acute for the next generation. People like Husayn would be more assertive and clear about their national movement and conscience, as would the rest of the Palestinians outside of Israel recovering from the 1948 trauma, and they would face a clear exclusionary policy, at every level from bottom to top, in the developing Jewish state.

Palestinians elsewhere were coping with double pressures of a similar, although not identical kind. Those in Jordan, despite the fact they were offered citizenship, preferred to remain stateless and refugee camp dwellers so as not to forfeit the right of returning to Palestine; and those in the West Bank and the Gaza Strip were trying to enlist the Jordanian and the Egyptian governments to support their struggle for liberation while remaining loyal residents in these host countries. In the refugee camps of Lebanon and Syria, the land in which Husayn lived was still the homeland for which many young people were willing to sacrifice their lives and many others dreamed of coming back to. Most of them were relatives or family members of the Palestinians inside Israel.

On the other hand, Israeli policy itself distanced the Palestinians from the Jewish state. Successive Israeli governments did not even try to hide their desire to segregate the two communities. There were other possibilities of much more integrated life, despite the *Nakbah* and military rule, but these possibilities wilted the moment they appeared. I am thinking here in particular about the unique but very natural dialogue that began to develop between Jewish immigrants from Arab and Muslim countries and the local Palestinians that was abruptly smashed by the state.

In 1954, the new Jewish immigrants from Arab countries were still communicating freely with the Palestinians as new neighbours and as connoisseurs of the same culture. The first group that sensed this inevitable affinity was the poets and writers. Some of the Jews coming from Arab countries were quite well-known poets and writers in their homelands. At first they united with Palestinian writers to form their own union as Arabic writers. In March 1955, Palestinian and Jewish poets convened a conference of Arabic poetry in Nazareth, organized by Michel Haddad, a Palestinian poet and editor of the literary monthly *al-Mujtama'*. Three famous Jewish Iraqi poets, Zakai Binyamin, Salim Sha'shu'a and Shalom al-Kitab, took part in the event, which was attended by more than five hundred people.[62]

For Jewish immigrants who had been artists in the former Arab countries – writers, poets or singers – the only ready-made audience in Israel who could consume their trade were the Palestinians. When the famous Jewish Egyptian belly dancer Zahara Yehoshua arrived in 1954 the only places she performed in were the Palestinian villages. Later she would be de-Arabized, with all the other members of her community, rename herself Dalya and desert her Arab culture.

One could only be an Arab Christian or Muslim in the new Jewish state, not an Arab Jew. When the Third Arab-Israeli War of June 1967 erupted, questions of loyalty, identity and culture once more disrupted individuals' ability to live a normal life in their own home country and they had to take difficult decisions even if they were not inclined to be politically active. Their national movement demanded a clear identification with, and even active support of, the overall struggle to liberate Palestine, and their state made it clear that any such conduct would end disastrously should Israel come out victorious from the 1967 clash.

ACCEPTING AND TESTING THE MODUS VIVENDI

After the Kafr Qassem massacre, it seems that many in the community understood that the military rule was nearly over. And yet they sensed then, as Palestinian citizens sense in today's Israel, that the basic discrimination was not the result of the military rule or the Emergency Regulations it was based upon. Their inferior position as citizens was not conditioned by a declared temporary measure – the military rule – but by a permanent reference of the state to them as aliens in their own homeland – through legislation. A series of laws passed by the Knesset in the early 1950s served to reinforce this discriminatory situation. Three such laws immediately affected, and continue to affect, the Palestinian citizens of Israel: the Law of Return, the naturalization law, and the law of the Jewish National Fund.

These citizenship laws gave precedence to Jewish immigrants – even to Jews who were only potential immigrants – over the indigenous Palestinian citizens in almost every sphere. In property, they created an apartheid-style system of land transactions. The laws passed in the first years of the state defined most of the land for sale in Israel as being the exclusive and perpetual property of the Jewish people. The result was that almost all Palestinian-owned land was taken by the government and turned into state land, which could be sold or leased only to Jews. By the end of the confiscation frenzy and the formulation of the policy legalizing it, 92 per cent of the country's land had fallen into Jewish hands. Palestinian land, which on the eve of the 1948 war amounted to 4.6 million dunams within the territory that became Israel, was reduced by 1950 to 0.5 million dunams.[63]

To summarize this period one can say that in the first decade of Israel's existence the basic parameters in the state's attitude towards its Palestinian minority were formulated and fixed. Many of these parameters have never changed. These parameters appear also as assumptions on the basis of which most government policies were pursued. It is crucial to remember that these assumptions were not the fruit of negotiations between the state and the minority, but were imposed on the minority first under the regime of military rule and against the backdrop of the 1948 trauma, and then reasserted and reaffirmed almost unilaterally throughout the years.

When translated into a reality, for the people themselves these assumptions were manifested first as a set of limitations on normal life through administrative and Emergency Regulations – which allowed the government to act outside the democratic laws. The adjective 'emergency' had very little meaning for the population in the first decade as the whole period was defined as one that justified the implementation of the Emergency Regulations. Later on they would be used less frequently but remained in the consciousness of the people and were easily accessible to the government for immediate use.

This was also the decade when the community as a collective adopted a strategy of non-confrontation with the state – apart from very focused and short-lived moments when individuals, leaders or vast numbers of people in the community felt that state had breached the delicate modus vivendi. Such a moment of near collapse happened in May 1958 when thousands of Palestinians went into the streets to celebrate Workers' Day on 1 May. This was at a time when the Israeli government was watching the rise of what it termed 'Arab radicalism' around it in the Arab world. Palestinians in Israel felt the need to show solidarity more openly with radical and progressive forces in the Middle East. There was a prospect of pro-Nasserite coups and revolutions in Lebanon, Jordan and Iraq, with an increase of support for the Palestinian cause from all over the Arab world. Britain and the United States were waging their own war against the progressive forces in the Arab world, regarding them as Soviet satellites that had to be defeated in the Cold War, and the Israeli government was also contemplating a military takeover of the West Bank, should the Hashemite dynasty in Amman fall. Therefore the Israeli reaction to the May 1958 demonstrations was particularly harsh. The demonstrators on the other hand were enraged by a fresh and extensive campaign of land expropriation, especially in the Galilee. This same month Israel celebrated a decade of existence and pressurized Palestinian dignitaries and leaders to take part in the festival, when they really wanted to commemorate their catastrophe.

The day before the main 1 May demonstration, on 30 April 1958, a procession was brutally dispersed in the main street of Nazareth. The Palestinians were told that no more processions and demonstrations would be allowed. Leaders and young members of the community nonetheless showed up in large numbers over the next days. The day ended with scores of wounded demonstrators and the arrest of some of the community's most well-known leaders, such as Tawfiq Zayyad and Emil Habibi. Throughout the month of May the picture was the same: processions met with a brutal policy and military reaction resulting in large number of wounded and arrested Palestinians.

The heads of the Jewish state were much more content with a poster prepared by a teacher from the village of Rami in the Galilee, showing a pre-state pupil being subjected to corporal punishment and ten years later an Arab pupil shown in healthy and happy educational surroundings. Both images distorted the complex reality in schools in rural Palestine before 1948 and after. Happiness depended very much on the parents and the teachers, not on the British government or the Israeli one.

This is not to say that Israel as a modern state, very much like colonial powers, did not have a positive impact on some of the negative aspects of the Palestinian society. This point is made very clear by As'ad Ghanem who writes, 'the traditional Arab society is closed and rigid [as well as] intolerant . . . It discriminates against women and rests on clannish and confessional affiliations', leaving the individual in an inferior position. Improvement in all these spheres of life are attributed by him both to Israel's modernity and to a more general Western influence.[64] But, ironically, with these transformations of course the nature of the oppression seemed even more hypocritical and unjust.

And indeed very few felt the Rami poster genuinely reflected what they felt ten years after being taken hostage as citizens in the new state. On an ethical and declarative level, the Jewish state broadcast a double message in those years: an invitation to join the state on the one hand, and a collective allegation of being a 'fifth column' on the other. The three laws mentioned conveyed the same double message of invitation and exclusion. The state symbols and the educational system as well as the media echoed this double message. In practice, in daily life, especially in the contact of the Palestinian citizens with the authorities, there was no place for the democratic part of the message.

It was, however, more than ambiguity; it was a geopolitical limbo in which the Palestinians in Israel could be neither people of the villages nor city dwellers. The members of the community were denied the benefits of urban life while slowly losing the defence and security mechanisms usually offered by rural society. Israel's policy of carrot and stick influenced their occupational and economic reality as well. Collaboration with the government on a local level brought financial rewards for the individual, but also, if one happened to be a head of council, it brought collective gains for the community.

Individuals and organizations played an important role in delineating the map of possibilities for the Palestinian community in Israel. During this period it was the journalists who played that role. Leading the way was *al-Ittihad*, the only daily newspaper in Arabic and the organ of the Communist Party. Every now and then the newspaper challenged the Emergency Regulations and paid for this with short periods of enforced closure. Twice, in January 1950 and March 1953, the paper was shut down for two weeks by a decree of the military governor, for criticizing the excessive use of the Emergency Regulations. Other means used against it included the prohibition of its distribution, as was done in January 1950 when its sale in the Triangle was stopped for 'security reasons'.[65]

Together with the activists this and other journals chose topics that were important to them and the community at large and pushed the boundaries by individual or collective action. It seems that the dictum of the journal of the Greek Orthodox community in Jaffa, *Al-Rabita*: '*Primum vivere, deinde philosophari*' ('First live, then philosophize') was the golden rule by which most people abided, although the editor of this paper also published articles calling upon the Palestinians in Israel to consider armed struggle – particularly when the oppression of the Israeli authorities seemed unbearable.[66]

NATIONAL ASSERTIVENESS AND RELIGIOUS COMMITMENT: AL-ARD AND ISLAMISM

But there were those who risked their lives by opting for a more confrontational way forward, like the al-Ard movement. While al-Ard can be, and should be, contextualized as part of the general pan-Arabism of the Nasserite variant, which was very popular during this period, it was also the end product of an incremental and somewhat incidental history of Palestinian responses to particular problems in Israel. It challenged not only the Jewish state but also the Communist Party's careful navigation around the issues of national identity. It reflected more than anything else the weariness with the ambiguity or the limbo imposed on the Palestinians in the Jewish state.

Al-Ard's beginnings reflected a desire amongst some Palestinians to take a more assertive position on the increasing number of political arrests being made in the mid-1950s. It was first named 'The Public Arab Committee for Protecting Prisoners and the Expellees', aimed, as the name suggests, at helping those who had been imprisoned or exiled from Israel as a result of their political activities. The bulk of the arrests, especially of young people, occurred each year on the eve of 1 May, the traditional day of demonstrations and protest against the military rule. Some of the youngsters arrested spent long periods in the unsavoury Israeli jails, as happened to a large group from the village of Arabeh who were detained on the eve of 1 May 1957. As noted before, Tawfiq Zayyad and Emil Habibi, among others, were frequently arrested for periods of nine months and more. Both, and in particular Zayyad, complained that they had been tortured when in the Tiberias jail in the summer of 1957.[67] Others were detained under administrative detention without trial for very long periods as happened to Khalil Khoury, a member of the Nazareth city council in November 1957; he was never told, even when he was released, what his alleged crime had been.

The common allegation was membership of an espionage network working for Arab countries. Announcements regarding the exposure of such networks included very few details and the archives of the secret service are not accessible with regard to these charges. The fact that many of those alleged to have been spying were released without trial may indicate how flimsy these accusations were, as in the case of a very bombastic declaration in August 1958, when the secret service announced they had discovered a wide pro-Syrian network in the north of Israel, among whom were large numbers of Communists.[68]

Quite often Palestinians who had been accused rightly or wrongly of espionage were offered the option of exile instead of imprisonment, especially in cases where the evidence against them was so thin that even a trial behind closed doors might not have produced the jail sentence coveted by the secret service. Such was the case of Ghazi Saadi, who for a while worked closely with the Office of the Advisor on Arab Affairs in the 1950s, but then began to regret this line of action and became more independent in his thinking and writing. He was a publisher and a journalist from Acre who was also a member of the Brit. When he changed course he was accused of spying for Syria but was offered the choice of exile, which he accepted in 1957.[69]

This committee that would become the al-Ard movement was another venue for national activity not controlled by either the government or the Communist Party. Public figures such as Yani Kustandi Yani, the head of the Kafr Yassif council, the lawyer Elias Kussa from Haifa and Jabur Jabur, the head of the Shefa-'Amr municipality, were prominent in the new committee. This body became the 'Arabic Front' and later the 'Popular Front', headed by Yani Yani.

The Arab Popular Front is often neglected in the history of the Palestinians in Israel due to its more famous offshoot al-Ard, but it was a crucial organization that served as the first representative body of the Palestinians in Israel. One of its major campaigns was aimed at preserving the Muslim holy places in the hands of the community in the face of Israel's decision in 1950 not to allow the Palestinians to manage the *Waqf* properties in the state.

The Front organized a congress in June 1961 and wished to convene it in the al-Jazzar mosque in Acre – a magnificent Ottoman building from the early nineteenth century, one of the few left after the country was de-Arabized, not only demographically but also architecturally. Thousands of people wanted to attend the congress, but the Israeli authorities ordered the custodians of the mosque to close its gates. The meeting was moved to a neighbouring coffee house, in which hundreds of people tried to convene. As Hanna Nakkarah, the Front's secretary, wrote about this amazing human gathering, 'The Congress was supported by the Arab people of Israel, irrespective of party affiliation or religious identity.'[70] The congress elected an executive committee that then led the struggle to retain some say in running the Muslim *waqfs* in Israel.

The same year, 1961, Yani Yani, the head of the Front, was conducting another struggle in which the Front would serve as a model for future political activity among the Palestinians in Israel. The arena was the north-western village of Kafr Yassif, where the government, with the full force of the military rule behind it, tried to secure permanent control over the local council for the dominant Zionist party, Mapai.[71] Yani Yani, as a representative of both the Communist Party and the Arab Popular Front, succeeded in defeating the government's candidate in a historical triumph, which would be repeated in 1975 when Tawfiq Zayyad won the elections in Nazareth (of which more is said later on).

This was all a good training ground for the young people who founded al-Ard, which sprang out of the wider movement in 1959 as a result of tactical debate and disagreement. Most of the founders were law students who saw themselves as *Usrat* ('the family of') *al-Ard* ('the land'). Reading its early publications, one can find many demands that would later be adopted by Israeli Palestinian political parties and movements, such as a call for the return of the refugees. In those pamphlets and its journal, edited by Salah Baransi, one can enjoy quite spicy caricatures of Israeli leaders, such as the depiction of David Ben-Gurion as the 'Jerusalem midget'.

Al-Ard was also unhappy with the way in which other organizations and individuals had resisted the land confiscation, and thought that a fiercer strategy was called for. Its early publications and discourse echoed Nasser's anti-Western rhetoric, and included vows to join the struggle against 'reactionary regimes' in the Arab world. In a way, they strove to open a diplomatic outlet for these ideas in what for them was occupied Palestine, although admittedly they supported the UN partition Resolution 181 of November 1947 as a basis for a new geopolitical solution. They were banned from activity, while some were arrested, and others exiled.[72]

But more than anything else, al-Ard was first and foremost a display of an assertive national position. It was also part of the fascination with pan-Arabist politics, which had been revived ever since Gamal Abdul Nasser came to power in Egypt in 1952. There was great excitement on the day of the Egyptian revolution on 23 July that year. When Nasser gave a speech that was broadcast by Egyptian radio, the streets of the villages and the alleys of the town would empty; everyone would sit around the wireless and listen attentively to the fiery rhetoric coming from Cairo. The new Egyptian leader symbolized courage and the promise of a better future, indeed a turning of the history clock backwards to a time before occupation and oppression had set in – until he proved to be a disappointment. Many young Palestinians were named after him, such as Gamal Zahalka, one of the leaders of the community in the twenty-first century, who was born in 1955. Only one other Egyptian could drag people from the streets to their transistor radios, and that was Umm Kulthum, the legendary Egyptian singer whose songs were hours long but filled the heart with emotion and offered a brief escape from the daily hardship and quite probably offered a sense of 'Arabism' in the newly Judaized Palestine. Many years later, the leader of Hezbollah, Hassan Nasrallah, would cast such a magical spell over the Palestinians in Israel – but this time it was the television screens that would be watched and the message would be Islamic as well as pan-Arabist.

When the Communist Party seemed to side with Nasser's great rival, Abd al-Karim Qasem from Iraq, in the new revolutionary world that had emerged in some Arab countries, the popularity of al-Ard grew accordingly since Nasser was still the most revered leader and icon in the Palestinian community in Israel. After the movement was banned, it attempted to continue its work as an economic outfit – a registered firm that managed publications, educational material and so on – but this mode of action was also barred by the government. The movement's able lawyer, Mansour Kardoush, succeeded in convincing the Supreme Court that an economic outfit could not be outlawed as a security risk and al-Ard was registered as such in 1962. Of course its business interest was quite limited and it continued to look for ways of acting as a political agency. Its attempt to run under the name of the Socialist List in the 1963 elections failed and it was outlawed once more and some of its activists fined and arrested. Among them was Muhammad Mia'ri, who would succeed in running on a similar platform and twice be elected to the Knesset in the 1980s as a member of the Democratic List for Peace.

No less daring and challenging to the Jewish state was politics in the name of Islam; political Islam was still in its infancy before 1967. The reasons for its emergence are similar across the region: a combination of socio-economic hardship, a lack of state welfare policies and the weakening of secular alternatives for action. Each Islamist movement in the Middle East was unique, with a particular agenda, whether national or social, that overshadowed the religious one. In the case of Israel, the national agenda was at least as powerful, if not more so, than the religious one, particularly later on in the 1980s.

Curiously, one factor in the rise of Islamism was the visit of Pope Pius VI to Israel in 1964. Young Christians enthusiastically embarked on preparations for the visit, and opened clubs and activity centres, especially in the Galilee. Their ardour was catching, and young Muslims responded with similar zeal, becoming involved in community work. Their main achievement was in occupying the days of the unemployed and underemployed in the Palestinian Galilee, Wadi Ara and the Triangle. The growing of beards, the wearing of traditional garments, and a more eager participation and interest in Islamic politics in the Arab world (voicing discontent with the way Nasser treated the Muslim Brotherhood in Egypt, for instance) were all part of this new phenomenon. An unofficial successor to the Grand Mufti during the Mandatory period, Sheikh Ahmad Abdallah, was the prime mover behind the scenes. He also collected funds for building more mosques and has had some able successors who expanded the movement into a significant political force on the map of Palestinians in Israel.

THE VARIETIES OF NATIONALISM

Al-Ard and the early activists in the name of political Islam tested the tolerance and boundaries of the regime under which they lived. They threatened to cross the consensual lines of those who represented politics inside the community and among the Israeli policy makers engaged with the 'Arab sector', as it now became known. The absolute prohibition imposed on such organizations by the Israeli authorities strengthened the Communist Party as the only body asserting the Palestinian national identity under military rule.

These were the two versions of Palestinian nationalism in the period leading up to the early 1980s. One implicitly supported nationalism within an outfit that ostensibly broadcast cosmopolitan and Marxist ideology, but which the regime knew represented national sentiment. The other was explicitly nationalist and pan-Arabist and was not tolerated by the regime. Both were political movements that saw democracy as a way of life and a desired political future. Espousing democracy in Israel, however, became a subversive act against the Jewish state. As mentioned earlier, the government also needed the Communist Party as a tool for keeping links with the Soviet Union open.

Although the authorities were aware that internationalism was quite often a cover for a national position, they were crystal clear when it came to anyone expressing open nationalist positions. These people paid a very high price. Some were punished via a heavy financial fine imposed on them for their political views, as was the case in 1959 for Salah Baransi, one of the founders of al-Ard and a key spokesperson for what As'ad Ghanem, calls 'the national stream' (one out of four tendencies he detects among the 'Israeli Arabs', the others being the collaborationists, the Islamists and the Communists).[73] Any of Baransi's writings would have been enough in the eyes of the Israeli security services to justify his arrest or expulsion. A typical comment of his was, 'Zionism is an ideology based on racism and discrimination. It used the method of racial discrimination to achieve its objectives and goals.' Anti-Zionist Jewish activists said the same at that time, but they were not treated as Palestinians were when openly pronouncing these views.[74]

There was an uneasiness among Palestinian members of the Communist Party, named Maki at the time, who wished to play a more national role – people such as Emil Touma and Emil Habibi, who were also taken by the powerful influence Gamal Abdul Nasser had on local and regional politics. But in around 1957 or 1958, they and others who were leaders of a sort took a strategic decision not to join in an active struggle against the Jewish state but rather to concentrate on a particular political agenda of their own, that of seeking an assertion of a national identity within the Jewish state. It would take some time before, in the early 1970s, this would be recognized as a legitimate mode of struggle by the PLO.

An illustration of what would emerge in the next decade as the Israeli Palestinian political discourse was already evident at the 1 May 1958 Nazareth march. Since the establishment of the Communist Party this had been a purely internationalist show of strength. In 1958, however, the Palestinian agenda substituted the more familiar Marxist slogans with calls for the right of return of the 1948 Palestinian refugees and support for the Palestinian national struggle, to which the response was, as mentioned earlier, a brutal police suppression of the march, leaving many wounded and many more arrested.

But it was not only the Israeli authorities who disliked the national content of the protest, so also did the Jewish leadership of Maki. As a result the tensions between the Palestinians and the Jewish activists in the Communist Party became unbridgeable. By 1965 it was impossible for them to be in one party. The Palestinian members left Maki, the old Communist Party, and created a new one, Rakah, the Hebrew acronym for the New Communist List. Even a desperate, intensive final attempt at reconciliation by the Soviet Ambassador, Comrade Zhubahain, did not help. Gradually Maki disappeared and Rakah became the Communist Party, with a far more distinct national character. Joel Beinin in *Was the Red Flag Flying There?* called it the triumph of nationalism over internationalism, a process he detected at the very same period in the Egyptian Communist Party.[75]

But one should be careful in summarizing this period only as an organizational or institutional history; it was also very much a personal history. By this I mean that, given the relatively small size of the community and its fragmented existence in a state that refused to recognize it as a collective, individuals could have an impressive impact on the community's ability to survive under a regime that at least until 1956 was keen to see it disappear.

A SMALL PANTHEON FOR FORGOTTEN HEROES

They may not have been leaders by the conventional definitions one finds in the political sociological literature, but in hindsight their stances were crucial for the overall existence of the community. Four stand out: Emil Habibi, Emil Touma, Hanna Naqara and Bulus Farah.

Habibi was a passionate orator and a charismatic leader, as well as a prolific writer and journalist. He had a column in *al-Ittihad*, the Communist daily, under the pseudonym 'Juhayna'.

Emil Touma was the editor of *al-Ittihad* (I had the honour of chairing an institute named after him many years later). He was the ideologue propelling the recovery of a Palestinian identity under a Jewish state. Hanna Naqara, already mentioned, was a human rights lawyer who questioned the legality of the very early land confiscations and paid dearly for it by having to spend long periods in jail. Bulus Farah, who quite soon retired to a private life as a businessman, was a respected figure in Haifa and attuned to the voices coming from the people themselves. He was the secretary-general of the Arab Front and of the committee for protecting the rights of the expellee and detainees, as well as being a member of the Communist Party secretariat.

Others like them were involved first in the Communist Party and then in the more national bodies, and contributed significantly through their writings and activities to the preservation of Palestinian nationalism within the new reality of the Jewish state. Tawfiq Tubi was a prominent and long-serving member of the party in the Knesset while other members were publicly active outside the Knesset, such as Fuad Khoury, Munim Jarjura and Saliba Khamis. Touma, Tubi and Khamis married Jewish women and in their personal lives thus embodied the alternative model to an ethnic and supremacist Jewish state.

Next to them I have already mentioned those who were more assertive of nationalism, and probably more aware of the dangers of Zionism. Salah Baransi, Sabri Jiryis, Habib Qahwaji, Ali Rafa, Muhammad Mia'ri, Mansour Kardoush and Mahmoud Darwish should all be remembered as people who struggled in the name of the natural and national rights of the Palestinians in the Israeli political arena and paid dearly by being either imprisoned or exiled. In the second rank of politicians who deserve to be mentioned are people like Uthman Abu Ras from Taybeh, who was the main activist in the southern Triangle, and Ramzi Khoury in Acre who, together with Gamal Mousa, the former a Greek Orthodox, the latter a Muslim, was influential in that part of the Palestinian community. The geographical distribution of Palestinians within Israel allowed figures in different regions, usually of the same generation and of different religious affiliations, to cement the ties between the community and the party in terms of politics, career and the elusive aspect of identity politics. For example, Yusuf Assad in Kafr Yassif and Zahi Karakbi, a Greek Catholic in Haifa, were active among grassroots members as well as among intellectuals and professionals, in keeping alive a national agenda – albeit one covered with Marxist discourse and Communist slogans.

THE END OF MILITARY RULE

In 1959 a new governmental committee headed by the Minister of Justice, Pinchas Rosen, was convened to evaluate the necessity of military rule. Unlike a previous committee headed by Yohanan Ratner, Ben-Gurion's chief Strategic Advisor in 1955, this one saw no point in the system's continuation. As the chair of committee put it: the 'Arabs' problem in identifying with the state was no reason for questioning their loyalty'. Rosen asserted that there was no precedent anywhere in the world for a group of citizens to be under state military rule for no apparent reason, that is without committing acts of terrorism or subversion.[76]

Interestingly, like the early academic researchers of that period, the committee also wondered why there was no 'terrorism or subversion'. The most elaborate explanation for this state of mind was given in 1968 by the American political scientist Ian Lustick, who developed a special conceptual paradigm to explain how co-optation and coercion had turned the Palestinians into a 'docile community'. Lustick attributed this docility to the efficient and sophisticated system of domination exercised by the government.[77] More loyal Zionist historians, such as Ori Stendel, singled out the lack of leadership and independent Arab organizations as the main reasons, and some Israelis such as Micha Nino credited the 'stable policy' of the state for the situation.

I hope this chapter in any case has shown that the community was not docile. Israeli researcher Elie Rekhess claimed that at various times, especially towards the end of the 1950s, some Palestinians in Israel contemplated an Algerian-like struggle, but eventually they decided against it.[78] Sabri Jiryis asserted that most of the Palestinians in Israel were reconciled to the existence of the state and those who were not realized that it was beyond their own power to change the reality. Moreover, he stressed that the Palestinians' uncertainty about the future solution for the conflict had caused a kind of paralysis at the level of action. This explanation is echoed by Elia Zureik, who explains the low-profile Palestinian resistance in Israel up to 1967 as the result of the government's policy of alienation and distancing the Palestinians from any share in power, as well as the role played by outside Zionist organizations such as the United Jewish Appeal and the Jewish Agency in providing the finance for the Judaization of the land. He also pointed to internal factors, such as the fragmentation of the society and its 'distorted class structure', as preventing active resistance.[79] Other researchers mention the military might of the state and the fact that the Palestinians were not called upon from the outside to take up arms against the Jewish state; neither did the state, as Zureik reminds us, demand full identification or assimilation from the Palestinian minority.[80]

My own conclusion, as I hope comes across clearly from the narrative so far, is that the Palestinians by and large accepted Israel as a *fait accompli* and in the early years of the state were not looking for an alternative framework, nor did they demand via the UN to be excluded from Israel. The aims of their struggle were to change the nature of the regime while not losing their affinity with their Palestinian and Arab identities.

So the chief policy makers in the early 1960s and the researchers of the period agreed that the community did not constitute a danger of any kind to Israel's security or existence. But the Prime Minister David Ben-Gurion and his Advisor on Arab Affairs, Yehoshua Palmon, were adamant in their refusal to abolish it. A few months before Ben-Gurion lost his premiership in 1963, he succeeded in orchestrating the last extension of military rule in the Knesset at a vote in February 1963. A wide alliance from left to right had expected to defeat the vote, but ironically, the Office of the Advisor on Arab Affairs recruited the vote of a Palestinian member, Diab Ubaid from Taybeh, to pass the motion to extend the military rule (there is no need to elaborate how this gentleman was viewed by most members of the Palestinian community). The government also had the support of the Druze Sheikh Ja'ber Madi, and the Christian Elias Nakhleh. To be fair to all three, they were under the heaviest possible pressure from the Advisors of the Prime Minister's Office.

Ben-Gurion's successor, Levy Eshkol, was less paranoid about the Palestinians in Israel and strove to abolish military rule. Since the military rule had been imposed by the sheer force of the Emergency Regulations, there was no need to pass a special law for its abolition. In 1966, Eshkol decided to take the initiative and declared the end of the military rule. However, the ban on free movement remained until September 1967 and several areas, such as the vicinity of the nuclear plant in Dimona and the Arava Valley, which stretched from the eastern side of the Negev all the way down to the Gulf of Aqaba and Eilat, alongside Israel's border with Jordan, were out of bounds for the Palestinians in Israel. But it was the beginning of a different era in the life and history of the Palestinian community.

CHAPTER THREE

MILITARY RULE BY OTHER MEANS,
1967–1977

IN THE MID-1970S the Palestinians in Israel comprised 13 per cent of the overall population. As a result of the Israeli law that annexed East Jerusalem, which was occupied in the June 1967 war, they became 15 per cent, that is, about half a million people.

The first twenty years of statehood were tough and anxious. At the time one suspects that many of them did not know that these were not objective hardships but the result of an intentional and systematic policy of discrimination. It was not only the visible aspect of military rule that oppressed the Palestinians during that era, but also the more invisible economic policies enacted from above. New research by Yair Bäuml,[1] based on recently declassified archives, has reaffirmed the suspicions of perceptive observers of the period under review, that the centralized and nationalized policy intentionally marginalized the Palestinians from the areas of agricultural production and marketing, and exploited them as cheap labour in other economic activities. A bisected economy on ethnic or national grounds was the result, with Jewish citizens forming the upper class and the Palestinians the lower class.[2] It was a starting point from which any community would find it difficult to take off economically and socially. By the end of this decade, the Palestinians were still by and large directed by governmental policies to work in industries that were traditional, offered low rates of pay and had no security of job tenure. Economists called this 'low occupational mobility' and the Palestinians remained concentrated in the blue-collar market, while the Jewish middle class grew enormously during this period, taking over more than three-quarters of the white-collar occupations.[3]

This decade's images are a mixture of humiliation and pride. They begin with Jewish society celebrating euphorically the June 1967 victory over Jordan and Egypt, conveying the impression that the mini-state of Israel was now transformed into a mini-empire: a force to be reckoned with, not only in the Palestinian world but in the Arab world at large. Quite a few Palestinians in Israel, secretly or openly, had believed Nasser's rhetoric about an imminent victory and his ability to return the historical clock to the pre-1948 reality. In some villages women vowed to delay indulgence in haircuts, jewellery or powder until freedom came. Despite the defeat, Nasser's reputation among the Palestinian people remained untarnished, and on his death in October 1970, hundreds mourned him publicly and vociferously.

But this secular 'messiah' of progress failed the masses and faded out of history in the year that followed the *Naksa*, the 1967 defeat in the Arab jargon. With Nasser's death pan-Arabism lost some of its attraction, and if there was any comforting image it would come a bit later, when a group of a few hundred young Palestinians, mainly students and refugees, waved their Kalashnikovs in a show of self-assertiveness and defiance. Soon this new group extricated the Palestine issue from the hands of politicians from all over the Arab world, who had ostensibly championed the 'Palestinian cause' ever since 1946 but done very little to advance it. As mentioned, Fatah was the largest faction within the PLO, which until then had been controlled by the Arab League. In 1968, in a quiet coup, Fatah usurped the PLO and replaced the officials appointed by the Arab League with its own members and other Palestinian guerrilla factions' members. This compensated a little for the humiliation and collapse of pan-Arabism and of the dream of liberation which had been put forward by the great leader of Egypt.

The images from the end of the decade were a direct result of the death of the big ideologies in the Middle East, and as a result not only life but also politics became more local. In the dictionary of Arab nationalism, the identification of the people moved from the *Qawmiyya*, the pan-Arabist sphere of identity, to the *Wataniyya*, the local identity. The latter distinction of course was much clearer in the case of the Iraqis and Syrians, and even easier to grasp for the Palestinians in the occupied territories and in the refugee camps; it was still blurred for the Palestinians in Israel. But the images of Tawfiq Zayyad, the first mayor of Nazareth, winning the municipal elections in 1975 were as exhilarating for the Palestinians in Israel as Nasser's triumphs had been at the beginning of his road to regional glory in the 1950s.

Zayyad threw out the collaborationist elite that had ruled the only real Palestinian city in Israel and those images are often conjured and remembered today. The elite comprised a number of families who had risen to power as a result of collaborations with the Israelis after the occupation of the city – they were not necessarily the notable families of the Mandatory Palestine era. Their claim to power was based on their willingness to cooperate – the most famous among them was Saif al-Din al-Zu'bi, a member of a clan that had collaborated with the Jewish forces during the 1948 war.[4] Tawfiq Zayyad was born to a farming family and as a teenager he had to work while he was still at high school to help the family survive the poverty which affected so many farmers in the north of the country during the Mandatory period. His teachers nonetheless remember him as a very industrious and committed pupil. As a young man he joined the Communist Party and was elected as a member of the city council of Nazareth in 1954.

It was not only the sight of Zayyad's triumph in Nazareth that stirred fond memories; it was also the sound of his voice that people of his and successive generations remember. He spoke with the enthusiasm of a proud Palestinian leader, echoing the discourse and narrative of other Palestinian leaders all over the Arab world. Although a leading member of the Communist Party, he was in many ways the successor of Yani Yani who, as mentioned, in 1961 headed a Communist–nationalist coalition which defeated the Mapai candidate in Kafr Yassif. Zayyad reiterated what many may have wished to suppress in the community, in his party and in the state: that the Palestinian experience inside and outside the borders of Israel was closely linked.

No less vivid in the memory of people are the images of what followed: a ruthless and immediate Israeli reaction in the form of massive land confiscation, leading in March 1976 to violent confrontations with the state that left several Palestinian citizens dead after being shot by the army and the police. This became engraved as the Day of the Land; an event commemorated annually ever since by the Palestinian community in Israel and about which more will be said later in this chapter.

LAYING THE LEGAL FOUNDATIONS FOR SECOND-CLASS CITIZENSHIP

In the years between 1967 and 1976 the Jewish state still considered the Palestinian citizens to be a potential security risk, but a lesser problem compared with the new occupied Palestinian populations, which required more attention, as well as the manpower that had been employed on military rule inside Israel until 1966. The structure of military rule was transferred almost as a whole to the West Bank and the Gaza Strip. Inside Israel it was replaced with a web of new legislation and rules on the ground which were meant to ensure segregation, obedience and co-optation, but which also displayed a willingness to consider some improvements in the general conditions of life.

While life was still lived, at least until 1976, with the same apprehensions and informal limitations as those imposed under military rule, the political and, especially, the legal elite in Israel did invest some effort into laying new foundations for the status of the Palestinian citizens. Only recently have legal experts developed a historical appetite, and thanks to their endeavours we have a better understanding today of the significance of the legislation and court rulings that took place in the first decade after 1967. In general the legislation had the appearance of guarding the rights of the Palestinians in Israel, but it formed a matrix of power that contained the Palestinians within glass walls, which they could only hope to break through if they were willing to be converted to Judaism. This tension was the result of the original contradictory legislation that at once granted equality before the law but qualified it by applying it only to Jews.

Second, this wave of legislation left immense power in the hands of the various government ministries to act outside the law in cases of emergency, which we now know in hindsight were hardly ever exercised against Jewish citizens but quite often against Palestinian citizens. A very illuminating example of this is the law and practice against those in the state who do not serve in the army. Two groups are exempted, although not legally: the Palestinians and the ultra-orthodox Jews. The former pay a high price in employment, welfare benefits, national insurance policy and other aspects of life, whereas the latter, if anything, get preferential treatment in some of these areas and equal treatment in others. Thus, initiatives to develop a basic law (a constitutional law which is very hard to abolish) ensuring human rights and equality were never completed in the period described in this chapter, while preferential laws for those serving in the army, code for Jews only, were pushed through.[5]

The first step towards articulating afresh the legal status of the Palestinians in Israel commenced in 1965. This was done within the framework of the law for the Population Registry. In brief, the law dealt with the question of who was an Israeli citizen, or rather, it answered the question of whether there was an Israeli nationality in the negative. As Nadim Rouhana has put it: 'there is no Israeli nation' as such; there are only Arabs and Jews in the Israeli state.[6] There was Israeli citizenship but only Jewish nationality and non-Jewish affiliation to religious groups (as mentioned in Chapter 2, the Druze community formed a separate religion). The very legal status of people with a national identity and others who were without nationality laid the foundation not only for discriminatory policies but also for a racist public mood. The differentiation between nationality, accorded to the majority group, and the sectarian or religious identity allowed to the others, created a legal discrimination that no future egalitarian law could alter. Thus, although during this period (from 1967 to 1977) several laws were passed that spoke the language of equality, nonetheless these made no difference to the daily experience of Palestinians in Israel. The main reason was that the basic laws, those constitutional laws that were there, as powerful as a constitution in other countries, remained discriminatory and biased. The amendments introduced to these laws did not change their spirit or impact. The most important law was the Israel Land Law, which still affirmed during that period that 90 per cent of Israeli land should belong to the Jewish people and therefore could not be sold to non-Jews.[7] The second was the basic law of elections that prohibited the eligibility of any party or list that did not recognize the Jewish character of Israel. And finally the basic law of the right of employment still connected the employability of a person with their respect for the basic values of the state of Israel, namely its Zionist character.[8]

The fragmentation of the Palestinian community into sects was part of the overall fragmentation of the Palestinian people, which was both the aim and product of the Zionist movement and later became the core of the Israeli strategy towards the Palestinians. In South Africa a similar concern about the majority of Africans potentially endangering the white supremacist minority led to a similar policy of fragmentation of the African community there into tribes, who were offered home-lands and even states.[9]

Another set of laws dealt with the educational system. Under military rule the educational system was practically, although never formally, segregated. The segregation was ostensibly the result of the restrictions on movement imposed on the Palestinians. After 1966, Palestinian citizens were allowed to travel into the Jewish areas and they could theo-retically join Jewish educational institutions. There was no law that prohibited them from doing so, but the establishment of separate educa-tional systems for them was a clear enough message. The segregation was not meant to allow Palestinians to develop cultural autonomy. Quite to the contrary, it was meant to supervise it closely so that such autonomy would not develop. It also allowed the government to discriminate in terms of resources and budgets. The standard of an average school or class in the Palestinian areas was much worse by any parameter or criteria compared to that of the average Jewish school.[10]

Interestingly, the segregation stopped at the level of higher educa-tion. The idea of an Arab university, which has surfaced every now and then from 1967 to the present day, was categorically rejected by the government, which feared that such an institution would become a hotbed of anti-state activity and radicalism. This loophole would both generate a culture of student activism in the community and turn the campuses into spaces where Palestinian–Jewish relationships would be contemplated, conceived and attempted. All in all, in hindsight one can say that segregation continued to dominate campus life as well, very much reflecting the segregated public life outside of the universities.

The legislation dealt less with the segregation in the educational system, which as explained above was taken as a given, and more with how to ensure total control and supervision within the system, now that the Emergency Regulations and absolute military rulers were gone. The law for supervision over schools was passed in 1969. The short message of a very detailed law was very simple and direct: any misconduct, in the eyes of Jewish supervisors from the bottom level upwards, of a Palestinian employee in the educational system would lead to dismissal or a very severe limitation of rights. During that decade, 1967–1977, the teachers' unions and the teachers–ministry committees that were meant to protect teachers from such abuses did not include the Palestinian citizens and, therefore, the few cases that were brought to their attention were decided in favour of the government and its representatives in the educational system.[11]

The legal glass ceilings or walls in other spheres of life came in the form of a very different legislation. In the early 1970s several laws were passed in Israel defining the privileges granted to those who served in the Israeli army. The national insurance authority granted them special welfare benefits, studentships, grants and loans, all of which were denied to the Palestinian population. Although not all the Jews served in the army – as mentioned earlier, ultra-orthodox Jews were exempt – only the Palestinians were discriminated against on the basis of their exemption from the army.

To complete this part of story one has to stress that it was not only demographic and Zionist concerns that shaped the legal reality after 1967, it was also the theories of modernization discussed in the Appendix. Therefore some of the laws were meant to improve the status of women and weaken the negative aspects of life in the clans and patriarchal societies, and may thus have created a different image of the Jewish state in the eyes of the minority. But since these laws were less significant in the eyes of the state, there was no real attempt to impose them, while in contrast every effort was made to impose discriminatory laws and regulations. The main problem in this area was that although the social services were equal by law, they were institutionally corrupt through their discriminatory practices. This could be clearly seen where two communities lived in close proximity, such as in Nazareth.

Throughout the period, the 10,000 or so inhabitants of the Jewish development town of Upper Nazareth were served by twelve social workers, while down below in Nazareth, the 100,000 Palestinians were served by a similar number of social workers. The same disparity in resources available to each of the two communities could be seen in every other aspect of social welfare and public services.[12]

Thus the bigamy, clannish hegemony, misogynist attitudes, corporal punishment of children and the negative aspects of an Arab rural society all over the region, which existed next to the positive features of egalitarianism, solidarity and the traditional defence mechanisms against the hardships of life, were not really confronted by the state that claimed to be the only liberal modern democracy in the Middle East. Some scholars, such as Alina Korn, stress that the policy also turned a blind eye to the inevitable criminalization of the Palestinians as a group living on the geographical and social margins of the society.[13] The pauperization of the society and its marginalization contributed to its criminalization and some of these petty criminals could be seen on the streets on days of national protest, adding a not always constructive contribution. But this fusion of criminality and nationalism served well those within the Israeli Jewish public who wished to demonize the Palestinians and delegitimize their right of self-determination and equality within the Jewish state.

THE UNBREAKABLE HOUSE OF GLASS

The new legislation and the continued sense of discrimination were far more powerful as factors shaping the life of the population than the hopes raised by the abolition of military rule. The reason was that the new goodwill on the part of some of the Israeli policy makers was less significant than it may have seemed on the surface, since the reality was still Jewish. And thus the official abolition of the military rule was followed by hopeful statements issued by the government to the press in 1967 and 1968. In fact in 1966 the official government agencies had already proclaimed proudly: 'The process of liberalization and concessions [to the Palestinian community] has reached an unprecedented peak after the 1967 war.'[14]

Later the official declaration talked about the newly won freedom of movement for the Palestinian citizens as an indication that 'almost all the restrictions that made life difficult and unnecessarily burdened the Arab population have now been removed'.[15] In fact, quite a few restrictions on movement had been imposed on the Palestinians in East Jerusalem, who were regarded officially as part of the 'Arabs in Israel' after 1968. But, more importantly, the civil administration, which was the informal branch of the military rule in the towns and cities, remained intact. This was a branch made up of members of both the Israeli police and secret service which possessed extended authority – almost unlimited – when it came to the Palestinian citizens of Israel. The police had a special section called the 'Board of Special Operations' (*Ha-Lishka le-Tafkidim Meyhuadim* or LATAM). Its terms of reference were to expose, report and prevent subversive, terrorist and espionage activity among the Palestinian citizens of Israel. This portfolio tells it all in a nutshell; even after the abolition of the military rule, the Palestinians in Israel were still considered to be the hostile aliens of the early twentieth century.[16]

This was reinforced by the national symbols of the state, which were exclusively Jewish and whose content owed much to the wars with Arabs and the Arab world. The flag, the national anthem and the state insignias were all not only Jewish but also anti-Arab in one way or another. The anthem craved for the return of all Jews to Israel while the flag resembled the Jewish *Talith* and the Jewish prayer mantle, and the parliament was represented by the *Menorah*, a seven-branched candelabrum used in the ancient Tabernacle in the Desert and in the Temple in Jerusalem. These insignias were not only meaningless to the Palestinians but actually hostile to their situation, representing as they did the Jewish right to the Palestinian homeland.

There was here an inherent paradox. On the one hand, from the moment military rule was lifted, Palestinians came into daily contact with Jewish society, from the lowest social strata upwards; the vast majority were employed by Jewish individuals or companies. On the other hand, there was no sign of any social or cultural interaction, while political cooperation happened only on the margins of the main stage. Thus cohabitation and coexistence were only temporary experiences for both communities rather than the result of a policy from above to produce a joint community or citizenship; if anything the government was quick to undermine any initiative for the creation of joint spaces, such as joint kindergartens and schools.

In December 1969, Arab and Jewish authors tried to create a joint union that did not last for long: A.B. Yehoshua, Dalia Rabikowitz, Yitzhak Orpaz, Mahmoud Darwish, Samih al-Qasim and Salim Jubran were among the founders of this hopeful outfit. The Palestinian authors demanded the abolition of the censorship of their work and an end to exile for some of the political activists and, in particular, to the administrative arrests (arrests without trial for unidentified terms), which by then had been imposed on hundreds of people in the West Bank and in the Gaza Strip (with a few cases also in Israel itself). It was difficult to secure their Jewish counterparts' support for this and the venture disappeared into thin air.[17]

A far more effective meeting was that organized by a new outfit: Siah, the Hebrew acronym for the New Israeli Left, which fought directly against the continued harassment of Palestinian writers, poets and journalists. In March 1970, the first meeting took place in reaction to the renewal of the Lydda-based author Fouzi el-Asmar's administrative arrest. By then he had already been interned in jail for a year and a half without access to lawyers and without having been brought in front of a judge.[18]

There were some attempts from above, though very short-lived and not genuine enough, to create some common cultural space. The Israeli television network opened an Arab section after the inauguration of Israeli television in 1968. While it would soon be seen as a collaborationist arm of the government by many in the community, in the early days it had the opportunity and the means to produce a different visual (if nothing more) reality, which it deserted later on. Particularly impressive was the children's programme *Sami and Susu*, a bilingual Arab–Jewish comic dialogue that had fans in both communities and addressed an audience on the verge of forming negative images of each other. (Research by the psychologist Daniel Bar-Tal proved that in Israel Jewish and Arab children subscribed to the demonized images of each other's community very early on in the segregated and indoctrinated educational system – even at the stage when toddlers supposedly live in a secure world of their own.)[19]

Participation in the common republican good, whether in culture or politics, was conditional, requiring acceptance of Zionism as the hegemonic ideology in the state of Israel. Hence in May 1969 a committee from the newly formed Labour Party (formerly Mapai) recommended that 'Arabs' could be party members as long as they accepted 'the guiding social and ideological principles of the party'.[20]

Palestinians lived in total segregation apart from a small urban minority who lived in proximity to Jewish neighbours. They had their own towns as well, Shefa-'Amr and Nazareth, which added to their sense of seclusion. As mentioned earlier, the educational system (apart from the universities where in that decade the presence of Palestinian students was low – around six hundred in 1971) was totally segregated.

The educational and cultural policy during the military rule was dictated by a wish to turn the Palestinian community in Israel into 'loyal' citizens. The secret service warned the government that without close supervision of schools and cultural activity, a nationalist Palestinian identity would develop. So Jewish officials were put in charge of curricula and censored cultural events as much as they could. The ability to appoint and fire principals and teachers added to the tight supervision of education and culture. The standard guidelines for the Jewish educational system included instruction to encourage students' love of their homeland and the strengthening of the national identity. Needless to say, these aims were not mentioned in the guidelines distributed among the Palestinian schools.[21]

The only 'mixed' school was a high school in Haifa, but even there the Palestinian pupils attended separate classes! By the end of the century several new mixed schools had appeared, though without either reflecting, or bringing about, a fundamental change in the segregated reality around them. In my class, graduating in 1972, there were two Palestinian students; the only ones in one of the biggest high schools in Haifa.

The strong limitations on expressing one's national identity and the imposition of severe control over education forces one to question the assertion of the mainstream sociologists in Israel who claim that with the abolition of military rule in 1967 Israel transformed itself into a liberal democracy. This is not reflected either in the recollections of the Palestinians themselves from that period or in the legislative programme. On the contrary, instead of referring to what unfolded as liberalization of the public space for the Palestinian minority, one can talk about a developing normalization in the relationship with both the state and the Jewish majority. This daily relationship was in itself a novelty compared to the reality under military rule, and may be considered an improvement, but it did not hide the inbuilt imbalance of the status of both communities, nor could it be taken as proof of the end of the de jure and de facto discrimination of the state against its Palestinian citizens.

Reading memoirs and talking to people about that period, it transpires that the most oppressive aspect of it all was not the laws, the seclusion, the segregation, the unemployment or the poverty. The impression one receives is that they were bad, but manageable. What was as intolerable as it was impossible to defeat was the attitude of those who represented power in the Jewish state: the officials in the Ministry of the Interior, the tax collector, the policeman, the judge or anyone who was supposed to provide service in the name of the state. The general experience was of abusive practices and humiliation that remained fresh long after the worst memories of military rule faded away, mainly because they are still there in the twenty-first century. Adnan Abed Elrazik, one of the first Palestinian lecturers in Israel (in the Department of Education in the Hebrew University), and Riyad Amin, who was one of the first Palestinian science PhD candidates (also at the Hebrew University; he later became a lecturer in Birzeit University), put together an evaluation of the situation in 1978. Looking back at the period after the abolition of the military rule, they found that discrimination had remained a salient feature in the life of the Palestinian citizens. They point to three areas – land expropriation, lack of employability and abuse in education – as the worst aspects of living as an Arab in the Jewish state during the period from 1967 to 1978.[22]

Those responsible for direct and indirect contact with the Palestinian citizens in the name of the state were still in the habit of providing benefits only in return for collaboration of a sort. If you wished to open a restaurant, to become an employee of the government, to expand your business or to embark on an academic career (a novel idea after 1967), some favour was to be expected in return. It could be active service for the Shabak, the Israeli secret service – just an occasional report, or grassing to the authorities, or an overt display of loyalty to the state. The relevant documentation that would prove or disprove how systematic or intentional this policy was after 1967 is not open as yet and one wonders whether it ever will be; in 2010 the Israeli government altered its policy of archival declassification, extending both the period and the terms for making new documents accessible to the historians. However, first-hand accounts suggest that attempts to get Palestinians to inform were common during that period, and that they still happen today.

Most of the Palestinians I know have succeeded in resisting both the temptation and the intimidation, but not everyone did. One of those who persevered under pressure is Hatim Kanaaneh, who returned from the USA to practise medicine in the Galilee during the late 1970s. He recalls how, quite soon after his arrival, the authorities tried to recruit him as an informer. As a returnee student he was entitled, as I was after finishing my studies abroad, for a loan to help set up life in Israel. But in his case, the Office of the Advisor on Arab Affairs sent an official to tell him that the loan depended on his willingness to serve as an informer. 'I'll scratch your back and you'll scratch mine,' Yorum Katz, the chief recruiter in the north in those days, told him. 'My itch is gone,' answered Hatim and ended the conversation. Katz possessed a lot of power in securing permits for businesses, trade and so on, and Hatim later discovered that Katz had banned his brother from trading with Gaza.[23]

In 1959 John Griffin, a noted white journalist, wrote a famous book, *Black Like Me*, about his experiences of living as a member of the black population in the American South. Three decades later Yoram Binur wrote an 'Arab like Me' book which reaffirms much of what is described above. Binur lived as a 'Palestinian' construction worker in Tel Aviv for six months and, although his account of the late 1980s is mainly about Palestinian workers who came from the West Bank, he also gives a vivid description of what it felt like to be an 'Arab' in Israel or the occupied

territories, and in Tel Aviv, the only Western city that has no Arab population in it.[24] In this context it is worth mentioning the work by Rebecca
Kook, the only one on the subject I know of, which methodically compares
the experience of African Americans with that of the Palestinians in Israel,
examining and evaluating latent as well as more obvious forms of racism
and discrimination. She concludes that the main difference lies not in the
practices and the daily reality of the community, but in Israel's willingness
to institutionalize the discrimination through legislation, whereas in the
USA, since the abolition of slavery and the segregation policies of the
southern states, the races have been equal before the law.[25]

The ability to engage for a while with wider Israeli society increased
the hopes of many among the minority for a better future in the years
ahead; these hopes were manifested in an increase in votes for Zionist
parties and a more open relationship with the main trade union, the
Histadrut, among other things. In fact, the high level of participation in
the various election campaigns was another indication of the aspirations
which people harboured during that period. When their hopes never
materialized, the frustration and depression would be immense. But this
was not yet known in the first decade without military rule.

THE SOCIO-ECONOMIC REALITIES OF LIFE

Some of the realities in the first decade after 1967 did not attract much
attention at the time, but nevertheless harboured destructive potential
for the future. One such slice of life was the economic imbalance
between the two societies. Jewish society began to thrive after the first
two decades of statehood, during which the economy had been
minimal and the state as a whole had been poor and struggling. Then
a new era of prosperity commenced. Reparations from Germany,
American Jewish money (particularly significant during that period),
various aid packages from successive American administrations, and
foreign investments all benefited Jews, mostly those of European
origin, but hardly affected the standard of living of the Palestinian
citizens of Israel. The annual income of a Jew was twice that of a
Palestinian as a result of the different pace of their economic development throughout the 1960s and 1970s.

The socio-economic reality at this time should be seen in a wider context. Twenty years of land expropriation had turned the Palestinian community, which had been principally rural and agricultural, into salaried workers, or rather semi-workers in the Jewish areas, who were underpaid and had very little hope for social and economic mobility. The Palestinians were clearly at the very bottom of the socio-economic structure with very little hope of leaving this unenviable position.

This, coupled with the different standards in education (the average Jewish child finished ten years of schooling, and the average Palestinian only six), meant that the disparity remained steady and was no less oppressive than direct military rule. A very detailed retrospective report on the employment situation found that between 1967 and 2000 the basic predicaments of employability among Palestinians in Israel have not altered much. Educated Palestinians more often than not were working in job for which they were overqualified. It stated: 'many Arabs suffer from discrimination in employment as many work places refuse to employ them'.[26] And thus although equivalent proportions of Palestinian and Jewish men were employed through the decade covered here, later on we learn that many Palestinian men became unemployed earlier on in their life due to the nature of their unskilled work (only 40 per cent of them remained in the labour market above the age of 50, while 70 per cent of Jews were still employed in the same age group).[27]

This polarization only increased over the next decades and contributed its share to the frustration and sense of oppression. Even those achieving a full cycle of higher education, including university, had very little hope of finding jobs that fitted their qualifications or expectations in a Jewish-dominated market; there is not sufficient data for the 1970s, but from the 1980s onwards, half of the university graduates did not work in jobs that fitted their qualifications.[28]

The economic situation was influenced by the prevention of governmental financial flows that would have encouraged economic activity. New Israeli legislation had encouraged such activity ever since the early 1960s but in practice these laws were not applied to Palestinian entrepreneurs and the Palestinian areas were not included in the state's infrastructural development planning. The result was that they lacked the developmental infrastructure necessary for beginning new economic projects, hence local entrepreneurs were not interested.[29] At the same time the general infrastructure for habitation: water, sewerage, roads, electricity and hygiene deteriorated.

Until the late 1980s the Israeli government gave precedence to what it called national interest over economic considerations. The national goals were encouraging Jewish immigration, the distribution of the Jewish population all over the country, a welfare system for all and high employment. This was achieved through a policy of centralization, including heavy regulation of the financial and banking system.[30] Even the rise of 'free market' parties took time to transform this facet of the economy.

In practice the centralized economy produced a complex bureaucracy that demanded permits for every aspect of life and allowed no free competition except on the periphery. Most of the economic power was in the hands of big governmental cartels and monopolies, many of which were run by government, the Jewish Agency and the Histadrut.[31] It was difficult to see how one could change the situation as the government had total control of development and strategy in the realm of economy, with the result that even when, in the next decade, liberalization was introduced to the local economy, the Palestinians could not exploit the free market reality to transform their conditions. Like democracy, the free market and privatization were conditional according to one's ethnic identity.

This was a typical colonialist dilemma for the Israeli policy makers; they insisted, as did those academics writing loyally in the name of the state and Zionism during that period, that the Palestinian society was modernized under Israel's rule. There is little doubt that they, or the natural progress of things in the Middle East, did contribute to the disappearance of some of the more negative aspects of the local indigenous society: there was less illiteracy, more opportunities for women, better health conditions, a higher level of education and so on. Again I would refer to the very honest summary of these advantages in As'ad Ghanem's work.[32] However, this was very limited progress in comparison with the Jewish society – a disparity which mainstream Israeli sociologists pinned on the nature of the Arab minority and which critical sociologists later on would blame on Israel's discriminatory policies. Like colonialist powers before them, the Israeli politicians and officials expected that this limited modernization would satisfy the Palestinian minority, but it did not. The undeniable improvement in the community's standard of living was judged by the Palestinians not according to past realities, but according to how they fared in comparison to the Jewish members of the society, and that exercise ended in great dismay and outrage.

Not all of the complex realities of the Palestinian society can or should be attributed to Israeli policy. This was a society in a Middle East that was transforming slowly and dialectically from the old world of Ottoman rule and traditional values into an age of nationalism and global capitalism. And, as elsewhere in the Middle East, old social patterns still affected life, even in places where brutal modern policies from above were trying to eradicate them, as was case in Ataturk's Turkey and in the Shah's Iran. Inside Israel, the clan, the *hammula*, was still the main centre of life in the rural areas, which meant both a source of solidarity and stability in the face of dire economic and social conditions, but also unchallenged patriarchy and only superficial ideological affiliations either to Communism, nationalism or collaboration with Zionism. The politics of the *hammula* and its main interests served as the principal political platform; any ideology that could serve this platform was welcomed. The younger generation, and wider sections of the small urban centres of Palestinians in Israel, had begun to drift away from this social reality but still found it difficult to assert life outside the extended family circle. This was particularly hard to achieve in the rural areas, where Israeli policies strengthened the power of clans, and very few alternative modern systems were open to individuals who were looking for new defence mechanisms that would replace the familiar traditional ones.[33]

A leading Israeli anthropologist at the time, Henry Rosenfeld, noted a new phenomenon emerging which was unique and had no comparable existence anywhere else in the region and this was the making of a young 'rural middle class' – almost an oxymoron.[34] The rural villages stopped being agricultural – they were now the residence of workers, employed and underemployed, mostly commuting to the Jewish areas. And in the village a middle class emerged. It was a process that took twenty years to mature. Alongside the workers there were the contractors, the lorry drivers, the restaurant owners, the lawyers and doctors and other professionals.[35]

Members of this middle class could not, even they wished, perceive Israeliness as an alternative to either traditional spheres of identity or the national one. Whatever we will call the process they underwent in the third decade of statehood, be it 'modernization', education or migration to the cities, the transformation of their lives deepened the rift between the Palestinian individual and the Jewish state. As Nadim Rouhana puts it, they developed a flawed national identity and one which was affected by the realities in Israel on the one hand, and the strengthening of the Palestinian national movement on the other; but whatever it was, it had very little in common with the Israeli Jewish identity.[36]

This was not the prediction of the academics in Israel who began to be interested in the Palestinian community as a subject matter. For them the Palestinians in Israel were a successful case study of 'modernization' under the guidance and impact of the modernizing state. These scholars equated modernization with greater integration in the Jewish state, an observation that was valid in certain aspects of life, but one which was wrong when it also included an assumption of *identification* with the state. Even if there were some indicators that Palestinians were succumbing to being a tamed national group within an exclusive Jewish state, given time, something more powerful seemed to be at work that tipped the balance against it: the unification with the Palestinians in the West Bank and the Gaza Strip.

THE IMPACT OF THE UNIFICATION WITH THE REST OF PALESTINE

As for everyone else living in Israel, the consequences of the June 1967 war, rather than the short-lived war itself, were formative events in the history of the community. For the Palestinians in Israel, the occupation of the West Bank and the Gaza Strip meant first and foremost a reunion. Nineteen years of living under Israeli rule had produced a variant of Palestinian identity that was different from that developing in the West Bank and the Gaza Strip. It was not a dramatic difference and, had the Israelis allowed process of a reunion and reunification by declaring the whole of the land west of the river Jordan as the state of Israel, or had the Palestinians in Israel, as a political community, opted for joining the struggle against the occupation, that difference might have been wiped out. But these options were not chosen and the two communities continued a separate, and at the same time parallel, existence until our century.

At first, Palestinians in Israel were barred from visiting the occupied territories for reasons the authorities at the time defined as 'security considerations'. The Ministry of Defense issued individual and collective decrees prohibiting visits. The secret service, it seems, feared that such visits would form political associations and produce synergizing impulses that in turn would create a powerful resistance movement on both sides of the Green Line. Even when the gates were opened around May 1968, nearly a year after the actual occupation, and Palestinians from Israel were allowed to visit the occupied territories, hundreds of Palestinians remained on blacklists prohibiting them from reuniting with their families and friends. Members of Rakah, the Arab Communist Party, had been on a special list since August 1967, preventing them from entering the occupied territories so that they could not 'incite the local population'.[37] Around March 1969, the Advisor on Arab Affairs' Office began a propaganda campaign aimed at preventing the outbreak of 'dormant national sentiments' among the Palestinians in Israel as a result of the reunion with the Palestinians in the West Bank and the Gaza Strip.[38]

When this ruthless effort subsided the Palestinians in Israel could move with relative ease into the occupied territories. The encounter was sweeping and exciting. Divided villages on the former border could rebuild bridges, families re-met after almost twenty years of separation and the traumas of being a Palestinian on different sides of the Green Line could be compared.[39] The reunion with the Palestinians in the West Bank and the Gaza Strip highlighted their unity of purpose, but it also exposed the conflicting agendas on both sides of the Green

Line, if not immediately then soon after. The political movement in the West Bank and the Gaza Strip focused on liberation from the Israeli occupation. The Palestinians in Israel, while supporting this cause, stressed as their priority the struggle for equality within the Jewish state.

But the differences were also exposed elsewhere. While the villagers of Barta (as was mentioned earlier, a village brutally divided by the 1949 Armistice Agreement with a line drawn in thick pencil by Israeli, Jordanian and UN officials, who created such tragedies in more than one place) were delighted by the reunion they also discovered that even their Arabic was not the same. Moreover, its inhabitants' willingness to learn or manage Hebrew was different: the eastern part of the village, which was on the other side of the border until 1967 and which was again separated from the other half after Israel built a segregation wall in 2001, was more reluctant to invest in the language of the occupier beyond functional words that allowed one to survive a checkpoint or a random encounter with the army. Meanwhile the children on the Western side were learning Hebrew and developing an Arabrabiya, a hybrid of Arabic and Hebrew, even after living for a relatively short time under Israeli rule. Standards of living were different, and despite a mutual desire to be reunited, it was clear already in June 1967 that it was preferable to hold the Israeli blue ID than the version designed for the occupied Palestinians. Nonetheless, the people of the eastern part of the village were much less confused about their collective identity, and, even if their hopes proved unattainable with the wisdom of hindsight, they could envisage life in the future without Israeli presence or control. By the beginning of the twenty-first century the physical separation of the two parts of the village would be more permanent, and the despair about any possible change would now be the same, but the political agenda was still different. The eastern part was fighting to end the Israeli military occupation and the western side was struggling to attain equal status within its own state.

While from a materialistic point of view, and that of basic rights, the Palestinians inside Israel seemed to fare better, the reunion also exposed how destructive the long separation of the community from the Arab world and its culture had been. Literature, poetry, theatre and films were victims of the military rule from 1948 to 1967 like every other aspect of life – not primarily because of censorship, but because they were cut off from their natural sources in the Arab world. These media were partly liberated after 1967 by the reunion with the occupied territories, and through them with the Arab world.

The recognition that the Palestinians in Israel were less well off when it came to cultural vitality and identity was triggered by the revelation of how Palestinian the culture of the occupied territories was, and the Palestinians in Israel craved to reconnect to this authentic part of their life that until 1967 had been forbidden and replaced with a culture from above prepared by the Israeli Jewish experts on Arab education and culture. Newspapers, short novels and books were devoured by hungry Palestinian readers when the roads to East Jerusalem, Ramallah, Nablus and Gaza were opened. Worried Israeli experts on Arab affairs who began to appear in Israeli academia after 1967 (many after long careers in the intelligence or secret service) warned that this would lead to the Palestinization of the 'Arabs in Israel'.[40] It did contribute to self-assertion and a clearer sense of identity, but it did not replace the unique experience of living as a Palestinian citizen in Israel, with its many ambiguities and the consensual choice by most to navigate carefully between sheer antagonism and base collaboration.

SEARCHING FOR THE UNIQUE AGENDA

After 1967, the official Israeli phobia about the existential danger posed by the Palestinian minority subsided and the Emergency Regulations and military rule were employed more infrequently and for shorter periods. The landscape was now more clearly charted. After 1967 the Palestinians were invited to protest against local and individual acts of discrimination within the Israeli legal system, but not collective ones. Any efforts to transform the Zionist reality in Israel and Palestine were clearly prohibited.

Although organizing politically on a national Palestinian basis was still forbidden, the public discourse during this decade became much more nationally oriented compared to previous years. The language of national liberation, and not that of Communism or democracy, was employed to show individual or public support for the PLO and its struggle to end the Israeli occupation of the West Bank and the Gaza Strip. More hidden, but again more visible than in previous decades, were the endorsements by Palestinians in Israel of the PLO vision of an Arab democratic secular state over all of Mandatory Palestine and the right of an unconditional return for the 1948 Palestinians.

The Israeli Palestinian community's agenda now gave equal weight to these two objectives: equal rights within the Jewish state and solidarity with the Palestinian resistance in the occupied territories. In around 1974 the leadership of the PLO gave clear recognition to the fact that the Palestinian way of struggle inside Israel differed from the struggle conducted elsewhere but was nevertheless legitimate. The acceptance of the unique role of the Palestinians inside Israel was helped by the appointment of Palestinians who left Israel to key positions in the PLO. One of them was Sabri Jiryis, who wrote that his appointment in 1973 as the new head of the PLO research centre, and that of others, expanded the knowledge in the PLO about Israel and introduced Hebrew to the PLO intelligence effort. Even more importantly, he felt that such knowledge allowed the leaders of the movement to accept the Jewish state as a *fait accompli*, rather than as a transient crusader state that would soon disappear. Some readers may find his latter claim exaggerated, but he certainly had an impact on PLO thinking about Israel.[41]

This was a crucial moment in the political history of the community. The fact that the community's unique version of Palestinian nationalism had been legitimized by the PLO meant that its future decisions on strategy and tactics would be taken without direction from the national leadership, and quite often without any consultation with it. At this point the Palestinian polity in its entirety was highly fragmented, with no clear centre or strong leadership. There were quite a lot of candidates for the burden of leader, of whom the one chosen, Yasser Arafat, was respected for his ability to keep some sort of structure alive in almost impossible conditions, but not for his statesmanship or leadership. One researcher at the time described the Palestinians in Israel as experiencing a transnational reality: their national centre was outside the border of their national homeland and yet they were a distinct national minority.[42]

At a time when other Palestinians communities were opting for the armed liberation struggle, the more nuanced approach of most Palestinians in Israel caused some unease in the community. It was particularly difficult for the younger generation. The heroism and glamour that surrounded the guerrilla movements and activities, especially in the refugee camps in Lebanon, and the more assertive national actions in the occupied territories, inspired a more active show of solidarity with the national movement. In Lebanon young Palestinians joined various guerrilla outfits and, even if only very few of them were directly involved in operations against Israel, many of them were trained and were an integral part of these units. Similarly, the attitude of the same generation in the occupied territories was not ambiguous as it was inside Israel: there the Jewish state was an occupier and a colonizer, nothing more and nothing less.[43] The action outside Israel was determined by Article 8 of the PLO constitution, which defined the armed struggle as a tactic and not a strategy. In the 1970s the concept of struggle was widened to include even an assertive membership of the Israeli Knesset or the pursuit of a successful individual career; this was helpful but not as attractive.

People today speak more openly about this period than about the previous decade. If one could talk about identities as a plethora of options which a person can choose to highlight or conceal, then one can see the various identities Palestinians in Israeli endorsed, that is, the national one, and the civic one which they were forced to adopt; each of these was displayed and hidden according to the circumstances. At times it was convenient to present a Palestinian identity, at times a religious one and, every now and then, an Israeli one. A similar predicament and complex usage of identity also prevailed in the case of the Palestinians in Jordan, who faced issues not totally dissimilar to those of the Palestinians in Israel, and like them had to navigate between a declarative and a behavioural mode of identity depending on context.[44]

The most elaborate analysis of this situation has been conducted by Nadim Rouhana, who is a political psychologist and a Palestinian born in Israel. He rejected the depiction of the community as Israeli Palestinian and rather talked about a state which had two groups with different identities. These identities are used in different contexts and meanings, and are almost unrelated to each other. He defined both identities as 'crippled' and 'incomplete'; what is missing is a core of cultural and social values, common political visions and rules of the game, and a formal legal component – a respect for the state and the citizenship in it.[45] Neither of the two identities, the Israeli or the Palestinian, has this complete scope. In more concrete terms, as noted by Rouhana, the Palestinians in Israel did not share any collective national experience with Jewish citizens, or a national museum, a national holiday or for that matter a national symbol.[46]

What was complex then would be even more complicated later on. The basic Palestinian national agenda until the Oslo negotiations in 1993 was clear – a democratic secular state and the unconditional return of the refugees. Once the PLO moved to full support for the two-state solution and became vague on the right of return, Israeli and Jordanian Palestinians' need to develop a particular and legitimate agenda became even more acute. This move for consolidating a more unique agenda for the community was accelerated by the events of 1973.

THE OCTOBER 1973 WAR – A NON-EVENT IN THE LIFE OF THE PALESTINIAN COMMUNITY

History has its own curves and junctures, and while the Palestinians in Israel were rethinking their identity and future, and those under occupation were contemplating how to survive and maybe even resist, the military rule was now transferred from one Palestinian community to the other, and the over-confident Jewish society of Israel was traumatized by the events of October 1973.

In October 1973, invincible Israel looked for a moment lost, confused and vulnerable. The Israeli army did succeed eventually in fending off a surprise attack by the Egyptian and Syrian armies, but it was caught unprepared and when the fighting subsided the mighty Jewish state looked distressed and weaker. The superiority of the army, and in particular the dominance of security issues were – briefly – questioned and challenged. Mizrahi Jews in deprived neighbourhoods, the right-wing opposition parties and new immigrants, all demanded more attention and were not satisfied any more with the government's tendency to attribute all of its failed policies to the security situation on Israel's borders.

Palestinians in the occupied territories too were now moving away from Jordanian patronage – a development which was discouraged by Israel but reinforced inadvertently by the Israeli decision to carry out municipal elections in 1976 – towards a more general Palestinian movement of resistance, spearheaded by the PLO. With the solidification of the PLO as the 'sole legitimate representative of the Palestinian people' – a claim supported by the majority of the world's states at the time, apart from the pro-Israeli West – and Israel's survival despite a relative defeat on the battlefield, the Palestinian community of Israel found itself being pulled between two powerful magnets: Israel and the PLO. The problem was that the Jewish state, and, for that matter, the Jewish public, did not show any appreciation for this kind of navigation between these uncompromising and demanding forces, and did not tolerate any political behaviour that did not represent a total acquiescence to the Jewish character and destiny of the state. When terrorist and guerrilla warfare reached the doorsteps of many Israelis after 1973 and endangered their individual security, this lack of tolerance became even more evident and dangerous to the community at large.

JEWISH MOOD AND RESPONSES

The popular ways of protest, even before the fateful events that close this chapter – the killing of six Palestinian citizens by police and the army at the end of March 1976 – were as dangerous in the 1970s as they had been under military rule. In the background were the wars of attrition with Egypt and Syria that lasted until 1973 (in which many soldiers were killed), and the intensification of the PLO guerrilla and terrorist activities against the state, its army and its Jewish citizens (including the hijacking of aeroplanes, the bombing of a Swissair flight to Tel Aviv and the shelling of the city of Tiberias). Against this backdrop it was easy to anticipate a total Jewish acquiescence in a daily routine of Palestinians arrests and even killings, which in most cases were not reported or noticed by the population at large.

When a bomb exploded in the central bus station in Tel Aviv, the mob tried to lynch anyone who looked like an Arab – in some cases Jews who came from Arab countries attacked other Jews with the same origin, mistaking them for 'Arabs'. These terrifying moments did not however help to change the attitude of the Mizrahi Jews towards the Palestinians – by and large as a political electorate they emerged as even more anti-Arab in general and anti-Palestinian in particular after 1973 (which explains their support for Menachem Begin's Likud Party during those years). It is beyond the scope of this book to delve too deeply into the attitudes of the Jews who came from Arab and Islamic countries. As mentioned before, their own low socio-economic conditions in comparison to the Ashkenazi Jews, their geographical location, on the borders with Arab countries where the conflict was felt more acutely, and above all the realization of many among them that self de-Arabization was the key factor that would ensure their full integration into the more veteran Israeli Jewish society, are the main reasons quoted by scholars on this subject.[47]

Some Palestinians from Israel were involved in planting bombs in busy urban neighbourhoods and others were members of Fatah and other Palestinian groups. A famous figure was Fawzi Nimr, who was responsible for planting a bomb in a residential area on Mount Carmel. Another famous case was the involvement of two Palestinians from the Galilee in planting a bomb in one of the Hebrew University's cafeterias on Mount Scopus.[48]

But all in all the numbers were very small. The Israeli government attributed this to a successful and ruthless policy of its security forces;[49] my suspicion is that in fact either the leadership or individual members of the Palestinian community made a strategic decision not to partake in this kind of action. The few scholarly analyses which exist point indeed to what Azmi Bishara defined as a strategic decision to accept the rules of the game within the state of Israel and to build a strategy upon them for transforming the oppressive reality.[50]

These disturbances were accompanied by the appearance of right-wing politicians and pundits calling for the transfer of Palestinians from Israel. Their intellectuals published a journal called *Ummah* ('the nation') in which academic articles appeared calling for transfer policies.

There were also ceaseless mainstream voices arguing that the birth rate among the Palestinians in Israel was a national security issue. In September 1969, the Demographic Council, appointed and supervised by the government, voiced its worries about the demographic balance between Jews and Arabs in Israel. This was the end of a process of research into the question begun in 1966 – the government decisions on which are still inaccessible to the historian. The council suggested a policy of promising tax benefits to Jews with large families and recommended a fierce policy against abortion.[51]

Any suspected cooperation with Fatah or the PLO, even if it only involved distributing leaflets or spraying graffiti, led to arrest. When three enthusiastic villages from Dir Hanna expressed their joy about Arafat's appointment in February 1969 as the new chair of the PLO by artistically drawing his picture on the walls of their homes they were immediately arrested.[52] Four youngsters in Arabeh in the Galilee were imprisoned for ten months for writing a slogan on a wall against the continued Israeli occupation of the West Bank and the Gaza Strip. At worst the demonstrators or the leaflet distributors were killed during the attempt to arrest them, as happened to three youngsters in the village of Touran in eastern Galilee in March 1970.[53]

Other political figures would find themselves in jail, even if they were not caught writing graffiti on walls or making public statements of their support for the national movement. This was the fate of the Haifa-based lawyer, Muhammed Mia'ri, who was occasionally put under house arrest. The most famous case from that period was the arrest and eventual expulsion of Sabri Jiryis. He was frequently detained for his open support of the PLO, which became more vociferous after 1967 when Fatah took over the organization. In 1969, he was summoned to the northern command and was handed an arrest warrant, according to which he was not allowed to live outside the city limits of Haifa, change home within Haifa without police permission or leave the city of Haifa without police permission, and had to 'report to the police every day at 15.45 and stay in his home from an hour before sunset until dawn'. And this, readers are reminded, was after the abolition of military rule within a liberal democratic state.[54]

On 20 February he was jailed on another administrative regulation. In March 1970, Jiryis was one of the initiators of a hunger strike by Palestinian administrative detainees, which attracted wide support, including demonstrations in Israel and across the world. He was allowed to leave Israel later in 1970, and moved to Beirut where he became the director of the Palestine Research Centre during the 1970s; he returned home to Haifa only after the signing of the Oslo Accords.[55]

The Israeli authorities seemed indifferent to the age of those arrested or interned for short or long periods. In May 1969, several pupils in Taybeh's high school painted graffiti in support of the PLO on every empty space in their village. They were interned without trial for several weeks. Their friends staged the very first Palestinian hunger strike in solidarity with them.[56]

Until 1976, Palestinian citizens who were bold enough to display any kind of solidarity with the PLO were arrested, expelled and had their houses demolished, although this happened on a much smaller scale to the Palestinians in Israel than to those in the occupied territories. Being subjected to similar treatment by the Israeli security authorities in time strengthened the connection between the Palestinians on both sides of the Green Line, although the strategy against this policy was still different in its means and choices. The Palestinians in the occupied territories regarded armed struggle and resistance as a legitimate and at times preferred mode of action. The legal source for Israeli actions against both Palestinian communities was also the same: the Mandatory Emergency Regulations. The sense that both communities lived under a similar regime was reinforced by the Minister of Defense's decision at the very beginning of January 1968 to grant the army even easier access to Emergency Regulations and allow commanders to declare any area in the whole space of Mandatory Palestine a closed military zone from which all its population could be expelled. Inside Israel, this policy was applied not for mass expulsion but for carrying out vast land expropriation and house demolitions, which occurred quite frequently after 1968, out of sight of the media and the public mind. There were three major waves of land expropriation in the Galilee during the early 1970s which were implemented by this procedure, namely declaring the area first a closed military zone and then evicting those living on the land and destroying their houses.[57]

This new licence further inflated the security system installed to monitor the Palestinians in Israel, which was already extensively deployed. Ostensibly its purpose was to prevent subversive acts against the state, but in practice the targets were, and still are, political bodies and individuals, who are constantly under surveillance.[58] This fact of life was known to those in the Palestinian community who decided to be politically involved in the new circumstances evolving after the 1967 war.

THE SEARCH FOR LEADERSHIP

Hostile legislation, oppressive practices and racist images in the background were a common dominator in the policy of Israel towards the Palestinian community on both sides of the Green Line. But inside Israel a more complex reality developed, beyond mere tensions or even direct confrontations.

The Palestinians in Israel were citizens of the state, as limited as this status was, while those in the occupied territories were stateless. More than any other distinction, this fact delineated the difference between each group's immediate agendas. The Palestinians in Israel were focused on citizenship, land rights and equality – those in the West Bank and the Gaza Strip on ending the occupation.

The hopes for a better and much improved life after the abolition of the military rule did not materialize, and despair more than hope set in – and in some circles signs of outrage began to bud. This mixture of feelings needed to be channelled and arrested for the sake of the community as a whole by a leadership that could not only engage with political issues but also take a lead on social, cultural and economic matters. When one reads the few newspapers of that time, one gets the impression that the main question asked was: 'Who could represent us?' The obvious choices were the few Palestinian members of the Knesset, who were totally ignored in the Israeli parliament and never considered when forming political coalitions or even opposition blocs. The Palestinians in Israel had no representation in the army, in the government, in the Supreme Court or in the leadership of the Histadrut, and needless to say they were excluded from the Jewish National Fund, the powerful body that decided how land would be allocated and distributed in Israel, and which also had an impact on the water quota, whereby the Palestinians had been discriminated against ever since 1948. Only 2.3 per cent of the water resources available in Israel were allocated to the Palestinians in Israel in those years, and the percentage has remained the same in the twenty-first century.[59]

There were no Palestinian industrialists or bank directors, and they were not represented in any of the professional guilds or associations. Their local councils were poor and very weak vis-à-vis the central government (this was the case for Jewish localities as well), and their only autonomous legal spaces were the old religious courts, which were confined to issues that matter in the life of the individual, such as weddings, divorce, inheritance and so on. The secular and state legal system more often than not discriminated against them in its judgement and did not provide a venue for a real challenge to the fundamental or whimsical discrimination of the powers that be. In all these spheres of life it did not matter whether one was a Christian or a Muslim, one could not escape on a daily basis the understanding that one was a second-class citizen of the Jewish state.

As before, the realm of politics was the principal arena for action. The political agenda in this third decade of Israeli statehood evolved around questions of self-assertion and ways of transforming an oppressive reality. Voting for the Communist Party, Rakah, was one way of trying to achieve this, and attempting to be organized in national parties was another even better way (in both cases the parliamentary representation was insignificant numerically – Rakah won three seats in the 1969 elections and very few Palestinians entered the Knesset with other parties). Prying open every possible door in the government was another means of protest. There was a dramatic increase in demands for improvements after 1973 and a very focused campaign against discrimination in the welfare system, the lack of teachers and classrooms, the inadequate medical services and, later on, even for a clear national agenda.[60]

After 1973, it was the Palestinian students at Israeli universities who moved ahead with presenting demands which represented in the boldest and clearest way the national agenda, whether it was the right of some internal refugees to go back to their villages (in the few cases where these villages were still there intact and not transformed, as most of them had been, into a Jewish settlement or a JNF forest) or protesting against demolition of houses or political arrests inside Israel and in the occupied territories. The students' input during those years was quite impressive, given that there were no more than 600 Palestinian students at the time at the Israeli universities.[61]

These processes culminated in 1975 with the appearance of new organizations on the political scene: a national committee for the Arab students, a committee of all the heads of Arab councils and a new Nazareth front that wanted to take the city out of the hands of the traditional pro-Zionist clans. The scene was ready for a show of force by the state, whose official or unofficial advisors on Arab affairs found this relative self-confidence and legal protest far too irredentist and nationalist in nature.

The heterogeneous composition of those now defined as a leadership indicated a significant transformation in the Palestinian community. Under the military regime it had been very difficult to lead, and indeed very few scholars who write on the Palestinian community refer to a leadership of any kind in the 1950s and the 1960s. Among the bodies mentioned above, the committee of the heads of local councils was the hub of the leadership; later on, as we shall see, the centre of power would gravitate towards a new body, the 'Follow-Up Committee' or Supreme Monitoring Committee as it is referred to in other sources, which included other members alongside the heads of councils.

There were still politicians, and maybe one could call them leaders of a sort, who continued the line of cooperation, and – in the eyes of their community – collaboration with the authorities.[62] Of course everyone had to collaborate as a Palestinian in a Jewish state, but there was a choice between only fulfilling the necessary minimal requirements and identifying totally with the state, its ideology and essence. This latter kind of collaboration was more typical under military rule but also persisted into the 1970s. Those involved were usually members of the Knesset for Zionist parties, more often than not benefiting personally from the association, but to their credit one should say that some of them believed they were also serving their community.

The gap between the various leaders who were working within a non-Zionist, and a national Palestinian, framework was narrowing (a process that would mature, as we shall see in the next chapter, after the outburst of the first *Intifada*). In party politics terms it was a rainbow that stretched between the Communist Party through to the new national parties and some members of the Islamic movement. They were all able to unite under the political slogan 'Two states for two peoples' for the Palestine question, while demanding cultural autonomy for the Palestinians inside Israel.

This clear ideological consensus among the Palestinians in Israel was, as before, more clearly articulated in the cultural sphere. During this decade, poetry and later on theatre were the main media for charting new waters of identity and association. The best-known poets among the Palestinian citizens in that period were either under house arrest or in jail for their more nationalist poems (although all of them had a sizeable share of love poems and more general poetry). When Samih al-Qasem published his collection *The Thunderbird Will Arrive* in March 1969, all copies were confiscated and the poet was arrested for not submitting parts of the book to the censor before publication. Two months later, the writers and journalists Salem Jubran and Ahmad Khatib were put under house arrest for publishing nationalist poetry. In September 1969, Jubran was exiled from his home in al-Buqaya (Pek'in in Hebrew) to Haifa. Nonetheless he would remain one of the most vociferous believers in Arab–Jewish coexistence in Israel. All that year, the year of 1969, Mahmoud Darwish, Palestine's foremost poet, was kept under house arrest, constantly renewed by the courts – until he had had enough and left the country. And there were others, such as Fouzi al-Asmar from Lydda, who was arrested in September 1969 for a suspected connection with the PLO, and Habib Qahwaji who after repeated arrests decided, like Mahmoud Darwish, to leave. The list is a long one.

Nonetheless, one cannot talk about that decade as one during which a unified leadership emerged. Personal ambitions, clannish affiliations, religious identities and the temptations of collaboration disabled any joint action, despite there being a clearer national agenda. There was thus an ideological consensus, very similar to the Zionist consensus on the Jewish side, but this did not provide the recipe for unified action. But it was powerful enough to bring about the worst clash since 1948 between the state and the Palestinian minority, the Day of the Land events of March 1976. The Palestinian protest on that day was a formidable display of political and social mobilization of a fragmented community navigating cautiously through the dire straits of nationalism and segregation, which some scholars already then chose to define as an apartheid system.[63]

This formative event was the culmination of twenty-five years of general oppression and a particularly harsh policy of land expropriation. More directly, it was a response to a new zealous Israeli policy of Judaizing the north of the country that produced the first serious clash between the state and the Palestinian minority.

THE STRUGGLE AGAINST LAND CONFISCATION

The most pressing issue after 1967 was land. After the June 1967 war, the Israeli governments of Eshkol, Meir and Rabin had given energetic Judaizing officials a free hand to wage another campaign of land expropriation in the Galilee. *Yehud hagalil* (Judaizing the Galilee) was a clandestine programme until 1976, when it became an open slogan of the Housing Ministry.

While the magnitude and the impact of the new wave of land policy would be realized and resisted after 1976, the continued undeclared land expropriation created the impression among the Palestinians in Israel that military rule still existed but under a different name. The Judaization policy of the Galilee was contemplated, quite openly, in the late 1960s and early 1970s. It was already then presented as an ideological plan to reduce the number of 'Arabs' in the north of the state. The *raison d'être* of this strategy was summarized in 1975 by an internal document of the Ministry of Interior, written by Israel Koenig, the official in charge of the ministry's activities in the north of the country.

Koenig was an appointment of the national religious party, the Mafdal, which had held the Ministry of Interior as a traditional fiefdom ever since the creation of the state. Typically for a moderate religious person but a narrow-minded nationalist, he saw the Palestinians very much as the early Zionist settlers saw them: as 'aliens' and 'foreigners' who were not supposed to be there in the empty land that was redeemed with the return of the Jews. He tolerated their presence, but was a strong believer in the need to limit it to a defined space and encourage more Jews to settle in the Galilee. He also suspected the Palestinians as an irredentist group who were waiting for the opportune moment to destroy the Jewish state from within. His direct successor in years to come would be Israel's foreign minister in the twenty-first century, Avigdor Lieberman, a secular Jew with similar phobias and attitudes. Koenig was supported by other politicians, openly or indirectly, holding positions in the Ministry of the Interior, police, internal security, housing and national infrastructures; these are all governmental agencies with a direct impact on the quality of life and conditions of the Palestinians in Israel.

The report he wrote in 1975 rebuked the government for its lack of effort in pushing forward the Judaization of the Galilee. He demanded vast expropriation of Arab land and massive settlement of Jews on it, as well as a tighter watch over the subversive nature of 'Arab' politics in the Galilee. When his report was leaked to the press, it was quoted as including the phrase 'the Arabs of Israel are like a cancer in the heart of the nation'. In fact, the actual report did not include this phrase, but it represented the spirit of the report.[64]

Far more important than the report was the fact that the Israeli government was willing to implement most of its recommendations. The 1975 Koenig Report became a brutal policy of land confiscation on the ground in 1976.[65] Jews were asked to settle in the Galilee in every possible way: new towns, new *kibbutzim* and new community centres. For this purpose, the Emergency Regulations were used again to expropriate land without compensation or the right to protest. The land was used for new Jewish towns and community centres (no new Arab towns were built despite the high rate of natural population growth and the limitations on Palestinians who wished to reside in Jewish areas) in order to attract upwardly mobile people from Tel Aviv. Land was also expropriated for the Israeli army, which was in constant need of more training grounds.[66]

Palestinian members of the Communist Party decided, after years of internationalizing their politics, to formulate a particular national agenda. They had some leverage in local Israeli politics and were not totally tabooed as the Palestinian national parties had been. After the cessation of diplomatic ties between Israel and the USSR following the 1967 war, the Communist Party was important to the authorities as a substitute for the embassy.

They, with the new enthusiastic student bodies, established 'The Committee for the Defence of the Land'. The charismatic Communist leader Tawfiq Zayyad, a national poet as well as a politician, took advantage of this new initiative to win the local elections in Nazareth, the largest Palestinian town in Israel. His ascendance on this wave of protest provided the community for the first time with a leader of a regional and international calibre. In 1976, Zayyad addressed the Association of Arab-American University Graduates in the United States and thus became the first elected politician of the community to appeal to the international community and stress the Palestinian aspect of the community inside Israel. 'The Palestinians in Israel', he said, 'support the right for self-determination, the right for a sovereign state, and the right of return to the homeland of their fathers and fore-fathers from which they were evicted by a criminal blow of the sword in 1948'.[67] His attempt to internationalize the issue crossed a red line in the eyes of the Israelis, and Palestinian activists who attempted the same thing in the next century would pay dearly for it.

The Communist Party, which had expanded to incorporate non-Communist Palestinian and non-Zionist Jewish bodies, declared itself as the new 'Democratic Front for Peace and Equality' (*Hadash* in Hebrew and the *Jabaha* in Arabic). This transformation enabled the party to enlarge its membership and become more active within Palestinian national politics in Israel, probably at the expense of traditional Communist goals, such as activity among the more deprived socio-economic layers of society. In Israel, ethnic origin corresponded so closely to socio-economic position that Jews who advocated equality and economic justice were doing so mainly for the sake of the Palestinians in Israel. At the time the Front was formed, and for a long time afterwards, the poorest Jewish town, Yeruham, had a much higher standard of living, by any known criteria, than Me'ilya, the richest Palestinian community in Israel.[68]

THE DAY OF THE LAND

The Jabaha, or the Front, channelled the dismay and wrath felt by thousands of Galileans whose land and houses had been taken from them by force. The emotion erupted on the last day of March 1976, in a protest remembered ever since as the 'Day of the Land'. The widespread demonstrations caught the government unprepared, coming as they did after a relatively calm period in the relationship between the state and the Palestinian community. The government, which naturally believed that it was pursuing the right policies, regarded the confiscation of the land as a priority, and did not anticipate any serious objections from the victims of that policy.

The direct trigger for the activists' decision to mobilize a widespread day of protest was a publicized governmental decision on 1 March 1976 to expropriate 20,000 dunams as part of the programme branded as 'Developing the Galilee'. By then, Israel had already confiscated 75,000 dunams during the previous decade – and this of course was after most of the Palestinian lands were lost in the 1948 ethnic cleansing. There was no pressure from anywhere in Israel to develop the area for further settlement – the only reason for the programme was to Judaize and de-Arabize the north as far as possible.

The governmental declaration was followed by an announcement from the Israel Land Administration (ILA) that detailed the location and function of the new wave of expropriation. The ILA managed the land regime in the state. It was made up of various governmental agencies but the dominant voice in it was that of the Jewish National Fund which, as we have seen before, had vast influence and had a charter to gain as much land as possible for the exclusive benefit of the Jewish people.

The target areas were lands belonging to villages adjacent to the town of Carmiel. The authorities wished to expand the town boundaries in all directions so as to disrupt a rural Palestinian continuity in the area. The town and the village lie halfway along the road between

Acre on the Mediterranean and the town of Safad in the upper western Galilee. Ever since 1974, members of the Committee for the Defence of the Land had known about these plans and tried to convince the government to jettison them, but to no avail. The Committee regarded the last wave of appropriation as a pure provocation and a direct act of dispossession. A day of national strike and protest was planned for 30 March 1976. The decision was made to demonstrate not only against the land confiscation but also against the overall discriminatory policy.

On that day, quiet demonstrations in the villages of Sakhnin, Arabeh and Dir Hanna were confronted by an aggressive police and army presence which later turned them into violent confrontations. Ten days before the declared day of protest, armoured cars manned by the border police drove back and forth through the main streets of the three villages. On 28 March, the Minister of Police declared that his forces were 'ready to break into the Arab villages' – he used the Hebrew word '*Lifroz*', which is usually employed to describe assaults on enemy lines and bases.[69]

In the few days before the strike the Hebrew press had already composed the narrative to explain where it came from. *Haaretz* called it the initiative of a violent group of people.[70] Earlier that month, the editorial of the Israeli daily newspaper *Yediot Achronot* called the initiative a Moscow-led operation to destroy the state of Israel. The Minister of Education, Zevulun Hammer, declared that the Arabs 'were cancer in the heart of the nation'.[71] And it seems that this was a kind of a general guideline for the police force when the protestors marched into these three villages on 30 March.

One of the main activists was Father Shehadeh Shehadeh. He recalls that about two weeks before the Day of the Land (on 18 March) the heads of councils convened in Shefa-'Amr and decided against a day of protest. When the news emerged, a group of angry youngsters stormed the municipality building in Shefa-'Amr, where the meeting took place – as the head of the local council committee at the time was Ibrahim Nimr Husayn, the local mayor. In those days most of the mayors and heads of council were members of the ruling Labour Party. The angry young men prevented the participants from leaving the building, so the police came and with tear gas dispersed the protestors. The participants moved to Sakhnin, a village affected most by the way of land expropriation; there they took a different decision and declared a national day of protest on 30 March.[72]

The heads of the three village councils approached the police on 29 March and requested that Border Police would not provoke the demonstrators the day after by being unnecessarily stationed in the villages' centre during the day of protest. Had this request being heeded, there probably would have been no casualties on that day.[73]

Shehadeh remembered vividly that his greatest shock was when he received the news on the morning of 30 March that the government had decided to send the army into the villages that participated in the national strike. It was the sight of the army, he concluded years later, that caused people to throw stones at them and Molotov cocktails and the army responded with live fire.

One of the organizers of the day recalled years later the dynamics that evolved:

> We had no intention for any violence, all we wished was to declare that we oppose the expropriation of land. We were near Arabeh, the policemen started shooting without any real provocation on our side . . . They also announced a curfew over the village at night; most people had no idea what went on. Then the police broke into the houses and arrested young people whom they claimed did not obey the curfew . . . in the chaos demonstrators were killed and wounded. And then you stop and think: when did the police in Israel ever shoot at Jewish demonstrators?[74]

The bloodiest confrontations took place in Sakhnin and Arabeh. A few thousand demonstrators headed towards the reviled police stations and surrounded them, hurling stones and in some cases Molotov cocktails, and shouted 'Fatah, Fatah'. In Arabeh, the youngsters among the demonstrators barricaded the road with burning tyres and came close to the military border and police forces, who were already there in great numbers the day before the general strike was announced. They chanted slogans such as 'This village belongs to us not to Israel.' The military response in all these three villages was the same: shooting with live ammunition into the crowd, killing six of the demonstrators.

Similar demonstrations took place in Wadi Ara. In one of them, Ahmad Masarwa, from the village Arara, took part. He reconstructed the events afterwards, commenting, 'what was amazing that we organised without anyone telling us to do so; we collected people and prepared pamphlets', all in preparation for a procession of protest in the village against the land expropriation. Before the procession began the activists, like Ahmad, went from door to door to convince people to take part in a national day of strike. This was a brave decision by the villagers as many of them were employed by Jews and risked losing their jobs for missing a day in their workplaces. As a reporter from the *Guardian* who witnessed the demonstration wrote, the 'strike was almost 100 per cent effective in the Arab towns and villages'.[75] Masarwa recalled that some of the people in the village told him they joined the strike not because of the land expropriation but because they could not afford proper schooling and health services due to the meagre salaries they received. The police brought in buses full of soldiers who kidnapped the young demonstrators and beat them up in the buses, arresting some of them while letting others go home.[76]

At the end of the bloody days, six people were buried. Khayr Muhammad Yasin from Arabeh; Raja Hussein Abu Riya, Khader Abd Khalila and Khadija Juhayna (sometimes spelled Shwaneh) from Sakhnin, Muhammad Yusuf Taha from Kafr Kana, and Rafat Zuhairi from Nur Shams (a refugee camp near Tul Karim), who was shot at Taybeh. The municipality of Sakhnin commissioned a monument from the Palestinian artist Abed Abidi to honour the three people from the village killed on the day. It took a long time before the village, which in the meantime had become a town, could secure a licence to build the exhibit, which is now a famous landmark in the Palestinian Galilee.[77] The poet Mahmoud Darwish wrote 'The Poem of the Land' in memory of those killed:

A small evening
A neglected village
Two sleeping eyes
Thirty years

Five wars
I witness that the time hides for me
An ear of wheat
The singer sings
Of fire and strangers
Evening was evening
The singer was singing

And they question him why do you sing?
He answers to them as they seize him
Because I sing
And they searched him
In his breast only his heart
In his heart only his people
In his voice only his sorrow.

As an act of solidarity other Palestinians, including in the occupied territories, joined in with the protest. It only lasted one day and yet it was, as we shall see in the next chapter, a monumental event in the relationship of the state with its Palestinian citizens.

The daily Israeli press described the events as pure fanaticism without any justified cause,[78] just as they later portrayed the demonstrations in 2000, without any sympathy or understanding of the Palestinians' motivations or the role of the military and the police in the violence. The public mood among Jewish society was such that this grave violation of the Palestinians' human and civil rights was condoned without any criticism.

The sight of the state security's forces killing its own citizens was one even the more hawkish Israeli politicians did not wish to see. However, if there was any shock it was short lived. This was just few months before the great political earthquake in Israeli politics, when the Labour government was replaced by a right-wing Likud Party, even more hostile towards the Palestinian citizens. In those last months of the Labour government the public attention was attracted to other dramatic events, such as the hijacking of the Air France flight to Entebbe, Uganda and the Israeli military operation to release the hostages. The West Bank was also boiling with the elections that for the first time put an end to the pro-Jordanian leadership, which was replaced by the PLO representatives.

The workers who went on strike were fired and the Prime Minister, Yitzhak Rabin, in a meeting with the heads of council declared that all the plans for expropriation of land would go through. Moreover the government decided to leak the Koenig document which was hidden from the public eye as it was deemed then, in 1975, to be too provocative. Although not all of Koenig's racist recommendations were adopted, it was never condemned by the government and it seemed to reflect the attitude of the senior Jewish officialdom involved in implementing the daily policy towards the Palestinians in Israel.

CHAPTER FOUR

BETWEEN THE DAY OF THE LAND AND THE FIRST *INTIFADA*, 1976–1987

THE DRAMATIC EVENTS of the Day of the Land led to a brief *rapprochement*, and a halt to massive land confiscation – although only for a short while. The Galilee was not totally Judaized, but Palestinian–Jewish tension remained high. In November 1978, the Jewish heads of local councils in the Galilee met with governmental officials and ministers in the newly expanded (on Arab land) town of Carmiel. Carmiel now stretched over the land expropriated, despite the protest and the sacrifices made by the local community.

The failure to stop the expropriation of land may be explained by the fact that such a day of protest on this particular question was not attempted again. The struggle, as far as the Palestinians were concerned, moved to the courts and even to attempts to involve the international community in its plight. In any case, the Jewish meeting ended with a call for the government to continue the 'Judaization' of the Galilee due to the 'radicalization' in the attitudes of the Arabs in the north of Israel. The slogan of the day was 'there is no shame in Judaizing the Galilee'.[1]

A prime mover behind such initiatives was the new Minister of Defense, Ariel Sharon, who already in September 1977, despite his more urgent concerns in deepening the colonization of the West Bank and the Gaza Strip, stopped any attempts to ease the expropriation policy or the land regime inside Israel all together. 'As it is,' he cried, 'alien elements [Arabs] take over the lands of the state. National land is robbed by others. Soon Jews will have no place to settle in.'[2]

Sharon orchestrated what Ghazi Falah described as the second wave of Judaization, which included almost doubling the Jewish population in the Galilee between 1960 and 1985. Sixty new Jewish settlements were added in three settlement blocks, Segev, Tefen and Talmon, all connected by a new web of highways, of a quality unknown before in the Galilee, where the roads to the Arab villages were never upgraded to such a level.[3]

Recollections of the decade that followed the Day of the Land are of individuals trying to rebuild a normal life after the frightening events, only to be faced twice, in 1982 and in 1987, with sharp reminders that normal life was a luxury no Palestinian, wherever he or she lived, could afford. But even before and in between the war in Lebanon in 1982 and the outbreak of the first *Intifada* in 1987, people could not keep politics out of their houses and private lives. In the age of television, and later on even more so with the advent of the Internet, even if one was not a victim of a particular policy, what happened to the other members of the Palestinian community or to the Palestinians at large was very much present and difficult to ignore.

However, this was also a period when individuals in the community reached senior positions as physicians, sportsmen and businessmen. The most impressive field was that of medicine, where thousands of doctors were employed in the governmental and private hospitals and medical services (although it should be noted that only in 2007 was a Palestinian, Dr Masad Barhoum, appointed to direct a hospital).[4] During this period the first Palestinians joined some of the top Israeli football teams and one or two made it into the national team (where the press watched nervously to see whether they would join in singing the Zionist anthem when required; needless to say most of the players of the national team did not, and still do not today, know the words off by heart. But the Palestinian players very honestly said they could not sing an anthem which craves for the return of the Jews to Zion.) Some very sanguine academic research was done following this, rather minimal, involvement of Palestinians in the Israeli football scene, in the hope that it would be a precursor of a more amiable relationship between the two communities. This was mainly due to the personality of Rifat 'Jimmy' Turk. A very kind soul born in the harsh neighbour-hoods of Jaffa, he became the first Palestinian footballer to play in Israel's national team in 1976. He moved later to work with youth and the community in Jaffa and symbolized a personal track out of the otherwise ghettoized existence of Palestinians in Jaffa.[5]

In the business sector, the first successes of construction and trade companies were noted, but again their ability to break into the Jewish market was limited and some later on were bought by big Israel compa-nies wishing to monopolize the market of coffee and dairies, which were traditionally advanced in the Palestinian sector.

But in hindsight these were not the crucial images that impacted on the life of the community as a whole. The relevant pictures are those of Palestinian leaders in the West Bank and the Gaza Strip arrested by a new fierce policy pursued by Ariel Sharon, or blown to pieces by a Jewish underground; or of Israeli tanks rolling into Lebanon in the summer of 1982 in a destructive campaign against the PLO and its leader Yasser Arafat; and finally of Palestinian children aged thirteen directing a rocket-propelled grenade against an Israeli tank in the Ayn Hilweh refugee camp in Lebanon, or hurling stones at the armoured cars in the Balata refugee camp near Nablus in the first *Intifada* against the Israeli occupation forces.

In between the political drama, in which the Palestinian community displayed solidarity with other Palestinians throughout the world and felt a part of a larger community of suffering and victimhood, more mundane and hopeful images infiltrate the collective memory. The first group of young lawyers and doctors began to make a difference to society; fresh plays and theatre in Arabic for the first time were shown independently and even documentary films were contemplated. More women were educated and worked, more babies were born, and people lived longer than in previous years.[6]

THE END OF LABOUR AND THE BEGINNING OF THE LIKUD ERA

For most Israeli Jews 1977 was as disturbing as 1973. The near defeat on the battlefield was followed by the demise of the Labour movement, which had controlled political life in Israel since the foundation of the state in 1948. It was replaced by the Likud coalition with a Liberal party and religious national Jews who represented the new drive in the Jewish society to settle in the occupied territories – a trend initiated by the Labour governments.

Menachem Begin, the new Prime Minister until his fall from grace in 1983 due to the drowning of the Israeli army in the Lebanese quagmire, was remembered among Palestinians in Israel as the man who led the struggle for the abolition of military rule. But soon this positive image was replaced with that of a political demagogue who did not hesitate to arouse the most basic racist and anti-Arab emotions to become Prime Minister. He was voted in by an Arab Jewish, Mizrahi, electorate, who were persuaded by an appeal to their anti-Arabism, among other issues. In their eyes, if I may recap what I have pointed out earlier on, and in the political manipulation of the political right in Israel, their ticket to full integration into the Israeli society was their ability to de-Arabize themselves: to wipe out their Arab traditions, roots and language so that they would become as Israeli and Zionist as the Ashkenazi Jews. Displaying a strong anti-Arab position, including vis-à-vis the Palestinian minority in Israel, assured success in the struggle for integration and with it, maybe, personal economic prosperity. Begin unashamedly exploited this impulse and these apprehensions. His other colleagues, such as Ariel Sharon and Yitzhak Shamir, were even more vociferous and anti-Arab than he was, at least in their speeches and discourses.[7]

But at the end of day, both from the vantage point of our time and when viewed through the eyes of Palestinians in Israel, this fault line of Israeli politics was quite meaningless in the lives of the Palestinian community. Likud and Labour may have differed on the fate of the occupied territories, but there was never any significant divergence of opinion between them as to what the status and the fate of the Palestinians in Israel should be. For both parties, from a Zionist perspective, it would have been better if the state had been emptied of its indigenous and local population, but this was an impossible dream. Instead they had to tolerate a Palestinian minority, provided it did not aspire to become a national group that could challenge, or even change, the Jewish nature of Israel.

Thus if you ask the Bedouin of the Negev about that decade they will recall that the last months of Labour in power were the worst. Driven by extra zeal, and without particular prodding from above, the officials in the Negev harassed this part of the community in the months leading to the election of the Likud. Ninety dunams of the land of the al-Sana tribe were run over by tractors to make them unusable while forty-five families from another tribe were moved from an area coveted by the Israel Land Administration to Wadi Ara in the north. They were first settled in area 109, as it was called, which was under the rule of Emergency Regulation No. 109 – which meant that for a while they lived in a closed military zone, unable to enter or leave it without army permission.[8]

As Ghazi Falah noted, the Bedouin discovered during that period that their problem was 'not so much of being Bedouin, but rather those of being Arabs in a Zionist state'; at the time Falah was a young Bedouin geographer trying unsuccessfully to offer a geographical perspective that was not loyal to the Zionist state or its assumptions. Geography, as Edward Said noted, is very closely associated with nationalism and patriotism; it was by far the most difficult position to hold within the Israeli academia and indeed Falah teaches it today in the USA.[9]

It seems that in the final days of Labour, its representatives on the ground were even less tolerant than during the decade as a whole. When the anti-Zionist movement Matzpen wished to screen a film about the 1956 massacre in Kafr Qassem, the film was confiscated. Even in 1977 it was not possible, either in the Arab or Jewish public space, to discuss openly what had happened in 1956. A similar attempt to silence discussion in cultural media about unpleasant chapters in the past occurred in the same month, when Israeli television wished to screen the film *Hirbet Hizah*, S. Yizhar's famous story exposing the violent side of Israeli conduct during the 1948 war. The month also saw the continued policy of house and administrative arrests for those who persisted in their criticism of the government, such as Ghazi al-Sadi, a publisher from Acre, interned for allegedly spying for the Syrians; he was offered release in return for exile and giving up his Israeli citizenship. Some even paid with their lives, as happened in Majd al-Kurum, a village on the road between Acre and Safad, where the authorities demolished a house and, in the process, when faced with demonstrators and protestors, killed one villager and wounded and arrested scores of others. This demolished house is still visible today from the main highway as a commemorative landmark of past tragedies and evils.[10]

Begin lost his seat to the more extreme right-wing leader Yitzhak Shamir, whose reign of power was short-lived and who therefore left no enduring impact on any aspect of life in Israel. From 1984, it was back to Labour, although this time within a unity government. As could have been anticipated, on the issue of Palestinians in Israel there was no dividing line between the two major political blocs of Labour and Likud.

THE AXIS OF EXCLUSION AND INCLUSION: LIFE IN THE FOURTH DECADE

The two dramatic events of this decade, the 1982 Lebanon war and the first *Intifada*, were not powerful enough to determine the troubling questions of identity, navigation, citizenship and survival, which remained insoluble and as problematic as they ever had been.

The limited possibilities open to Palestinian citizens were the result of the previous governmental policies. Since the policies in the new decade did not fundamentally challenge these early ones, the political options and strategies for the individual and the Palestinian community as a whole were pretty much the same as before. The most significant fact in this respect was the economic gap between the Jewish and Palestinian communities in the late 1970s. It was so wide that one can now say with confidence, and in hindsight, that it defeated the chances for real reconciliation, even without the particular pressures on the relationship brought by the 1982 Lebanon war and the first *Intifada*.

For political and academic observers at the time, the main change between Labour and Likud was the espousal of an extreme capitalist economic policy by the latter (advised directly by none other than Milton Friedman), and this was the main reason for the economic polarization in the Jewish state. This analysis was favoured by the Communist Party, which asserted that a more egalitarian economic and social policy would have produced a Jewish state in which the minority could live on equal terms with the majority (next to a Palestinian state in the West Bank and the Gaza Strip).

While important sections in the Zionist left, for instance a new group of leading professors and intellectuals in the Labour Party, Kevuzat 77, the 1977 group, began to adopt this analysis and prognosis, young intellectuals in the Palestinian community, many of them originally members of the Communist Party, saw the problem as originating elsewhere. They still believed that the source of the problem was the ethnic ideology of the Zionist movement and its adoption as a hegemonic strategy by the Jewish state. Therefore the solution in their eyes was to substitute the regime in Israel for any political outfit that would be liberated from this hegemonic ideology, regardless of its economic nature. So while the Communist Party opened a huge Soviet book festival in 1977, other activists were pushing forward either more purely national agendas or Islamic ones.

Whatever was the cause, one point is very clear from a historical perspective: in terms of expectations and realities, the socio-economic conditions seemed to have a decisive impact on the vast majority of the Palestinian community, as now a second generation of children born into post-Mandatory Palestine was growing up. The economic reality affected the social one in particular for this new generation. Israel in the late 1970s was a state where Palestinians, unlike Jewish citizens, had very limited options for social mobilization. For example, official Israeli statistics showed that only 1 per cent of Palestinians were enrolled in the official education system beyond the age of sixteen, and only 4 per cent were enrolled between the ages of thirteen and fifteen.[11] The low percentage of Palestinians accepted into Israeli universities did not meet their drive for higher education; hence many young people found their own way to Europe, and those connected to the Communist Party to Eastern Europe, in pursuit of academic careers.

Given the economic deprivation and these social limitations, the prevailing experience of many in the Palestinian community at that time was of a growing sense of alienation from the state, even thirty years after its foundation and a decade after the abolition of the military rule. The problem was not only the policies of the Jewish state, but also the expectation, at least among the educated elite, that life was about something more than mere existence. Against this background one can appreciate how the Jewish state seemed to the more politicized Palestinians in Israel at the time. The state excluded them as full citizens, occupied their nation state, and refused to recognize its responsibility for the *Nakbah* and its consequences.

On the other hand, new avenues opened up for those who sought an individual career. This did not amount to being integrated or included in the community of equal citizenship, but it posed a question for those who would portray their situation as straightforward oppression and occupation. As is later elaborated in the Appendix of this book, when academic research inside Israel on the community developed in the 1980s and 1990s (very much thanks to the emergence of a community of Palestinian scholars in Israel and the appearance of progressive critical Jewish social scientists), this mixed reality of collective repression, but with individual opportunities, was depicted as an ethnocracy. A minority in the form of an excluded ethnic group was allowed certain freedoms and opportunities, as long as they did not undermine the hegemony and control of the majority ethnic group. The end result of this formula is a serious and systematic abuse of basic civic and human rights of the minority group. But away from academia in the world of political activism, where the mixture of limitations and openings was on offer not as an abstract idea but as a daily reality, the discourse of human and civil rights was at times less appealing than the national dictionary and images; the latter seemed more apt as a compass for those in the Palestinian community who wished to alleviate the yoke of decades-long oppression.

But as this book insists, life as lived – rather than academically defined, analysed and described – did not move that schematically between inclusion and exclusion. The worst aspect of it, one assumes, was that every now and then the Israeli Jewish society, mainly through its intellectuals but at times even through its state agencies, conveyed a false message of a wish to make Israel a more pluralistic and open society. While the older generation within the Palestinian community were experienced enough to view these promises with healthy scepticism, the younger generation – in this decade becoming an overwhelming part of the community – were at first more optimistic about the options open to them. When these promises turned out to be mere words and the reality remained more or less the same, the younger generation would be even more assertive in its conviction that change would not come from Israel's goodwill, but only through a struggle from within.

The first disappointment in this regard occurred in the decade under review here, when even the Ministry of Education in Israel declared its wish to make Israel into a multicultural society in the early 1980s.

A NEW MULTICULTURAL SOCIETY?

Life inside Israel was more intricate than it appears in the works of those who commend Israel for finally building a democracy in those years and those condemning it for running an apartheid state. The social and political intricacy can be partly explained by the complex relationship between the Palestinians in Israel and other groups in society. The Palestinians were part of the emerging multicultural reality in Israel, in which the politics of identity fragmented the political scene into groups representing particular ethnic, religious and cultural agendas; some of these group formed political parties on the basis of their particular identity: a feminist party, a Russian Jewish party, a Mizrahi party, an ultra-orthodox party, a Mizrahi ultra-orthodox party and more. Each in its own way felt victimized by the state in the past or in the present.

Similar predicaments could have served as a basis for a common political action. On an intellectual and theoretical level, the fragmentation of Israeli society due to the politics of identity did encourage some new perceptions among Jewish academics, journalists and (more than anyone else) film-makers about Palestinian conditions inside Israel. After the Lebanon war several very commercially successful Israeli feature films represented this new sensitivity. Three such films, *Hamsin*, *A Very Narrow Bridge* and *Behind the Bars*, dealt in one way or another with the Palestinian–Jewish relationship in Israel. The Palestinians in general, and the ones living in Israel in particular, appeared in those movies as heroes rather than as villains, and even as freedom fighters, whereas their image in previous films had been that of members of a demonized and anonymous enemy. These films were less about the Palestinians than about the moral tribulations of the film-makers or the conscientious Jews in Israel. But they did humanize for the first time the 'Arab' on the Israeli silver screen.[12]

This hesitant engagement may explain the lack of political alliances between the Palestinians in Israel and the other groups. Even the political cooperation between the 'peace camp' – representing that section in the Jewish society pressuring for the end of the 1967 occupation in return for peace – and the Palestinian minority was limited. This was mainly due to the clarification of the national position of the Palestinians in Israel on the one hand, and on the other the new political interpretation of what passed as 'left' and 'right' in the Jewish community, which focused almost exclusively on the debate over the future of the West Bank and the Gaza Strip while displaying a unity of purpose and position towards the Palestinian community inside Israel. In other words, the Israeli peaceniks were bothered about the occupied territories – which they wanted to give up – but were less concerned about the Palestinians in Israel with whom they had to contemplate a joint life.

For an alliance to work either the 'peace camp' had to abandon Zionism or the Palestinian minority had to ignore its national affiliation. In relative terms, there would have to be a pact between critics of Zionism, whom I termed elsewhere 'post-Zionists' – Jews willing to forsake all or part of the Zionist interpretation of reality – and Palestinians prepared to put their civic agenda above the national one. Few in both groups were willing to go that far; the majority of the Jewish critics of Israel remained within the Zionist mindset and the new activists asserted that their immediate struggle was national and not civic. The gap grew in intensity and conviction and dismantled any potential alliances that might have been contemplated or attempted.

If it was difficult to create an alliance between the post-Zionists and the new national forces, one can understand how impossible it was to build such bridges between the mainstream Israeli political forces and the Palestinian community at large. During this decade, while individuals continued to cooperate with the state, its organs and representatives out of necessity, or even at times to collaborate out of personal greed, there was very little room for collective cooperation with the state based on confidence or mutual interest.

Even in the more hopeful years leading to the Oslo Accords in 1993, at which it was alleged that Israel and the PLO officially reached a historical compromise on dividing Palestine into two future states (although we now know that this failed accord should not have been read in such an optimistic way), there was no room for improvement in the relationship of the state with the minority living inside it. While there was a new willingness to be dovish on the question of the occupation – namely to consider partial withdrawal and a solution – there was at the same time, and as a direct result of this flexibility, a strengthening of the hawkish attitudes towards the Palestinians inside Israel, which could be expressed in these terms, 'If we recognize your right to a state in the occupied territories and you do not like our state in pre-1967 Israel you now have an option.' This would become the platform of a very important party of Russian immigrants and extreme Mizrahi Jews, led by a former bartender from Moldavia, Avigdor Lieberman.

But at the time we are discussing here, the main process was the emergence of the national parties inside the Palestinian community, while the divorce from the Jewish peace camp would come only later, in 2000. The reason that the clear difference in the agenda between the Zionist left and the Palestinian community in Israel was not apparent yet was that they both shared the same hope during the days of the Oslo Accords, and as long as the PLO still believed in the chance of peace through that accord, both the Zionist peace camp and the major parties within the Palestinian community supported the process. These new national parties associated the question of peace with the Palestinians with their own future and as such located themselves outside the 'legitimate' boundaries of the Zionist left or 'peace camp'. What they did not know at the time was that the PLO also excluded their fate from a possible peace process in the future. Such stances opened up the whole question of Israel's identity, democratic conduct, and its future between Europe and the Middle East. There was nothing a Zionist party could offer on the horizon that promised a significant change in the reality of a Palestinian citizen in the 1980s, so aptly described by the writer Anton Shamas after the first Lebanon war: 'I am a second-rate citizen, nationless in the Jewish state of Israel.'[13]

THE NEW NATIONAL FORCES

In the Palestinian community at that period, the search was more and more for self-assertion and a national modus operandi that did not rely on Jewish coaching or cooperation. The Day of the Land was the first national day of protest in this respect. The event itself institutionalized political activity in the community through the formation of the 'Committee of Heads of Local Arab Councils', which now worked alongside, and at times fused into, the 'Follow-Up Committee'. This body was the final version of previous committees that had been seeking since the 1970s to coordinate the political activity of the Palestinians inside Israel. In 1981, the main politicians and the heads of councils created the coordination committee, but it did not last for long.

A more successful attempt at coordinating the political activity of the community came in 1982, in the wake of the Lebanon war in general, and the massacre in the Palestinian refugee camps of Sabra and Shatila by Maronite militias strongly connected to the Israeli army. The angry protest all over the Palestinian villages and urban neighbourhoods led to the founding of the 'Supreme Follow-Up Committee' (which we will refer to hereafter as the Follow-Up Committee). The idea was conceived by Ibrahim Nimr Husayn, the mayor of Shefa-'Amr and the chair of the committee of local councils. He also became the first chair of the new committee. At first it included eleven heads of the main local councils and towns and the members of the Knesset. By 1990 other representatives of various NGOs and citizens living in mixed Arab–Jewish towns also received representation on the committee, which became a mini-parliament for the Palestinian community. It created subcommittees for dealing with various aspects of life in the community: education, health, sport, social services and agriculture. Its inaugural meeting was in Shefa-'Amr where it sat until it moved to Nazareth where it sits today.

In the main the Follow-Up Committee charted basic guidelines or general positions on issues that troubled the community at large, such as relationships with the Jewish state, the PLO or the Arab world. Like the other NGOs, the Committee had no power of sanction and their declarations were effectively recommendations to the community, sometimes heeded and sometimes not (for instance the call for a national strike was not always accepted – but more often than not, it was). The Follow-Up Committee later became a more significant body. Its members did not seek total obedience to their policy proposals but rather wished to offer their community a compass with which to navigate in the stormy and dire straits of life in the Jewish state; or, more precisely, its statements had recommendations of how best to build a golden mean between the national demands and the pressures of the state. Very rarely did it call for direct confrontation as it did in 1988 and in response to the events in Jerusalem in 2000. A good example of its attempt to be a consultative body can be seen in the educational work of the Follow-Up Committee, which in 1984 was taken over by a body under its supervision called the Follow-Up Committee on Arab Education in Israel. This body responds to the needs of parents and teachers within a system that is closely supervised, monitored and managed by Jewish officials in the Ministry of Education. Navigating between the requirements of the segregated educational system that demands total obedience to the Jewish state and the natural impulse to provide national education for the younger generations requires daily decisions on how to deal with the curriculum dictated from above, the content of official ceremonies such as the problematic Day of Independence celebrating Israel's foundation, while totally ignoring the catastrophe that befell the Palestinian people in 1948, and similar issues.

In other areas, it was the Committee that suggested how best to react to events in the first and second *Intifada* and later on to other Israeli operations in Lebanon, the West Bank and Gaza, and it suggested what content to give to days of commemoration, be they for the *Nakbah* of 1948 or landmarks such as the Day of the Land, in the history of the Palestinian community inside Israel. In most cases where events organized by the Committee deteriorated into direct confrontation, the feeling among the Palestinian Israeli observers (and of this writer as well, but not however in the Israeli media) was that the trouble began with an overreaction on the part of the troops facing the demonstrators.

But the major change in the political scene was the appearance of purely Arab parties. Two political formations stand out in this period as offering a national outlet separate from both Communism and Zionism. The first was led by Muhammed Mia'ri, a former founder of the al-Ard movement. He and his former colleagues produced a new parliamentary party, Hareshima Hamitkademet Le-Shalom, 'The Progressive List for Peace'. The members of this new outfit had to fight in the Supreme Court of Justice for the right to participate in the national elections in Israel. The main opposition came from the Israeli secret service, and it was a high hurdle to get over.[14] Only when it was considered in comparison with a fanatical right-wing Jewish party did the court allow it to take part in the Knesset elections. It was the first political party to take part in the democratic process that declared openly its unambiguous support for, and identification with, the Palestinian national movement.

Initially the party had a few Jewish members in it, but they soon left and it developed into the 'Arab Democratic Party', soon to become the 'National Democratic Party', Balad, which is the acronym in Hebrew of the title but also means the 'land' or the 'village' in Arabic (it was later known as Tajamu – 'the block'). Obviously, for the secret service, it acted outside the tolerated boundaries of Arab activism in Israel but the authorities in general tolerated it, although they suspected and monitored it very closely.

The PLO's Declaration of Independence (adopted by the Palestinian National Council in Algiers on 15 November 1988) unilaterally declared the establishment of the State of Palestine and declared the chairman of the PLO, Yasser Arafat as the president of the new state. The principles of the state were the acceptance of the two-state solution and the need for a peaceful solution with Israel. This declaration, and of course the Oslo Accords of 1993, strengthened the acceptance, albeit grudgingly, of such political parties.

The second alternative followed a very different line of thinking that would become popular in the Islamic movement and with the Palestinian public at large in the next century: acting as a political movement and yet refusing to partake in the parliamentary process. Anti-Zionist activists with some Palestinian friends had already done this in the previous decade in Matzpen but it remained a very small and marginal group. In its stead emerged a purely Palestinian national movement with Jewish solidarity. The new party went by the name of Abna al-Balad, 'the sons of the land' or 'the sons of the village' in Arabic. It had been founded in 1969 but became publicly known after the 1976 Day of the Land events. It defined itself as 'a Palestinian movement operating within the Green Line of Israel'. Among its main demands were an unconditional right of return for the 1948 refugees, the end of Israeli occupation all over Mandatory Palestine and the creation in its stead of an Arab, secular and democratic state.

Adopting such positions required a fair share of personal courage as arrest and harassment were an inevitable risk one took when joining the movement (although the worst action against them by the state took place only in 2004, when its leadership was arrested for alleged cooperation in terrorism with Fatah activists in Jenin). When Balad became a parliamentary party in the late 1980s, led by Azmi Bishara, some members of Abna al-Balad joined it, forsaking the principle of not participating in the elections, while the others continued to operate as the original movement, as they still do.

THE IMPACT OF THE 1982 LEBANON WAR: A CRISIS WELL-NAVIGATED

The forced eviction of the PLO headquarters from Jordan to Lebanon in 1970 strengthened the political and military presence of the Palestinian guerrilla movement in Lebanon. PLO political, cultural and military activity was directed from Beirut, while the scattered refugee camps served as a launching pad for operations inside Israel. One of these was the attack on a bus at the northern entrance to Tel Aviv in 1978, which triggered Operation Litani in which Israel occupied the southern part of Lebanon, up to the river Litani, with the help of Maronite militias. This happened three years into the Lebanese civil war, which erupted in 1975, and continued until the late 1980s while involving a long period of heavy Syrian presence in the country at the behest of the Arab League.

Israel created what it called a security zone in southern Lebanon against which Palestinian forces fought together with Muslim militias.

Qatyushas (Second World War Russian-made missiles) were fired into Israel's northern towns and settlements, and Israel retaliated with heavy bombardment from the air, the land and the sea. In 1981, the American envoy Philip Habib secured a ceasefire between the PLO and Israel. Israel decided to violate this ceasefire after an assassination attempt on its ambassador in London, Shlomo Argov, on 3 June 1982. One suspects that the Israeli Minister of Defense, Ariel Sharon, who had tried ruthlessly to crush the PLO influence in the Gaza Strip and the West Bank, was looking for an opportunity to destroy the PLO in Lebanon. The assassination attempt provided the necessary excuse; although the assassins, as was well known to Sharon, were Abu Nidal's people, who vehemently opposed the PLO and who were supported at the time by the Iraqi regime. 'Abu Nidal, Abu Shmidal,' replied the Chief of Staff of the IDF, Rafael Eitan, when he was told this was not a PLO operation. 'We need to nail the PLO.'[15] So Israel violated the ceasefire by bombing nine PLO camps in Lebanon and the organization retaliated by heavy bombardment on Israel's north. This was the sign for the Israeli forces to roll in and occupy Lebanon as far as Beirut and the border with Syria.

Prime Minister Menachem Begin – always the constitutional gentleman – brought the decision to go to war for hindsight approval by the Knesset. Only Hadash (formerly Rakah, the Communist Party) voted against it, and even tabled a no-confidence motion against the government. 'The country will regret this war for ever,' declared its Jewish member, Meir Vilner. The chief editor of *Yediot Achronot*, Israel's foremost daily at the time, demanded in response that Vilner and the Palestinian members of the Knesset be brought to justice on charges of treason.[16] Only when the Sabra and Shatila massacres were carried out did a mass movement develop in Israel in opposition to the war.

The 1982 Lebanon war produced new dilemmas in the relationship between the Palestinians and Jews in Israel. As the late poet and novelist Emil Habibi put it, in the phrase first uttered by Mapam MK Saif al-Din al-Zoubi (long before the 1982 war), 'My country was at war with my people.'[17] The whole war was a bizarre experience for the Palestinians in Israel, in particular for those living in the north. The Israeli government euphemistically called the war, 'Operation Peace for the Galilee'. In fact, of course, the Galilee was mainly populated by Palestinians who identified with the organization branded by Israel as the enemy of peace in the Galilee: the PLO.

All in all, the war against the PLO, which ended with the removal of the PLO headquarters to Tunis and the death of many Palestinians and the destruction of their homes and refugee camps, did not change the political strategy of the community. Israeli policies were still regarded as oppressive, but the struggle against them was played out within the set of rules formulated by the Jewish state. This was not a democratic game in the eyes of the activists and politicians, but it required more democratization in the politics of the community itself.[18] By this time the nature of the Israeli oppression was understood better by leading academics in the community. Many of them rejected the state's depiction of them as immigrants who should accept the code of the host country, and instead defined the Palestinians in Israel as an indigenous community to which a foreign state had immigrated, and yet were excluded from nationhood in their own homeland.[19]

The political struggle was expanded after the Lebanon war. Intellectuals, students, workers and women (highly visible on the ground, though not in the leadership) were the main agencies moving the struggle ahead. Political identity and the land question were still the two main issues at the heart of political life. Something else happened in this respect: after 1982, the struggle in the occupied territories and inside Israel had much more in common than in previous years. The difference in the nature of the Israeli control over the life of Palestinians in the two localities still determined the particular experience of each community, as either second-class citizens of the state of Israel or inhabitants of occupied territories ruled by a military regime. But in both cases there was a need to use diplomacy in dealing with Israeli and international law, and other means, alongside the armed struggle still adhered to by the PLO until 1988.

THE TIME OF THE STUDENTS

This was the decade of the campus as the main locus of political happenings. Members of the various student committees, still not recognized by the universities, protested against the occupation and in solidarity with the PLO. Each such demonstration was either prohibited by the universities' management or, if allowed, ended with severe punishment for its organizers. The students organizing one such demonstration at the Hebrew University were arrested by the army (the IDF not the police) and forced to remain in their villages by a military decree that prohibited their travel to Jerusalem, thus risking losing their academic year. Needless to say, the army would never have engaged with Jewish students in this way. A constant source of clashes on the campus was the repeated attempts throughout that decade by the general, that is, the Jewish student union, to invite the anti-Arab politician Meir Kahana to the campuses, while leading figures in the Palestinian community, such as Tawfiq Zayyad, were barred from speaking there (for instance in the Technion in May 1979).[20]

The decade began with Rakah dominant in student politics but soon that part of the community was drawn first towards more national agendas such as the one offered by Abna al-Balad, the official successor of the al-Ard movement, and later on to the Islamic movement. The chairman of the student committee at the Hebrew University, Azmi Bishara, later formed his own political party, but like other colleagues of his, Issam Makhoul in Haifa and Mohammad Barakeh in Tel Aviv, used this as a launch-pad for a career in national politics. The price, which was quite often beatings by the police and arrests, was balanced by the growing respect among the community for this new mode of national resistance and steadfastness.

CRAVING A THIRD SPACE

But not everyone was a student or an activist. The community, now around 600,000, was mostly made up of normal people craving a normal life but hardly finding it. The complications after 1982 lay not only in the relationship with the state but also with the rest of the Palestinian national movement. Now that all of historical Palestine was under Israeli control and the Jewish state had gone to war against the Palestinian leadership in exile, the Palestinians in Israel were required to decide whether they were once more '*Dukhala*' ('insiders'), the derogative term applied to them by the press in the Arab world until 1967, or partakers in the national struggle.

At the end of the day, the politicians, and the public at large, remained loyal to the old patterns of behaviour and did not deviate from the rules of the game that they themselves had set. The support for the PLO in Lebanon was limited to the theatre and editorials in the press. As mentioned in the Appendix to this book, this decision brought home forcefully to the academic observers the double marginality in which the minority lived – marginal both within Israeli society and within the Palestinian national movement. But whatever reservations academics may have had about it, this way of life was still the preferred golden mean as far as political activists and indeed regular members of the community were concerned.

Inside the borders of pre-1967 Israel, citizenship in the 1980s allowed more freedom to express political goals, whereas in the West Bank and the Gaza Strip occupation necessitated a more subtle and convoluted approach through political poetry, the attribution of heroism to remaining in Palestine and not emigrating, and through a strong belief that powers such as the PLO, the Arab world and the international community would rescue the occupied society. When these methods proved futile, large sections of the younger generation opted for open resistance, leading their society to the uprising of 1987. It is worth remembering that at that time, even after the 1982 Lebanon war, when the PLO headquarters moved to Tunis and lost both control over and direct contact with many Palestinian communities within Palestine, there was a third Palestinian agenda, different from the one born in the refugee camps in Jordan, Syria and Lebanon. The refugee camps were still the location which determined the theme of the Palestinian national struggle, its essence and its goals, but in the occupied territories and inside Israel new variations on the theme of 'struggle' developed according to the particular circumstances in which each community lived.

The Palestinians in Israel employed for most of the time a mode of national struggle that differed quite significantly from the uprisings and direct confrontation chosen by the Palestinians in the occupied territories. Even when pushed hard by the state in October 2000 (when thirteen Palestinian citizens were killed in clashes with the police in circumstances described later in this book), which regarded their mode of protest during that month as being akin to a Palestinian uprising in the occupied territories, their strategy remained intact – although it became more and more difficult to maintain.

It can be best described as a third-space strategy, in the meaning of the term as articulated by Cornel West when discussing the options of the African-Americans in the USA.[21] It is the wish to be free from the need to be fully integrated and co-opted by the state on the one hand, but also not to succumb and be totally consumed by the homogenizing collective identity of the Palestinians, on the other. One could chose between those two, one could move from one to the other, even in a single day, and one could find ways of fusing them together, in the sense that one could decide, for instance, to become pious and religious as a preferred way of protest rather than participating in an organized activity in a party or a movement.

For those exhausted by the endless navigation through the matrix of a reality full of contradictory demands from the state, the national movement, the old social structure and the temptations offered by new political forces radicalizing the demands from the individual in the name of nationalism and liberation, there was always a sphere of an individual or collective nature. For most of the time this was a respite from the magnetic field of identities and loyalties demanding an individual decision or choice. In other words, members of the community tended, and may still tend in the future, to retire to the domestic sphere because they were and are so stressed by everything else. This could be the source of a future strategy that might defeat the big ideologies and grand schemes of colonization and liberation – the harbinger of a new dawn for Israel and Palestine as a whole.

In more simplistic, and maybe realistic terms, this sphere was the space between the demands of cooperation and surrender to the state, and the growing pressure to partake in a Palestinian struggle either in its typical pre-1967 Israel mode of operation or the more confrontational one offered by the Palestinians in the occupied territories. When one was in the third space, one did not have to decide which struggle suited one best, nor participate in the new debate which emerged in the 1980s:

whether to support the old PLO charter of one independent Arab state as the ultimate solution or to adopt the new line of the PLO in Tunis, that of following the old and hated solution of a two-state settlement. Viewed from the third space in any case, and in practice, the whole of Mandatory Palestine was one state ruled by Israel.

But it was difficult to remain for long periods in this individual space, a natural and human desire, as the 1980s drew to a close. The process described before of an Israeli Jewish polity willing to discuss a compromise over the occupied territories, but unwilling to accept the bi-national reality in the pre-1967 Israel, continued with greater force and animosity.

THE UNYIELDING ZIONIST ANIMOSITY

As mentioned, the absence of a regulated, voluntary, cooperative contact between the majority and the minority was also due to the crystallization of a new consensus in Jewish society on the linkage between peace in the occupied territories and the unwillingness to succumb to any Palestinian demands in pre-1967 Israel.

This was not only the result of the 1967 war, it was also the inevitable logic of Zionism and its ability, or rather inability, to accept another national minority in the midst of the Jewish state. While in the previous decade Israeli academics had attributed the problem of the Palestinians in Israel to their unfulfilled modernization, a new, more critical generation of sociologists accused the state of Israel of excluding the Palestinians from the republican 'common good' and questioned the benefit of a democratic system for the non-Jewish minority. To progressive Jewish thinkers the exclusion from the nationhood of the state seemed to be the problem. The lack of any reference to such a problem from anyone with authority in the political elite undermined the possible civic agenda for a joint struggle towards a more inclusive policy. It would be replaced by a clear national and even Islamic agenda.[22]

The unwillingness at the high political level to absorb at least some of the criticism these sociologists voiced in the early 1980s was not surprising. As this book has tried to show so far, the political elite in the main suspected the Palestinian minority of being a fifth column until at least 1966, and still regarded it as a hostile element, even after the abolition of military rule. Opportunities for individuals had opened up, but the possibility of the Palestinians in Israel belonging to, or acting as, a collective was deemed an existential threat to the state. Therefore the main agencies that were engaged with this community, as individuals and as a group, were the secret service, the police and the army, where it should have been the government ministries and agencies. For all intents and purposes the Palestinians were still treated as the enemy within.

In the decade we are covering in this chapter this governmental mood, and in a way strategy, was reinforced by the growing and now powerful racist attitudes towards Palestinians in Israeli Jewish society. The staggering results of frequent surveys of public opinion reveal that a majority of Jews supported the exclusion of the Palestinians from any equal footing in the society, contemplated and dreamed about their disappearance, and suspected them of constantly planning to destroy the state of Israel.[23]

THE POISONOUS FRUIT OF KAHANISM

This mood produced even more extreme phenomena. The worst was the appearance in 1978 of Meir Kahana and the Kach movement. This American Jew was the founder of the Jewish Defense League in the United States, which began as an organization harassing, quite violently, the official Soviet representatives in the USA and in the UN as part of the struggle to allow the immigration of Jews from the USSR to Israel. The Zionist establishment in America, however, abhorred the man and his tactics and in 1971 he immigrated to Israel, where he founded the movement Kach ('So be it' in Hebrew). He narrowly missed being elected in the 1973 election and became a popular public figure among the settlers in the occupied territories and the Mizrahi Jews in the deprived social and geographical margins of the Jewish society.

In the first press conference Kahana convened in Tel Aviv he preached openly for the forced transfer of the Palestinians from Israel. He then began collecting signatures to this effect, later accompanied by provocative marches into heavily populated Arab areas in the country. But when he tried to lecture at Tel Aviv University in that year, having been invited by the students' union, which was exclusively Jewish, a group of Palestinian and Jewish students prevented his entry to the campus. The next step in his racist career was to target Arab individuals in high places, such as Rafiq Halabi, the correspondent of Israeli TV in the occupied territories, whom the Kach pamphlets defined as the 'arm of the fascist left in Israel'.[24]

Kahana ran for the 1984 elections under the slogan 'Give me power to deal with them' (them being the Arabs in Israel) and adopted a yellow flag on which an aggressive fist was directed at the map of Israel with the word Kach on it (this was taken from the insignia adopted during the Mandatory Palestine period by the Irgun of Menachem Begin). The movement was barred from participating in those elections due to its racist agenda, but the Supreme Court decided to lump together the discussion of this movement's admissibility to the Knesset with that of the 'Progressive List for Peace' party of Muhammed Mia'ri. The balancing act, which equated a rabid racist with a moderate national party, deflated any hopes for the legitimization of the Arab minority in Israel as a national Palestinian group. Even after the List was allowed to compete for a Knesset seat, Palestinian members of the Knesset were regarded as part of the same equation, namely as the counterpart of the most extreme right-wing personalities and organizations in Israel. This was another indication of the exclusion of the Palestinians as a political community from the civic space of the state.

Thus Kahana became a member of the Knesset in 1984, preaching openly for the establishment of a hardline Jewish theocracy and using his parliamentary immunity to conduct a campaign of intimidation and terror against the Palestinian citizens in Israel. His list was barred from the 1988 elections and in November 1990 he was murdered in the USA; al-Sayyid Nusair, an Egyptian who was allegedly a member of the group that later became al-Qaida, was tried but acquitted for this crime.

Kahana's popularity, and (even more so) a softer version of his kind of racism in Jewish society at large, led critical scholars in the 1990s to apply the model of ethnocracy not only to the regime and the state, but also to the society at large. This meant that the real or alleged democratic features of Israel were exclusively the prerogative of the Jewish majority.

THE DOUBTFUL SALVATION: THE SUPREME COURT OF JUSTICE

The Supreme Court, regarded as the watchdog of democracy in Israel, was the only bulwark limiting the political strategy from above and the public mood from below. In the 1980s, the Zionist political parties made an effort to delegitimize any organization that did not recognize the Jewish nature of Israel; this would have led to the exclusion of all the Palestinians parties and NGOs from legal activity. However, the Supreme Court passed several rulings that at least de facto enabled non-Zionists, in the sense of outfits that do not accept the Jewish nature of Israel, to play a part in the political game. So while the Knesset passed a law to such an effect in 1985, the Court found ways of allowing non-Zionist parties to participate in the elections despite the law (later on, as this book was being written, the right-wing parties in Israel were looking for a new phrasing for the 1985 law that would prevent any Supreme Court in the future from finding any such loopholes). This balance of power would change in the next century, but more on that in our concluding chapter.[25]

There were however cases, and quite a few, where the 'national interest' rendered the Supreme Court decision irrelevant. Such was the case of the villages of Iqrit and Kafr Bir'im. These two Maronite villages lay on the beautiful tops of the upper Galilee mountains near the border with Lebanon. They surrendered without resistance in the October 1948 Israeli *Hiram* operation that ended the war in that area, assuming that this would secure their stay and prevent their expulsion. In November that year the Israeli army asked them to leave the village just for two weeks and then promised them a safe return. As happened in scores of other villages that surrendered in that area, within those two weeks the Israeli army demolished the village and prevented the repatriation of its people. In a typically cynical act the demolition was carried out in the Christian village on 24 December 1948. The villagers were moved to al-Jish, one of the villages which was allowed to stay intact in the 1948 ethnic cleansing operation and which already hosted the people of the nearby Qadita, which had been emptied in precisely the same way as Iqrit and Kafr Bir'im.[26]

However, these two villages' case was different from many similar examples because they appealed to the Supreme Court with the original documents clearly stating the army's promise of safe return. The Maronite Patriarch kept pressuring the government on this issue and was told first by Ben-Gurion, and then by Eshkol, Meir, Rabin and Begin, that the 'security situation' prevented their return. In the meantime the villages' area was declared a closed military zone, despite the fact that in 1951 the Supreme Court ruled that they had the right to return, but postponed a final verdict on the question to a later date. In 1953, the army blew up the houses which were still intact and the village was transformed into yet another 'deserted' 1948 village, which meant it was transferred into the hands of the Custodian of Absentee Property, who had the right to decide to give it to whomever it chose. It chose to give part of the land to a nearby Jewish *kibbutz*, with a similar name, built on the villages' land: *kibbutz* Baram and several collective settlements (*moshavim*).

In 1972, the steadfast villagers succeeded in recruiting some famous Jewish figures to their renewed campaign and even the great ethnic cleanser of the war, Yigal Alon, now a minister in the Golda Meir government, supported their repatriation. The Likud leaders before the 1977 elections promised a solution. But the Labour Party, now in opposition, opposed the move and the Likud rank and file were also less enthusiastic about the move. The struggle still continues today, but it is unlikely that the Supreme Court ruling on this will ever be respected.

THE ISLAMIC ALTERNATIVE

Without even the more progressive Zionist sections of the regime displaying any genuine desire to work jointly towards a civic agenda, a national and especially Islamic agenda became more attractive. And indeed in this decade, in about 1985, the previously marginal Islamic movement became a social and political force to reckon with. It began modestly in a congress convened in Nazareth in October 1977 and then developed into a meaningful movement. The first cadre of activists were the first alumni of the Islamic colleges in Hebron and Gaza, and it was strengthened by ties with similar groups in the occupied territories – groups which for a while Israel nurtured as a counterforce to the secular Fatah movement.[27]

It also matured as a political movement. Until 1981, some of its main activists tried to organize as a proper guerrilla organization under the name Usrat al-Islam ('the family of Islam') and planned some sabotage operations. They were caught, court-martialled and imprisoned. Two years later, the discourse and modus operandi of the movement changed. A charismatic leader, Sheikh Abdullah Nimr Darwish, from Kafr Qassem in the Triangle, emerged as a pragmatic leader working closely with the other politicians of the Palestinian community and leading the movement to its early local and national successes.[28]

The movement grew for two reasons. First, the more secular forces, inside Israel and in the Palestinian world in general, did not deliver. It was time in the eyes of many who were not necessarily 'religious' in their private life to give someone else a chance to change the reality. Second, the economic hardships endured by most of the Palestinians inside Israel were as oppressive, if not more so, than questions of identity and political orientation. The religious way of life offered a defence mechanism and a way of coping with the scarcity of housing, jobs and food. It was easier from that perspective to support a more comprehensive dogma of Islamism that demanded more pious public space and envisaged an Islamic theocratic future. This may have deterred middle-class urbanites, but not the villagers who had already lived for years within a tradition and religious values. However, there was already in the 1980s a substantial secular element within the Palestinian community, with a clear value system and a history, which delineated by its very existence the boundaries within which the Islamic movement could grow and expand.[29]

THE POLITICAL ECONOMY OF MODERN ISRAEL, 1980–1987

Beneath the discussion of identity and political orientations that seemed to dominate the Palestinian scene in Israel after the Lebanon war, there were harsher economic realities that not only did the government decide to ignore, but also the political leaders themselves at times seemed to repress. As mentioned in the previous chapter, one of the main problems of the Palestinian leaders was their inability to transcend their personal rivalries, despite their ideological consensus about who they were and what their main agenda was.

In the mid-1980s, the only significant expansion in the economic life of the Palestinian community was the appearance of low-capital industries and business catering for the Palestinian market in Israel, which was unable to break into the general Israeli market. Hundreds of small factories in the realms of food, textile and construction materials sprang up in the 1980s and early 1990s.[30] The businesses were operated from within their owners' private property, quite often in the space created between the traditional pillars on which houses were built (originally to host the family's livestock or grains and foodstuffs). The infrastructure was inadequate in most cases for producing businesses at the level of the Jewish competition, which was subsidized and fully supported by the government. The Jewish periphery at the time was recruited to work for the huge economic concerns and companies that had already emerged in the 1970s; but these economic octopuses skipped the Palestinian community. The exceptions were the spinning mills, which employed 12,000 women by the end of the 1980s. They were also exceptional in the sense that they triggered other processes in the community, mainly of women's empowerment and independence, and they also increased family income.

The most uncomfortable new element in the economic lives of the Palestinians in Israel was the arrival of Palestinian workers from the occupied territories who took over the jobs traditionally done by the Palestinians in Israel, working in the services, tourism, construction and agriculture. Compared to the Palestinians in Israel, this labour force had no basic protection or elementary rights and was poorly paid. It was impossible to compete with them. The economic boom in Israel and the destruction of the economic infrastructure in the occupied territories attracted 75,000 workers from the West Bank and the Gaza Strip by 1982. However, spiralling inflation under the new Likud government in 1984 devalued even the meagre money they made in

Israel, such that working in Israel was more akin to being recruited to a slave market than an immigrant capitalism that could benefit those who left their host countries. But, until 1987, their presence diminished the job opportunities of some sectors of the Palestinians in Israel; this was a fact of life that added to the already existing hardships incurred by unemployment, the lack of social services and the limited allocation of public money.[31]

As a result of the new set of pressures, especially in the rural areas, immigration from the hinterland, such as the Galilee, to the urban centres such as Haifa and Nazareth, increased. More importantly, as is normal in urban realities, the places taken by the newcomers were vacated by those who were relatively well-off. Their destination was in some cases the nearby Jewish development towns. Despite the official policies of Judaization, the inherent racist attitudes of the Jewish population at large and that of the development towns in particular, the temptation to lease or let a flat at a price far higher than its actual worth was too much. Palestinians residents appeared in Nazareth Ilit, the Jewish town built to counterbalance old Nazareth demographically and spatially, in the Jewish neighbourhood of Ramleh and Lydda, in Carmiel and in the Jewish sections of Acre and Haifa, as well as in Rehovot, Beer Sheba and Eilat.[32]

Their main drive was not ideological; it can easily be found in the official *Israeli Statistics Book* of 1987. The 643,000 Palestinians (not including the 137,000 residents of East Jerusalem and the 14,400 Syrian Druze of the Golan Heights), comprising 15 per cent of the population, lived in seven purely Arab towns out of Israel's one hundred towns with 10,000 or more inhabitants.[33] Jaffa is a case in point. This was one of Palestine's main cities, in many ways its cultural and political centre and its gate to the outside world. Most of its population was expelled in 1948, but the Palestinian population grew as a result of internal immigration from the villages around the town that had been evicted during 1948.

In the late 1980s, about ten thousand Palestinians lived in Jaffa in three neighbourhoods: al-'Ajami, al-Jabalyyah (Ha-Aliya in Hebrew) and al-Nuzha (Lev Yafo in Hebrew). Seventy per cent of the houses in al-'Ajami were destroyed by the authorities by the 1980s under the pretext of their being illegally built after 1948 and 30 per cent of the buildings in al-Nuzha were demolished (in all more than three thousand units were destroyed). No new apartments were offered and as a result makeshift huts took their place. There were no nearby Palestinian villages and the Jaffa population felt isolated and segregated from the rest of the metropolis of Tel Aviv. Less than a third of the inhabitants owned their flats and the rest depended on Jewish landlords who could quite easily evict them at any given moment. Riots and widespread squatting of new flats led the government in 1987 to include the Palestinians in Jaffa in a project of neighbourhood rehabilitation and there was a promise, still unfulfilled, to build new homes. The inevitable result was the emergence of intensive criminal activity and a gangland whose victims are quite often innocent bystanders and inhabitants.

The town of Ramleh has had a similar history and went through an identical crisis in the late 1980s. As in Jaffa, here too the average family had two persons living in tiny rooms, located all over the city, where about another ten thousand Palestinians lived. A few thousand lived in the old city of Ramleh in houses which had been earmarked for demolition as illegal – a common scene in those days and still today – with the tin roofs of temporary abodes which hardly provided shelter from the heat of the sun or the wrath of the rain. The most notorious Palestinian urban neighbourhood in Israel is the Jawarish quarter in Ramleh, almost synonymous with crime and violence, ruled by iron fist gangsters from one *hammula* mastering the drug trade in the area. In the early 1990s, the Jewish municipality found a solution to the problem: it encircled the neighbourhood with a fence and ghettoized its poor dwellers, leaving them at the mercy of these criminals. The eastern neighbourhood was bisected when an industrial plant was built in its midst and around it.[34]

Israeli geographers and demographers, such as Arnon Soffer of Haifa University, regarded this development – namely the move of Palestinians to Jewish towns and even the move of Palestinians citizens in Haifa from the city centre to the mountains – as a grave danger and warned the authorities against it.[35] But the bi-national reality that unfolded in Israel during the 1980s was stronger than the ideology of the ethnocratic state (a concept we explain in more detail in the Appendix).

Worst hit were the Bedouin in the south who lived in non-recognized villages. Their lives became impossible due to two efficient agencies which dealt with them. The first was the Administration for the Development of the Bedouin, which was part of the Israel Land Administration. This body was responsible for transferring the Bedouin into reservations of a kind. The other was the Bedouin Education Authority, which determined the level of education those communities were to receive. It was founded in 1981 and from 1984 one person ran the show: Moshe Shohat. The head of the educational system for all the unrecognized villages in the Negev, his main power was his ex officio position in the committee that appointed teachers and principals for the few schools in the villages. The state policy which dictated where they should live and where children should study meant that the Bedouin had to live in villages without elementary infrastructure, having been driven from their traditional locations and robbed of their land, and their children had to walk hours to get to the scattered schools offered to them. Employment in these schools was a privilege for which one paid with loyalty and obedience. During the period covered in this chapter, this quid pro quo in the educational system was a widespread phenomenon. The Deputy Minister of Education Yitzhak Cohen, suspected by many to be a Shabak member, supervised the vetting of teachers and principals, according not to their qualifications but to their 'loyalty'.[36]

Unlike the previous decade, the government made promises to the Bedouin that they would stop the land confiscation and the harassment – but the policy on the ground remained much the same. The victims approached the Israeli Supreme Court, which in April 1979 condemned the government for its policy of land expropriation. In its final statement the esteemed judges wrote: 'The court has never encountered such a stark violation of a governmental promise.'[37] It is worthwhile mentioning once more that these were the 'good Arabs', serving in the army and thus expecting preferential treatment; not only did this not eventuate, but they seemed to fare worse than the rest of the Palestinian community.

The other community of 'good Arabs', the Druze, fared a bit better, but not much. Unemployment, poverty and the lack of spatial development produced feelings of resistance and frustration. In September 1978, a group called the 'Druze Initiative Committee' was formed, becoming a home for youngsters who regretted the historical pact made with the Jewish state and in particular the obligation to join the compulsory service in the army.[38]

Probably the only group that found more employment during that period was women, and especially young women. Women still comprised a mere 10 per cent of the working force but this was much more than it had been in 1948. Traditional attitudes to women working outside their home were a disincentive, but the demand for cheap, unskilled labour pushed the trend in the opposite direction. It was only later that the significance of this change would become apparent. Men, however, were pushed out of agriculture at an even greater pace during this decade. The decade began with a quarter of the men being involved in agriculture; by its end the figure had fallen to just a little more than 5 per cent.[39]

Among the younger members of the community, university graduates were significantly more common, though they were still small in number compared to the Jewish population. But they were frustrated by the lack of any proper opportunities to make use of their newly won educational background. No wonder the educated elite of the Palestinians in Israel during that period became an attractive case study for scholars who were researching the connection between unfulfilled social and economic expectations on the one hand and political frustration and ideological outrage on the other. The trend would only get worse in the years to come. A survey conducted at the University of Haifa covering the years from 1982 to 1987 found that almost half of the university's Palestinian graduates were unemployed or employed as unskilled workers.[40]

The exception was the medical profession – the only environment where relative integration occurred. Palestinians had always been employed as staff in Jewish hospitals, and by the 1990s some had achieved high managerial positions. Immigration from the ex-Soviet Union in the late 1980s curbed Palestinian employment opportunities, but they still have an impressive presence from the lowest levels upwards.

Only recently has there been an attempt to explain the unique role of medicine in the economic map of the Palestinians in Israel. Israel has suffered from an acute shortage of physicians ever since the 1980s. For a while the immigration from the ex-Soviet Union seemed to fill the gap, but the demand for doctors remained high in the rather hypochondriac Jewish society and the system became more receptive to absorbing Palestinian doctors. The governmental service did not offer high salaries as it did for instance in the hi-tech industries, which have been by and large inaccessible to the Palestinians in Israel. Most of the economic incentives offered by the Israeli government were aimed at forcing the Palestinians to stay in the Palestinian areas – working in a central urban hospital was one of the few options for geographical mobility beyond the Israeli boundaries of segregation. In the 1990s, the number of Palestinians employed in the medical services rose to almost 10 per cent (from 1 per cent a decade before) and as this book is being written the percentage is growing exponentially. Today 25 per cent of medical students are Palestinians. In 2008 the Israeli universities unashamedly decided to raise the age of acceptance from eighteen to twenty. The Palestinian students, since they do not serve in the army, could join the Israeli universities at the age of eighteen. However, now they cannot be admitted or even apply until two years after they have graduated from high school; they are more likely to try abroad or maybe pursue an alternative career.[41]

A DE FACTO CULTURAL AUTONOMY

The educated elite therefore needed to express their growing disenchantment with the Jewish state. This may explain why the first half of the 1980s saw the blooming of new energies in the Palestinian press in Israel. The main newspaper, *al-Ittihad*, published by the Communist Party, became a daily in 1984 (and in it was the literary supplement *al-Jadid*, which became an independent monthly publication), while at the same time the government's mouthpiece, *al-Abna*, was closed from lack of interest. Moreover, a new non-partisan and purely commercial newspaper, *al-Sunara*, appeared in Nazareth; others would appear later on such as *Kul al-Arab* and *Panorama*.

The Israeli government thus tacitly admitted that it could not engage any longer with the Palestinian minority via the official press and organs. This not only represented an ideological shift, but also recognized the need to treat the Palestinian community with a businesslike approach in the capitalist and privatized society that Israel had become in the early 1980s. Thus the official press was replaced by national and local papers and journals. The Islamic movement attempted such a project too, but at that time it was a total failure, with their paper, *al-Qalam*, closing down after two years through lack of funds and readers. Later on it would become much more successful and popular.

Against this background, it was surprising to see the Israeli government investing more money in official radio and TV stations during the 1980s. These were propaganda tools directed both at the local Palestinian population and at the Arab world at large. But already in the 1980s, it was clear that this kind of broadcast was ridiculed and considered suspect by most of the Palestinians in Israel, and until they had their own radio stations – they still do not have a TV station – they preferred to listen to the Arabic stations from neighbouring countries.

The mushrooming of journals was matched by a new theatrical energy, especially after the Lebanon war. Young playwrights such as Riad Masarweh found a way of displaying solidarity with the PLO in theatre pieces, hoping that they would not be immediately censored, as an explicit political article or demonstration would have been. His adaptation of Ghassan Kanafani's *Men in the Sun* with the setting of the Israeli invasion of Lebanon in 1982 landed him in trouble with the authorities, who censored and barred his play. Like him, writers and poets were now far more open in their support and identification with the Palestinian struggle – willing as before to pay a high personal price for their opinions. The Likud government, like the Labour government before it, regarded such expression as tantamount to terrorism, and although some key figures in the Israeli public scene called for a dialogue with the PLO, the official policy was to prosecute and persecute any Palestinians in Israel with such ideas.

It was not the first time that that particular text by Kanafani had caused trouble for the Palestinians in Israel. The short novel is very human and universal, telling of the tragic trip of three Palestinians in a water tanker, searching for work and life, from Iraq to Kuwait, only to suffocate to death before reaching their destination. The text was targeted by the philistine Israeli secret service because of the author's deep involvement with the Popular Front for the Liberation of Palestine (PFLP), which caused him to be assassinated by the Israelis. This was enough to turn his writings into forbidden material. In October 1977, the police banned the opening of a play based on Kanafani's novel presented by the Al-Sadiq theatre in Nazareth since the text, and this was a common allegation, had not previously been sent to the censor.

Other more original texts were also treated in a similar way, especially if they were staged as plays. This was ridiculous as Palestinians, like the Israeli Jews, visited the theatre in the same limited numbers as is common worldwide since the destructive advent of television and cinema. When, in December 1978, members of a local theatre company, al-Balad, performed a play under the title *The Lost Peace* they were arrested, again for allegedly not showing the script to the censor beforehand.

The drive to create despite censorship was propelled, as mentioned before, both by the reunification with the West Bank's cultural milieu and by the new connection with the cultural capital of the Arab world, Cairo, in the wake of Israel's bilateral peace deal with Egypt, signed in 1979. The political bravado of President Anwar Sadat's historical visit to the Knesset in November 1977, and the subsequent peace treaty which was engraved as a formative event and image in the album of every Israeli Jew from that generation, left very little impression on the Palestinians in Israel, who like the Palestinians elsewhere felt that the Camp David Treaty signed by Sadat and the Israeli Prime Minister Menachem Begin, on the White House lawn with President Jimmy Carter as the midwife, was an illegitimate one. Egypt received back the Sinai Peninsula, to the very last inch of it, at the cost of leaving the occupied territories in Israel's absolute control.

Culturally, however, the treaty did transform the Palestinian cultural scene. Books, plays and journals from the Arab world were now more available, not just from Cairo but also from Beirut. The three years of direct Israeli occupation of Lebanon (1982–5) allowed book traders – as well as drug traffickers – easier access to publishers, bookshops and cultural centres in Beirut. Palestinian writers, poets and playwrights travelled more easily to the Arab world and became more familiar household names there. The poet Siham Daoud was published for the first time in the region in 1979 and others followed suit.

But, as always, the lives of everyone in Israel, the trends, the processes and the general development, were interrupted by political upheavals and earthquakes. The next stop in this story was the outbreak of the first *Intifada* at the end of 1987.

CHAPTER FIVE

AFTER THE FIRST *INTIFADA*

BETWEEN PALESTINIAN ASSERTIVENESS AND JEWISH UNCERTAINTY, 1987–1995

THE IMAGES OF YITZHAK Rabin shaking the hand of Yasser Arafat on the White House lawn on 13 September 1993 have long been shelved, and rightly so, as an embarrassing moment of staged histrionics that utterly failed all those living between the River Jordan and the Mediterranean. Such cynicism and frustration are warranted in hindsight, given the dismal reality that developed on the ground. But at the time, the Palestinians in Israel, clinging desperately to any sign of better things to come, were moved deeply by the ceremony and could hear, or so they thought, the clatter of the wings of history passing near them before disappearing again – God knows for how long.

Their leaders were endlessly photographed with Yasser Arafat in Tunis and later on in his new presidential seats in Gaza and Ramallah. These photos were framed and proudly displayed in the mayor's office, the lawyer's chambers and the physician's clinic. No less inspiring was the picture of the Palestinian members of the Knesset asked to be part of a coalition government for the first time in Israel's history. True, they were not asked as legitimate sons of the family, more like stepchildren, but still. They were not invited to be ministers, but were allowed to serve as deputies to the speaker of the house and were offered membership of parliamentary committees from which they had been excluded ever since 1948.

Even the most prestigious committee in the Knesset, the Foreign Affairs and Defense Committee, on which usually only ex-generals and security service people sat, was now opened to them. In the past the Knesset had passed a regulation that restricted participation in this committee to parties with a minimal number of representatives – which was calculated as that of the largest Arab party plus one. Now this was changed and Hadash's member of Knesset, Hashem Mahamid, was filmed entering the chamber where military and intelligence operations were supposedly discussed. But not really: the Knesset immediately appointed a sub-committee within this committee for intelligence matters that of course excluded Mahamid and any other Palestinian members of the Knesset.

But still these were hopeful images. The Palestinian members of the Knesset became the 'Blocking Bloc' as it was called in the local political jargon after the 1992 general elections. This meant that the second Yitzhak Rabin government – returning Labour to power after fifteen years in opposition or as a junior member of a coalition – could only be voted in on the basis of the Arab members of the Knesset, despite their willingness not to receive full membership of the coalition.

When Yitzhak Rabin was murdered, his assassin said that one of the reasons for his actions was that Rabin was elected on the votes of 'Arabs'. Palestinians remember the murder as an anxious moment. One teacher in a progressive kibbutz in the north recalls that he was advised not to stay the night because when the news of the murder appeared everyone suspected the assassin was a Palestinian, and the teacher might have been at risk of a revenge attack. This was shortly after a Jewish settler in Hebron, Baruch Goldstein, massacred people while they were praying in the mosque there. The desperation over the continued occupation led to the phenomenon of Palestinian suicide bombers sowing havoc in Israel's public transportation, shopping malls and restaurants (inspired also by the first acts of this kind, which were performed by the Shiites in southern Lebanon, in their war initially against the multinational force led by the Americans and later on against the Israeli army there). Although quite a few Palestinian Israelis were among the victims and one could very rarely prove that there had been collaboration by the Palestinians in Israel with the suicide bombers, in the Jewish public mind the terrorist attacks were associated with the Palestinians in Israel. '*Eyn Aravim, Eyn Piguim*' ('No Arabs, No Terrorist Attacks') was a very popular sticker on cars in those days.

These images thus formed a mixed image of hope and hate, of 'peace' of a kind and a 'war' of a kind. Soon however this became a spiral of descent into an unknown future, triggered by the uprising in the West Bank and the Gaza Strip against the twenty-year-old occupation.

THE IMMEDIATE IMPACT OF THE FIRST *INTIFADA*

After twenty years of occupation, life in the West Bank and the Gaza Strip consisted of familiar, but almost intolerable, routines for most of the Palestinians there. By the beginning of 1987, it was clear that no outside forces would help extricate the people from their harsh situation. The international community, the Arab world, the PLO and the Israeli peace camp were all in one way or another unable or unwilling to intervene in the lives of those imprisoned under the reality of occupation and oppression.

Against this background, one can only wonder why an uprising was so late in coming. It finally began in December 1987, when its leaders chose a term already in use by the grassroots movements in the Arab world, *Intifada* ('shaking off'), to describe their attempt to end the Israeli presence in the West Bank and the Gaza Strip. The rising started in the Gaza refugee camps, probably the most politicized group of Palestinians at the time, who also bore the brunt of Israel's retaliatory action. There it was translated into a declaration of the camps as being free from Israeli control, non-violent demonstrations and attacks on isolated Jewish colonies. The wave of protests moved from there to the rural areas of the West Bank, where young people bravely faced the strongest army in the area, but of course eventually succumbed to its power. The last were the city people, who provided both leadership and political orientation, as the PLO, at that time based in Tunis after having been expelled from Lebanon in 1983, was slow to react and absorb the new energy that was bubbling on the ground.

Fault lines, such as the *Intifada*, extract the individual from his or her daily sphere of life, but more in the sense of awakening them to the wider historical and ideological context and explanation for their predicament than of transforming their lives on the ground. For Palestinians living in Israel, before, during and after the *Intifada*, daily mundane activity was a luxury not always attainable, and it certainly did not ensure immunity from the grip of politics and ideology. The policeman on the road reminded them of their second-rate citizenship; the security officials in the airport humiliated them even if they happened to be a professor in the university; the deputy principal in the school, with a forced or voluntary connection to the secret service, assessed their loyalty; and the judge of minor crimes more often than not discriminated against the unfortunate Palestinians sitting in front of him, while exonerating Jews accused of the very same offences.[1]

But before and after the *Intifada*, it was possible to find factors balancing and easing this oppressive reality. Private businesses prospered, good grades were attained in high school, the universities made possible a better career during this period, and the normal cycle of birth, marriage and death still created joyful or sad moments regardless of politics and ideology. Better TV antennas brought Arab culture via the television: there was no more need to cram around a squeaky wireless radio and listen to Umm Kulthum from Cairo or Fairuz from Beirut. The Israeli Television Arabic programmes were less needed and trusted, but at least they broadcast a long feature film in Arabic every Friday.

But the uprising did not allow too much indulgence in this daily existence. It was not only disruptive in the sense of needing attention, but it also tested a very delicate balance that had become the strategy of survival for the Palestinian minority in Israel. This strategy was based, according to Israeli Palestinian sociologists, on three elements: first, a total support for the official PLO position that demanded the creation of an independent Palestinian state next to Israel; second, a demand for equal civic and human rights for the Palestinian community in Israel; and, finally, a decision to employ only tactics that were possible within the Israeli legal system. Except for meetings with PLO leaders, which until 1993 were illegal according to Israeli law, only very few individuals diverted from this modus operandi. Strikes and demonstrations were always held with official permission and carefully pre-planned.

Individual acts in connection with guerrilla or terror warfare were condemned by the leaders, although admired by the society.

At least to begin with, this three-tiered strategy facilitated a swift reaction to the events in the occupied territories in December 1987. The Palestinians in Israel were quicker to respond than the PLO. A few weeks after the uprising started, they began organizing strikes and demonstrations on a special day called the 'Day of Peace', at which for the first time political action was coordinated between Palestinians on both sides of the Green Line. The first big demonstration took place in Nazareth in January 1988, while food and other essential material was collected then, and on a monthly basis thereafter, to be sent to the besieged Palestinians in the West Bank and the Gaza Strip.

The Palestinians in Israel preceded the Jewish 'Peace Camp' in drawing attention to the particularly brutal and callous manner in which the Israeli army and secret service were reacting to the *Intifada*. This included mass arrests without trial, torture during interrogation, and assembling all the men in the reoccupied villages and in some cases subjecting them to merciless beating and similar atrocities. Even with strict censorship, pictures of most of these atrocities reached the television screens of the world at large, and the Arab world in particular.

The volume of outrage among the Palestinians in Israel could have led to a massive deviation from the strategy of working within Israeli law. The demonstrations were accompanied by stone throwing, and tyre burning at the first demonstration on 21 December 1987. The leadership condemned these actions, unhindered by the PLO leadership, which made it clear that it was aware of 'the special circumstances and constraints of the Arabs in Israel'. And yet each such isolated case was blown out of all proportion by the pundits of the Israeli media.

Solidarity with the Palestinian uprising was not only translated into demonstrations and strikes: the Follow-Up Committee and leaders in the trade union movement responded to local initiatives by activists and by people who usually refrained from political activity to help the Palestinians in the Gaza Strip and the West Bank. These outfits began organizing collections of food, money, medication and clothing for the occupied territories. It was not much, but symbolically it was very significant.

The contribution from the Palestinians in Israel, later supported by some sections of the Israeli left, was reciprocated by the Palestinians in the occupied territories who decided in 1988, despite their own struggle, to commemorate the Day of the Land as a significant juncture in the rural uprising. This act of solidarity formed an association in the public mind, on both sides of the Green Line, between the land confiscation and killings in the Galilee in 1976 and similar acts, on a wider scale, in the occupied territories in 1987. It also brought home the nature of neo-colonialist economic dependence, so strikingly similar in the relationship of Israel with both Palestinian communities.

THE ISLAMIC MOMENT

In both areas of historical Palestine the uprising gave impetus to the political Islamic forces on the ground. Hamas, Islamic Jihad and the Islamic movement in Israel were now powerful political actors. They were part of a wider Middle Eastern phenomenon termed 'political Islam' by those who rightly refuse to use the more popular Western reference 'Islamic fundamentalism'. In general, the term is a scholarly attempt to assess the impact of religion on politics in the Arab world and beyond. It is by no means definitive, and each religious movement needs to be understood in its own context.[2]

The Islamic movements on both sides of the Green Line had several features in common in the immediate years after the first *Intifada*. They were very assertive in their position on the political agenda of the day, which was an American attempt to impose a Pax Americana on the Israeli–Palestinian conflict. The movements were opposed to American-brokered peace deals. The close association between the USA and Israel, and its impact on the fate of the Palestinians, was an easy agenda to pursue. But this interest in current politics was only one aspect of political Islam in Israel and the occupied territories.

The introduction of Islamic concepts into the political scene was based on a genuine return to religion and tradition in Israel. The wish to reconnect with past codes of conduct was not limited to the Muslims in the late 1980s but was evident in the Jewish community as well. Religion in Israel proved to be a resilient and adaptive force, rather than the dwindling relic of traditionalism so easily dismissed by the gurus of the modernization theories. By offering a redemptive outlook on life lived in harsh conditions, religion also proved to be an effective response to the pressures of endless uprooting, deprivation and discrimination experienced by the Palestinian minority in Israel. Thus, the political aspect of religious survival was an attractive alternative, not only as a daily way of life but also as a plan that promised change, in a situation where the worst was already experienced.

The religious politics of identity differed from the other groupings in Israel in that they also aspired to be a substitute for nationalism, or at least an improved version of it, but one which would inevitably lead to a more uncompromising confrontation with the 'Other'. The national Palestinian leadership inside Israel, and even the PLO, had lost some of their hold over their communities. This meant that there was more space and motivation for individual and collective adaptations of more pious modes of behaviour. This was evident both in the countryside and in the poorer section of the urban communities. In the rural areas, traditional concepts and beliefs had been maintained for centuries and could easily be given a more political orientation – especially given the encroachment of the Israeli authorities into the lives of the Palestinians. They were also apparent in the poor neighbourhoods, such as eastern Nazareth, which felt alienated not only by the Jewish side in Israel but also by the socio-economic polarization in their own locality. The fact that many of the more fortunate city dwellers were highly secular in style and outlook only made those in more deprived areas more antagonistic towards wealth and intellectualism.

It was not a unified picture. Despite the overall deprivation of the Palestinian community, there were still striking socio-economic imbalances between the two geographical centres of Palestinian life in the Jewish state. In the north, the Galilee was generally better off than the Triangle and Wadi Ara, where the population was crammed into a small space and only allowed access to a limited spectrum of jobs. Not surprisingly, petty crime and unemployment soared. It was there that political Islam sprang up, where life was lived in even more miserable conditions than in the refugee camps in the West Bank.

Contrary to the conventional modernization models, the more secular and affluent Palestinians in Israel gravitated towards, and sought inspiration from, their more traditional and much worse-off compatriots in the West Bank and the Gaza Strip. The young people and a relatively high portion of women – sections within society who were not given a decisive role in the political struggle – were most attracted to the path of personal salvation offered by various interpretations of Islam. These ranged from the mystic Sufis to the fundamentalist offshoots of the Muslim Brotherhood. One already mentioned was Abdullah Nimr Darwish, who dominated the politics of Islam in Israel in the 1980s before losing power to more charismatic young leaders emerging in the deprived and densely populated area of Wadi Ara. Like many leaders, he received a formal Islamic education in Nablus and Hebron in the early 1970s, where he was introduced not only to the world of learning but, more importantly, to the varied activities on offer for a militant politician in the Islamic mode. These ranged from the *Risalat*, epistles originally sent by the Prophet to the community of believers but now turned into modern-day political messages, to clandestine cell organization, sabotage and violence. Preaching in the mosques, however, became the most visible part of that activity. The sermons called for the restoration of the golden Islamic age in Palestine, that is, the revival of Muslim control of the country in strict adherence to the Quranic code. The basic message could be peppered with references to the Jews, imperialism and, more significantly, with commentary on current politics, usually reflecting the PLO's position on the Palestine question. Any combination of these ingredients was enough to get someone such as Abdullah Nimr Darwish into trouble, and indeed he spent long periods in Israeli jails, as mentioned in the previous chapter. But after 1987, he watered down his criticisms and became a founder member of al-Haraka al-Islamiyya ('The Islamic Movement'), a legally registered NGO.

In the late 1980s and early 1990s, the movement participated successfully in municipal elections, defeating both the veteran Communist politicians and the agents of Zionist parties. The victory in Umm al-Fahem, on the northern part of the Wadi Ara Road and adjacent to the Green Line with the West Bank, of a young preacher, Sheikh Raid

Salah, in the 1989 elections signified a change in the movement's orientation and composition.

Unlike Darwish, Salah rejected the participation of the Islamic movement in the national election, although accepting it in the local one since the latter in his mind did not signify recognition of the Jewish state. He also demanded more pious behaviour from believers and a strict imposition of Islam on the public space. He and his friends in this section of the movement later adopted the struggle over Jerusalem's future as a major point of action and worked closely with the Islamic organizations in the West Bank and the Gaza Strip. A split was inevitable. Salah's followers were known as the northern Islamic movement – since geographically Umm al-Fahem is north of Kafr Qassem, the stronghold of Abdullah Nimr Darwish (although less than 30 kilometres separate the two villages). As time went by the southern wing would join other parties and the northern one would be the only recognized Islamic movement in Israel.

In some cases, the newly elected mayors and heads of local councils of the Islamic movement excelled in running their municipalities and solving long-standing problems. They were eventually hampered by government animosity and, more decisively, by internal schisms and corruption. The Islamic movement took about a third of the electorate share among the Palestinians in Israel. Their strength was less the result of the Islamization of the society as much as it was the Palestinization of it (if the counter-process was Israelization, a term used by the Jewish mainstream scholars to describe willingness to cooperate, collaborate or modernize). The 'Palestinian consensus' among the Palestinians in Israel, namely the three-tiered strategy mentioned above, after the uprising broke, included not only the 60 per cent who voted for Arab parties in the 1988 general elections, but also quite a few who voted for Zionist parties.

It was easier to adopt such a consensual position in light of the dramatic changes that occurred in the official position of the PLO in 1988. In November that year, the PLO explicitly endorsed a Palestinian state alongside Israel and the view that Palestine and Israel should be one secular democratic state became a minority view. There were now two options for those members of the community who bothered to think about the reality beyond the immediate future. One was to accept the new PLO position as indicating that, as Palestinians, they would remain citizens of a Jewish state and a second was to view this as a temporary stage on the way towards a more utopian united Palestine.

THE NATIONAL MOMENT

On the secular side of things three main political forces competed in a society that was less and less convinced that parliamentary Palestinian representation meant much in terms of improving daily life, but did feel that it expressed some sort of national pride.

Hadash, formerly Rakah, had now consolidated the new organization founded back in 1977. Through connection with Mizrahi activists such as Charlie Biton of the local Black Panther movement, Hadash hoped to expand into the Jewish working-class electorate. Biton, a Moroccan Jew, and other friends had already emulated the African American Black Panther movement in the early 1970s when they tried to improve socio-economic conditions for Jewish immigrants from Arab countries and their second generation. The location of these communities on the social and geographical margins of the Jewish society was attributed by these activists, and later by some leading intellectuals in that community, to an intentional policy of discrimination sustained by the Ashkenazi – European Jewish – establishment.[3]

Alas, the disgruntled masses of these communities preferred clerical or anti-Arab Jewish nationalist parties to Communism and even more so to an alliance with Palestinians in Israel. Hadash remained within the boundaries of its previous electoral successes, between three and four out of one hundred and twenty members of the Knesset.

They were joined by Azmi Bishara's Balad, mentioned in the previous chapter. Bishara was born in Nazareth in 1956 to a Communist family. He studied at the Hebrew University, where he was a leading force in the Arab student committee, and completed his academic studies with a doctorate from Humboldt University, at that time East Germany's leading university. Upon his return he joined Rakah but very soon, in around 1995, he founded the new party, which had a clear national agenda although it did not differ much from that of Hadash. His charismatic personality, and then the presentation of the consensual

Palestinian position without a Communist or Arab–Jewish comradeship scaffolding, attracted many of the young educated and professional Palestinians to his party. In the 1995 national elections he joined forces with Hadash, and then in the next campaign his party ran alone under his chairmanship. I will discuss his party in greater detail at the appropriate chronological location, in the next chapter.

The third more marginal force was the steadfast Abna al-Balad movement. Its explicit support for one Arab secular democratic state quite often landed its leaders in jail for long periods. Raja Aghbariya and Hassan Jabarin were put under administrative arrest for most of 1988, mainly for openly declaring themselves as members of the movement.

As mentioned, this movement split into two and in 1995 part of it joined Balad, as did Muhammed Mia'ri's 'Progressive List for Peace', not before its leaders were tried in June 1988 for peace contacts with the PLO, and four Jewish peace activists were arrested on similar charges; at the time the legendary Ezer Weizman, a minister in the unity Labour–Likud government, declared his willingness to talk directly to PLO representatives in August. The emergence of more central voices on the Jewish political side calling for *rapprochement* with the PLO was a precursor for a short-lived Arab–Jewish cooperation in the 1990s, which disappeared again in 2000. Even in the heyday of joint actions it was clear that this was not a highly important issue as most of these demonstrations were in support of a peace process which, in the eyes of members of parties such as Abna al-Balad, deepened the occupation rather than terminating it. But these joint demonstrations and activities should be recorded in a people's history as potential precursors for a different future. In the period under review most of the more daring and impressive demonstrations and other modes of protest were carried out by Arabs and Jews jointly, many of them by joint women's groups.

The role of women in creating a bi-national agenda for peace deserves a book in itself and indeed some pioneering work has already been done on it. It seems that feminist awareness developing in the 1970s within the Jewish society produced more cooperation between women of the two communities, especially on the issue of violence towards women and the impact of the conflict on this violence. The search for a role for women with the Jewish communities coming from the Arab world also produced, in some cases, a stronger affinity between Palestinian and Jewish women.

By 2000 the emergence of a feminist base for joint action produced the Coalition of Women for Peace, an umbrella organization for NGOs and movements of Palestinian and Jewish women struggling for democracy and equality inside Israel and against the occupation of the West Bank and the Gaza Strip. Other groups which were not members of the coalition similarly, and at times more poignantly, challenged the Zionist nature of Israel and displayed more clarity about the solutions they would support in the future.[4]

Balad's way of presenting politics at the end of the period covered in this chapter was also supported by Abd al-Wahhab Darawshe, a member of the Labour Party who was ousted for his insistence that his party should have open and direct contact with the PLO and Arab leaders. He formed his own party, the Arab Democratic Party, but then also joined, not personally but ideologically, the Balad's national platform in struggling for national and cultural autonomy for a Palestinian minority within Israel next to an independent Palestinian state in the 1967 occupied territories.

Two different kinds of political conduct appeared during that period. One was the very unique mode of action adopted by the internal refugees or, as they became known, the displaced persons in the community, and the other consisted of individual enterprises which sought to achieve what party politics had failed to deliver.

The internal refugees were the Palestinians expelled from their homes in 1948 and later on until 1952, but who remained in Israel living in other villages and towns (one estimate is that a third of the inhabitants of Umm al-Fahem, which is today a town, are internal refugees, that is to say that most of these city dwellers or their families came originally from nearby villages). The conservative estimates are that today those refugees, which includes those uprooted in 1948, around 40,000, their immediate families and others dislocated by force within the state of Israel ever since, number around 250,000–300,000. The numbers are still an issue for an ongoing discussion and have been recently covered by a book devoted to the issue.[5]

Around the fortieth anniversary celebration of Israel's independence, the main activists in this community coordinated what hitherto had been the local committees of each deported village into a national committee of internally displaced persons based in Nazareth, initially in Safafra, the western neighbourhood which hosted most of the refugees from the nearby village of Saffuriyya, destroyed by the Israelis in 1948 and on whose ruins, under the watchful eyes of its former inhabitants, Jewish settlers built the settlement Zipori.[6]

The committee developed a new national ritual that would become a focus for a novel kind of activism in the community. This consisted of annual pilgrimages to one of the destroyed villages, where a ceremony of commemoration took place, with eyewitnesses telling the story of the village and in particular the days of its destruction; this was followed by the cleaning of the area and the leaving of some sort of a commemorative mark. The villages chosen for this ritual, which still continues, are those with relatively easy access – others are impossible to reach because there are Jewish settlements there, or because a forest has been planted over the village by the Jewish National Fund. Once the pilgrimages began, JNF officials encircled the remains of the villages with barbed wire to make them inaccessible.

Other activities included the creation of a museum of a sort commemorating the *Nakbah* in Nazareth, the convening of meetings and conferences on the 1948 Palestinian refugees' right of return and attempts to recruit, with little success, local politicians to their cause. Their activity was reciprocated by one small Jewish NGO, Zochrot, 'remembering' in the female form in Hebrew, which took upon itself the mission of informing the Israeli public about the 1948 events with the help of the work of the Israeli new historians and the Palestinian historiography that challenged the accepted Zionist version of the war and, in particular, debunked the myth of a voluntary Palestinian flight in 1948.

The second unique feature of this period was individual and independent political careers. There were some independent voices in those days which sought their own course of navigation through the murky waters of local Israeli politics. An outstanding figure in this respect was Ibrahim Nimr Husayn, the long-reigning mayor of Shefa-'Amr and the head of the Follow-Up Committee. He was chosen for the latter position precisely because he had no clear party affiliation and seemed to be respected by all concerned (the Committee preferred to have a non-partisan head and, later on, Husayn's neighbour from Kafr Madna, Muhammad Zeydan (Abu Faysal), would be twice elected to this position because of his lack of affiliation with any recognized party). Inevitably, Husayn's decision to avoid any direct confrontation with the Israeli Ministry of Interior, which was the bread and butter of any Arab council that wished to survive, led some to accuse him of unnecessary collaboration with the state. Young members of the public in his hometown disliked his approach; one of them threw a Molotov cocktail at the municipality building, burnt the Israeli flag there and wrote graffiti against the mayor, who responded by organizing a rally of support.[7]

HARSH ISRAELI REACTIONS: BACK TO THE SHABAK

That there was another option, and an impulse not to be content with being second-class citizens, was shown by the positions adopted by the Islamic movement and its powerful appearance on the scene, and the consolidation of the national secular position by the new national forces and even inside Hadash. The emergence of a more assertive Islamic and national Palestinian voice within Israel led the Israeli political elite to put strategizing about the issue back into the hands of the security octopus. Instead of employing human rights lawyers, political scientists or social welfare specialists, the government gave the secret service the 'Arab file'. As before, the drive to continue the undemocratic and racist policies led to a deterioration in the personal security of Israelis as a result of the ongoing Palestinian national struggle, which in the period under discussion focused on the settler communities in the West Bank and the Gaza Strip. The bloody retaliation by the settlers and the army heightened tension between Arabs and Jews inside Israel.

One result was the growing popularity of Meir Kahana and Kach, whose imagery and language was adopted by the mainstream press when referring to any Palestinian in Israel who did not succumb to Zionism or the state as an 'enemy'. This was not a phenomenon confined to the extreme margins. The support (which, one should reiterate, was democratically expressed) given by Palestinians inside Israel to the uprising unleashed verbal attacks on them from the centre, the left and the right. The basic message was in some way a return to the 1950s images and perceptions of them as a dangerous fifth column in the midst of Jewish society.[8]

There was, as mentioned in the previous chapter, a new presence of Palestinians in the very towns and settlements that were meant to keep them in their own habitual enclaves. Although these individuals were the last to express support for the uprising publicly or openly, the two disconnected phenomena were fused into one.

This could be detected around the government's discussion table. After years of neglecting the issue and not discussing the situation of the Palestinians in Israel in any serious manner, the government convened a special meeting in May 1989. It was probably the first cabinet meeting devoted to the subject since a special meeting convened in the aftermath of the Day of the Land in 1976. Then Yitzhak Rabin had appointed the ex-general Matti Peled to look into the Arab educational system and try to improve Arabs' sense of belonging. Not much happened in this respect apart from some multi-cultural masterplans devised by the Ministry of Education that included sections on educational workshops focused around 'coexistence'. With the appointment of Shulamit Aloni as Minister of Education to the 1992 Rabin government, more content and purpose was cast into these official schema and, at least theoretically, there was a space for a less segregated educational reality, but this hope did not last for long. It evaporated with the rest of the promising indicators of a possible better future with Rabin's assassination in November 1995.

This may be a good point to discuss Rabin's legacy in Israel in general, and in the life of the Palestinian community in particular. This writer does not share the assessment of many of his colleagues of Rabin's drive for peace during the days of the Oslo Accords, nor the assertion, put most eloquently by my friend Avi Shlaim, that Rabin's assassination was the main reason for the collapse of the Oslo Accords.[9] The Oslo process was the brainchild of Rabin's arch-rival in Israeli politics, Shimon Peres, and was never fully endorsed by the late Prime Minister. Like all the Israeli negotiators before and after him, he saw peace negotiations as offering the Palestinians terms of surrender, rather than a genuine attempt to reconcile and live jointly in the disputed land.

However, I do believe that he was unique in his approach to the issue of the Palestinians in Israel, not during his first term in office (1974–1977) but during his second term (1992–1995). I was already participating in Israeli politics in those days, as part of the Palestinian political scene, and he was one of the few who treated fellow Palestinian politicians as human beings and legitimate members of the political scene. Rabin approached the Palestinian parties immediately after the election in the summer of 1992 and offered them, for the first time in the history of the state, a partnership in government. As discussed, it was very limited; he did not dare to offer them a place in the formal coalition, but in return for their support in the parliament, they were given senior positions in the Knesset and his government pursued some policies of positive discrimination in state employment (granting an assured place and quota for Palestinians among senior officials), increased educational budgets and some improvements in the social welfare system. This also included a dialogue, interrupted by the Likud government which came into power in 1996, about allowing more say to the Palestinians regarding the content of their educational system. Some of these achievements were taken away by future governments; others were kept and helped to mitigate the overall and continued oppressive reality.

The 1989 cabinet meeting on the 'Arabs' in Israel was similarly futile. The leading voice in that meeting was that of the Communications Minister, Yitzhak Modai, and the discussion evolved around the radicalization in the attitudes of Palestinians in Israel. 'The intifada has spilled over into Israel,' declared Modai and 'there are villages which the police are afraid of entering'.[10]

Local politicians spoke in a similar vein when asked about the Palestinians in Israel. In an interview the Mayor of Carmiel lumped together what he saw as increased support by the Palestinians in Israel for the *Intifada* with the continuous move of Palestinians into his town, commenting, 'Carmiel was built in order to Judaize the Galilee, it is too early for joint life. They should stay in their village.'[11] This kind of official apartheid discourse and attitude was tolerable worldwide at a time when apartheid in South Africa was about to crumble.

The irony was that at that time governmental policies openly favoured the Jewish citizens in the Galilee and the Negev. The Israel Land Administration, now operating in a more regulated and organized manner (a process begun in 1977), introduced the five-year masterplans for spatial expansion in the early 1980s. Whereas in the case of the Jewish population these plans were meant to allow expansion, in the case of the Palestinian minority they were aimed at limiting expansion rather than aiding it. Cheaper services were provided to the Palestinian population in the name of efficiency, while the main impulse for this was in fact ideological. As noted by many researchers, this discrimination still continues today.[12]

These problems were reinforced by the lack of any public land accorded to the Palestinians for developing industry, public housing or commercial centres. A mere 0.15 per cent of the state land during that period was given to Palestinians in Israel for non-agricultural use, of which the vast majority was used for building shanty towns for the Bedouins in the Negev and better housing for the Druze (5 per cent of the 0.15 per cent).[13]

The Israeli press followed these statements by national and local politicians with distorted reports on the youth and educational initiative taken by Palestinians to improve the poor services provided by the state. Any attempts to find something for teenagers to do during the long summer vacation were reported in the press as '*Intifada* youth camps'.[14] Such attitudes were translated into other forms of harassment and intimidation. A typical case was when a coffee-house owner in Haifa demanded that seven young Palestinian customers should not speak in Arabic. Worse, Palestinians overheard speaking Arabic in shopping malls were attacked in Ramleh, Tiberias and Migdal Haemek, and one villager from al-Makr was murdered by a Jew. Palestinian fans of a local Nazareth football team were attacked viciously by the Jewish fans.[15]

From official circles, then, down to the hooligans in the streets there were days when anyone speaking Arabic was immediately suspected and feared. No wonder, in the 1990s as well as in the 1950s, the principal governmental agency entrusted with formulating and executing the policy towards the minority was the Shabak.

One of the major decision makers in this organization, Nachman Tal, summarized the outfit's aim as keeping the temperature at a reasonable level. As he explained:

> Even if the Arabs in Israel attained full equality, they will never be fully satisfied and would not change their national and ideological preferences. A national minority will always find it difficult to live in the state of the majority, therefore there is no solution to the problem. One has to keep the temperature low.[16]

He used this reference to temperature as he was impressed by something a veteran French colonialist from the days of the struggle for Algeria told him: that the French mistake was noting too late that the temperature had risen; as if 'detecting' in time the Algerian resistance to the French occupation would have left the country in French hands. However, in the same piece in the newspaper a veteran of the Shabak noted that 'keeping the temperature low' was a euphemism for pursuing a very aggressive and hostile policy towards the Palestinian citizens and he doubted the wisdom of such an attitude. Tal claimed that it was a carrot-and-stick policy, but the problem was that the carrot, constant improvement of the citizens' standard of living, was the politicians' job and in most cases they were unwilling or unable to fulfil it.[17]

This analysis and prognosis is quite bewildering as we know now in hindsight that the secret service predicted that the Palestinians in Israel would join the uprising. These Shabak experts should have (but could not have, due to their prejudices) listened to the leaders of the Palestinian community who repeatedly declared and explained that not only they, but also the PLO, did not expect the Palestinians in Israel to take part in the uprising. Nadim Rouhana asserted at the time that the Israeli 'experts' on the Arabs mistook very emotional identification with the uprising with a wish to take an active part in it.[18] Even groups of the Palestinian community branded by the Israeli establishment as 'Israelized' – and therefore ones which sent their sons to serve in the army – such as the Druze and the Bedouins shared this emotional identification. The result was a new discourse in the main Arabic newspaper in Israel, the official organ of the Israeli Communist Party, *al-Ittihad*. The national PLO discourse, when employed by Palestinian media in Israel in the past, would have led to the closure of newspapers and the arrest of journalists. Now it poured out like a tidal wave – everyone was using it. The Green Line in this respect disappeared – the prisoners of the uprising in the occupied territories were regarded by the Palestinians in Israel as if they were their own prisoners in Israeli jails. This is why for Palestinians on both sides of the Green Line the uprising had no political boundaries; it was a revolt which encompassed every Palestinian living in the historical homeland.

CULTURAL BOOM

This discourse was already there, as we mentioned in the poetry of the 1950s, in the novels of the 1960s and in the plays of the early 1980s. The trend had been reinforced by the uprising. Now it also penetrated the more folkloristic genre of local poetry – it appeared in the traditional praise local poets and storytellers recited at weddings, sometimes in an improvised duo between two poets, 'competing' on who could best extol the virtues of the bride and groom. Popular songs as well began to incorporate more political and ideological elements.

This was a very prolific period for the written word within the Palestinian community of Israel. There was a booming new literary energy across different gender, religious and sectarian backgrounds, including authors such as Munim Haddad, Naji al-Dahir, Dib Akkawi, Naila Azzam-Labes, Shakib Jahshan, Ussaman Halabi, Admon Shehadeh and Afif Shalhut. As a result their works have touched on almost every aspect of life. In response to Edward Said's famous article after the Lebanon war, 'Permission to Narrate', in which he urged Palestinians to retrieve and protect their narrative in the face of Israeli propaganda over the years, one of the local poet laureates, Samih al-Qasim published a new collection under the title *Do Not Ask Permission from Anyone* and Munim Haddad in Taybeh opened in 1988 a centre for Arab heritage with the publication of a book *The Arab Heritage: Erasure and Awakening*.[19]

But if previous decades were those of poetry and then theatre, this one was the epoch of the documentary, and, to a lesser extent, the feature film. It began with films made by Michel Khalifeh from Nazareth, who produced both documentary and feature films dealing with the Palestinian experience inside and outside Israel. *Pages from Ripe Memories* told the story of two women, one of them the famous Palestinian novelist Sahar Khalifeh and the other a villager from Yafat al-Naserh. In 1987 he filmed *A Wedding in the Galilee*, the second-ever Palestinian feature film and the first shot inside Palestine.[20]

Khalifeh belonged to a group of Palestinians from Israel, mainly from Nazareth, who studied and worked abroad and then came back and produced films on the Palestinian reality in Israel. Others included Rashid Masharawi, Eliah Suleiman and Hani Abu-Assad. The boom in cinematic production was important because, apart from individual Palestinians in exile, the communities of refugees and those under occupation were too preoccupied with the existential struggle to bother with this crucial medium. The PLO while in Beirut had put some effort and money into making documentaries about the Palestinian condition, but since it moved to Tunis, and then during the Oslo days, partly to Ramallah, its cultural production had subsided. Whether it was Masharawi in his film *The Shelter* or Khalifeh in his various films, their depiction of life reflected the Palestinian existence inside and outside the homeland. The films moved between the personal and the national experience as sharing the same features of safety, danger and aspirations.

While such contributions to the cinema were crucial, the input as far as other aspects of general Palestinian culture were concerned was also much less marginal than it used to be. An Islamic or rather a neo-Islamic take on culture developed in Israel as it did in the rest of the Muslim world. When the Salman Rushdie affair exploded all over the Muslim world, it had a faint echo in the Palestinian community as no one thought of publishing the book in Arabic. It appeared in Hebrew despite a single protest letter send by Adil Zaydan, the secretary of the religious scholars in Israel. But in Israel at least in those days you could ridicule any religion in a novel, including Judaism. Later on, the Islamic movement, unlike the established Islamic bodies, would have an impact on culture in certain spaces where it was politically powerful. This was manifested in events where women were separated from men during musical performances but, all in all, Islam in the public sphere was more political and social than cultural: by this I mean that the theatre, films and shows by Palestinians in Israel were not censored, and not even self-censored, on matters of Puritanism and modesty, only by the Israeli authorities if the works of culture were regarded as subversive or against the state.

Palestinians were reading Hebrew novels more than ever before, although they would be translated into Arabic only in the late 1990s and the beginning of the next century. Few of the Palestinian writers wrote in Hebrew themselves, but one, Anton Shammas, produced what many local critics regard as one of the best novels in this language, *Arabesques* (in the twenty-first century his successor in a way is Said Qashua who has already produced three novels; they are more lightweight but have been written by someone also deeply in love with the Hebrew language). Shammas' novel was the tale of one Palestinian village destroyed by Israel in 1948; a tale beginning in a Syrian village in the nineteenth century and ending in the United States in the 1980s. This work landed its writer in the spotlight and later on involved him in a famous public debate with one of Israel's leading novelists, A.B. Yehoshua, who famously invited Shammas to leave the country if he was unhappy with the Zionist regime and the success of the Jews in dispossessing the Palestinians.[21] Alienation, namely the depiction of the Palestinians in Israel as aliens in their home country was not just a governmental policy, but also a private crusade by a liberal author.

As before there was no real and significant dialogue between authors, poets and journalists. The cultural life reflected the segregated socio-political reality which had been built and sustained by successive governments. This is also why the number of mixed marriages, in this period a more common phenomenon, remained too marginal and negligible to warrant any serious mentioning in a book like this. To be fair, one should say that traditional Palestinians did not welcome such marriages or connections any more than most Jews did. Yet a woman or man could easily convert to Islam for the sake of marriage, but was less welcome to convert to Judaism. Films and novels had many such romances as their main plots, however in real life there were far fewer. One could possibly agree with the Haifa-based sociologist, Yuval Yonay, that the number of interracial marriages was 'too small to be studied since separation between Jews and Arabs is so ingrained in Israeli society, it is surprising that anyone manages to escape these central controls'. And indeed those who do, risk the wrath of the Jewish society at large.[22]

In response to the involvement of two young Jewish women from Petach Tivka, a large city near Tel Aviv, in an alleged attack by Palestinian youth on a Jewish citizen in Tel Aviv, the municipality of Petach Tivka announced it was establishing a team of youth counsellors and psychologists whose job it was to identify young Jewish women who were dating Arab men and 'rescue' them. But this brand of policy was usually not triggered by the alleged involvement of young women with criminal activity by Arab youth. In Pisgat Zeev in Jerusalem the residents formed a vigilante-style patrol to stop young Jewish women meeting with Palestinians. And in 2007, the municipality of Kiryat Gat launched a programme in schools to warn Jewish girls of the dangers of dating local Bedouin men. The girls were shown a video titled 'Sleeping with the enemy', which described mixed couples as an 'unnatural phenomenon'.[23]

Even at that period cultural production was deemed dangerous in a state where its value was judged by the secret service and not according to artistic critics. Thus when the painter Jawad Ibrahim from Umm al-Fahem opened an exhibition displaying images from the *Intifada* and life under occupation, he was arrested and spent a long time in the notorious Keziot jail, where people were held for terrorist offences.[24]

A PHONEY CRISIS: THE FIRST IRAQI WAR

At the time the first Gulf War seemed to present a moment of serious crisis in the relationship between the Jewish state and its Palestinian minority. But its short duration did not significantly transform the attitude of the state to its Palestinian citizens. What it did do, however, was to expose, and very forcefully so, the fragility of the fabric of coexistence in Israel.

At the beginning of the crisis, when Saddam Hussein invaded Kuwait in August 1990, no particular tension was felt in the relationship between the two communities; despite the animosity of most of the Palestinian political bodies to the al-Sabah dynasty in Kuwait, the legitimacy of the princedom was not challenged. Saddam Hussein too, until the outbreak of the crisis, was not one of the popular Arab leaders in the eyes of the local community. The Communist Party, in particular, had not forgotten Saddam Hussein's cruel treatment of the Iraqi Communists throughout his rule.[25] Even the Islamic movement did not seem very impressed by Saddam Hussein's alleged return to religion in the early days of the war.

But the American declaration of Operation Desert Storm in January 1991 changed this picture. *Al-Sirat*, a new publication of the Islamic movement, was the first organ to transform its attitude as soon as the US forces arrived in Saudi Arabia.[26] In less than two weeks Saddam Hussein was rehabilitated in the local press and even inside Hadash there were sharp divergences of opinion, quite visible in the various articles written in *al-Ittihad*. Incidentally, the paper was much democratized as a public arena after that debate, in the sense that it was much more open to printing various viewpoints.

It is also important to mention that the Iraqi crisis coincided with the demise of the USSR. *Zo Haderech*, the Hebrew weekly of the Communist Party ('This is the way' in Hebrew), adopted the Russian stance in the crisis, less out of obedience as in the past, and more as a reasonable and cautious position that eventually was accepted by the Israeli non-Zionist left as the best take on the crisis.[27] The gist of this position was a sharp condemnation of the USA for a cynical manipulation of the Kuwait crisis, while at the same time refraining from supporting the Iraqi occupation. And yet it accepted Saddam Hussein's famous linkage between the withdrawal of his forces with the Israeli withdrawal from the occupied territories – that is, he promised to withdraw his army from Kuwait if the Israeli army left the Palestinian occupied territories.[28]

In hindsight, it seems that the crisis contributed to the consolidation of the Arab national position as a much-preferred option to the Arab–Jewish solidarity promised by the Zionist left and Hadash. The Progressive List for Peace, and politicians such as Abd al-Wahhab Darawshe who proposed a politics of identity evolving around Palestinian and even pan-Arab issues, became more popular – ironically at the time when Hadash succeeded for the first time in significantly enlarging its support among the Jewish electorate.

When the heavy American bombardment on Iraq began and Saddam Hussein sent the first Scud missiles to fall on Israeli towns – causing a lot of damage but hardly any casualties – the tension between national and 'coexistential' options became higher. At one moment the national tone seemed to go even further than the politicians of the community wanted. On the morning the Scud missiles landed on Israel, Hashem Mahamid, a member of the Knesset who was the chair of Hadash in those days, told *al-Ittihad*, 'by invading Kuwait Saddam redeemed the honour of the Arab nation'.[29] His colleague Ahmad Tibi explained that these words reflected a great support for Saddam Hussein among some Palestinians in Israel but added that this did not mean that they would have liked to see the Iraqi ruler ordering a chemical attack on Israel (which was in those days the unfounded doomsday scenario sold to the Israeli public) and this not because of the fear that Palestinian citizens could also be hurt, but because even Saddam Hussein was not seen as someone who would go that far.[30]

In some circles Saddam Hussein was hailed as the new Salah al-Din and yet one could not escape the many displays of solidarity with the Jewish citizens hurt by the missiles. Mustafa Abu Riya, the mayor of Sakhnin, orchestrated an operation of offering safe houses to Jews in the Tel Aviv area who were the main target of the Scud attacks on Israel. 'There is nothing unusual in this initiative,' he told the press, 'I see it is an obvious reaction.'[31] Abd al-Tariq Abd al-Hay, the head of the local council in Tira in the Triangle undertook a similar initiative and said 'We are both peoples of this land, with the same fate of life and death, and therefore our doors are open for anyone needing a safe place.'[32] And a local politician from Baqa al-Gharbiyya explained that these initiatives came, 'from the people, themselves'.[33] When Palestinians became victims of the Hezbollah missile attacks on the Galilee in the summer of 2006, there were no such initiatives on the Jewish side.

The only casualty of the missile attack was a Palestinian baby from Taybeh, suffocated to death in the oxygen mask she was mis-fitted with. 'There is a need to introduce to every household in Israel the notion of a common fate,' wrote Emil Habibi. He was writing an opinion piece for the Israeli daily *Davar*, while sitting in the sealed room which each family in Israel had prepared in anticipation of a chemical attack on the state. 'Both peoples have to go out of the sealed rooms and the shelters with the conviction never to return to them,' he finished optimistically.[34] Alas, this lesson was not learned by the Israeli Jewish majority.

The very same Palestinian politicians and intellectuals would return to a more complicated and delicate analysis once the fighting subsided and the excitement on all sides petered out. As always it was the writer Anton Shammas, inspired by Milan Kundera's famous novel, who found the right way of expressing the problem, talking about the 'Unbearable Lightness of the Arab Citizen in the Jewish State'. The total disregard by both Israel and the PLO of the Palestinians in Israel during the Oslo Accords process drove home strongly his encapsulation of the predicament of the Palestinians in the Jewish state.

A HUGE NON-EVENT: THE PALESTINIANS IN ISRAEL AND THE OSLO ACCORDS

The first *Intifada* came to an end with the signing of the Oslo Accords in September 1993 and the attempt to implement it over the next two years. The Accords were presented worldwide as an agreement between the PLO and Israel to create an independent Palestinian state in the occupied territories in return for mutual recognition and peace. In practice, very soon it transformed into something else, either because it was not meant to be a peace agreement but an Israeli *diktat* to the Palestinians or due to good intentions going wrong. I tend to agree with the former analysis. In any case, in reality, the Accords were translated into an agreement that divided the West Bank and the Gaza Strip into three categories: areas still directly occupied and colonized by Israel; areas jointly ruled by Israel and the Palestinian Authority (a new body created by the Oslo Accords to run the West Bank and the Gaza Strip); and areas independently ruled by the Palestinian Authority. The power of the Israeli military and security presence was such that it reigned in all three areas, frustrating the Palestinians' hopes for independence and self-determination and the Jewish Israeli aspirations for peace.

In any other history book this juncture should form a separate chapter; but from the perspective of the Palestinian community inside Israel, as indeed that of the Palestinian refugees and exiles, this peace process intentionally left them out of its terms of reference. The exclusion was not only on the part of Israel, but also accepted by the PLO leadership as part of the boundaries of discussion when they first met their Israeli counterparts in Norway in the spring of 1993 and when the two sides finalized the historical Oslo Accords there in the summer of that year. There were some voices asking the Israeli government to involve Palestinian politicians and experts in the bilateral and multilateral discussions that formed the Accords, but to no avail. There was no Israeli Palestinian influence on the process.[35]

This did not mean that (as mentioned in the opening sentences of this chapter) the very acceptance, albeit a short-lived one, of Arafat and the PLO as peace partners in Israel did not raise many hopes among politicians and citizens alike. But even before the rest of the Palestinian groups despaired of a process that proved to go nowhere, the community inside Israel realized that its implementation would, at best, ease life for those occupied after 1967 – and even that proved to be too sanguine an assumption – and at worst would produce another wave of violence in reaction to its failure to satisfy the hopes it raised in the first place.

But the eventful years from the outbreak of the first *Intifada* to the apparent failure of the Oslo Accords in 1995 were important for the Palestinians inside Israel as they helped to define them clearly as part of the Palestinian world at large, as fragmented as it was, while at the same time highlighting the crisis that such an attachment produced in the relationship with the state.

What emerged was not that the community was unique in comparison to other Palestinian groups but rather that it had a unique problem. Zionism was the exceptional factor, not being a Palestinian in Palestine, or what used to be Palestine. This strong affirmation of the connection to the country and not to the state was the end product of a long internal Palestinian analysis of the predicament, crisis and nature of the community, which was followed by a prognosis and a kind of action plan for how to deal with the crisis of being a national indigenous minority within the Jewish state. I would like to end this chapter with this insight because on the basis of both this analysis and prognosis, the community went from a very hopeful and assertive period, 1995 to 2000, into a very precarious and dangerous existential period after 2000 and until today. And yet the analysis is still valid and the action plan has not changed.

This new analysis was possible because of the new national role Palestinian academics began to play in the life of their community. Khalil Nakhleh, Sami Mar'i, Elia Zureik, Mahmoud Miari, Said Zaydani, Sharif Qananeh and many others contributed to this new understanding (their work is discussed in the Appendix). Notable was the work of Ghazi Falah, a geographer who almost single-handedly challenged the hegemonic Israeli Jewish scholarship on the Palestinian minority, laying the foundation for critical work in the future.

What these scholars and their successors did was to map the fluctuations in the construction of a clearer identity for the community. While the first *Intifada* strengthened the identification with the Palestinian struggle, the initial stages of the Oslo process created a false impression that part of the struggle for statehood was about to be fulfilled. In this respect there was no difference between the Palestinians on both sides of the Green Line, who moved in the same way from a willingness to confront the occupation into a hopeful mood that Oslo would bring a peaceful end to the occupation; and then shortly after entered a state of despair once it transpired that there was no real Israeli desire for peace.

No less important was the clear distinction made by the new body that Oslo created, the Palestine Authority, and the leadership bodies of the Palestinians in Israel. When the president of the PA, Yasser Arafat, arrived in Gaza in 1994, a huge delegation, representing all the political groups in the Palestinian community in Israel came to greet him (apart from factions in the Islamic movement, who must have known better than others that this was not a triumphant moment).

The PA and the Palestinian political parties and movements inside Israel were two discrete outfits that cooperated intensively and saw eye to eye on all the national issues, but did not involve each other in taking decisions on the ground. There was more indirect involvement.

Some Palestinians from Israel, such as the politician Ahmad Tibbi, served for a while as an advisor to the PA and at times of crisis – such as the rift between Muslims and Christians about ownership of holy sites in Nazareth – the Palestinians in Israel sought the advice of the PA, and especially that of President Arafat in a search for a solution. The PA also had a special liaison office for maintaining contact with the Palestinians in Israel, headed by Fawzi Nimr, originally from Acre and who was mentioned in our chapter on the 1960s as one of the few at the time who actively joined Fatah's struggle against the Jewish state from inside Israel.

The mutual respect shown in not interfering in each other's local agendas misled some of the most prominent Jewish scholars who were experts on Arab affairs in the Jewish state, such as Sami Smooha and Eli Rekhes, who assumed that the Oslo Accords accelerated and strengthened the process of 'Israelization' among the Palestinians in Israel, namely a distancing from the pan-Palestinian issues and a focus on local issues. When Said Zidani and As'ad Ghanem chose to differ and highlighted the issue of crisis, rather than separation, they were (we can say now in hindsight) far more accurate. The crisis was visible even before it was clear that Oslo was going nowhere. The crisis was how to bridge over the gap between the natural impulse to act for and belong to the Palestinian national movement as a whole on the one hand, and to obey the rules of the game in Israel, for the sake of local struggles, on the other. The inevitable result was that, politically at least, the community of activists and politicians deserted the navigation and preferred to change the paradigm, asking the Israeli Jewish society how they would cope with a pure national minority in their midst on the one hand, and their claim to be a democracy on the other.

The first *Intifada* and the Oslo process thus removed some, but not all, of the false distinctions between the 'Arabs of Israel' and the Palestinians in the occupied territories and elsewhere. This new recognition was reinforced by a better comprehension of the connection between the socio-economic conditions in Israel and the fate of the Palestinian community in it. After 1993 these conditions were closely connected to the reshaping of the national agenda. Academics articulated the reality in clearer terms than ever before: Israel was an ethnic state in which a national minority lived in a segregated manner, either in the countryside or in the neighbourhoods in the city.

But there was, as mentioned, a new action plan and the gist of it was to build a civil society made out dozens of new NGOs and community-centred organizations. Those activists who founded the NGOs did so with a conviction that the Jewish state was not theirs, although they were part of it and therefore they were catering and working solely for the benefit of their community in all aspects of life, including those for which the state should have been responsible. This was done as a result of Israel's refusal to recognize the Palestinians either as a national minority or equal citizens. So in 1981 the Galilee Society – the Arab National Society for Health Research and Services – was founded in Shefa-'Amr. Its aim was to improve the health conditions and services for the Palestinian citizens who were neglected by the state's health services just because they were not Jewish. Its programme included scientific and field research, data analysis, and litigation on health and environmental issues.

The Arab Association for Human Rights (HRA), was founded in 1988 in Nazareth. Its declared aim was to promote and protect the civil, political, cultural and economic rights of the Palestinians in Israel. They prepared human rights educational programmes for secondary schools and developed strong ties with UN agencies dealing with these rights. This association would become extremely important in monitoring the pollution of several rural areas, predominantly Palestinian, as a result of the toxic and dangerous industries which had been moved there. Some of the state's most poisonous chemical industries were situated around the city of Nazareth, in an industrial plant called Zipori and near the Bedouin habitat south of Beer Sheba, Ramat Hovav, dramatically increasing the number of associated illnesses. The Galilee Society's monitoring and protest work is one of the few success stories of Palestinian civil society in Israel.[36]

This Galilee Society was in many ways the first of its kind and others followed suit. Palestinian intellectuals and graduates who failed to find jobs in the academic system channelled their energies and capabilities into these new outfits, advancing both the research and the activism on behalf of the community as a whole. The HRA and the Galilee Society were behind the establishment of Adalah, the 'legal centre for Arab minority rights' in Israel, officially opened in 1996. It began by providing legal assistance to Palestinian NGOs in Israel and to community-based organizations, organized study days and trained young Palestinian lawyers. Their main aim was to make use of the Israeli legal system so as best to serve the Palestinian community as a whole. But they were also engaged with comparative and international law with the intention of enhancing the status of the minority. It would become itself the most important Palestinian NGO, and is discussed as such in the next chapter.

Women's organizations also began to focus on the special needs of the society rather than join in the international feminist struggle. The first organization in this vein was 'Women Against Violence', founded in 1993 in Nazareth. Their aim was to identify the level and causes of violence against women in Palestinian society, to create and provide services for victims of such violence, and to promote the status of Palestinian women in Israeli society.

Influenced by these developments, the Arab Follow-Up Committee ceased to function in a haphazard way and registered as an official NGO in 1992, preparing a clear programme for leading the civil society in promoting the educational, social, economic and political conditions and rights of the Palestinian minority in Israel.

Soon many other NGOS would spring up and pay attention to additional aspects of life, the most important of which were the cultural and educational fields. Although Arabic was and still is an official language in Israel, with an equal status to Hebrew, this status was totally ignored in practice. The struggle that began in the 1990s to force governmental agencies and municipalities to use Arabic was quite successful. Much less successful was the struggle for autonomous status in the Palestinian educational system. Despite all attempts, Jewish Zionist officials and politicians continued to control the curricula and teaching in the Palestinian schools, especially in the fields of history, culture and politics. However, the NGOs managed to create an alternative and adjacent environment where the Palestinian perspective and narrative on all these issues was accessible to wide sections of the society. In fact, it would become so successful that in the twenty-first century, the Israeli government would try to limit the works of such NGOs and activists.

Such civil society activity can create a false impression of the crystal-lization not only of an autonomous existence within the Jewish state but also one which separated 'the 1948 Arabs' from the rest of the Palestinian people. As already noted in this book, the history of this community, despite the endless Israeli efforts to fragment the Palestinian people and existence, was still an organic part of the history of the Palestinian people. The carving-out of an autonomous existence through the encouragment of the civil society was done in order to maintain the links and association with the rest of the Palestinian people to weaken those with the Jewish state.

All these new insights and actions were crystallized when Yitzhak Rabin was assassinated by a Jewish terrorist in November 1995. In many ways this announced the end of the Oslo process. By the time the process died it was deemed irrelevant by the Israelis, and disastrous by many Palestinians. Instead of bringing healing to the torn country, the peace efforts led it into yet another wave of bloodshed by the end of the century. As early as 1995, most Palestinians had labelled the Oslo process as yet another form of occupation, and most Israelis felt it had failed to safeguard their personal security.

The combination of possible new thinking in the corridors of power, Yitzhak Rabin's need to rely on the Arab parties to form a steady coalition after the 1992 election and the hopes, proven to be false, that the Oslo Accords had produced, means that the year 1995 stands out as an aberration; it was an exceptional year, displaying at last the potential for an alternative reality.

CHAPTER SIX

THE HOPEFUL YEARS AND THEIR
DEMISE, 1995–2000

1995 DID NOT START well for the Palestinians in Israel. The year began with a huge demonstration in Nazareth against the settlement of Palestinian collaborators in Arab communities. The Oslo Accords meant that the new Palestinian Authority would now have jurisdiction over sizeable parts of the occupied territories. As a result, tens of thousands of Palestinians who had been working – either willingly, or, in most cases, reluctantly – with the Israeli secret service feared that they would now be identified and brutally punished by the new regime.

The Israeli government's decision was typically insensitive. Their policy of ethnically segregating their citizens meant that it was unthinkable that these collaborators would be relocated into Jewish areas. Sending them to live in Palestinian areas represented a show of force to the population, alongside perhaps a hope on the part of the authorities that their collaborationist background might be useful. The collaborators were never accepted as part of the community, and the end result was an alienated existence that drove many to crime and despair. When the Palestinian actor Yussuf Abu-Warda was asked to appear in the role of a collaborator in a play performed at the municipal theatre of Haifa, he categorically refused to do so, despite pressure from the management.[1]

But many of the images that come to mind from that year are more hopeful. In 1995, the Palestinians in Israel formed 18 per cent of the overall population. The increase in their numbers and the consolidation in their living spaces (or what professionals call habitats) led to greater self-confidence within the Palestinian community. The end of agriculture as a way of life in the villages meant that the gap between culture and attitudes in rural and urban areas narrowed. This was a year in which entrepreneurs showed a significant increase in willingness to venture out of the traditional occupational boundaries of the community, into the areas of hi-tech and tourism; it was also a year in which the number of Palestinians in senior civil service positions was higher than ever before, although still very minimal.[2]

The community's overall strategy remained the same and the number of citizens involved in modes of resistance beyond the conventional was still very small. They included those who adopted an active confrontational attitude in demonstrations and a few hundred youngsters who out of frustration occasionally threw stones at cars passing by their villages or set fire to tyres.[3] But the rest were now reconciled to the modes of action open to them legally and politically.

If you ask members of the Palestinian community who were born in the first decade of statehood in Israel, and are today not involved in politics, what picture they recall from that period as encapsulating its mood, for good or ill, many would point to the return for two days of Mahmoud Darwish to Haifa. The exiled writer, by now the best-loved poet of the Palestinian world, had previously asked to come to Haifa to see his relatives and been refused. He reacted then by commenting, 'The Israelis read me in a poetic way, but it is always the reading of the Other.'[4] But when Emil Habibi died in 1995 Darwish was allowed to attend his funeral. One wonders what his inner thoughts were when he saw the lines engraved on Habibi's tomb: 'Stayed in Haifa'.

1995 was also the year that the Israeli Association for Civil Rights (IACR) highlighted discrimination against Palestinians as Israel's greatest civil rights problem. This may seem trivial, but never before – and never since – has any mainstream Israeli organization been willing to cast such a strong light on the plight of the Palestinians. The IACR annual report noted that even after almost fifty years of statehood, Israel did not have any fundamental law – Israel has no constitution as such – that ensured the equality of the citizens before the law, while there were laws that directly discriminated against Palestinian citizens. In fact, in theory it would have been possible to enforce segregation in public spaces between Arabs and Jews, as no law prevented it.

The IACR also attracted attention to the discrimination against the spouses of Palestinian women in Israel. Since 1948, the Ministry of the Interior had made it almost impossible for a Palestinian woman to marry a non-Israeli citizen and stay in the country. Worse was the situation of Palestinian women marrying Palestinians from the occupied territories, who were tricked into signing away their Israeli citizenship and were thus forced to live in the occupied territories rather than Israel itself.

But in 1995 the first ever law to grant full equality to its citizens regardless of their ethnicity or religion was passed in Israel – though, needless to say, it has been ignored in the years that followed. According to this law employers could no longer discriminate against Palestinians. However, Jewish employers continued (and still do) to advertise vacancies for employees 'after their military service', a clear code in the Israeli society for 'Jews only'. Palestinians also continued to be discriminated against in terms of university admissions and welfare benefits, which were also partially dependent on military service. However, in 1995 some of the discriminations under this framework were discussed by the Israeli Knesset and an initiative to increase the child benefits to Palestinians was put forward. Like almost every other promising pledge made in 1995, however, this never materialized.[5]

Why was 1995 so different? I have tried to hint at possible explanations in the beginning of this chapter: Rabin's coalition government and the hopes of the Oslo Accords. An additional factor was the privatization of the economy, which for instance allowed the first appearance of a totally independent Arabic radio station run by Palestinians, Radio 2000 in Nazareth (hosted in the same building as the Follow-Up Committee). But probably more important than anything else was that for a short while a different kind of Israel seemed to emerge in academia, media, culture and even on the margins of politics. This was all part of a post-Zionist era that allowed some more conscientious academic Jews who entered the public service to have a slight influence on governmental policy and practices vis-à-vis the Palestinian citizens; a notable example was the Civil Service Commissioner between 1994 and 1996, Professor Yitzhak Galnor, who introduced an affirmative action scheme to increase the number of Palestinians in the public service.

A NEW POLITICAL SCENE?

In 1996 came a significant development in party politics. A group of young Palestinian intellectuals headed by a university lecturer, Azmi Bishara, registered as a political party. Despite the clear ruling of the law and even a Supreme Court judge that a party that did not recognize Israel as the state of the Jewish people, or as a 'Jewish state' would not be allowed to take part in the elections, the national Palestinian agenda of the party was accepted. Balad, an acronym for *Brit Leumit Democratit* (National Democratic Alliance) in Hebrew (*al-Tajamu' al-Watani al-Arabi* in Arabic), expressed a wish to transform the state of Israel into a genuine democracy for all its citizens, regardless of their national or ethnic identity. It also supported a two-state solution and the implementation of the UN Resolution 194 that called upon Israel to allow the unconditional return of the 1948 Palestinian refugees. As mentioned in the previous chapter, Balad ran together with Hadash as one proud national list in the 1996 Knesset elections. For the first time in that year the Palestinians had the option to vote for a national party: not a Zionist one, not a Communist one and not an Islamic one.

This apparent new openness continued during the campaign for the 1996 elections. The southern wing of the Islamic movement – led by Abdullah Nimr Darwish – decided to take part in the elections and joined others to form a united list, Mada', the acronym in Hebrew for Arab Democratic Party. The de facto split between this and the northern wing, led by Sheikh Raid Salah, now became a formal separation. Two of the southern wing leaders succeeded in entering the Knesset in the 1996 elections.

But these encouraging signs did not last for long. In May 1996, in order to impress voters in the run-up to the national election, Shimon Peres, the prime minister and leader of the Labour Party, wanted to show his more hawkish face. Always wounded by his lack of career in the army, he took every opportunity to be photographed wearing a military blazer and commanding this or that military operation. In retaliation against the Hezbollah war of attrition against the Israeli occupation of southern Lebanon, which finally drove the Israel Defense Forces out in 2000, he ordered a massive attack on the organization's installations. This was stopped when a refugee camp in the village al-Kana was bombed and more than a hundred refugees were killed in what the Israeli army code-named Operation 'Grapes of Wrath'. Palestinian students at Haifa University demonstrating against this operation were arrested, leading to further demonstrations and a new period of uneasy relations between the management and the Palestinian students there.

As it turned out, Benjamin Netanyahu led Likud into a victory in the 1996 elections – against a background of a particularly bloody suicide-bombing campaign in Israeli shopping malls and public transport. This was a surprise in a way for two reasons. First, since experts assumed that the Labour candidate, Shimon Peres, would win the elections as a result of public sympathy for his party following Rabin's assassination, and, second, Netanyahu was clearly one of the vociferous and prominent voices demonizing Rabin and inciting anger towards him before the murder. But the Jewish electorate of the country it seems, judging by these results, were less shocked by the murder than one assumed at the time, and it does seem that Netanyahu cleverly exploited the public rage in the wake of the suicide bomb attacks.[6]

In September of that same year, Netanyahu ordered the opening of a tunnel under Haram al-Sharif (Temple Mount) in Jerusalem. Interpreted by many Palestinians as an act of sabotage, this triggered riots that threatened to spill over into Israel proper, but fortunately subsided quite quickly without anyone paying much attention. However, none of the problems that triggered this unrest were solved, and thus the more serious second *Intifada* was just around the corner.

THE POLITICS OF RELIGION: POLITICAL ISLAM AND CHRISTIANITY IN ISRAEL

The split into two of both main Islamic Palestinian parties did not signal any weakening in the popularity of the return to Islam as a way of life and a solution to individual and collective issues. The rural land-scape in particular changed accordingly: new minarets and golden domes appeared on the skyline and many more women and men were seen wearing traditional dress, although other styles and fashions were still on display in the urban centres of Haifa and Nazareth.

After the election the main bone of contention between the two factions of the Islamic movement was the Oslo Accords. While the leader of the southern wing participated in a rally supporting the peace process, the leader of the northern movement, Sheikh Raid Salah, condemned the agreement and rejected its premises, branding Yasser Arafat's arrival in Gaza and the establishment of a Palestinian Authority in the occupied territories as an act of treason. And while all the other politicians in the community went regularly to visit and consult with Arafat in Gaza or Ramallah, the leaders of the northern wing made a point of not being seen with him or any other senior member of the Palestinian Authority. But Salah emphasized that changing the course of politics in the occupied territories should be done only by democratic means. A new journal, *Sawt al-Haq wa al-Huriyya* ('The Voice of Justice and Freedom'), became the main venue in which these views were expressed.

In the West, it was reported that the increasing power of political Islam was causing the Palestinian Christians to emigrate. The percentage of Christians in the Palestinian community did indeed decrease during that period, from 12 to 10 per cent; this was a blow to the community as a whole, particularly given that many worked in skilled professions. But it is not clear, and we still have no professional research on this question, what role political Islam played in their decision making. It seems that a more important factor was the arrival of one million Russian Jews and non-Jews, who were pushed by the government into occupational spaces usually dominated by Palestinian Christians. This was particularly evident in the health and social services. Majid al-Haj, a Palestinian Israeli sociologist from Haifa, conducted a comprehensive study on the impact of the immigration of Russian Jews on the Palestinian community in Israel already in 1996. Two salient negative influences were noted as affecting the Palestinians in Israel as whole. The first was the transfer of budgets originally meant to enhance the community to the project of integrating the new immigrants; and, second, the immigrants tended to vote, and still do today, for right-wing parties with particularly racist and harsh positions against the Palestinian minority in Israel.[7] With an arrogance and aggressiveness nurtured in the *Ulpan* (Hebrew schools) system in Israel, the newcomers treated the indigenous population as aliens. The occupational cake in Israel was not huge in any case, and those belonging to the wrong ethnic or religious side found it even harder to keep their slice.

But Christians had always been a minority in Palestine, and a minority inside a minority in Israel. Moreover, they formed a better-off segment of the population that could therefore afford to emigrate. For most of the state's history, and despite governmental efforts to divide and rule, it had not mattered whether Palestinians were affiliated to Christianity or Islam. A more complex matrix of identities developed with the beginning of the twenty-first century, as we shall see in the next chapter.

THE SEARCH FOR JUSTICE (*ADALAH*)

Literary Arabic is a very rich language, with plenty of synonyms for precious words such as justice. *Al-Haq*, often used by the Islamic movement, is one such word. Another kind of justice was sought by a very different enterprise in those years: *Adalah* ('justice' in the legal sense) was founded at the end of 1996. It began as a very modest outfit with one lawyer and a part-time secretary. By 2000 it was employing seven lawyers and another ten members of staff and had become the leading NGO in Israeli-Palestinian civil society.

Adalah's work began with a modest but successful campaign to force municipalities to add Arabic to signposts and street names, and increase the budgets of Arab schools and welfare outfits. After 2000, it began to represent the Israeli Palestinians both as citizens and as members of a national minority. Its philosophy – articulated from very early on – was that the personal autonomy of the individual was a right that had to be fiercely protected, and that this right included also the collective rights of the group to which the individual belonged. In fact, as Adalah's activity expanded in the first years of its existence, its efforts to enhance the former also seemed to strengthen the latter.

Adalah's contribution went beyond its legal activity. Together with more progressive and non-Zionist thinkers, it transformed the public discourse on the Palestinians in Israel. It contributed to protecting, through legal means, their right to their own narrative and collective memory. And, more importantly, Adalah, its supporters and the few Palestinian scholars who were part of Israeli academia and whose work forms an important part of the bibliographical infrastructure of this book, clarified the distinction between an immigrant community (the conventional Jewish description of the Palestinians in Israel) and an indigenous people to whose land an alien state immigrated.

Adalah's initial modus operandi was centred around appealing to the Israeli Supreme Court, a bastion of democracy that often turned out to be as discriminatory as the rest of the state agencies, but still harboured the potential, which was sometimes realized, of doing things differently. Between 1996 and 2000 it submitted more than twenty cases to the court that dealt with equality for Palestinian citizens. In particular, towards the end of this period, it focused on the plight of the non-recognized villages in which 10 per cent of the Palestinian population lived.

At the time, one hundred and twenty such villages existed in Israel, each lacking electricity, a water supply, public services, schools and health centres. Moreover, their inhabitants were all theoretically, and sometimes not so theoretically, in imminent danger of being forcefully evicted. In Adalah's campaign their plight came to symbolize the situation of the Palestinian community as a whole. And this struggle, in the years 1996–2000, exposed the plight of the Palestinian community, which could have been addressed by the Israeli government, but was not.[8]

THE STRUGGLE FOR RECOGNITION

As mentioned, Adalah focused on the unrecognized villages. As we have seen, the Palestinians who had been expelled from their houses in

1948 encountered various different fates: some were forcibly expelled from the country or left of their own accord, while others joined the villages left intact or became part of the small urban minorities. Some tried to form new small villages or returned to cleared villages that for some reason had not been taken over by the Jewish National Fund for building settlements or planting forests. Occasionally, Palestinians were expelled and returned in a cat and mouse routine. In 1965, a new law of planning and building redefined the areas in which unrecognized villages existed as 'inadequate for residence'. All these villages were erased from any official register, which meant that no state or municipal services were available for them. Those living there could not vote, receive mail or maintain community life, and could not put the village's name in the address section on their ID card. If residents tried to pave roads or dig a sewage system or build new houses, the state's bulldozers would appear and destroy them. Between 1995 and 1999 almost 400 houses were demolished in the unrecognized villages.

Among other things, Adalah campaigned for residents to be allowed to use their village's name on their ID card, thus giving their dwelling place some official recognition. The particular village which Adalah chose as a case, Husniya, was eventually added to the list of recognized villages after a long struggle. Other cases, such as a village near the town of Sakhnin and a large number of villages in the Negev, were less successful.

Struggling on behalf of the unrecognized villages exposed other problems suffered by the Palestinian population as a whole. One was the attempts by Jewish municipalities to expand at the expense of the unrecognized villages. One such project that incrementally over took such Bedouin space was the exclusive Jewish community centre in Omer, near Beer Sheba, whose council tried to confiscate the land of two unrecognized villages, Umm Batin and Al-Maqiman, and expel its inhabitants. Ironically, Omer is also home to some of the more conscientious Israeli academics, who fight relentlessly for the rights of the Bedouins to remain in their villages and be recognized.

Ten of the largest unrecognized villages were in the Negev. In December 1997, Adalah represented them in a demand for the establishment of basic medical clinics. Mothers whose babies needed simple treatments were forced to walk for hours through the Negev desert as there was no public transport connecting the villages. An additional problem was that traditionally Bedouin women were unable to travel outside their homes without a male escort, limiting their ability to move even further. The villages had the highest rate of infant mortality in Israel (16 out of every 1,000 births) and a very low level of immunization. Half of the children in these ten villages were hospitalized in the first six months of their lives, half of these for anaemia and malnutrition.

In the 1990s Israel enjoyed one of the most advanced public health systems in the world, and therefore it should have been possible to apply these progressive policies throughout the state. But the long history of colonization, the ethnic ideology and more than sixty years of discriminatory practices created a formidable barrier to turning laws into a new more hopeful reality. Similar problems existed in the arena of social services. In the needy Jewish areas there was one social worker for each 600 inhabitants. The 6,500 inhabitants of the ten villages had one social worker attached to them. Even that person was removed by the local authority for 'lack of funds' in 1999.

In the 1990s serious attempts were made to pass laws that safeguarded human dignity and the right to life, which were broadcast throughout the world as the latest product of the only democracy in the Middle East. In 1992 the Law of Human Rights was passed, which decreed that freedom and dignity were core values, and was given a status of a 'basic' law by the Supreme Court, meaning that it fulfilled a constitutional role and could only be abolished with the consent of the Supreme Court. But these noble aspirations and declarations did not amount to much, either in the occupied territories or inside the Palestinian areas of Israel.

THE STRUGGLE FOR SPACE

Away from the unrecognized villages, the official villages and towns in the Palestinian areas suffered from an acute problem of space. Most of the Palestinian land had been expropriated in the 1950s and 1960s and in their place only one small neighbourhood was built from scratch for the Palestinian community, compared to hundreds of new towns and settlements for Jewish citizens. This was the western neighbourhood of Buqia in upper Galilee, which was built as a safe haven for the Greek Orthodox community, who were driven out of their village by the Druze after centuries in which Druze, Jews and Christians had shared the village in harmony and peaceful coexistence.

Adalah and other NGOs tried to use the legal system to pressure the government into allowing the expansion of the space allocated to local municipalities and councils so that new land would at least be added to existing settlements. The Palestinians' frustration grew in the 1990s, when it became clear how generous the government was when it came to building and allowing planning permission for new Jewish settlements. The two cities of Nazareth were a case in point. Upper Nazareth, as mentioned previously, was built under David Ben-Gurion's orders to kick off the Judaization of the Galilee and strangle the old Palestinian city of Nazareth. In the late 1990s it housed 50,000 people living in an area of 40,000 dunams, while Nazareth with its 70,000 inhabitants had to be content with 16,000 dunams.

Israel in the 1990s was rich enough to offer some areas a 'status of national priority' – in terms of lower taxation, building permits, more public services and so on. Not one Palestinian village or town was included in this preferential treatment. Moreover, the authorities were very reluctant to impose the law on Jews who illegally expanded their homes or built new ones, while not one Arab balcony escaped the alert eyes of the supervisors. Each demolition of a house or part of it became a show of force, a source of outrage and frustration, drowning the hopes triggered by the Oslo Accords or the more progressive legislation. A famous example of one such demolition was brought to public attention by a court case involving the Sawai'd family near Shefa-'Amr in the lower western Galilee, who built a house on a land they bought in 1959. The authorities claimed the land was for agricultural use only and demolished the house. There were thousands of cases like this in the 1990s.

The absence of master plans, a systematic refusal to grant permits for expansions and, as mentioned, the refusal to allow the establishment of new villages and towns led quite a few among the Palestinians in Israel to build 'illegally'. Between 1993 and 1996, the authorities demolished more than 2,000 houses belonging to Palestinians (during that same period only 130 such houses were demolished in the Jewish sector). Each such demolition was planned like a military operation. I witnessed several myself: helicopters hovering in the air, the military sealing the area with plenty of heavily armed troops, creating the impression of an attack on an enemy outpost rather than an engagement with citizens of the state. The house's inhabitants were evicted without due notice and found themselves literally in the street.

Not only were houses demolished, but land was still expropriated, either for the purpose for Judaizing the Galilee or the Negev, or for the army's training grounds. In 1998, 18,000 dunams were confiscated for security reasons in Umm al-Fahem in Wadi Ara. A demonstration by the people who owned the land was brutally dispersed, reminding everyone that the hopeful years might have been an illusion. The brutality of the police and the army was a direct import from the means employed in the occupied territories: potentially lethal rubber bullets left many badly wounded wherever Palestinian citizens protested against such demolitions and confiscations. In one case, the immunity of Azmi Bishara and Muhammad Barakeh as elected members of parliament did not protect them from a rubber bullet in a demonstration in the city of Lid, where 15,000 Palestinians were crammed into three slums, crime-ridden areas where all the buildings were illegal in one way or another.[9]

THE DEMONS OF THE *NAKBAH*

The scars of 1948 reopened in 1998 in a state that celebrated the jubilee of its founding, and ignored the commemoration of the catastrophe that came with it. In the legal sphere this meant reopening the question of absentee property. The Palestinians in Israel were not only those left behind by the millions who became refugees, they were also eyewitnesses to the pillage that followed the exodus: not only the lands that were turned into forests and the houses turned into rubble but also the looting of what was in the houses. From 1950 the Israeli Absentee Property Law enabled the state to take over the property and land of all the Palestinians who did not reside within the borders of Israel. The law also covered the property belonging to the internal refugees, those Palestinians who became refugees in their own state, as they were not counted in the October 1948 census (as discussed in the first chapter of this book).

In 1998, Adalah approached the Custodian of the Absentee Property in Israel, demanding a list of the properties involved and their location. In 1991 the state controller had criticized the state for not keeping orderly records of these properties, and not surprisingly the state now replied to the court that the files were lost and that the Custodian could not provide such a list. Adalah would demand this information again and again, but to no avail.

The jubilee celebrations encouraged a small NGO to become more vociferous and visible in the public arena. This was the Committee for the Defence of Displaced Persons' Rights, representing the internal refugees in Israel. In 1998 the committee decided, in alliance with the Jewish NGO Zochrot, that in addition to making annual visits to former Palestinian villages, as mentioned in the previous chapter, they would also encourage ceremonies inside some of the Israeli settlements and kibbutzim built on the sites of these villages.

They first attempted to do this in the remains of the 1948 village Umm al-Faraj in the Galilee, where a mosque and a graveyard remained on the outskirts of the *moshav* (agricultural community) Ben-Ami, which had been built on the village's ruins. These remnants were now bulldozed by the people of the *moshav*. The police refused the request of the committee to demonstrate there, claiming the site was private property. After a legal struggle a limited demonstration was allowed.

And thus *Nakbah* day became a new landmark on the calendar. It was first commemorated around 15 May 1998, the day of Israel's foundation – as it still is around the world – but it was later decided also to mention it during the official Israeli independence celebrations, which are fixed according to the Hebrew calendar. The Jewish public, and quite a few Palestinian families, use this holiday for picnics and recreational activities in the forests, many of them planted on the ruins of Palestinian villages. These two very different types of visit to the Jewish National Fund parks so far precariously coexist.

The first such day, on 15 May 1998, was impressive, with demonstrations, commemorative ceremonies, the waving of Palestinian flags and carrying of posters showing the names of the destroyed villages. *Nakbah* day was also commemorated in the occupied territories and a growing sense of joint fate and future was strengthened. In the 1998 commemoration a speech by Mahmoud Darwish was broadcast to a huge gathering in Nazareth. In it he said: 'As the Jews have the right to demand from Europe reparation for the damage caused by the Nazis in Europe, so do we have right to demand reparations for the damage caused by the Israelis.' Still, only a few villages went as far as the people of Ailut west of Nazareth, who built a memorial listing the names of the people in the village massacred by Israeli troops in 1948. The absence of other landmarks of this sort reflected not so much fear of the official Israeli response as a wish not to deal openly with a repressed and painful past.

The awareness of the crucial role played by the *Nakbah* in the Palestinian identity reinforced the links between Palestinians in Israel and the occupied territories, both in the political and in the cultural realms. During this period, Palestinians could holiday in Egypt and Jordan (where they could take their cars after Israel signed a peace treaty with the Hashemite Kingdom), and could also visit Damascus and Beirut as politicians and public figures, especially from 1997 onwards, when the government in Damascus and Hezbollah became more interested in the fate of the Palestinians in Israel and started to invite them. Of course these visits were widely condemned by the Israeli authorities and eventually landed some of the visitors in Israeli courts for allegedly 'conspiring with alien states'. But culturally this also fortified the Palestinians' sense of belonging to the majority culture in the area.

The other side of the cultural coin was the beginning of the artistic appreciation in Israel of works produced by Palestinians. Asim Abu Shaqra from Umm al-Fahem, Abed Abidi and Issa Dibi from Haifa exhibited their work in Jewish galleries, heralding a new era in which cultural identity expressed from below challenged the values imposed from above. Documentary and feature films continued to be an important medium through which national affiliations and aspirations were expressed, as poetry and plays had been in the past. The annual convening of the Palestinian film festival in Nazareth was one manifestation of the institutionalization of the new cultural assertiveness. There was one new and crucial development: in the vast majority of cases, these displays of cultural autonomy were tolerated by the state, even if not officially recognized. In around 2010, important sectors in the second Netanyahu government, elected in 2009, would try to turn the clock backwards and brand this autonomous behaviour as a kind of treason and disloyalty to the Jewish state.

The Islamic movement was less concerned with films, but found its own way to connect with the past, turning scores of destroyed mosques and tombs of holy Muslim men all around the country into sites of pilgrimage and landmarks. Most notable is the tomb of Izz al-Din al-Qassam, a Syrian preacher who participated in the Syrian revolt against the French in 1925 and was tried *in absentia* for his role and fled to Haifa. He became a popular preacher there, calling in his sermons for a personal return to Islam alongside a fervent collective struggle against the pro-Zionist policy of the British Mandate. He recruited Palestinians from the shanty towns around Haifa and made guerrilla units out of them that attacked British installations and Jewish settlers, until he was killed by British forces in 1935 and was buried in the Palestinian village Balad al-Shaykh. At the end of 1947 the village was attacked by the Jewish militia, the Haganah, which massacred many of the villagers in retaliation for a bloody assault on Jewish workers in the nearby refinery complex. The rest of the villagers were expelled in May 1948 and in its stead a Jewish settlement was built by the name of Nesher. Only the graveyard and a few houses remained.

Al-Qassam is revered by the leaders of the Hamas movement, who named after him both their military wing, the Al-Qassam Brigades, and the primitive missiles they launched into Israel in the early twenty-first century. The movement's activists cleaned up his deserted tomb and the al-Istiqlal mosque where he preached in Haifa, even though the municipality had surrounded the mosque by a new highway, which drives through the adjacent Muslim graveyard. In September 1997 Jewish activists of the right desecrated the tomb with a pig's head and the Nesher municipality refused to allow easy access to the devoted activists. But they continued to keep clean the tomb of this man who is a hero in the Palestinian pantheon and a villain in the Zionist narrative.

NEW POLITICS OF IDENTITY

If the Islamic movement and Adalah demonstrated two ways by which the Palestinians in Israel could seek change in the last years of the twentieth century (and their limitations), Azmi Bishara showed a third one. His own personality and the circumstances of the 1990s led him to venture not only to head a national party but also to stand as the first Palestinian for the post of prime minister, in a state where this should at least theoretically be possible. The Israeli electoral system had been changed in the 1990s and the electorate now voted separately for a party and a prime minister. Bishara presented his candidacy for the 1999 elections and immediately the Israeli right appealed to the Supreme Court to nullify it. They based their claim on an interview Bishara gave *Haaretz* on 29 May 1998, in which he said that Israel would have to be a state of all its citizens, and expressed his vision of a bi-national state covering all of historical Palestine. The right-wing parties lost and Bishara ran. Of course he did not win, but he made his point. It gave many Palestinians pleasure to hear the secret service offer to give Bishara an escort, as they had to for every candidate for such a high post, and to hear Bishara decline.

Other political attempts to assert a national position were also relatively successful despite the efforts by the Israeli right to stop them. But more often than not there was a limit to how far this freedom went. A new party emerged in the late 1990s, Ra'am (acronym in Hebrew for Joint Arab List); it was banned from showing footage of the violence of the police against demonstrators in its party political broadcasts, and the comparison made by one of its leaders, Hashem Mahamid, between the treatment of Palestinians in Israel and apartheid in South Africa, was censored. Even images of the harassment of the Bedouins in the Negev were omitted.[10]

These broadcasts would have shown Jewish viewers a reality they were not informed about, although probably many would have not been moved by it. The Ra'am video depicted the activities of the

'Green Commandos', whom we mentioned before as the special section of the 'Israeli Nature Reserve Authority' that perceived the Bedouin in the Negev as a disruptive element in the southern desert. The clip showed the commandos at work, setting fire to and spreading poison in the Bedouin's fields, and confiscating their herds in the name of ecology and environmental policies. The Bedouin were pushed into new areas allocated to them by the government, like the reservations of Native Americans in the USA. All these images were removed from the small screen to avoid any potential incidents of incitement arising from the material shown.

This period ended with Hadash, the Communist Party, for the first time attempting to submit a draft law that specifically stated the need to grant equality to the Palestinian citizens of Israel and defined Israel as a democratic and multicultural state. The party felt that the afore-mentioned Human Rights Law was too vague to address to the needs of the Palestinian community in Israel. The legal advisors of the Knesset argued that the proposed Hadash law would negate Israel as a Jewish state, and, as expected, it was rejected by the majority of the Jewish members.

By this time the transformation of Hadash into a more determined, national party was completed. It still had a Jewish constituency of a few thousand, which grew a little in the next century with the total demise of the Zionist left in the wake of the second *Intifada*. This is why it was not surprising to see Hadash organizing the main demonstrations in support of Iraq when, in 1998, it seemed for a moment that another Gulf war was about to erupt. The village of Tira witnessed the largest demonstrations in support of Saddam Hussein in that year. As in 1991, the despairing perception of the American–Israeli alliance as the major obstacle to any chance of alleviating Palestinian suffering led to this show of support for a ruler who had done very little himself to help the Palestinians.

A NEW CIVIL SOCIETY

The creation of a Palestinian civil society, partly in response to the failure of the Oslo Accords, meant the emergence of quite a few new

NGOs pushing forward the civic agenda, even at times at the expense of the national one. At the very end of the twentieth century and the beginning of the new one, even more NGOs appeared, expanding further the areas in which Palestinians took their destiny into their own hands.

One such was Mada al-Carmel, which appeared in 2000 as the main intellectual and academic Palestinian research body outside the state and private universities. In this modest outfit in Wadi Nisnas in Haifa, doctoral as well post-doctoral Palestinian graduates could, for a while at least, put their academic qualifications to good use for their own community without worrying about political censorship or ideological monitoring. Another important NGO was Mussawa ('Equality'), created for the purpose of monitoring, as it has done since 2005, the level of racism and discrimination inside Israel. Together with the Follow-Up Committee for Arab Education it pressured the Israeli Ministry of Education to increase the budgets and reduce the oppressive supervision of the Arab school system.

The initiative for more equal footing within the universities was also pursued towards the end of the twentieth century by the 'Arab student committees', who organized demonstrations, often (unlike in the past) authorized by the university authorities, at which they showed their solidarity with both the general Palestinian struggle and the other forces fighting for civic development. The sense that the oppressive features of life could perhaps be removed by legal and civic action was made manifest in the struggle against the authorities of the University of Haifa in 1997, when protestors challenged the long-established managerial practice of punishing students for participating in unauthorized demonstrations with sanctions including expulsion from the university. This struggle continued until 2000, with partial successes.[11]

In many ways the mushrooming of NGOs was the result of the failure of the political parties of the Palestinians in Israel to deliver tangible changes in the reality – although the latter nonetheless faithfully represented the collective identity and aspirations of the community. There were more than fifty such organizations by the end of the century, and a particular NGO, Ittijah, was formed to direct and coordinate this vitality and energy. In a more theoretical book this activity would be contextualized in a deeper analysis of what is fashionably called 'civil society'. But this author is not a keen admirer of the term or the concept, and I will just list the works which have done this in an endnote.

Here it will suffice to note that all of them had two features in common, which probably amounts to a 'civil society' in the making or the emergence of a 'third sector', another favourite term that Israeli sociologists in particular like to use. The first was a critical examination of the level of discrimination against Palestinians in Israel: in education, welfare, health services, communication and media, employment and so on. The second was an attempt to empower citizens to improve some of society's malaises themselves: abuse of women and children, poverty, and hereditary illness born out of tradition and prejudice, to mention but a few.[12]

There was a third agenda in between the civic and the national one, which at the time was defined as cultural autonomy. All the outfits and individuals mentioned so far contributed to its emergence. Legally, this was the struggle to protect collective cultural rights, inspired by the model of the French Canadians, the Swedes in Finland and other minority populations. The modest request to have signposts in Arabic was the precursor to a wider campaign, which amongst other things demanded more influence on the content of the curriculum such that the Palestinian narrative would be taught in schools. One particular NGO, Ibn Khaldun, founded by As'ad Ghanem and based in Tamara in the lower Galilee, was particularly effective in pushing forward this agenda.

But the reference to culture should not mislead the reader; nationalism was still a potent force, which defined not only the collective but also individual and even gender activism. This predominance of nationalism caused a split within feminist activity in Israel. Jewish feminists saw a-nationalism, or even anti-nationalism, as crucial, but Palestinian women activists felt that, despite the centrality of the gender issue, they did not wish to give up their national framework and identification. A small group of Mizrahi activists felt the same and founded a group called 'My Sister', Achoti, with a stress on Arab culture alongside gender as a point of reference. A particularly delicate issue was the abuse of women, which in Western professional literature was attributed to religion and tradition. Feminist activists in Israel such as Nabila Espanioly and Aida Touma-Suliman and many others decided to establish their own asylum centres for victims of such violence in 1997, explaining that their 'mission is to return to separate frameworks in which we can develop and maintain a distinct national Palestinian identity'.[13]

The invasion of ethnic and national questions of identity into the overall struggle against state co-optation and oppression left very few aspects of life outside the realm of ideology and politics. And when it came to negative aspects – for instance, of traditional patterns of behaviour – the only way to cope with them was, as in the case of women's abuse, by assigning it to 'the civil society' and not to a governmental agency, or to an Arab–Jewish venture. The positive side of this reality was that, at the very end of this century, the society did indeed begin to tackle questions of bigamy, corporal punishment in schools and honour killings of women.

But there was also space for those who wished to enhance individual rights. There were Palestinians both in the exile communities around the world and inside Israel who were not deeply or even slightly involved in politics, even if they were looking for individual ways of expressing their identity and vision. One such person was the film-maker Elia Suleiman, one of the few Palestinian artists whose work, as he put it, gave 'vent to an absolutely individualistic point of view'.[14] His many films, the most famous of which was *Chronicle of Disappearance*, tried to challenge the collective memory and its obedience to a nationalized space or present. This was probably the boldest attempt to think of the Palestinian condition away from the usual advocacy of the right of return and the unification of old Palestine as a nation state. Suleiman's work was critical of the old ways of articulating identity, and could have opened the way for different thinking, had there been a reality to which this courageous view could relate.

All these demands and possible avenues were still part of the agenda after the outbreak of the second *Intifada* in 2000, but some of them were marginalized for a long while as a result of this most serious crisis between the Jewish state and its Palestinian citizens. The first sign of things to come was during the 1999 elections. On the face of it there was a successful constellation of political forces of the Israeli left organized to topple the right-wing Netanyahu government. For liberal Zionists, another term in office for the Likud leader seemed the worst-case scenario. The mood in the Palestinian community, however, was different. On the eve of the elections a movement appeared calling on voters to cast a 'white ballot', to express a total mistrust in the system. For the first time in years, the number of Palestinian voters – traditionally it was higher than the Jewish vote, at around 80–85 per cent of the electorate – dwindled. With the obvious danger of generalization, they had developed a different position from that of their traditional allies on the Jewish side. They felt they could no longer see much of a difference between the right and left in the Israeli Jewish political camp.[15]

The aftermath of the 1999 elections proved their point. The new government did not include the Israeli Palestinians in its coalition, and the exclusionary policies of the past Labour governments were now adopted by the newly elected Prime Minister Ehud Barak, formerly the IDF Chief of General Staff, delivering another blow to the hopes of the previous five years. It was clear now that despite the discourse before the elections of 1999 being Israel's moment of truth – in particular concerning the Palestine issue, where almost seven years after Oslo no significant progress towards peace had been recorded – there was no genuine internal debate. Politics reflected inertia rather than the power to change.

ON THE WAY TO THE SECOND *INTIFADA*

The first task of the government was indeed to try to bring the negotiations with the Palestinian Authority to a fruitful end. The heated debate within Jewish society in the wake of Rabin's assassination had totally subsided. The Israeli government called upon the PLO to accept unconditionally its peace programme: the creation of a demilitarized 'Bantustan' without independent foreign or economic policy and without the huge settlement blocks in Gaza, the Greater Jerusalem area, the Hebron Mountains or the Jordan valley. In return for this reduced concept of a 'Palestine', the PLO was asked to declare the end of the conflict and the end to all its previous demands, including the right of the Palestinian refugees to return to their homes. Needless to say, the future of the Palestinians in Israel was not part of the programme.

This *diktat* was accepted by the majority of Jewish members of the Knesset, and even the right-wing opposition accepted the basic outlines of the programme with few reservations. From Peace Now on the left – once a natural ally of the Palestinians in Israel – to Gush Emunim on the right, there was a wide consensus on the nature of the conflict's solution. Unfortunately, it was a position that only deepened the already wide gap between Palestinians and Jews in Israel.

It became painfully clear to the Palestinians in Israel that the old dichotomy between Labour and Likud no longer reflected the Israeli internal debate on the critical issues concerning the minority. Indeed, Labour (the hegemonic representation of Zionism since 1882 until its fall from power in the 1977 elections) and Likud (the heir of the Zionist faction, Herut, an alternative, more ethnocentric and segregative variant of Zionism known as Revisionism that rose to challenge Labour's Zionism as of 1922) had effectively coalesced into one major ideological stream.[16] For despite the bitter antagonism that has separated them historically, and despite Labour's loss at the polls in 1977, it was Labour's vision that prevailed over the Revisionist commitment to total sovereignty over the whole of historical Palestine. It was Labour's vision, in which Likud essentially acquiesced, that became the principal prism through which the political centre and professional elites in Israel viewed the Israel–Palestine reality.

To be fair one should add that the above analysis was clear in the mind of academics and professionals who closely followed political developments in Israel. The Palestinian citizens themselves were still more apprehensive of a Likud government in 1996 than a Labour one. And thus for instance in the village of Tira in the Triangle a black flag was waved after Netanyahu's victory and, as retaliation, an unknown person planted a bomb in the town hall.[17] But after the 1999 election of Ehud Barak and Labour, this sense of a united Zionist front was also shared by the vast majority of the Palestinian citizens in Israel.

But Israel was not a totally homogenous society in 2000, at least less so than it would be nine years later. Despite the convergence of the two mega-parties into one stream, there were still two main variants to the hegemonic ideology: post-Zionism and neo-Zionism. The first, articulated more clearly in 2000 than it had been in the late 1980s when it first came to prominence, strongly criticized Zionist policy and conduct before and after 1948, accepted many of the claims made by the Palestinians concerning 1948 itself, and envisioned a non-Jewish state in Israel as the best solution for the country's internal and external predicaments. As such, it presented a point of view acceptable to large numbers of Palestinian citizens in Israel. But due to the events described in the next chapter, the movement itself almost disappeared and therefore the potential political alliance that it could have produced did not materialize. Thus post-Zionism did not become a political challenge. The post-Zionist success was in legitimizing abroad, more than in Israel, hitherto taboo topics of great relevance to the internal debate in Israel: the nature of Zionism, Israel's moral conduct in 1948, the refugee problem and so on. The impact was felt mainly abroad since academia and the educational system in Israel succeeded in eliminating the post-Zionist challenge in the next decade.[18]

The main political challenge to traditional Zionism came from the right, from a fundamentalist Zionism termed by some as 'neo-Zionism'. From the perspective of the Palestinians in Israel, neo-Zionism was a violent and extreme interpretation of Zionism. It existed as a marginal variant of Zionism both in the Labour and the revisionist camps and was nourished in the teaching centres controlled by the religious Zionist Hapoel Hamizrachi (which became the National Religious Party, Mafdal). It burst forth as an official alternative after the 1967 war, pushed forward by expansionists among the Labour movement, leaders of the newly established Likud, and leading rabbis. In the 1980s, neo-Zionism widened its constituency by forming alliances with the settlers in the occupied territories and the deprived and marginalized sectors of Jewish society. Whether North African Jews, or immigrants from the ex-Soviet Union who had not made it in Israeli society, the neo-Zionist outfit sold them anti-Arab racism as the best and lowest common denominator for political action. When rabbis threw in a theological flavour for such ideas they became even more powerful and threatening to the Palestinian minority in Israel. It began with a whisper, but by the beginning of the next century it was common to read, especially in the local regional newspapers, the chief Sephardi rabbi of Safad, or Lid, warning against too many Arabs roaming their cities or 'kidnapping' innocent Jewish girls. When these people had access to a local radio station, in what became a kind of Israeli bible-belt broadcasting, their poisonous and racist tongues would know no boundaries. This kind of rhetoric was accompanied by the establishment of special organizations to protect Jewish lives in these areas, mostly underdeveloped towns on the margins of the state, and 'salvage' the few hundred Jewish women who – God forbid – fell in love with Palestinians from nearby villages.

This was part of a wider problem. The Jews who came from Arab countries have traditionally been an electorate of the right in Israel, in terms not so much of the debate about the future of the occupied territories as of their attitude towards the Palestinians inside Israel. However, the sociological research is not definitive nor is this group homogenous. They were nonetheless an important part of the alliance that maintained the neo-Zionist point of view: an uneasy pact between expansionist nationalists, ultra-orthodox rabbis and ethnic spiritual leaders of the Mizrahi Jews, all presenting themselves as champions of underprivileged Mizrahim. One important party, Shas, through its spiritual leader, Rabbi Ovadia Yosef, resorted more and more to racist remarks about Arabs as part of its attempt to widen the ranks (often including references to the right to conduct genocide on them: 'We should destroy and eliminate the Arabs,' he said).[19] Shas being a very cynical political movement, however, when holding the Ministry of Interior it did not refrain from promising benefits to the Palestinian community should their representatives in the Knesset support the religious legislation Shas wanted to push forward. Parties like Shas, and its predecessor in the Ministry of Interior, the national religious party Mafdal, were also able to persuade and sometimes bribe a few *Hammulas* in the rural areas to vote for them *en masse*.

These political and ideological developments inspired considerable apprehension among the Palestinians in Israel. The move to the right had commenced with the election of Netanyahu in 1996, but the whole political leadership now lost any interest in advancing the Oslo Accords and missed opportunities to mend fences and maybe leave some hope for the future – opportunities which had been spotted very clearly by the Palestinians in Israel. One such was Yasser Arafat's visit to the Holocaust museum in Lohamei Hagetaot (a kibbutz in the north of Israel) after he was disinvited by the Holocaust museum in Washington. The visit was condemned from left to right and the process of reconciling the traumas of both sides was cut dead when it was just beginning to bud. Azmi Bishara, who wrote several articles against Holocaust denial in the Arab world and among the Palestinians, commented despairingly, 'Finally a Palestinian leader acknowledges your suffering and you reject him.'[20]

In September 1997, Prime Minister Ehud Barak asked for forgiveness from the Mizrahi Jews for years of discrimination, a gesture ridiculed at every level by the Palestinians in Israel, who had organized a national strike on the same day to protest against their discrimination. *Al-Ittihad* called upon Barak to ask for forgiveness from the Palestinians in Israel, a request that, needless to say, went unheeded. On the other hand, at an official ceremony in October 1997 commemorating the Kafr Qassem massacre, the President, Moshe Kazav, asked for forgiveness in the name of the state. For many Palestinians this seemed too late, and was christened by the press as the butcher's apology (*Kazav* means 'butcher' in Hebrew).

Many felt that it was too late for Israeli gestures. When the Israeli Association for Civil Rights demanded that a Palestinian Israeli be a member of the Israel Land Administration, Amir Makhoul, a leading figure in the developing civil society (and the brother of Issam Makhoul, a long-serving Hadash member of the Knesset) wrote that this was a patronizing act that was not genuine or practical, since the Palestinian representative would be a lonely voice in a body which would continue to adopt plans for further expropriation of Palestinian land and space.[21]

The relationship between the Jews and the Palestinians in Israel would worsen in the next century, but it was already bad enough. When an Israeli helicopter in southern Lebanon crashed in an air accident and more than seventy soldiers died in February 1997, Azmi Bishara explained to *Haaretz*, Palestinians in Israel 'are barred from joining in the mourning as this was not an innocent accident; it occurred during an occupation of an Arab country, an occupation with which they could not identify'.[22] In Israel's only Arab–Jewish community, Wahat al-Salam or Neve Shalom ('Peace Oasis'), one parent who lost his son in the accident sought to call a sports facility after him, creating the worst crisis in the relationship between the two ethnic groups, from which they still have not recovered today. As Bishara mentioned, for the Palestinians, even within the context of a mixed community, there was no problem in respecting the private grief of a member of the community, but commemoration in a public space in their eyes endorsed the legitimacy of the occupation of Lebanon during which the accident occurred.

Despite this difficult atmosphere, however, individuals, parties and NGOs continued trying to communicate with government in the closing years of the twentieth century. In one area, that of schools, an uneasy dialogue continued throughout the 1990s with some relative success in getting bigger budgets, more schools and more freedom in determining the curriculum.

The movement to the centre of politics of ideas and platforms which had previously been confined to Kahana and Kach explains why his son and successor, Binyamin Zeev Kahana, was such a failure. He did send threatening pamphlets everywhere suggesting that Umm al-Fahem, the major Palestinian town in Wadi Ara, should be bombed and that sort of thing, but he was also prosecuted by the State Attorney (although the Supreme Court let him go unpunished). He was killed in an attack on his car in the occupied West Bank. His successors continued to try to provoke in a similar way, but they have become less significant in the overall deteriorating picture.

With the demise of Oslo, even before the outbreak of the second *Intifada*, the gap between neo-Zionism and mainstream Zionism regarding possible solutions about the occupied territories narrowed to insignificant proportions (although it would be revived for a short while over the decision of Ariel Sharon's government to evict the Jewish settlers from the Gaza Strip in 2005). But the vision of the future was not just a matter of defining borders or containing Palestinian national aspirations. It was also a matter of identity and the essence of the society. This vision was formed by an alliance of settlers, ultra-orthodox and secular Russian immigrants, who had their own party, Israel Beitenu ('Israel is our Home'). The leader of the latter was Avigdor Lieberman who would become a senior minister, and, as we shall see in the next chapter, would contribute more than anyone else to the dissemination of a racist anti-Arab discourse and legislation. The alliance also had scholarly support in the form of a think-tank, modelled on similar neoconservative outfits in the USA. They all offered a simplistic image of the reality whereby the fault line of exclusion and inclusion in the common good was clearer than ever before: the Palestinians in Israel were not included.

Against this background, at the very end of the twentieth century, a sort of Palestinian elite emerged that would succeed in mobilizing its community in the next critical juncture – that of the second *Intifada* of October. Who was this elite made of? This was a much more educated, some would say more modern, group of leaders and activists. They understood better than their predecessors the nature and loopholes of the Israeli political, legal and social systems. But this was also a very frustrated professional elite. The dramatic increase in the number of high schools and high-school graduates over the previous fifty years meant that a large number of them had gone to university, although many fewer Palestinians applied and were accepted compared to Jewish applicants. Some suspected this gap was ideologically motivated and engineered by means of psychometric exams; the little known and still inaccessible information concerns quota policies in the professional courses such as medicine and law.

The second source of frustration was the lack of job opportunities for those who graduated successfully from the universities. Their best chance was usually a teaching position in a school. Seventy per cent of the teachers in Arab schools in the 1990s held university degrees that had very little to do with the careers they have chosen.[23]

Employment in areas which were security-related, even loosely so, such as the national telephone or electricity companies, offered hardly any positions to Palestinian citizens. This included El-Al, the national air carrier, the water authority and governmental ministries in general. An intriguing exception was the tax collection agencies; there seemed to be fewer objections to installing Palestinians in the most unpopular governmental agency. Knowledge and education also made people more informed about the level of discrimination. The official publications, which proudly proclaimed that resources were more equally distributed between Palestinians and Jews, were now closely read and examined against a reality of disparity that hardly changed.

The effect of these socio-economic realities was heightened by consistent references to the Palestinians in Israel as a demographic danger.[24] Such references became very common in the closing years of the twentieth century. They were made by leading academics, senior ministers including the various prime ministers, the daily newspapers and anchormen and women in the media. As a headline in the daily newspaper *Yediot Achronot* cried, 'The demography of the Arabs in Israel is the next ticking bomb threatening the state of Israel.'[25] These references were far more important signifiers of the regime's attitude than the nice poster the government prepared for the Israel jubilee celebrations, showing the children who made up the new Israeli society: a Russian Jew, an Ethiopian Jew, a religious Jew, a secular *Sabra* (a native-born Israeli Jew) and an Arab. This was the second version prepared for the Day of Independence; the first one did not include the Arab boy.

The twentieth century closed with a bitter but poignant letter by the Palestinian author Anton Shammas from his voluntary exile in the USA to his many Hebrew readers in the fashionable weekly, *Hair* of Tel Aviv: 'The Zionist adventure has been an utter failure. True, the desert bloomed, but in its stead intoxicated wilderness covered the land.'[26]

CHAPTER SEVEN

THE 2000 EARTHQUAKE AND ITS IMPACT

IT IS NOT DIFFICULT to choose the image to represent the last decade of our story. All the possibilities come from three days in October 2000. It could be the picture of police snipers shooting at a gathering of youth who were throwing stones and blazing bottles. It could also be Asil Asleh, aged eighteen and a member of one of the very few Arab–Jewish youth peace movements, Seeds for Peace, who was shot at close range by a police officer when sitting under a tree as he watched the demonstration and clashes in his town of Sakhnin. It could be the image of twenty-six-year-old Wesam Yazbak, the nephew of the leading Palestinian historian in Israel and later president of the Israeli Oriental Society Mahmoud Yazbak, who was shot in the back while trying to calm down his comrades in the narrow alleys in Nazareth. It could be the two young women being beaten in front of the camera by the special police units for just walking along the main road between Yafat al-Nasrah and Nazareth.

The images presented to the Jewish public were different, of course. The keynote of their newspapers and radio and TV contributors was 'back to 1948', showing isolated Jewish settlements in the Galilee stormed by masses of people, cut off by stoning on the roads leading to their homes and a sense of insecurity unknown before. It was the age of the second *Intifada*, which had subsided by 2010 in the West Bank and inside Israel, but which still smoulders on in the Gaza Strip.

THE OCTOBER 2000 'EVENTS'

The second *Intifada* raged from October 2000. It spilled over into Israel itself, where the old frustrations of the Palestinian minority burst out in solidarity with the Palestinians killed in Jerusalem in the confrontations that followed the visit of the then opposition leader, Ariel Sharon, to Haram al-Sharif, the holiest Islamic site in Palestine and the third sacred site after Mecca and Medina. Unarmed Palestinians went out to protest against the Sharon visit as well as against the failure of the Oslo Accords and promises. Palestinians on both sides of the Green Line rejected Israeli and American accusations that the extremism of the Palestinian leadership was responsible for this failure. Despite his declining popularity, large sections of the community resented the demonization of Yasser Arafat as a warmonger for refusing to accept the Israeli *diktat* for peace in the Camp David Summit in the summer of 2000.

But more than anything else, Sharon's visit triggered a response from people whose hopes had been falsely raised for a moment only to be hurled to the floor as unattainable and illusionary. Thirty-three years of occupation seemed to be far from reaching an end, notwithstanding the charade of peace and negotiations. And when women, men and youngsters went into the streets to demonstrate, they were met by the fully equipped Israeli border police.

The Follow-Up Committee and leading politicians among the Palestinians in Israel proposed days of solidarity in the old way of calling a national strike and a huge public gathering. In response, a huge demonstration was staged in Umm al-Fahem in Wadi Ara in a show of solidarity with the Palestinians in the occupied territories. More spontaneous demonstrations took place in villages located near some of Israel's main highways and newly built outposts, recently erected as part of the Judaization of the Galilee. On these spots, sensitive locations for both communities, the demonstrators blocked the roads and in some cases began marching into these settlements, many of them gated communities where people had been oblivious until that moment to how Palestinian was the environment in which they had settled, on land confiscated from the locals.[1]

It is worth mentioning that the Judaization of the Galilee, which was the main trigger for the Day of the Land events in 1976, was an ongoing process. And therefore even when the agenda of a particular juncture such as the one in October 2000 was outrage against the Israeli occupation of the West Bank and the Gaza Strip, the two agendas, the land confiscation and the occupation, fused into one. This connection was recognized by the Orr Commission, the official inquiry committee appointed by the government to investigate the causes for, and the events of, October 2000, of which more is said later. The report summarized what various Palestinian NGOs and human rights activists had been saying for years, in Hebrew, and what had been written in the numerous memoranda submitted since 1976 to government agencies, which it seems no one had read or paid any attention to.[2]

The Orr Commission singled out the Israeli policy of land confiscation as one of the main causes for the frustration among the Palestinians in Israel. The problem was the absence of any master planning that would have approved expansion and building of new houses and flats. The official excuse for not allowing any new building, or extensions to existing buildings, between 1976 and 2000, was the absence of these master plans. But of course they were not created because ideologically the Jewish state did not want to allow its Palestinian community to improve its living conditions, or at least did not care about the predicament of insufficient living space.

The committee, in a very subdued tone compared to the one used by the investigative NGOs, including the Israeli Association for Civil Rights, stated 'that the natural rights and needs of the Arab population were not met or cared for'.[3] What they did not mention was a far worse aspect of the land policy of Israel. These natural needs led to illegal building on a large scale, which was met by an aggressive policy of house and flat demolitions. As mentioned earlier, in Jaffa and Ramleh alone during that period, thousands of flats and houses were demolished and a similar policy was implemented wherever Palestinians lived in the Jewish state. In October 2000, it was the sight of a demolished flat or house and not a knowledge of the discriminatory policy that impelled demonstrators to risk a direct confrontation with the might of the Israeli forces.[4]

The organized demonstration in Umm al-Fahem and the sporadic protest marches began on 1 October 2000. From the Israeli police's point of view the most dangerous development was the actions by a small number of demonstrators who left the main event and stationed themselves on the Wadi Ara highway connecting the city of Hadera to the city of Afula, blocking it and stoning passing cars suspected of being driven by Jews. The police reacted with live ammunition, which was unprecedented inside Israel but quite common in the occupied territories. Whether from above, or on the ground, commanders and officers decided this was the West Bank and not Israel proper. The uprising spread elsewhere, with the same scenes of demonstrations and retaliation with rubber bullets and live ammunition. It lasted for a week and became known as the 'Events of October'.

A second wave began on 7 October and involved violent attacks by Jewish citizens on Palestinian cars, neighbourhoods and citizens, propelled not only by the disturbances elsewhere but also by the kidnap of three soldiers by Hezbollah in the north. The battlefield between the citizens was the border zone connecting Nazareth and Upper Nazareth. By around 10 October it was all over. The balance of dead and wounded was worse than that of 1976. Thirteen Israeli Palestinian citizens had been shot dead by the police; one Jewish citizen died when a stone hit his car on the Haifa–Tel Aviv road. Hundreds were wounded and thousands were arrested.

These violent confrontations have already been the subject of scholarly research. Several reasons were suggested for their ferocity, making the same points as those mentioned by the inquiry commission appointed by the government at the end of October 2000. The first is the conventional sociological theory of uprisings, which is depicted as an accumulative process of oppression that becomes at one point unbearable – quite often due to a mundane rather a dramatic event – and then the volcanic mountain erupts. This was also used to explain the connection between a road accident in December 1987 in Gaza and the eruption of the first *Intifada*.[5]

Other explanations were more specific, such as the disappointment with Ehud Barak's government, which had been elected in 1999 with the help of the Palestinian electorate. The religious aspect of Sharon's visit of course touched a nerve in the more Islamic sections of the community, and even in those who were more secular and saw the violation as a national rather than a religious slur. The Israeli authorities and the official inquiry committee also blamed the politicians of the Palestinian community for incitement – but this does not appear as a significant cause for the consequences of the clashes with the police and indeed 'incitement' when used by governments on such occasions quite often could mean motivation to respond to, and representation of, the people's own feelings on a given issue – which is how most scholarly analyses of the event tend to explain it.

One of these leaders, Azmi Bishara, asserted that the main reason for the vast demonstration, overshadowing any other agenda, was solidarity with the Palestinians under occupation. He pointed out that a consensual body, the Follow-Up Committee (made up of all the Palestinian members of the Knesset, directors of NGOs and heads of municipalities), had called for the general protest and was fully heeded. In other words, it was not the actions of some radical elements that dragged the community as a whole into the demonstrations; it was a reflection of wide sections of the community and a position that united all the political parties and factions in it.[6]

But Bishara's main point was that it was not meant to be a violent clash, and when such days of solidarity were organized again, when Israel attacked Lebanon in 2006 and carried out its Operation 'Defensive Shield' on the West Bank in April 2002 and 'Cast Lead' in January 2009, a restrained police and army reaction produced very different results. It is I think now clear that the reaction of the police and the army, prodded by the Shabak's insistence on the need to be ruthless in such scenarios, inflated and inflamed a crisis that could have ended differently. Bishara's point has been substantiated by a recent PhD dissertation on the issue of mobilization in the October events. The high level of mobilization of the community, by a leadership that carried very little authority, lacked organizational skills and was not always respected, was remarkable and unprecedented.[7]

What all concerned agree upon was that somehow things got out of hand, whether the narrative is the official Israeli one of an 'incited mob' that had to be contained, or the more suspicious Palestinian one that the security octopus of Israel had been looking for a long time for an opportunity to intimidate and silence the assertive national minority. The first official narrative described a violent demonstration, not enough policemen on the spot, a real danger to neighbouring Jewish settlements – towards which some groups of demonstrators gravitated with anger – and the use of live ammunition by one or two demonstrators, all of which resulted in an excessive police reaction that ended in the killing of thirteen citizens (mainly from snipers' fire).

The Palestinians in Israel's narrative, to which the author of this book also subscribes – not as an objective observer but as someone who was there on the ground – is summarized well by several Palestinian scholars who wrote on the affair. They suggest that the Israeli modus operandi became evident when the first demonstration gathered in October 2000. The police, the border police, the secret service and the *Mistaravim* (covert agents disguised as Arabs and already used to infiltrate the occupied territories) infiltrated the Palestinian villages and towns and were supported from above by snipers who fired live ammunition into the crowd or coldbloodedly approached the demonstrators and killed them. If one can summarize the Palestinian take on what lay behind October 2000, it would be to say that this was an institutional use of state power to deliver a message to a fifth of its population: be docile and accept your status as second-class citizens, or encounter the wrath of the army and security forces.

The Palestinian NGO Mussawa ('Equality' in Arabic) probably represented the consensus in the community well when it depicted the events as the following: 'in response to a demonstration by unarmed Arab citizens in response to the violation of Haram al-Sharif by Ariel Sharon, the Israeli police shot live ammunition at the demonstrators and killed thirteen citizens'. A similar depiction can be seen in Adalah's detailed examination of the report:

> At the beginning of October 2000, many of the Arab citizens of Israel protested against the oppressive Israeli policy in the occupied territories. These protests developed and were directed against the lethal actions by the police. As a result thirteen citizens were killed and hundreds were wounded. The police shot live and rubber bullets at the demonstrators, and even used snipers. All in direct violation of the police's own code and regulations.[8]

The clash, namely a national day of protest spilling over from the areas where Palestinians live into exclusive Jewish spaces, roads and highways, was indeed an eruption of frustration over many years of discrimination. But it need not have ended the way it did, had the Israeli police not employed – as they did in 1976 – live ammunition against unarmed citizens. Already in 1998, it was possible to gather from the Israeli mainstream media that the security apparatuses were seriously discussing how to fend off what they saw as a dangerous radicalization among the Palestinians in Israel. From the election of Benjamin Netanyahu as Prime Minister in 1996, the political elite supported the scenario that in times of emergency the traditional policy of co-opting the Palestinians through integration should be pushed aside and a green light be given to the security forces to deal with such a situation according to their understanding.

The excessive use of force was seen before the events of 2000 in the increased number of house demolitions within the Palestinian areas in Israel. In April 1998, helicopters hovered in the air above a small neighbourhood in the south-western margins of the city of Shefa-'Amr. The army and the police encircled this place, Umm al-Sahali, in numbers unseen before in such operations. Similar might was used in the Daliyat al-Ruha area in Umm al-Fahem, and in Wadi Ara, where the army confiscated 500 dunams from the inhabitants to turn them into training fields. The land had been used for pastoral and agricultural purposes for years and its takeover in March 2000 was deemed a pure provocation rather than the result of any shortage of firing spaces for the army.

But the main indicator and precursor for the drama that unfolded in October 2000 was hidden from the public eye. A month before the events the Israeli police ran through a simulation of a large-scale confrontation with the Palestinian population in the north.

> Welcome to the war game 'Tempest'. We are hosting you in the Centre for Police Studies [in Shefa-'Amr]. Fifty-two years ago, this very front, was occupied by Brigades 7 and Golani . . . and here we are still engaged with the same problem as then, not occupying the country but keeping it safe.

Thus opened the commanding officer of the manoeuvre, or more precisely the war game in which the police practised confronting a national day of demonstrations by the Palestinian community in the north. For him such a scenario represented a continuation of the 1948 Israeli War of Independence, when the Palestinian community was the enemy and was ethnically cleansed as a result. The 'Front' was dozens of villages occupied and uprooted, and on one of them the police built its school for junior officers where the meeting took place.[9]

As noted before, reality is murkier than plans, and although the role of the security forces seems to me, ten years later, to be the crucial factor in explaining the severity of what happened, far more important is what this clash revealed. The historian of the Spanish Civil War Professor Shlomo Ben-Ami, who entered politics and was tricked by Ehud Barak into taking the impossible portfolio of the Police Ministry, observed rightly that the fracture exposed the 'genetic code' of the conflict.[10] He was less well-suited to overseeing a police force that, contrary to his orders, used snipers and assault units that were trained to deal with terrorists assaulting civilians; not civilians demonstrating against terrorist policies. He lost his job after that.

MENDING THE FENCES?

Theodore Orr, a judge of the Supreme Court, headed the official inquiry commission that looked into the events in retrospect. He is a Polish Jew who arrived in Palestine in the 1930s and, after practising in private law, entered the judicial system. He was chosen to head the commission as he had worked for most of his career as a judge in Palestinian areas. His main claim to fame until this appointment was his releasing of a well-known Israeli industrialist, Eli Hurvitz, who had been sent to jail by a regional judge.

Established after the leaders of the Palestinian community exerted heavy pressure on Ehud Barak's government, the committee also included the Israeli historian of the Middle East Shimon Shamir and the Palestinian judge Sahil Jarah, who resigned soon after the committee began its deliberations, unhappy with its course, and was replaced by another Palestinian judge, Hashem Khatib. The official website of the

Israeli Ministry of Justice reports that Khatib was born in Israel in 1941 (when of course Israel did not exist). He also served in Palestinian locations such as Acre and Nazareth and of course being a Palestinian in Israel added more symbolic credence to the committee.

The committee began real work only in November 2000 as the leaders of the committee were displeased with its initial limited authority and succeeded in expanding it. The bone of contention was the committee's insistence that its recommendation should lead to the prosecution of those found guilty of violating the law (at the end of the day no such indictments were ever submitted to the Attorney General, despite the promises to do so, nor were post-mortems conducted by the government to confirm or refute the results of private autopsies by the families of the deceased that showed the victims had been shot in the back at close range).

The meetings took place in the Supreme Court building, a new additional bizarre-looking complex on the government hill on the western side of Nazareth. During the early days, one of the police officers accused of shooting unarmed demonstrators, officer Reif, gave testimony. Abd al-Muni'm Add al-Salih, whose son Walid was killed in that incident, could not bear what he felt was the officer's distortion of the truth and approached the bench and kicked the officer in the face. As a result the next testimonies, and there were many of them, were given behind a glass screen that segregated the witnesses from the public. Another police officer, Ayino Attalah, who stood next to Reif – there were quite a few Palestinian policemen and a few officers present during the police attempt to control the demonstrations – testified that Reif was shooting live bullets not only at demonstrators in the village of Kafr Manda, but also at the village's elders who tried to calm down the situation. Reif was the commander of the Misgav police station. Misgav is the main Jewish settlement in the settlement bloc, named Segev, created in the 1970s as part of the second wave of Judaization, referred to earlier on in this book.[11]

The police used this incident as a pretext for limiting the public presence in the committee to forty people, including journalists. Each of the families of the bereaved was allowed only one representative. 'The murderers sit in the hall, and we are thrown out,' commented Asali Hassan, a representative of the families. Jamila Asala, the mother of the youth Asil, told the press that her family got up at 4 a.m. in the morning to get to the hearings and was refused entry: 'Not only did they kill our children, they do not allow to sit in the hall.'

Adalah represented the community at large in these discussions, and the families also established their own committee to make sure that neither the government nor the Palestinian politicians would forget what happened or neglect the inquiry. Palestinian politicians asked, without success, to have a similar standing to that given to the Northern Irish community in the Saville Inquiry into the events of the 1972 Bloody Sunday killings by the British Army, at which the Northern Irish community were treated as equal parties to the government and the army, and their representatives were allowed to be present at all of the proceedings. (Coincidentally, Bloody Sunday also involved the death of thirteen citizens at a demonstration, in that case Irish Catholics killed in Derry. The inquiry, which took place in Derry itself, was established by the British government in 1998 after years of campaigning and following an earlier inquiry that was widely seen as a whitewash of the British forces involved.)

Two years later, letters warning some police officers that they might be prosecuted were sent, but were never acted upon. Apart from the obvious reluctance of the authorities to bring the policemen to trial, it was also a time of political upheaval and instability. During the inquiry the Barak government fell and the first Ariel Sharon government was elected (it was re-elected in 2003). Sharon and his Minister for Internal Security (formerly the Ministry of the Police), the right-wing hardliner Uzi Landau, were hostile to the committee and the submission of the final report in September 2003 was a low-key event. Its conclusions, that blame should be shared between the Arab politicians for 'inciting' the protestors and the police for being ill-prepared, disappointed many Palestinians and left the scars open and wounds still bleeding.

Despite the inquiry, the fences between the two communities were not easily mended. It took time before Jewish customers returned to shop on Saturdays (when Jewish shops are closed) in nearby Palestinian villages and neighbourhoods and dine in their restaurants. But ten years later one can say that slowly this dynamic and active cohabitation is back to what it used to be.

Politically, however, the divide grew and the fences remain broken. In the aftermath of the killing, a new assertive young generation of Palestinians stuck to the strict definition of their community as a national one and demanded in an even clearer voice than before that Israel be made into a state for all its citizens. In turn, they faced an even more ethnocentric, quite racist, Jewish majority, for whom removing the Palestinian minority if things got out of hand was a serious possibility.

One of the most striking absences in the Hebrew and Jewish media discussion of the Orr Report was the apparent lack of interest in the backgrounds of those shot by the police, which did not match in any way the depiction in the Commission of an incited mob or a gang of hooligans, or even over-enthusiastic demonstrators. Similarly, in 2010, following the attack by Israeli commando units on the Turkish flotilla that attempted to break the siege on Gaza, the Israeli press claimed that the initiative was led by terrorists; the local media did not provide the profiles of the nine Turks killed, who were ordinary citizens and not members of al-Qaida. In contrast, any Jewish Israeli soldier or citizen who is killed in a terrorist attack is described in detail and mourned at length in the printed and electronic media.

LONG-TERM IMPLICATIONS

The impact of October 2000 over the next few years was more disastrous than predicted by even the more pessimistic observers. The police legitimized in its own eyes and in the eyes of the public the killing of demonstrators as part of its response. Forty Palestinian citizens were killed by the police in the next few years, although in incidents involving petty crime or mistaken identities rather than at demonstrations. However, demonstrations after these dramatic events were relatively peaceful as the police did not use snipers again, nor did they enter the villages and towns when commemorations of October 2000 and other events took place.

No less worrying for the Palestinian community was the full support the Israeli media gave the police and the lack of any sympathy or solidarity with the victims and their families. Very few critical voices were heard in a democracy when thirteen of its citizens were shot dead. Those who remained silent included some who had been regarded in the past as natural allies of the Palestinian cause inside Israel.

If this narrative of events and its aftermath is accepted then one important fact of life emerges for the first decade of the twenty-first century, which brings this book up to the present. There was nothing spontaneous on either side of the divide about the October 2000 events. The Palestinian community was building a civil society that was able to do what the political elite had failed to do for years – mobilize people to participate in a mass civil disobedience at the right moment. On the other hand, the police were ready for such mass action, responding with a prompt violent reaction, which was meant to send a message that such demonstrations would not be tolerated. The latter message may have been successful for a while, as can been seen by the very low-key mobilizations in response to the 2006 Lebanon war and the 2009 massacre in Gaza.

The structure of this book suggests, however, a more intricate reality. The second half of 1990s was a moment of hope unfulfilled, and the frustration over the false liberal discourse inside Israel and the language of peace in the occupied territories augmented the outrage and the willingness to confront a very powerful regime despite the imbalance of power and past experience. When the bullets began flying on both sides of the Green Line – directed at Palestinians opposing the occupation and against discrimination – the positive energy still remaining in the realm of peace and reconciliation petered out. The Israeli society closed its ranks and talked in one voice, which left the Palestinian minority even farther away than before from the republican common good and located it in the enemy camp with whom official Israel had once more been at war since 2000. The political and educated elites of the Palestinians in Israel lost all belief in 'coexistence', liberal Zionist discourse or a future of change within the present parameters of the Jewish state. 'This is a humiliated, hurt community still able to contain its rage, but only just,' wrote a journalist in *Haaretz* who covered the commemoration of the October events in 2009.[12]

THE POLITICAL DEMISE AND ELIMINATION OF AZMI BISHARA

The public arena for Palestinians in Israel was now moving from one pitfall to another, although none was as bloody or traumatic as the October 2000 events. A year after the October events, public attention was drawn once more to Azmi Bishara.

Since 1999 Bishara had run an individual campaign inspired by his vision for Israel as a state for all its citizens, which the powers that be found difficult to tolerate and accept. His eloquent appearances on television had defeated both many of Zionism's best spokespersons and the Palestinians who collaborated with the state. In 1999, he nearly ran as a candidate for the Prime Minister's post, stretching the pretence of equality almost to breaking point.[13]

Bishara had roamed the Arab world ever since he founded his party: kings, prime ministers and leaders of revolutionary organizations such as Hassan Nasrallah were among the many he embraced and with whom he discussed the future of the area in general and of Palestine in particular. Some of the leaders he met – such as Bashar Assad of Syria, who still holds political prisoners without trial – did not add to his popularity among his voters. But during his decade of activity, no other minority intellectual or politician has achieved what he has in the field of self-assertion and self-dignity.

In November 2001 the Knesset decided to revoke Bishara's parliamentary immunity to open the way to indict him for violating the Prevention of Terrorism Ordinance from 1948 and the fifth regulation of the Emergency Regulations (which covers participation in subversive action against the state). He was accused of twice giving speeches which supported the Palestinian resistance in the occupied territories and praising Hezbollah for forcing the Israeli army out of southern Lebanon.

This was a serious escalation in the authorities' interference with Palestinian freedom of speech in Israel. Can Palestinians support the right of the Palestinians in the occupied territories and the Lebanese forces to resist the occupation by Israel? The answer to this, as rightly pointed out by Richard Falk, depends on whether one interprets this resistance according to Israeli law or to international law. From the international perspective Bishara's speeches were totally legitimate and legal; however, according to the Israeli Emergency Regulations they were deemed to support terrorism.[14] The idea that international law is relevant to the relationship between the state and the national minority is at the heart of the matter of Palestinian citizenship in Israel. After 2000 the 'internationalization' of this issue, or rather predicament, seemed to many Palestinian activists in Israel to be a proper and fruitful strategy. The Israeli authorities, for their part, rejected vehemently such an expansion and struggled hard against those supporting these views.

Bishara won that legal struggle but the campaign against him was not over. In September 2006, he went on a visit to Syria with several members of his party. This was a month and a half after the start of what was called the second Lebanon war: a widespread Israeli military operation against the Hezbollah in response to the abduction of three soldiers on its borders that ended with more than a thousand deaths in Lebanon and hundreds in Israel. Bishara openly backed the Syrian position of supporting Hezbollah and demanding the return of the Golan Heights, and struggling against the Israeli hegemonic position in the area.

On his return, the Attorney General declared he would consider another legal action against him. The public was in the dark about what happened next. In April 2007 it was announced that Bishara had left Israel and on 22 April Bishara handed his resignation letter from the Knesset to the Israeli consul in Cairo. He left because he was about to be arrested for allegedly contacting a Hezbollah agent and providing him with information on the strategic location of potential targets for the organization's missiles. It was also rumoured that he would be accused of smuggling funds from 'subversive' elements for his party's activity. The first and more serious allegation, which would be repeated against several leading members of the Palestinian community in 2010, was totally ridiculous. Palestinians in Israel know very little about these matters; they do not serve in the army and what they know can be gathered from Google Earth. More plausible was the allegation that Bishara personally transferred money from outside sources for maintaining his political career. The secret service made a connection, not necessarily correctly, between the money and the alleged passage of information. One way or another it was clear that Bishara was targeted as a leading political personality who contributed significantly to the newly won self-assertiveness, confidence and identity of the Palestinian community in Israel in a way that troubled the powers that be.

A similar attack was launched against Sheikh Raid Salah, the leader of the Islamic movement, whose greatest achievement was that of putting the issue of Jerusalem, and the related Israeli policies, into the centre of the global Muslim and regional Arab consciousness. In his case the allegation was contacts with Hamas, but he stayed on, sat in jail for a year without trial and won the legal struggle when no serious allegations were proved in court (Bishara might have not survived a year like this in jail, suffering as he did from serious kidney problems).

A CLEARER VIEW ON THE ETHNOCRACY

Bishara was not the only Palestinian Member of the Knesset, or activist, to be targeted by the authorities on charges of potentially collaborating with the enemy; as if Palestinian leaders inside Israel could develop an anti-Palestinian stance to satisfy the apprehensions of the political and security establishment of the Jewish state.

The growing numbers of both Palestinian academics at Israeli universities (in relative terms; they are still a tiny fraction of overall numbers) and critical sociologists interested in the topic produced a clear definition of Israel, at least from the perspective of its national minority: ethnocracy. In an ethnocracy, the minority is granted partial equality and a limited integration as individuals into its political and economic life. At the same time, a long-term and unchanging policy of control and surveillance guarantees the continuation of the majority's dominance and the minority's marginality.[15]

The adoption of the paradigm of ethnocracy also helps to reshape the historical narrative of the Palestinians in Israel. The model included the explanation of how an ethnocracy was formed: when a dominant group seizes control of the mechanisms of the state and makes ethnicity, rather than citizenship, the key to the distribution of resources and power.

The next historical chapters are also easily explained by this paradigm. Politics undergoes a gradual process of ethnicization, according to ethnic-based classes: in this instance the introduction of the Law of Return and the land policy from the 1950s onwards. If one visits the Hebrew Wikipedia, dominated by Zionist discourse, and reads the entry for the October 2000 events, the background section starts with the early Zionist colonization of Palestine, and although the discourse is different, as is the music, the factual analysis and the lyrics are the same. There is a direct line, even in this popular presentation of history and politics, between formative periods in the life of both ethnic communities and the eruption of violence in 2000.

It is a very useful perspective, allowing those who subscribed to it to understand better how to locate the formal side of democracy from which the Palestinians in Israel have undeniably benefited. The basic rights such as suffrage, the right to be elected, freedom of expression, movement and association are there, but they are all identified with a single and superior ethnic group. These basic rights are granted not by the rule of the majority, but from one ethnic group to the other.

The links between economic and social deprivation and ethnocracy were also clarified through this prism. The demographic growth of the Palestinians in Israel, much faster than the Jewish equivalent, has not been met by an adequate economic, occupational and spatial development.

It is not clear if everything can be pinned on the ethnocratic nature of the state, but if one accepts this is the best way of describing the Israeli regime, one can also clearly detect its impact on other aspects of life in the twenty-first century, which do not originate with its power but are highly affected by it. One such issue is the prominence of the clan, the Hammula, in social life, especially in the rural areas. Despite the key economic role played by the nuclear family, the traditional hierarchal and patriarchal structure of the clan still played a dominant social role at the beginning of the twenty-first century. This is best demonstrated by the detailed research on the topic by As'ad Ghanem, who noted the resurgence of the Hammula as an alternative and retrograde political grouping. It affected a variety of decisions taken by the community: from who would marry whom to who would win the local elections and how the economic resources of the community would be divided.[16]

BEYOND POLITICS: THE SOCIAL MATRIX OF TRADITION AND MODERNITY

The average Palestinian citizen encountered ethnocracy less as an abstract political or legal structure and more as a matrix of walls and glass ceilings that prevented integration or equality. The walls were not only imaginary. More and more Jewish communities living in proximity to Palestinian villages or neighbourhoods wished to emulate the segregation wall Israel built in the West Bank. As the *Haaretz* journalist Lili Galili put it (in her case it should be read as a sarcastic remark): 'Who wants to wake up in the morning and see an Arab? Alongside the big separation wall from the Palestinians, national and social separations emerge inside the state. Fences, walls, ramps, bisect the land and turn it into a huge maze.'

A case in point is the village of Jisr al-Zarqa, one of only two villages remaining on the Mediterranean coast, out of the sixty-four which were cleansed by the Israeli forces. Its location, far away from the rest of the Palestinian community, turned it into one of the poorest villages in Israel. It lies 30 kilometres south of Haifa near Kesaria (Caesarea), built on the ruins of the Palestinian village Qaisariya, one of the first to be cleansed in 1948, and now the home of many of Israel's richest Jewish citizens. In 2002 the Kesaria development corporation began to build an earthen embankment dividing their town from Jisr al-Zarqa.

Izz al-Din Amash was the head of the village's council for twelve years. He was the first academic graduate of the village and a member of Meretz, a Zionist party on the left. And yet he said in an interview when trying to climb on the ramp the people of Kesaria built, 'I am afraid to come here. I feel like I need a special permit to do so.' A local physician, Raji Ayat, explained two months after the embankment was built that the main reason was not racist but economic – the houses in proximity to the village had a lower value in the housing market and it was hoped the separation would put them on a par with the rest of the housing in Kesaria.

The people of Nir Zvi, a wealthy settlement near Ben-Gurion Airport, live in proximity to the city of Lod (in Arabic al-Lid), a Palestinian neighbourhood. They also built a wall of separation. Ahmad Abu Muamar, a seventeen-year-old dweller in the nearby Arab neighbourhood, commented cynically, 'Even in the occupied territories they did not built such a huge wall.' Ali Abu Qtaifan said, when the wall was finished and was located two metres from his home, 'I cannot see the sky and the sun. My house has vanished away and so did I.'

The people of Gani Dan in Ramleh also built a wall between them and the Jawarish neighbourhood. A year before the building of the wall, a huge police force – 'larger than the one the Americans used for capturing Saddam Hussein', said one of the dwellers to *Haaretz* – came and demolished houses that were too near to the wall, so as to create a wider distance between the Jewish citizens and unwanted Palestinian ones.[17]

BREAKING OUT OF THE WALLS

It is mainly the poorer sections of the Palestinian community that have been the victims of these policies of gates and enclavements. Among the better off, the first decade of the twenty-first century was a period to try to break out of the ethnic disadvantages imposed on them by the Jewish state. This was possible since not everyone was an activist struggling all the time, and not every field of life demanded activism in order to succeed or to integrate.

Browsing through the new public space, the Internet, with all its meeting places such as forums, websites, Facebook, Twitter and similar virtual arenas, one can see an individualization of the Palestinian experience in Israel. The anonymity and the nature of the intercourse and discussion that characterizes the Internet enables Palestinian and Jewish citizens to interact without the continual need to flag their identity or wave their ethnicity. The Internet can be a tool to advance political and ideological causes, but it can also be blind to ethnicity and race.

Interesting examples are forums that seem on the face of it totally void of any relevance to ethnicity, such as forums of car lovers, those suffering from particular medical complaints or other social forums. A random example would illustrate this point. In April 2004, a young Palestinian, Nur from Kafr Qara in Wadi Ara, was trying to join a car forum, and was very honest about his anxiety about how he would be treated as a Palestinian; to be on the safe side he reminded the other participants that two of Israel's best rally drivers were Palestinian Israelis. Either this information or the relative depoliticization of car lovers helped him to be enthusiastically invited to join the forum. This could go on as long as he kept silent about current events, on which the other members began to comment in a typical anti-Arab fashion; his association with the forum did not last for long.

But boundaries in this century, as in the previous one, are charted from above, and not by the bi-national reality on the ground. Jewish society, self-centred and still licking the wound of the Rabin assassination, is looking for a new consensus. The one constant feature in it has been the absence of the Palestinians in the redefinition of Israeliness in the twenty-first century.

THE VISIONS CONTEST

On the shores of the Sea of Galilee at the end of 2001 about fifty Jewish academics and intellectuals, journalists, military men and politicians gathered. They included well-known figures from the Zionist left, right and centre. And they came as 'Israeli citizens of the Jewish people', according to their self-declared definition.[18]

It was a very well-publicized event, one can say with confidence, the first of its kind attempting to formulate an intellectual and civil Zionist attitude towards the Palestinian minority in Israel. That this was done within civil society and not in the governmental corridors of power is not surprising. The mushrooming of NGOs and the privatization of the political and ideological scene (in the sense of offering either a substitute for parliamentary politics or a parallel form of it) moved the debate on the Arab–Jewish relationship from the government to the public arena of civil society. According to As'ad Ghanem, in 1990 there were one hundred and eighty NGOs and by 2001, more than six hundred had been added. One should stress that only the debate was moved across – policy was still the domain of the government and its agencies.[19] When Palestinian NGOs modestly and cautiously initiated polices of their own – for instance preparing curricula for the Arab schools – this would be brutally blocked by the government.

Not much united the luminaries and pundits who came to spend a few days on the lake's shores. The only issue that bonded them together was the demographic fear: the number of Palestinians inside the historical space of Palestine. For the politicized and activists among the Palestinians in Israel this became a landmark in their relations with the Zionist left. The latter's discourse of 'we have to keep our state Jewish' did not sound very different from the extreme right-wing call for the transfer of the Palestinians in Israel. The way in which the main spokesperson of the Zionist left and centre presented the demographic discourse was akin, in the eyes of the Palestinian Israeli observers and citizens, to the most racist discourse now delegitimized in the West.[20]

These views were summarized in the document which emerged from that meeting: *Amant Kinneret*, the Kinneret Charter. A Jewish democratic state within the boundaries that the government would delineate in the future was an old vision repackaged as a new one. According to this point of view, democracy and solely Jewish ethnicity were not mutually exclusive but rather compatible, and anyone who rejected this future was disloyal to the state and its values. How would the Palestinian citizens fit in? As one of the leading thinkers behind the Kinneret Document, the author A.B. Yehoshua, commented: 'We have a real problem and this is how to make the Israelization of the Arabs work.'[21] It is indeed a difficult task if one considers a later interview he gave to *Haaretz*, in which he stated that he would rather not live in a building where Arab families resided.[22]

His literary work, like that of other famous Israeli writers such as Amos Oz, reflected this wish to modernize the Arabs, to get rid of them or to turn them into Jews.[23] In the first decade of the twenty-first century scholars produced some illuminating work on the representation of the Palestinians in canonical Israeli literature, films and theatre. But these rather one-dimensional, negative, and at times demonized images did not shock anyone in the Jewish public after the October 2000 events, if indeed anyone bothered to read about them, as surveys of public opinion confirmed that these images and perceptions were deeply rooted in Israeli Jewish society.[24]

It seems the authors, academics and state officials were particularly desperate about, or rather fearful of, the Bedouin in the Negev. The officials we have mentioned in an earlier chapter, who were responsible for the transfer of the Bedouin into reservation-like enclaves in the 1970s and early 1980s and monitored their lives closely in unrecognized villages, shared the same image of this more nomadic section of the Palestinian community with the producers of high and popular culture in Israel, even at the beginning of the twenty-first century; to quote a description in *Jewish Week* from 1992:

> Bloodthirsty Bedouin who commit polygamy, have thirty children and continue to expand their illegal settlements, taking over state land . . . In their culture they take care of their needs outdoors . . . They don't even know how to flush a toilet.[25]

These images conjured up by the officials were not a far cry from Amos Oz's description of the Bedouin in his novel *Nomads and a Snake*, a 1965 tale about an Israeli retaliation against Bedouin stealing the local kibbutz's water:

> In the defence of the retaliators I will say that the Bedouin shepherd has the shiftiest of faces: one eyed, broken nose, drooling mouth full of long and sharp twisted foxy teeth. One who looks capable for perpetrating any atrocity.[26]

Four Palestinian NGOs, the Follow-Up Committee, Mussawa, Adalah and research institute Mada al-Carmel, published their own vision documents, not only in response to the Kinneret Charter but also in reaction to a vision master document prepared by the 'Israel Democracy Institute', a leading think-tank which is highly influential in Jewish Israeli politics. The Institute's project, which did not diverge much from the Kinneret principles, but was more professional and academic in tone and content, described a 'consensual constitution', which was deemed provocative by many intellectuals in the Palestinian community, who were not taken into account in the process of its preparation and did not see even their most basic aspirations reflected in it.[27]

The countering Arab visions were also a reaction to the October 2000 events and the eventual crisis that followed this juncture. They were also, as one of their authors Shawqi Khatib, who was the chair of the Follow-Up Committee at the time, explained, a response to the continued fractions fragmenting the community's political scene, and thus a straightforward attempt to present a more unified position in the future.[28]

The four documents do not differ much from each other and the absence of one single document was the unfortunate result of the internal personal and organizational strife in the Palestinian community, which affects not only parliamentary and party politics but also the world of the NGOs and the civil society. They all shared a historical narrative that depicts Zionism as a colonialist movement that dispossessed the indigenous people of Palestine by force. They question Jewishness as a national identity but recognize the ethnic rights of the Jews who settled in Palestine to live within a bi-national state within the pre-1967 borders.[29]

They seek a concessional democracy, like the one that was intact for a while in the post-Soviet Czech Republic and those that still survive in Belgium, Switzerland and Canada, in which the right of the 1948 refugees to return would be recognized and the Palestinians would enjoy cultural autonomy; according to their demographic share they would be represented in the legislative, executive and constitutional arms of the state and hence in the distribution of resources and budgets. Finally, the documents demanded an equal status for Arabic and national Palestinian insignia in the state. Some documents also suggested a power of veto over crucial strategic decisions pertaining to the society as a whole.

The vision documents also later facilitated the construction of national bodies to deal with the rise in crime, family and gender violence in the community, as well as jointly tackling widespread corruption on a local level and dysfunctional administrative services on a regional level. The authors pointed out that as intellectuals and professionals they had a duty to face the apparent decrease in the level of education and even of the number of Arab students in recent years. In short, the authorities displayed indifference and a lack of agency, hence the need to take the initiative. In some of the documents the Israeli governments are blamed for manipulating these internal rifts and weaknesses to their advantage, but that does not absolve the community itself for bearing some responsibility for the dismal reality.

Gender issues too were very high on the agenda and were engaged with in a progressive feminist way. Written and based on the liberal feminist approach, the documents isolated religious fanaticism as the main cause of the abuse of, and discrimination against, women. The documents include far-reaching statements about the advancement of women's rights within the Palestinian community, with strong condemnation of honour killings and violence in the family. There was even a clause about the future of gays and lesbians in the future society, but there was a last-minute decision to exclude this very sensitive issue. This was too progressive for the Islamic movement, which did not endorse the vision documents, partly because of this but mainly because they conveyed a vision of a secular state as the best solution in the future.

The section on women's rights brought to the fore a subject that needs further elaboration: the status of women in Palestinian society in Israel. So far in this book we have stressed the connection between the socio-economic development in the rural areas, most importantly the semi-proletarianization of the farmers' lives, which enabled women to go out to work and to seek a greater role in running family affairs. This was a process that began in the 1960s and continued until the early 1990s, when the entry of Russian immigrants limited the employment choices for women.

In the sphere of education and career, the numbers of independent women grew, not due to Israeli policy, but as part of a much wider phenomenon in the whole Arab world of women's emancipation and empowerment. Social and educational achievements were also bringing women to the fore in political life, although by the beginning of the twenty-first century women were still under-represented in political parties. The situation in the NGOs was much better as one could easily notice their growing numbers among the student community and, as in Israel, they were the main teaching force in the educational system.

The feminist impulse was studied closely by the Palestinian research centre Mada al-Carmel, which showed that assertive action on women's rights, life and dignity went hand in hand with a stronger belief in and determination to struggle for the overall rights of the Palestinian minority.[30] The fusion of these two agendas can be seen in the personality of the only national Palestinian member of the Knesset, Hanin Zuabi, from Nazareth, whose rights as a member of the Knesset have been recently partly denied due to her participation in the Turkish flotilla to Gaza in 2010. In that same year, the Minister of Interior, Eli Yishai, sought a special legislation against her, claiming she was a traitor with no right of citizenship. It is both her feminism and her national stance which the Israeli male politicians find hard to digest and accept.

No less impressive was the struggle of women in several spinning mills ever since the 1990s for better conditions and against widespread sacking. This hard labour was undertaken by Palestinian women for many years, especially in the north, but after the Israeli–Jordanian peace agreement in 1994 and the globalization of the textile economy, they lost their positions to even cheaper labour in Jordan. Those who remained in the industry had to struggle hard to maintain a reasonable level of pay. They could only work in factories next door, partly due to traditional suspicions about working far away from home, partly due to the fact that most Palestinian villages are still not connected by public transport, while all the Jewish settlements are (which inadvertently accelerated the number of independent women drivers within the Palestinian community, which is now at a level similar to Western societies). According to some very recent research, quite a large number of women sacked from the textile industry have moved into the tourist industry, a previously exclusive Jewish domain where there is now a significant Palestinian presence for the first time, as staff and owners of guesthouses and restaurants.[31]

Yet even given the considerable transformation in women's status, the vision documents went further into feminist issues than some of the more conservative sections of the Palestinian society would have wanted them to go; this brings home again As'ad Ghanem's assertion that to define streams in the politics of Palestinians in Israel only on the basis of people's attitudes to Zionism is too reductionist and that a fuller picture emerges if one assesses their stances towards wider issues of tradition and modernity.[32] The assertion was that the Islamic movement did not endorse fully the vision documents due to the question of women's status.

The vision documents, claims Mary Totary, a Palestinian political scientist from Haifa, reflected a desire for a change in a society that, due to its long years of deprivation and oppression, succumbed too easily to the simplistic, traditional and religious ways of life offered by the Islamic movement or existing in nearby Arab countries. According to her analysis, in such circumstances traditional organizations seem safer and more attractive than an unclear modern chaos. This explains, Totary argues, the huge popularity in 2007 of the Syrian soap opera *Bab al-Hara*, 'The Gate to the Neighbourhood', broadcast on the Saudi channel MBC, which had one of the highest ratings among the community's viewers. This is a story of the victory of the traditional Arab way of life over modernity, showing all the former's positive aspects – hospitality, solidarity and honour – and also the negative ones – degradation of women and disrespect for individuality.[33]

But criticism of the visions came also from other quarters. Abna al-Balad rejected the documents since the party was opposed to the partition of the land, but otherwise these documents did seem to represent faithfully the aspirations of Palestinians in Israel. However, it should be noted that Sammy Smooha claims otherwise and insists that his findings show that 65 per cent of the community accept life in a Jewish democratic state and therefore condemn the documents as too radical. There could be indeed a gap between reconciling with a reality and hoping for something better; however, Palestinian sociologists who carried out their own survey of public opinion vehemently reject Smooha's findings and claim very strong support for the vision's basic features.[34]

From left to right, the Israeli Jewish public, through its newspapers, members of the Knesset, government ministers and populist pundits, declared the vision documents as a statement of war. The worst part for them was the fact that, for the first time in sixty years, the Palestinian community had taken the initiative itself and adopted the language of the indigenous people versus the settler state. Yet a far more existential danger for the Palestinian community in 2007 was the demographic and geographic, rather than academic, struggle over the future. In this realm time seemed to be frozen and the strategies, policies and discourse employed were those heard for the first time in 1948.

THE UNENDING CONTEST OVER SPACE

Although limited new areas were allocated for physical expansion of the Palestinian habitat, for the first time since the creation of the state of Israel, they were insignificant and – more importantly – insufficient for the demographic growth of the community, which is still double that of the Jewish one. This was due to continued expropriation of land and the lack of urban planning for the vast majority of the Arab towns and villages. Hence the trends begun at the end of the previous century continued with force in the new one. Despite policies of segregation, individual Palestinians disrupted this master plan by continuing to move into Jewish neighbourhoods in mixed towns and to rent houses in Jewish development towns.

The message from the government, Jewish mayors and the press was the same: the growth of the Palestinian community in Israel is a national threat. Writing this sentence, I wonder whether readers can imagine how it feels for the birth of your child to be perceived as a threat to the state of which you are a citizen?

From the Prime Minister to social organizations to proposals and legislative debates in the Knesset, there is an almost obsessive interest in increasing the Jewish birth rate or Jewish immigration to confront this 'demographic danger', wrote one Palestinian scholar, depicting faithfully the mood and policy in Israel.[35]

In the first decade of this century the Judaization of the country continued to be a high government priority and a major concern for Jewish individuals and collectives, which were now able to expand already existing ownership of their land due to the continued privatization of the land regime in Israel – a major reform promised and executed by the newly re-elected Benjamin Netanyahu in 2009. But even before 2009, under the Sharon and Olmert governments (2001–2009), the distribution of the Arab population in Israel, its demographic growth and political tendencies were all lumped together into the alarming concept of a 'strategic threat' – a term used frequently when the heads of states, leading academics and experts meet annually at the Centre for Interdisciplinary Studies in Herzliya, a private university run mainly by retired professors from other universities. Kenes Herzteliya, the Herzliya Conference, became the principal platform for the heads of states to give their equivalent of the American State of the Nation address (this is where Prime Minister Ariel Sharon declared his Disengagement Plan from the Gaza Strip in 2005).

The second wave of the Judaizing the Galilee (*Yihud Ha-Galil* in Hebrew), as mentioned, began with the first Rabin government, which was keen to diminish the number of Arabs in the Galilee by increasing the numbers of Jews in it and by strangulating the Arab rural population, forcing it to either emigrate or stagnate. The three blocks of settlements built throughout the next thirty years were meant to disrupt the natural geographical continuity of these villages by driving Jewish wedges in between them.[36]

The Jews came, but the Palestinians did not leave, so a third wave of Judaization began in 2001. This time the Judaizer of the past, Shimon Peres, now a minister for developing the Galilee and the Negev, joined Ariel Sharon, the Judaizer of the West Bank. This was also not very successful; Jews, for all their sins, preferred to live in Tel Aviv. In 2002, Prime Minister Sharon declared: 'If we don't settle the Galilee, someone else would do it.'[37]

It was in such a speech that the plans for the most recent wave of Judaization in the Galilee, Wadi Ara and the Negev were announced in 2005. (It is not a coincidence that this was the same year of the disengagement from Gaza: a seemingly dovish move in the occupied territories had to be 'compensated' by a hawkish move inside Israel.) Worried Palestinian heads of councils met in the village of Kafr Manda to oppose a plan for expanding territorially more than one hundred Jewish settlements at the expense of land belonging to Arab landowners. The other side of the plan (not stated openly, but presumed by the participants in the Kafr Manda meeting) involved disallowing the expansion of Palestinian villages.

The architect of the 2005 plan was Sharon's deputy prime minister, Shimon Peres, who also suggested at a Jewish meeting in Carmiel before the Manda meeting that 10,000 units would be sold cheaply to Jewish citizens to enhance the plan of Judaization. 'The development of the Negev and the Galilee is the most important Zionist project in the next years,' he declared. The costs for this project were supposed to come from the American administration as part of the $2.1 billon promised by President George W. Bush in compensation for Israel's withdrawal from the Gaza Strip in 2005.

In those days, the Israeli policy makers realized that they could no longer rely on Jewish immigration from abroad as the best means of maintaining their demographic superiority in the state, however its future borders were demarcated. These human resources were running out so all they could do was to encourage Jews to leave the metropolitan centres of Israel and resettle in the north and the south, encouraging them with tax exemptions, the quality of life and an 'Arab-free' environment. In 2010 one can say with some confidence that this drive has totally failed. The Jewish population of both these peripheries remains as it was in 1950: poor, unemployed and with weak occupational and service infrastructures. The few spots of wealthier middle-class suburbia that have emerged are the exceptions to the rule, and not enough to attract other people. The next shots in the struggle to Judaize Israel are two new towns with a population of more than 10,000 orthodox Jews, with the highest birth rate in the country: one near Nazareth on land confiscated from the village Ayn Mahel, west of the city, and one in the midst of Wadi Ara.

A fourth wave of Judaization began under Ehud Olmert's government (2006–2009). This cabinet went into a destructive war against both Lebanon in 2006 and the Gaza Strip in 2007. But it was also very active in the 'Judaization' project especially in three areas: Greater Nazareth, Wadi Ara and the Negev. The aim was to look for new ways of de-Arabizing and Judaizing these regions.

This last and present project was continued with even more zeal by the centre-right government of Benjamin Netanyahu which came to power in 2009. This wave was motivated by the failure of the previous policies to make all these areas, and the greater Nazareth area in particular, Jewish. People and economies move in mysterious ways and instead of the Nazarethians leaving, the well-off among them began purchasing homes in the very citadel that was meant to evict them.

In his speeches as the leader of the opposition in 2005 Benjamin Netanyahu made it clear that he already regarded this new reality as a grave danger to Israel's national security. But if you want to know where the governmental consensus lies in twenty-first-century Israel, you listen to the members of the Labour Party – partners in the coalition government of both Olmert and Netanyahu. One such representative is the head of the regional council of lower Galilee, Motti Dotan, who said in 2008: 'If we lose the Jewish majority in the Galilee this is the end of the Jewish state.' This member of the allegedly left-wing Zionist party added: 'I would like to imagine a Galilee without Arabs: no thefts, no crimes . . . we will have normal life.' If the 'left' talks in such a manner, you can imagine what the language used by members of Likud and Israel Beitenu (Lieberman's party) might be.[38]

A new aspect to the current attempts to Judaize the Galilee has been the open support given to it by ecologists, industrialists and academics, including the Jewish National Fund and the Society for the Protection of Nature in Israel. Diminishing the Palestinian presence in the Galilee was also fully endorsed by the prestigious union of Israeli wine producers, who adopted a new plan prepared by leading academic figures from the Technion. The plan was publicized in 2003 and stated that the Jewish 'takeover'[!] of the Galilee was a national priority. It began by saying: 'It is either them or us. The land problems in the Galilee proved that any territory not taken by Zionist elements is going to be coveted by non-Zionists.'[39] The gist of what they suggested was to seize land by force in any territory deemed important strategically and to keep it until Jews settle on it. The director general of AMPA, the leading Israeli electrical manufacturer proudly stated in 2004 that his company was not only making refrigerators but also supported the 'Judaization of the Galilee' by building new communities in the area: 'We are not ashamed to say that our plans [for building villages for the company's veterans] have a Zionist element of Judaizing the Galilee.'[40]

This and other plans became governmental policies when Shimon Peres was the deputy prime minister responsible for the Galilee in Ehud Olmert's government in 2006. The first victim of this new strategy was the beautiful village of Ayn Mahil, east of Nazareth and adjacent to Upper Nazareth. It was already only accessible in 2006 by one road that went, purposely, through a Jewish religious neighbourhood in upper Nazareth (thus for instance on the Day of Atonement, the people of Ayn Mahil could not leave or enter their village). In the new plan they will be encircled by a new town called Shacharit ('dawn' in Hebrew, and also and more importantly the name for first Jewish prayer of the day). The intended population are 10,000 ultra-orthodox Jews. The officials of the state do not hide their hope that this community will procreate at an exponential pace and rectify the 'unfavourable' demographic balance, as well as physically strangulate Ayn Mahil and separate it from the greater Nazareth area. The village's ancient and famous olive groves have already been uprooted in 2009 in preparation for the new town. Needless to say, it will be built on land exclusively expropriated from the village and its people. The construction of the new town is accompanied by an additional web of roads and highways that separate other villages from each other and from Nazareth.[41]

In this new matrix, another two villages are facing a far graver danger than losing their living space. Under Emergency Regulations available to him as Minister of National Infrastructure in the 1990s, Ariel Sharon decided to further the cause of Judaization by building a new heavy industrial site on land expropriated from the Palestinians in the midst of the Palestinian villages surrounding Nazareth. Named Ziporit, the site houses a glass factory Finicia and a poisonous aluminium factory – both not allowed by international law to be built in proximity to human habitation. The nearest village is Mashad and since the opening of the new industrial site the number of deaths from cancer there has risen by 40 per cent.

Similar tactics, of building new cities, disrupting the geographical continuity between Palestinian villages and a large urban centre and between themselves by the erection of walls and roads, are occurring wherever there are Palestinians in high concentration in Israel: in the Galilee, Wadi Ara and the Negev. In 2006, the government announced its plan to create a town, called Harish with 150,000 ultra-orthodox Jews, for the very same reasons that Shacharit was contemplated. The ultra-orthodox colonization worked well in increasing the number of Jewish settlers in the occupied territories and it was hoped it would be beneficial here as well.

This new policy is not surprising. It is another chapter in the history of Palestinian fragmentation. Ever since 1948, the Palestinians have been dispersed and divided into different communities, each suffering the consequence of Israeli policies in a different way. The bifurcation and bisection of the Palestinian existence by Israel enabled the Jewish state to deal more effectively with a people and a society that cast a huge question mark on the state's legitimacy, prosperity and, from a Zionist point of view, existence.

The division of the Palestinians in the 1967-occupied territories into the mini-states of Gaza and of Ramallah plays ideally into this Israeli strategy of control and oppression. The smaller the Palestinian community and the more isolated it is, the better it can be ruled. This sense of having things under control also characterized the relationship of the Jewish state with its own Palestinian minority.

The model for these new Israeli policies is the strategy pursued over the last twenty years in the Greater Jerusalem area. The aim of the policies against the two holy cities of Jerusalem and Nazareth is the same: to disrupt physical and geographical continuity. In the Greater Jerusalem area villages are separated from one another and from Jerusalem itself by Jewish neighbourhoods, bypasses, military camps and the infamous apartheid wall. This matrix of control must have been visible to the Pope when he visited both Jerusalem and Nazareth in 2010 but he chose to remain silent.

In 2009, many of my Palestinian friends inside Israel were alarmed by a rumour that the Egyptian foreign minister had been told by Israeli generals of a master plan to ethnically cleanse all the Palestinians from Israel. This was probably unfounded and the Egyptian politician denied it later. However, the faked (in this case) smoke emanates from a real fire of hate and racism. In a lecture he gave at Tel Aviv University the former and esteemed President of the Supreme Court of Israel, Aharon Barak, summarized the Israeli attitude towards democracy:

'If you ask the Jews in Israel whether they would like to live in a democracy, the vast majority would say yes. The same vast majority would say yes to the proposition to expel all the Palestinians from Israel.' He and his happy listeners giggled when he said this. This is however, no joke. Given Israel's history, the nature of Zionist ideology and the present policies on the ground, it is quite possible that the democratic wish of the Jewish in Israel will become a nightmarish reality in years to come.

It is important to stress that these efforts have the widest possible consensual support from the Jewish population, intellectuals, educated people and academic experts. Businessmen who are involved in production of goods traditionally provided by Palestinians also chipped in enthusiastically in favour of Judaization: olive growers, coffee makers, tourist agents and similar trades. Some do it from a cynical economic evaluation of the benefits reaped from such projects, but most out of obedience to the hegemonic ideology controlling the state since its foundation. *Yeshua*, 'salvation', and *Geula*, 'redemption', previously ecclesiastical terms describing the individual road to heaven, are now state jargon for the land policy of Israel.

The lack of space increased the movement of Palestinians into 'Jewish areas'. The successors of Kahana were now supported by a party which had senior representatives in the government, Avigdor Lieberman's Israel Beitinu ('Our home') party, which employed the familiar language of rabid racism and anti-Semitism to warn against the 'Arabs' harassing 'our daughters', committing crimes and contemplating a total takeover of 'our houses'. Violent eruptions were around the corner; the worst were a few days of clashes in Acre where Arabs and Jews live precariously in joint houses in the modern part of the city.

But life sometimes is more complex than the simplicity of governmental racist policies or politicians' ideologies. The situation over the last few years in Upper Nazareth is a good example of this.

If you call the spokesperson of Upper Nazareth, a city overlooking the old Nazareth, and ask how many Palestinians live in the new 'Jewish' city, the answer would be long and winding but would lead you nowhere. Officially, there are none. This is also the impression you get if you visit the city's elegant website (which appears only in Hebrew and in Russian). But wait, you may insist, as I did, 'I am standing in front of a house which is decorated by an engraved epitaph which states: ' "There is no power but in God" in Quranic Arabic.' And I added, 'I know there are two Palestinian members of your city council.' 'We still do not have enough information about the numbers,' is the official reply and so to all intents and purposes there are no Arabs in Upper Nazareth.

Twenty per cent of this city's population are in fact Palestinians. They moved into the city mainly from the crowded city of Nazareth and from the villages surrounding it. Some of them had to pay as much as three million shekels (the equivalent of about £500,000 or $800,000) for a flat or a house, three times more than its market value. The people who sell the houses are Russian immigrants gravitating towards Tel Aviv. The Palestinians in the city have no schools or kindergartens, thus the roads connecting the real Nazareth with Upper Nazareth are overcrowded when schools open and close. But Israel being Israel, the non-existent 20 per cent have representation in the local municipality and demanded, and received, a promise to build an Arab school in Upper Nazareth for the absent Palestinians. They are sitting together in a coalition with the ultra-right-wing party of Avigdor Lieberman, who declared in August 2009 that stopping the immigration of Arabs into Nazareth, as he calls it, is a national priority. His representative in the town, the mayor, needed the two Palestinians to defeat the rival Labour Party. But he is also committed to the 'Judaization', namely the de-Arabization, of his city.

A huge pressure on this delicate reality were the wars in Lebanon in 2006 and the attack on Gaza in 2009, and alongside them the issue of the media's credibility. By 2006, during the second Lebanon war, it became clear that, for more than a decade, the Palestinians in Israel had been using the Arab satellite media, and especially but not exclusively the television channel al-Jazeera, as a far more reliable, informative and inspirational source of information than the Israeli equivalent. The misinformation by the Israeli army's spokesperson, exposed by the leader of Hezbollah, accentuated this process.

The networks in the Arab world opened a window not only to current news and developments, but also the dynamic and vibrant cultural scene all over the Arab world. New books, poems and songs can now reach and enrich the Palestinian community in Israel (among them those written by the Palestinians from Israel who would rather publish in Beirut, Cairo or Amman than in the very few publishing houses in Palestine, which are located mostly in Jerusalem and the West Bank). Ever since 1987 there has been a process of strengthening the ties not just with the Palestinian polity and nationality, but also with Arab heritage and culture. Unlike the 1950s, this was not done in secret, but as part of a new assertion of a cultural and not just a national identity. Mada al-Carmel, the Palestinian research institute in Haifa, found that 75 per cent of the Palestinians in Israel accepted the Hezbollah and al-Jazeera narratives of the second Lebanon war in the summer of 2006.[42]

In 2005 the Palestinian NGO I'ilam and Tel Aviv University political scientist Amal Jamal conducted a very comprehensive survey on the level of confidence in the media in the Middle East. This exposed what Jamal called 'a serious crisis of confidence of the Arab citizens in the Israeli media'. Sixty-five per cent of the Palestinians believed al-Jazeera more than any Israeli new channel.[43] This crisis of confidence only accentuated other fractures in the already fragile edifice of the Arab–Jewish relationship in Israel. As before, both the majority and the minority survived these tensions well, but I fear that, as such episodes accumulate, as an inevitable consequence of the historical circumstances in which the Jewish state was born and of its hegemonic ideological nature and stance, the likelihood of similar crises passing peacefully in the future looks more and more doubtful.

Meanwhile, as Nadim Rouhana has noted, a unique Palestinian identity has developed: segregated from the Israeli Jewish one, but also different from that of the other Palestinian community. Its language is Arabrabiya – an Arabic in which words of Hebrew are now an integral part of the dialect (vividly demonstrated in the most famous Israel film in recent years, *Ajami*, a tale of the tough Jaffa or Yafa neighbourhood, played by the citizens themselves and not by professional actors). This Palestinian way of life can for the time being be protected by a very low profile, not attracting the attention of the authorities, or maybe at the price of total depoliticization. But life is not just made up of material needs, and it is almost impossible to divorce cultural from political questions. Moreover, safety from individual or state harassment is not guaranteed if one wanders outside the Palestinian areas into the more public space in Israel.

But the issue that most significantly clouds the growing number of individual success stories is the shape of the regime in recent years, and in years to come. For the Palestinians in Israel, the Jewish state has legally become a secret-service state, with dire implications for the future.

EPILOGUE

THE OPPRESSIVE STATE

ON 29 MAY 2007, the Israeli Knesset duly revalidated, as it has done annually in recent times, the Emergency Regulations that had been imposed in Palestine by the British Mandate in 1945 and readopted by Israel on its day of foundation in 1948.[1] On paper, even today in the twenty-first century, there are almost two hundred such regulations, which enable the state to legally declare any part of the country a closed military area, exercise administrative arrest without trial, expel and even execute citizens.

From the creation of the state until 1996, there was no need to extend this validation annually as it was regarded as a permanent situation. In 1996, in a celebrated display of democratic histrionics, official Israel announced the annulment of the regulations' permanent status and the government decreed a need for an annual approval. The recurrent approval, needless to say, was taken for granted (partly because, even without the annual approval of the Emergency Regulations, the government was still able to impose the same discriminatory regime on the basis of the general State of Emergency declared in Israel on the day of its creation and which was still intact in 2007). But for many observers, the 1996 annulment, or rather charade of annulment, was the last attempt to democratize the country. After that, and particularly in the wake of the second *Intifada*, the legislative effort in Israel focused on restricting even further the limited rights citizens had enjoyed under the State of Emergency Rules and Regulations.

As mentioned throughout this book, critical scholars, both Jewish and Arab, inside Israel have chosen recently to define the state in which such realities are tolerated as an ethnocracy. I think that this is not a complete picture and would like to refer to Israel in this epilogue as a State of Oppression; not for all its citizens, only for its Palestinian minority. Oppression in the modern era can only be fully achieved with a developed security apparatus and I argue here that the worst aspect of the minority's existence is that its daily and future fate is in the hands of the Israel secret-service apparatuses. There is no parallel example for such total securitization in any of the states that make up the democratic world. The only states which apply similar methods of control are to be found in the very region where Israel's founding fathers attempted to build a European enclave: several states within the Arab world (and some African states). Of the models typifying the Arab world, one in particular applies to Israel: the Arab *Mukhabarat* (secret-service) state.[2] As such, the processes taking place in the state of Israel in recent years do not belong to the twilight zone between democracy and dictator- ship, which was of concern to perceptive thinkers such as Giorgio Agamben, nor is it enough to define Israel as an ethnocracy. If it were, the deterioration could then be halted or slowed down by reinforcing democracy; but, as this book tries to argue, such a fundamental change would be a total sell-out of the most basic assumptions on which the Jewish state was built and on which it is currently maintained.

Israel controls the whole area that was formally Mandatory Palestine and the examination of its oppressive nature relates to its relationship with about five million Palestinians who live in the Mandatory Palestine area. In more ways than one, the oppression also affects the lives of the millions of Palestinians who live in exile or in refugee camps as a result of the ethnic cleansing Israel carried out in 1948.

The professional literature also offers models of such oppressive regimes beyond the Arab world, such as the term 'Masters' (*Herrenvolke*) democracy', chosen by some scholars to describe the apartheid regime in South Africa.[3] For the lack of a better paradigm I opt here for the 'Oppressive State' as the paradigm that can best describe the current reality for the Palestinian minority in Israel. In reality, and in our analysis, the paradigm is applied to only a part of the population in the country, while the other part of the population is aware of the oppression and fully endorses and supports it. Therefore this paradigm of the Oppressive State is not an attempt to analyse Israel or Zionism in their totality as a historical, cultural or political phenomenon, only its relationship with its Palestinian inhabitants. The democratic paradigm assumes that there is one state, one society and one territory. Such a paradigm could never apply to apartheid South Africa and does not apply to the reality in Israel, a country whose founders wanted to build a central European liberal democracy, but instead created a hybrid between a settler colonialist state and a secret-service (*Mukhabarat*) regime imposed on its Palestinian population.

This is a dynamic model and its version in 2010 is not the same one employed in the days of military rule. Moreover, throughout the years of its existence, there have been attempts, wholesale or piecemeal, to strengthen the democratic variable in the impossible equation of a democratic Jewish state.[4] But it seems that in the last few years an opposite trend has emerged that indicates that the Jewish state has given up on the charade of democracy due to navigation fatigue and, as a result, has escalated its oppression of the minority in an unprecedented manner.

THE HISTORICAL CONTEXT OF THE OPPRESSIVE STATE

Zionism was born out of two impulses. The first was a wish to find a safe haven for Jews after centuries of persecution and maybe an insight that worse was yet to come. The second was the desire to reinvent Judaism as a national movement, a drive inspired by the Spring of Nations, the 1848 wave of national uprisings in Europe. However, as soon as these two impulses were territorially realized in Palestine, the national and humanist project became a colonialist one. Inside Palestine a third impulse was added, the wish to create a pure Jewish space in whatever part of Palestine was coveted as the future Jewish state. And when that part was finally delineated in 1947/1948, consisting of 80 per cent of historical and Mandatory Palestine, it was clear that the only way of achieving it was by ethnically cleansing the one million Palestinians who lived there.[5]

The ethnic cleansing of Palestine that depopulated half the country's people as it destroyed half the country's villages and towns has never been acknowledged or condemned worldwide. The Jews became a decisive majority in the land as a result and claimed their state was a democracy, with its leaders committed to ensuring that 'the democracy' meant the permanent dispossession of the indigenous population of Palestine.

The global message for the state of Israel was that it could be included in the democratic world despite its actions in 1948. The result was that the value of ethnic supremacy was cast as superior to any other values. Most importantly, it was maintained as such, despite Israel's wish to be recognized as the only democracy in the Middle East. Indeed it was the only democracy in the world where the ethnicity and religion of the natives defined their citizenship, and where a suprema-cist ethnic state posed as a democracy. Moreover, the ethnic cleansing left 160,000 Palestinians inside the Jewish state, whose territorial expansionist appetite led to the incorporation of another 2.5 million Palestinians in 1967 (now there are almost 4 million). Indirectly the state also controlled the lives of the 5.5 million refugee community emerging out of the 1948 ethnic cleansing and subsequent waves of expulsion. While after 1967 Israel chose not to use the same drastic means for ensuring its ethnic supremacy, its substitute for them was the creation of an oppressive state.

The presence of Palestinians in what was supposed to be an exclusive Jewish space determined the nature of the state, which was dictated by a set of presumptions manifested in daily realities rather than in the law. However, a certain foundational legislation was deemed necessary, and was useful, as it attracted very little external attention, despite Palestinian scholarly attempts to show that even this minimal legisla-tion was sufficient to brand Israel as a non-democratic state. The end result of minimal legislation and extensive practices was a total violation of the right to own property, land, identity or culture, or to receive full state benefits and rights. Sometimes this was achieved through mili-tary rule, sometimes by direct or indirect occupation, and sometimes through its semi-apartheid policy.

However, the wish to be recognized as a democracy demanded impressive navigation skills of the political class in order to steer the state between segregation, oppression and occupation on the one hand, and the pretence that these did not exist on the other. With American backing and European support this pretence became strategy, enabled by the quality of the leaders and a certain regional and global constellation, as Israel was accepted as a member in the world of Western democracies and recently as a member of the OECD. This could not have been achieved without the assistance of Israeli academia, the Supreme Court and the media, which re-cast the oppressive reality as democratic.

While liberal Zionists were at the centre of power in Israel, the navigation produced two golden rules about the Palestinians governed by Israel. One is that there are two kinds of Palestinians: the 'occupied', with no rights whatsoever, and 'our Palestinians', the citizens of the state who have no collective rights – apart from formal democratic rights such as voting. Unlike the Jewish majority, they have no right of land ownership, cannot identify in public with their national movement and cannot build autonomous educational or cultural systems. For most of the time this was sufficient for presenting Israel as the 'only democracy in the Middle East', but the apparition disappeared when, after 1975, the Palestinians in Israel increasingly demanded collective rights. Then, in October 2000, the state reacted brutally and violently to drive its message home.

THE NAVIGATION FATIGUE OF THE OPPRESSIVE STATE

This navigation fatigue was fully exposed when the Palestinians citizens of Israel fundamentally challenged the definition of the state as a democracy. The serious challenge commenced in 1976 with the campaign against the vast land expropriation in the north and culminated in the widespread show of solidarity with the second *Intifada*, resulting in six deaths in the first instance and thirteen in the second, not to mention hundreds of wounded and thousands of arrests, marking the beginning of the end of the navigation efforts.

But these two challenges, in 1976 and 2000, were low-intensity actions compared with the deeper process of change that affected the Palestinian minority in Israel and which has produced unprecedented challenges to the state in the first decade of the twenty-first century. The more active and self-assertive sections of that minority clearly and unequivocally demanded the construction of a genuine democracy in a state which they branded as a supremacist ethnocracy. This was a new chapter in the life of a community that used to respond to governmental initiatives rather than initiate action itself. Whereas in the past the state had responded with violence, it now responded via its security apparatuses by dispensing with the charade of democracy, among other things through legislation. This could be analysed as democracy deteriorating into a 'state of exception' (to use Agamben's term, applied to the West's reaction to the events of 9/11), but as argued here in the case of Israel, this same curbing of civil rights had a different root and purpose.

The recent challenge revolves around one party, Balad, one movement, the Islamic Movement, and the four vision documents mentioned in the previous chapter. One could add to it a special antagonism towards the return of the *Nakbah* as a major constituent of the collective identity of the Palestinian citizens. The state's response came in 2007 as Bishara was expelled from political life via allegations that he spied for Hezbollah in the Second Lebanon War. At the same time, as we have seen, the leader of the Islamic movement, Sheikh Raid Salah, was charged with similar crimes and imprisoned for more than a year without trial before finally being brought to court, when it transpired that none of the charges against him could be validated.

The second challenge was the vision documents. On 13 March 2007, the daily *Maariv* reported on a closed meeting of the Shabak (the Israeli secret service) at which the head of the organization described these documents as indicating a 'dangerous radicalization of the Israeli Arabs; they tend not to identify with the state and this is caused by the rise of subversive elements among them'. When asked to respond to the piece in *Maariv*, Yuval Diskin, the head of the Shabak, reiterated his view that the documents were subversive, endangered state security and could lead to the closure of the NGOs involved.[6]

The vision documents and the reassertion of the right to refer to the birth of the state in 1948 as a Palestinian catastrophe were fought with new legislation. And thus Diskin's remarks were accompanied by legislative efforts to curb this 'subversive' trend. These amendments to the laws de-legitimized and stripped the citizenship of anyone who did not declare his or her faith in the Jewishness of the state or who supported Palestinian organizations such as Hamas.

The new discourse signalled a violent response to any attempt to express a collective Palestinian identity or challenge the ethnic state, denoting clear signs of the descending fatigue. At the beginning of the twenty-first century official Israel was tired of navigating between an actual policy of ethnic discrimination and the formality of a democratic state. The regional and global balance of power – as understood in Israel – made such navigational skills redundant. No one in the USA or the Arab world seemed to expect Israel to be a democracy.

The fatigue was also the inevitable result of the mediocrity of the political leadership, whose capacity to navigate seems to be significantly less than that of the previous generation of leaders. This came to light in the summer of 2006, when the Prime Minister and several ministers were busy fighting a legal battle against charges of corruption, and their skills of navigation were called for. In fact they showed very little skill and dragged Israel into the Second Lebanon War, which was universally regarded as the first-ever Israeli military defeat. The vacuum of military rule was filled by two outfits that had never had much faith in the need to appear 'democratic' for domestic or foreign consumption, that is, the army and the secret service. These two organizations were above the law anyway, and their position testified to the fact that Israel was not a democracy transgressing into a state of exception, but rather a secret-service – Shabak – state, a local Arab and Middle Eastern variant of the Oppressive State.

THE PARALLEL MODEL: THE *MUKHABARAT* STATE OF THE ARAB WORLD

Politically, the *Mukhabarat* state exists only within the boundaries of the Arab world (although there are similar states elsewhere). Such a state is characterized as a mass mobilizing state, run by an all-pervasive bureaucracy and ruled by military and security apparatuses.[7] The variants of this model range from robust to liberal autocracies and the span is wide enough to include Israel.

What characterizes such states more than anything else is the sustainability of their security establishment (the *Mukhabarat*) in the face of internal challenges and external pressures. This sustainability is ensured by a strong connection to an outside power; to quote John P. Entelis, 'the *Mukhabarat* state cannot long endure if it lacks the financial resources to pay its soldiers, purchase arms, upgrade equipment, maintain supplies, and acquire externally-gathered intelligence data'.[8]

One of the experts on the subject, Nazih Ayubi, described such states as 'fierce', as distinguished from a 'strong' (democratic) state.[9] The relationship between the state and its citizens is not a legal one, but purely a function of fierce power relations (remember that this is a typology of Israel's relations with the Palestinians, not with its Jewish society). A fierce state resorts to the use of raw power as its default function – whereas in democracies which find themselves in crises such as the 9/11 bombing, the use of such power is a deviation from a set of non-violent default means of maintaining the state.

Readers versed in the critique of Israel are familiar with its depiction as 'an army with a state'. This is actually a common reference to the *Mukhabarat* state of Algeria, about which it was written that 'every state has an army but in Algeria the army has a state', describing how deeply enmeshed the linkage between the state and the security apparatuses is.[10] To be fair, this is not far from the very bold attempt by several critical Israeli sociologists to define Israel as a militarist society.[11] The role of the army or the security apparatuses in these studies appears not to be the outcome of anomie, as it would be in the state of exception, but appears to be a part of the state's foundation and *raison d'état*. Critical sociology points to the oppression as stemming from a non-democratic founding ideology and a colonialist reality, not from any internal contradictions in the democratic system that can produce states of exception. The ideology and the colonialist reality have produced a state in which the army and the security services reign not in exceptional situations, but as a rule. The militaristic model mobilizes Jewish society, but, as a typical *Mukhabarat* state, oppresses the Palestinian population.

The authoritarian, rentier militaristic state of the Arab world is a model that better corresponds, historically and theoretically, with the state within the state of Israel: the state of the Palestinians within the Jewish state. However, as argued by others before me, it is a hybrid with another model, the settler-colonial state, which can be presented as a mixture between an Arab post-colonial model and a colonialist model, such as South Africa during the days of apartheid.

CONCLUSION AND FUTURE TRENDS

The deep knowledge of theory and the equally deep involvement in their community's fate have led Palestinian scholars in Israel to intertwine theoretical paradigms with straightforward political polemic. A favourite source of inspiration that was exhumed from relative darkness was the work of Carl Schmitt, the German jurist and political theorist who, in one way or another, blessed dictatorship as a functional and just political system. Raef Zureik and others have wisely and sensitively tackled the uneasy dialectical relationship between romantic nationalist Germany and an analysis of present-day Israel. One can see why recent policies and discourses adopted in Israel, especially towards the Palestinian citizens, seem to come directly from Schmitt's theorizations.

Issam Abu-Raya, in response to the remarks of Yuval Diskin, head of Shabak, wrote: 'Diskin's statement fits beautifully with [Carl] Schmitt's arguments' about the sovereign having the final say under the law of a defending democracy.[12] This was a line of reasoning that pushed Schmitt into the Nazi embrace. However, although – if one follows Diskin's words on several other occasions – one can see the similarities with Schmitt, the story of Germany and Schmitt is of a deteriorating democracy that became a dictatorship and was salvaged once more. This trajectory is inapplicable in Israel unless one accepts the liberal Zionist claim that pre-1967 Israel was different. My argument is that the Israeli paradigm is a colonialist and post-colonialist mixture, a political outfit of a settler state ruling through a *Mukhabarat* state.

Israel's brand of oppression is the one that typifies both settler states and *Mukhabarat* states. Therefore the navigation fatigue, the harsh response to new challenges and the overall political situation at the beginning of the twenty-first century are indicators of an escalating cycle which carries the potential to end the pretence and the false inclusion of Israel in the frame of analysis of Western democracy. This escalating cycle is made up of a series of legislative measures, all intended to continue the oppression of the Palestinian population under the Israeli state rule.

The first wave was in 1948, leading to the rights to own land, water and buy and sell land being denied to the Palestinians by law, as was the right for full citizenship. This was followed by discrimination in every aspect of life, including welfare, education and protection from abuse of the law, all practised systematically and efficiently but not legalized.

The second wave was the legislation through the imposition of the Emergency Regulations on the occupied West Bank and Gaza Strip in 1967 that denied basic human and civil rights to the millions who lived there. It began with ethnically cleansing 300,000 Palestinians and then constructing the oppressive regime we are familiar with today. All this was achieved without undermining Israel's membership in the exclusive democratic club.

The third wave is the one that points to navigation fatigue. It concerns greater Jerusalem, defined as one-third of the West Bank, where potential Palestinian citizens of Israel have lived since it was officially annexed to Israel in 1967. A set of municipal regulations and town-planning ordinances have enabled the ethnic cleansing of the 200,000 Palestinians who live there – an operation that needed time and had not yet been completed at the time of writing (40 per cent have already been transferred).[13]

And there has been a fourth wave of legislation that began in 2001. A series of parliamentary initiatives led to new discriminatory laws, among them the 'nation and admittance to the country' law which bans any reunion for whatever reason between Palestinian couples or families living on different sides of the Green Line. In practice this is a means of preventing the return to the homeland of any Palestinian who 'overstayed' abroad. Other laws institutionalized discrimination in the welfare and educational realms (for instance the right of the secret service to determine the employment of school principals and teachers). And finally there are the laws, already mentioned, that equate objection to the Jewishness of the state with treason. These laws do not change the reality, but attest to the state's ability to forsake the charade and work more freely against the Palestinians wherever they are.

According to the scenario described and analysed in this epilogue, the short-term repercussions may be catastrophic; we expect either escalating state violence against the Palestinians, wherever they are, or further oppressive legislation. However, in the long run, they may rob Israel of the moral and political shield with which the West has provided it. If it continues its oppressive regime, Israel may be South Africanized or Arabized and thus judged by harsher criteria that the elite would take more seriously culturally and economically, much more than the current soft rebukes Israel receives as a democracy. This may mean that Israel will come to be regarded as a pariah state and that an end is brought to the dispossession and occupation. Moreover, de-democratizing Israel could give Palestinian resistance hope for change and lead it to abandoning its tactics, which are rooted in despair and anger, born not just as a response to the actual oppression but also as a reaction against the hypocritical, dishonest brokery of the West in the conflict from its very first day. If Israel is seen as a permanent oppressive state, the Palestinians may see a light at the end of their tunnel of suffering and abuse.

But I would like to leave the readers with some positive images. There are now five mixed Arab–Jewish schools in Israel, defying the educational system's total rejection of these brave attempts to create alternative enclaves for the future.

There are growing spaces of leisure and pastime, such as the German colony in Haifa, the promenade in Tel Aviv and the green parks on the boundary line between East and West Jerusalem, where Palestinians and Jews share a restaurant, a coffee house or a recreation park. There is no segregation in public transport, air travel included (although there is still abuse and maltreatment of Palestinians at the security checkpoints in the airports), and unlike in the occupied territories, apartheid walls are still scarce (although most Jewish villages and suburban areas are gated communities, in the main to keep the 'Arabs' out).

One does not want to idealize the situation. In many other places of pastime and leisure, Palestinians are not welcome because of who they are and the daily abuse by whoever represents the government continues. There are two forces at work in 2010. One is the Arabrabiya, mentioned before as a distinct Palestinian Israeli dialect of Arabic inter-twined with Hebrew words; it is a functional language spoken between members of the community. It broadcasts a clear message to the Jewish majority and the state: we are, so far, the only Palestinian group that knows you well, accepts your presence in our homeland as an ethnic group and wishes to share life with you despite everything that your state and movement has done to us.

The other force is the language of demographic danger. The headline of the newspaper *Yediot Achronot* in the early days of July 2010 was 'We Are Losing the Negev'. To whom? To the Palestinian citizens of Israel; not to a foreign army, illegal immigrants or to cynical profiteering from the outside, but to our own citizens. The media and political language of middle Israel is that a new Palestinian baby is a grave national danger to the state's existence. No affirmative action, no drastic improvement of standard of living or symbolic inclusion of Palestinians politicians as ministers in the government (which was done only once and hailed by the Zionist left as a genuine revolution); none of any of these theoretical and actual improvements could transform in any meaningful way the fate of the Palestinians in Israel and that of the Jewish state as a whole. Time will tell whether the articulate and impressive new member of the Knesset from Balad, Hanin Zuabi, who, as mentioned, lost some of her privileges due to her participation in the Turkish flotilla to Gaza in June 2010 (a loss greeted by some Jewish members of the Knesset parties with a toast) represents the future because of her excellent Hebrew and intimate knowledge of what it means to be an Israeli, or whether she too will be trumped by a state and a public that still believes in the twenty-first century that it is possible to create an exclusive Jewish space in the midst of the Arab world.

NOTE ON THE SCHOLARSHIP

RESEARCH ON THE PALESTINIANS in Israel was first undertaken by non-professional writers who wished to present either the official Israeli line or individual grievances of members of the community.[1] This genre continued to appear later on, mainly from Israelis who were involved in one way or another in shaping the policy towards the Palestinian minority in the state. So this was a literature informed by one's stance in the ideological debate inside Israel and did not attempt a professional approach – nor did its writers possess such qualifications.[2]

The ideological or political divide was also explicit when the professionalization of the research on the Palestinians in Israel commenced in earnest during the 1970s. Very broadly defined, research lay on a spectrum between a Zionist thesis and an anti-Zionist antithesis on this charged topic. By this we do not mean that every academic work is a political statement or an ideological tract, far from it; but that the author's ethical and moral departure point is important in deciding where their professionalism will take them. Support for the hegemonic ideology of the Jewish state was more explicit in the less professional books, such as those written by Ori Stendel,[3] and less so in the academic research that appeared mainly in the social science departments. But it was present in both types of literature. The more implicit support for the hegemonic ideology, as this term is defined by Noam

Chomsky,[4] came from the field of modernization theories which main-stream academics used to analyse the case studies of the Palestinians in Israel. Hegemonic ideology, according to the Chomskyan approach, prevails in almost every modern society in the West and it is a powerful concept that governs the life of every citizen. This ideology is a conceptual and ethical value system that interprets and explains the reality to the society at large. More often than not, this interpretation fuses with the interest of the powerful sections and groups within the society. The theory of modernization is one such hegemonic ideology and it is still the main theoretical infrastructure for Israeli academic study of the topic today. Due to the impressive scholarly output it has inspired it also informs this book, which tries to challenge some of its basic assumptions, as discussed below.[5]

THE AGE OF MODERNIZATION

The first decade after the 1967 war was one of euphoria in general in Israel: the victory was sweet and its bitter fruits recognized only by very few. Politicians and generals, who continued to regard the minority community of Palestinians as a 'fifth column' and a grave security risk, were willing to let military rule continue, and even contemplated the Palestinians' forcible removal from the state. At the same time, however, academics were developing hopeful scenarios for the future. In both its self and external image, Israel was a new super-regional power ruling over vast areas of Egypt, Palestine and Syria. Academically this translated into a sense of a mission, subscribed to by many members of the scholarly community in a way, as argued convincingly in a recent book by Gabriel Piterberg, that did not differ significantly from academic writing in other settler colonialist societies in the past.[6] When leading researchers wrote about Mizrahi Jews (who came from the Arab world) or the Palestinians themselves, their work bore the unmistakable overtones of the 'white man's burden'. Israel, and in particular its Ashkenazi citizens, had a mission to modernize everything in sight, be it the Mizrahim or the Palestinian minority. The 'mission' was not easy. Sammy Smooha, one of the most progressive of those who chose the Palestinians in Israel as his subject matter, nevertheless wrote about difference in core values between Arabs and Jews as part of the reason for inequality, although emphasizing the role of discriminatory policies.[7]

In short, Smooha saw the Jewish community as a progressive, modern society while the Palestinian minority was a primitive one. He argued that there was a modernization process going on, but that it was slow and might lead to a clash of civilizations that, due to the balance of power, would end in the demise of the Palestinian minority in Israel, or alternatively their integration as a modern society. Smooha predicted that the former scenario was more likely to occur. To his credit, in later works he would move away from this essentialist and orientalist depiction of Palestinian society and would cast as much blame on Israel's discriminatory policies as on the intrinsic problems of 'Arab' society and culture.

However, his articles from that period indicate that inside and outside Israeli academia the Palestinian minority was not only considered to be primitive and non-modern but – as surveys from the period among Jewish citizens showed – also one which would never become modern unless it was de-Palestinized and de-Arabized. Since these perceptions were prevalent in academia and the media, as well in the corridors of power, one can see why the removal of military rule after 1967 did not change much in practice, as the third chapter in this book tries to explain.

The dominance of the modernization theory as the principal prism through which the reality of the Palestinian minority should be viewed was helped by the august presence in Israeli academia of one of the world's most renowned theorists on modernization, Samuel Noah Eisenstadt, who died in 2010. His students at the Hebrew University examined the Palestinians in Israel as a classical case study of a successful modernized and Westernized community in transition and added scholarly weight to the more ideological aspirations of the political elite.[8]

The basic assumption was that the community at large was a traditional society that was modernized through its incorporation within the state of Israel. More specifically, it was seen as a society in 'transition' between traditional and modern phases. These academic observers were looking for quantifiable evidence of the transformation of an Arab society and its adoption of a Western way of life. At the same time, this methodology was applied in a similar way to the Jews who came from Arab countries, the Mizrahim. Both were conceived as ideal objects for the study of modernization and Westernization.[9]

This school of thought would have a large number of successors, who followed the search for modernization with a more focused examination of the chances of 'Israelization' versus 'Palestinization' of the community. In other words, successful Westernization was equated with a collective acceptance of being part of the Jewish state, while adhering to a national Palestinian identity was considered a failure. The problem with this approach was that it was not clear whether the political elite in Israel wished to Israelize the Palestinians in the state and, far more importantly, whether a successful modernization could have led to extra 'Palestinization' of the Arabs in Israel. As the theorists among these researchers knew only too well, the politicization and nationalization of communities such as this one was a common predication by modernizationists around the Middle East and beyond. Thus a bizarre model of modernization developed, one which saw the acceptance of Israel as a Jewish state as a positive outcome of the process and regarded modernization as questionable if it produced an impulse among the Palestinians in Israel to continue their struggle in the name of Palestinian nationalism and against the Zionization of the country.

The most advanced and comprehensive attempt to deal with the subject matter from this perspective has been attempted in the last decades by Sammy Smooha, mentioned above, whose many professional and meticulous books and articles defined the state as an ethnic democracy, which was the end result of the push for Palestinization of the Arabs in Israel and the limited Israelization the Jewish state allows them. This is probably the farthest one could go without directly challenging the basic assumptions of Zionism or modernization theories.[10]

This was until recently a dominant feature of the research, but it is much more marginalized today as a result of the overall decline of modernization theories and the new tensions that have emerged in the twenty-first century, which cast doubts on the sanguine assumptions of such researchers. What caught the critics' eyes were also some method-ological questions. The common methodological approach in terms of research on the Palestinian community, throughout its history, has been the in-depth interview. Given that this is an oppressed community that conceives any questionnaire, whether official or academic, as an attempt to invade its privacy and expose its disloyalty, relying on the answers to questions asked by Israeli Jewish scholars is the least scholarly method one could think of.

This was the major problem in authenticating the reported answers on Palestinian attitudes in Israel towards either 'Israelization' or 'Palestinization'. But in more general terms, even when they have been carried out in a more open atmosphere free from exogenous pressures, such interviews quite often provide an incomplete picture of people's political or ideological attitudes. The analysis in the mainstream research on the attitudes of Palestinians towards Israel was based on the common social-science practice of dividing a political attitude into three components: cognitive, behavioural and emotional. The social-science research in general, and not only in this case, fails constantly to deal with the last of the three, which in the case of nationalist senti-ment and attitude is crucial.

This book has attempted in a modest way to examine the positions of individuals and groups as they were manifested in the realm of emotions. One helpful approach is that which draws on various disci-plines and recent developments in cultural studies, and in particular from the new meeting point between historiography and hermeneutics. This last juncture has produced some excellent conceptualizations of human behaviour as a textual representation. Further developments in this particular aspect of research have also opened new vistas to those who sense that the researcher's own understanding of someone else's under-standing of a reality – an area developed by the late Paul Ricoeur – plays a crucial part in books like this one.[11] Very few, if any, academics who have written about the Palestinians in Israel are detached enough from the issue; in fact most of them are deeply involved in the affairs of the community in one way or another. Hans-Georg Gadamer has suggested, compellingly, that we should accept historiographical understanding as a limited affair by which the historian's contemporary interpretation of reality, familiar and clear, fuses with that of his subject matter, distant and murky, and it is impossible to turn them into two discrete explanations.[12] But more important for our case is the ability, with this interdisciplinary approach in mind, to extract the attitudes and positions of Palestinians towards the Jewish state from cultural works, be they poems, novels or movies, in addition to the more conventional sources concerning the Palestinians in Israel's attitudes towards the Jewish state and to their Palestinian affiliations.

Adopting the modernizationist paradigm did not necessarily mean condoning Israeli policies. During the 1970s, Israeli anthropologists, like their peers in the general field of Middle Eastern studies, condemned the accelerated modernization that undermined the rural areas without providing adequate infrastructure elsewhere. One should also say that although this mainstream anthropological effort came under severe criticism from non-Zionist scholars[13] – and it was very valid criticism in most cases in my view – these anthropologists developed closer human ties with the Palestinians themselves, their language and culture.[14]

It should be noted that modernization is still an approach that is present in the continuing research on the Palestinians in Israel, although it is much more marginal than before. It was first challenged from outside Israel in the early 1970s by Palestinians researching abroad and by some interested scholars who began to appreciate the value of examining these case studies more closely.

EARLY CHALLENGES

The opposing theory developed in three different locations simultaneously. It was a mixture of individual and collective effort. The first impressive push of the envelope was done by Elia Zureik, originally a Palestinian Israeli who left to study and teach abroad in the early 1970s. His *The Palestinians in Israel: A Study of Internal Colonialism* (1979) was the first Palestinian scholarly attempt to engage with the issue and analyse the Palestinian community within the framework of critical sociology that examined them as an ethno-national group surviving within a colonialist model.[15] Zureik himself noted rightly how different his study was from all the previous works on the subject, the vast majority of which were written by Israeli sociologists who focused more on Israeli policies and less on the Palestinian community itself.

Zureik's book not only posed a theoretical challenge, but also demanded that critical analysis of Israel be seen as legitimate, at a time when any criticism of Israel's policies was attacked as being anti-Semitic. Zureik realized that any book on the Palestinians in Israel was also a book about Israel, and that any book written from the minority's point of view was quite likely to challenge the Israelis' self-image, endorsed by many people in the West at the time, of Israel as being a progressive, socialist and democratic society.

Zureik located the Palestinian community in what he called the third cycle of colonization in Palestine: the first being the Ottoman, the second the British and the third Zionist/Israeli. This was also the most modern and institutionalized form of colonialism because the modern state was the vehicle, the infrastructure and the justification for the discriminatory policies towards the Palestinians. Zureik was the first to expose, layer by layer, the tightness of the administrative, legal and educational grip the Jewish state had over the Palestinian population.

His very lengthy and loaded theoretical preface to the book implies a comparison of Israel with apartheid South Africa and a rejection of Israel's new face in the 1980s, that of the pluralist society. The pluralist model implies a soft criticism of modernization, and suggests that there was no need for the brutal elimination of traditional ways of life and modes of behaviour but rather demands that the state allow the various communities that made up the Israeli society to keep their individuality to some extent. Zureik demanded the exclusion of the Palestinians from this benevolent model as they were not just a community in the multicultural fabric of Israel but a colonized minority.

Co-optation and control was the theoretical matrix the American political scientist Ian Lustick chose to challenge the accepted research agenda for the study of the Palestinians in Israel. His book, *Arabs in the Jewish State: Israel's Control of a National Minority*, was a novelty even down to its title, since the American academic establishment followed the Israeli suit and did not refer to the Palestinians in Israel as a national minority (and the PLO was still regarded as a terrorist organization and not a national movement).[16]

While Zureik was interested in offering a new paradigm for understanding Israel's policy, Lustick wanted to know why the Palestinian minority in Israel was 'quiescent'. He recorded the modes of protest, individual and collective, of Palestinians in Israel but concluded they did not amount to sustained political activity. His answer to the question was that the Jewish state constructed a very intricate system of control that kept the Palestinians oppressed on the one hand, but also disinclined to rebel on the other. Lustick's work was impressive, not the least because it was a PhD turned into a book. Very few doctoral students in the USA showed either an interest in, or an empathy for, the Palestinians in Israel. Lustick did not go as far as Zureik in adopting the colonialist paradigm – he preferred the pluralistic one. But his depiction of the daily realities conveyed a picture of anything but pluralism in Israel's relations with the Palestinian minority.

In this respect it is important to mention the pioneering work of Khalil Nakhleh and Sami Khalil Mar'i. Nakhleh was a native son of Rameh in the Galilee; he was one of the first Palestinians to graduate from an American university, in anthropology in the early 1970s, and later became the first director of the Arab Institute in Belmont, Massachusetts. His work posed the first challenges to the hegemonic anthropological Zionist depiction of the Palestinians in general and those in Israel in particular. This was one of the first affirmations of the possibility of basing the Palestinian identity of the community on sound academic research.

Sami Khalil Mar'i was one of the first Palestinian lecturers in the Israeli academy to write critical books and articles on the Arab education system in the Jewish state. To appreciate his work, which in hindsight seems to be much more tame and cautious than twenty-first-century work on similar subjects, one has to realize that he began writing when the political elite outside the ivory towers was still following a hesitant and careful line, and was only at the beginning of escaping from the oppressed margins into which it was squeezed by the Jewish state.

CRITICAL PARADIGMS

This was the early 1980s, and what followed was the entry of local and younger Palestinian academics into the research fray. They were not a homogenous group: some of them followed their Jewish teachers and looked at the minority as a case study of failed modernization, but cast the blame on Israeli policies rather than on an essentialist analysis of the community's 'backwardness'. Others, the majority, continued Zureik's work but with an additional theoretical framework that helped in one way or another to explain both the nature of the Israeli oppression and the relatively muted Palestinian reaction inside Israel. Several of them, such as Nadim Rouhana, Majid al-Haj, As'ad Ghanem, Ramzi Suleiman, Adel Manna and Ahmad Sa'di, to mention but a few, were focused on the double marginality model, which explained not only their location within the Jewish state but also the changing relationship with the Palestinian national movement. On the margins of double marginality and impressive, though very limited in numbers, a feminist critique emerged of a triple marginality, that of women inside the community.[17]

One of the first voices in this respect was that of Said Zaydani, now a scholar and resident of the West Bank, but formerly a Palestinian citizen in Israel. He went further than some of his other colleagues by offering not only an analysis of the situation but also a prognosis, and introduced the term 'cultural autonomy' as a kind of a minimum demand on behalf of the national minority. Zaydani was not the only one to leave the confinement of Israeli Jewish academia and prefer an occupied, but distinctly Palestinian, academic milieu in the West Bank. Sharif Kannaneh moved from the north of the country to Bir Zeit, but before that contributed significantly to the research on culture and history and laid the foundation for a more Palestinian-orientated historical research.

His general work was followed by other Palestinian historians in Israel, but, unlike him, very few went back to write the history of the 1948 catastrophe. Even today this is still chiefly the domain of critical Israeli Jewish historians; one can venture a somewhat psychological explanation for this reluctance, that of repression: an unwillingness to confront the trauma of loss and destruction. In any case, this has been changing in recent years. Recently Mustafa Abbasi of the University of Haifa, Mustafa Kabha of the Open University and Adel Manna, head of the Arab Society section at the Van Leer Institute in Jerusalem produced straightforward historical work on the 1948 period.[18] Before them, the historians of the Ottoman period, Butrus Abu-Manneh and Mahmoud Yazbak, explored the history of the land through a narrative that challenges the Zionist myth of a 'Land without People waiting for a People without a Land', whether before or during 1948. Others began writing about the history of military rule and particularly challenged the depiction of Israel as a liberal democracy.[19]

Parallel to these individual efforts, in the late 1970s and early 1980s a group of scholars at the University of Haifa started to develop a more critical engagement with the topic. Their works came out in a short-lived Hebrew publication, *Notes of Criticism (Mahbarot Bikoret)*, part of an overall Marxist critique of the Israeli society. Hence it included not only an examination of the situation of the Palestinian minority but also that of workers, women, Jews who came from Arab and Islamic countries and other marginalized groups, including the Druze community.[20]

In their wake the beginnings of a more systematic view of Israel as a settler colonialist society followed, while at the margins of the argument committed anti-Zionist activists and academic members of Matzpen added their own, at times feverish but very poignant, critique of the state. Matzpen was an offshoot organization that separated from the Israeli Communist Party in 1962, criticizing the party's obedience to Moscow and its support for the idea of a two-state solution in Israel and Palestine. It had in its midst, before it dissolved in 1982, quite a large share of academics and scholars.

In 1985, Nira Yuval Davis and Oren Yiftachel introduced another fresh perspective that would be adopted by others later on: the indigenous versus settler colonialist theoretical paradigm for understanding spatial and demographic policies against the Palestinian community in Israel; in effect, that the settlers' community received all the advantages at the expense of the indigenous population.[21] While the mainstream academia did not adopt this vocabulary, it did accept, even when it was pro-Zionist in its inclination, that ethnicity is the most powerful ingredient in the relationship between the Palestinians and the Jewish state; so powerful that it affects cultural, political and economic relationship.[22]

THE PRO- AND ANTI-ZIONIST CRITIQUE

The last wave of innovative thinking appeared in the 1990s, and though its impetus weakened at the beginning of the twenty-first century it is still present in the research on the Palestinians in Israel. Elsewhere I have termed this wave post-Zionist research, referring mainly to Jewish scholars who have written critical works on the Zionist past and the Israeli present.[23] During that same period, however, Palestinian researchers in Israel have expanded their research, which became more professional and assertive than ever before, bringing them closer to direct confrontation with the state, especially after 2000 when the whole political system in Israel moved to the right.

An important part of the post-Zionist phenomenon has been the work of the critical sociologists in Israel. Theirs was a frontal deconstruction of the modernization theories and assumptions. In addition the research was boosted by developments elsewhere. While Jewish scholars developed a more critical approach to Zionism, past and present, Palestinian scholars looked for academic freedom outside the university and developed their own think-tanks and research institutions so as to be able to widen the scope of the research even further.

An intriguing precursor of this critique was provided by an American-Palestinian scholar, Raja Khalidi. In the late 1980s he identified the strong connection between the application of the modernization theory and the Israeli policy towards the Palestinians in Israel. The Israeli Zionist scholars have attempted to portray the benefits accruing from Israeli citizenship rather than the problems. The stress was thus placed on economic performance in comparison to neighbouring Arab states or to the Mandatory period; the theoretical rights granted by law – in particular the right to vote and to be elected; and the right to education and health services. Khalidi showed that this depiction was based on the conceptions of the modernization theories and their distorted tools for measuring success and development. Thus movement away from traditional patterns of economic production and political behaviour was depicted as morally desirable, and intensified contact with Israeli Jews was seen as improving life for the Palestinians in Israel. In fact, modernization moved economically at two different paces, and thus the Palestinian economy in Israel was an enclaved market within the Israeli economy.[24]

IN SEARCH OF ACADEMIC AUTONOMY

Leading this trend was by now the famous politician Azmi Bishara, still in his role as an academic, who contributed extensively both theoretically and practically to the study of the community. His main impact was in locating the Palestinians in Israel firmly within the overall Palestinian history and even beyond the Arab world as a whole. In a pioneering article written in 1993 he argued forcefully for the inclusion of the history of the Palestinian community within the general Palestinian and Arab histories. The Palestinians in Israel, he wrote, 'have the same historical departure point as the other Palestinian groups'.[25] This observation enabled him to chart more clearly the uniqueness of the community's national agenda within the general Palestinian reality.

What made them different is their location as a national minority on the margins of the Jewish state. They became citizens of a state they had not chosen to join and it had not elected to have them as citizens.

Bishara's personal history, as well as the growing involvement of Palestinian Israeli scholars in the research into the group, indicates how superfluous it would be to look for 'objective' or even neutral research on the topic. Similarly, the counter-narrative of a community enjoying a benevolent modernizing state that offers them a better future than that of other Arab peoples is only provided by Israeli scholars who declare themselves to be loyal Zionist citizens of the state. This is not to say that the research is not professional, but it is full of contradictions because, apart from a very few outsiders, the subject directly affects those who write about it. The history of the research is thus marked by these affiliations and identities as much as by the declassification of new material or the development of new theoretical approaches.

In the 1990s a plethora of articles and books enriched beyond recognition the study of the Palestinians in Israel – ironically at a time when the overall peace process totally ignored them. This author contributed, and subscribed to the more critical point of view, as this book clearly shows, but nonetheless has relied heavily on the works and professionalism of the more conventional and mainstream scholars with whom he disagrees ideologically.

The critical, and one can say currently the dominant, view is that of Israel as an ethnic state imposed on a bi-national reality. The tension between the practical and symbolic representations of the state as purely Jewish in an absolute reality of bi-nationalism has been the main source of the tensions in the past and could be crucial in determining Israel's fate in the future. So far, governments and the establishment have succeeded in maintaining by force a correlation between the Jewish national boundaries and the civil one, which has left the Palestinians outside the common good, in republican terms, and made them stateless members of the state. Growing numbers of researchers have warned that this may not be sustainable in the long term.

What has marginalized the more loyal research are the facts on the ground. Even mainstream scholars could not deny that sixty years of continued discrimination could be explained merely as a policy; it reflected a strategy. Through analysis of the education system, the official language, spatial policies, legal practices, media treatment[26] and other aspects of life, the discrimination has become more evident, even if at times subtle. All this essential research has been done by Palestinian scholars teaching and working in Israel.[27] This academic representation challenges the Israeli pretence that it is the only democracy in the Middle East (which it is, but only for its Jewish citizens). It is also impressive as an interdisciplinary scholarly effort that at times has needed collaborative work, quite often by Arab and Jewish academics working together, to provide a comprehensive picture of the reality in which the Palestinians in Israel live.

Some (for example the human rights and peace activist Uri Davis) went as far as to define the state as an apartheid state on the basis of its present laws, practices and realities.[28] The record in terms of economic policies is from any theoretical perspective damning, but the record in terms of standard of living and health (for instance) less so. The colonialist paradigm was also introduced to the study of the Palestinian community; the methods employed by the white settlers in South Africa were emulated by the early Zionists and the discourse explaining why White had a supreme right over the land was echoed by some of the writings of the mainstream Zionist ideologues, as can be seen from the studies by the Palestinian scholar Nur Masalha.[29] This model, as can be seen from a later book by Jimmy Carter,[30] is reserved more commonly for the Israeli occupation of the West Bank and the Gaza Strip. This is a good place to highlight the importance of Nur Masalha's contribution over the years. Born in Daburiyya in the Galilee and blocked from pursuing a decent academic career in Israel, he moved to England but never lost his interest in the community. His knowledge of Hebrew and of the Israeli Jewish mindset enabled him to analyse and explain Israeli policies over the years. He was also one of the first scholars to highlight the plight of the internal refugees in Israel.

The new research has also contributed to a different vocabulary and political dictionary. In Israel the term 'Arabs' has been replaced with all kinds of variations on the theme of the Palestinians in Israel. The new discourse also includes dichotomies that have never used before, such as settlers versus native or indigenous population.

THE AGE OF THE ETHNOCRACY

The preferred term for the Israeli state now seems to be an ethnocracy, or the alternative (invented by Sammy Smooha, who is still an important voice in research on the Palestinians in Israel) of an ethnic democracy.[31] The former does not recognize the constitutional and political regime in Israel as democratic, apart from superficial and formal democratic procedures, whereas the latter includes Israel as one possible sample, albeit a flawed one, of a democratic regime. In this respect, the works of Nadim Rouhana, Oren Yiftachel and As'ad Ghanem are important consolidations of this conceptual approach.[32]

Whether Israel is analysed as an ethnocracy or as an ethnic democracy, in both models it is a regime obsessed with demographic questions, an obsession which has overridden any other considerations when it comes to the formulation of policies towards the Palestinian minority. Thus even sixty years on, the academic research navigates between a meta-narrative of oppression, internal colonialism and discrimination on the one hand, and individual stories of relative success and loopholes in the system that enable some sort of equality and normality on the other. In the background also are hopeful statements by the government about allocating more money to the 'sector' (as official Israeli discourse defines the Palestinian minority) while at the same time every political representative who is not a member of a Zionist party is frequently called in by the police to be investigated on charges of treason or incitement.

The bottom line is a very rich literature which, especially in recent years, covers almost every aspect of life in the Palestinian community. It forms an articulate position not only about the Palestinians in Israel but also about the history of knowledge production on them. This literature has not always resonated with the agenda and the problems of the Palestinian community itself, but its discussions, even in the most abstract way, of issues such as identity, tradition and dignity, often echo less academic and more popular discussions within the Palestinian community.

The obsession with demography should have given demographers an unprecedented role in academic research on the community, and there is a high proportion of that kind of research in Israel. Most of it is still in the form of very professional, jargon-heavy, quantitative social-science articles. Some of these works are not even overtly ideological or political. Thus the demographers were able to extract more information from the Palestinian community, not only as a result of political awareness or commitment, but by the improvement of the techniques in this particular field.[33]

Demographers have also done essential work over the years in exposing the improvements in the community's living standards, the decrease in death and birth rates, the rise in the age of those getting married and similar features that have breathed fresh air into the unfashionable modernization theories of transformation. While the data reaffirmed a process of change within the recognizable parameters of modernization, when compared to the patterns of change in the Jewish community it suggested the same oppressive, and in part stagnant, picture depicted by the other academic disciplines. And, as mentioned, nowadays the preferred explanation for the gap is the ethnocratic model, that is, an intentional discrimination and favouritism towards one ethnic group at the expense of the other.

I have not mentioned every type of research that has been carried out, as the Palestinian community has been the subject matter of almost every theory in the human and social sciences that one can think of. Thus, for example, psychology students quite often targeted the Palestinian community in order to test the validity of socio-psychological theories, and through them tried to understand the relationship between the Jews and the Arabs in Israel – a pioneer in this field was Ramzi Suleiman of the University of Haifa. Theories that engaged with inter- and intra-group conflicts, self and external images in the making of conflicts – the work done by Daniel Bar-Tal and his associates at the University of Tel Aviv has been particularly extensive – and the role of group therapies in solving the tensions are quite abundant and useful.[34]

But the most important work has been and is still being done in political sociology, geography, political science and cultural studies. Put together, as has been attempted in this book, they compensate for the lack of media attention and for the world's indifference to this crucial group of people on whom much of what happens in Israel and Palestine may depend in the not-so-distant future.

NOTES

PROLOGUE: HOSTILE ALIENS IN THEIR OWN HOMELAND

1   These entries can be found in Bracha Habas, *The Book of the Second Aliya*, Tel Aviv: Am Oved, 1947 (Hebrew), which is a collection of letters and diary entries of the settlers who came around 1905. See also Nur Masalha, *Expulsion of the Palestinians: The Concept of 'Transfer' in Zionist Political Thought, 1882–1948*, Institute of Palestine Studies, Washington DC, 1992.

2   Herzl's diary, 12 June 1895, translated from German by Michael Prior; see Michael Prior, 'Zionism and the Challenge of Historical Truth and Morality' in M. Prior (ed.), *Speaking the Truth about Zionism and Israel*, Melisende, London, 2004, p. 27.

3   Ibrahim Abu Lughod, Review: *Palestine Arabs in Israel* by Sabri Jiryis, *MERIP Reports*, no. 58 (June 1977), p. 19.

4   The Center for National Security, Univeristy of Haifa Report, 2007.

5   Oren Yiftachel, 'Ethnocracy, Geography and Democracy: Comments on the Politics of the Judaization of the Land', *Alpaiym*, vol. 19 (2000), pp. 78–105 (Hebrew).

6   Arnon Golan, 'The Settlement in the First Decade' in H. Yablonka and Z. Zameret (eds), *The First Decade, 1948–1958*, Yad Ben Zvi, Jerusalem, 1997, pp. 83–102 (Hebrew).

7   Reported in *Haaretz*, 25 January 2006.

8   Amany Dayif, *Palestinian Women under the Yoke of National and Social Occupation*, Pardes, Haifa, 2007, p. 48 (Hebrew).

9   *Haaretz*, 9 January 2002.

10   The amendments to the law and an interpretation of its significance can be read on various websites such as that of the Physicians for Human Rights, *B'Tselem* and the Israeli Association for Civil Rights (mainly in their annual reports for 2006).

11   On the Jewish National Fund Law, the former Israeli Minister of Justice and Foreign Affairs, Yossi Beilin, wrote: 'this is one of darkest, racist and illegitimate laws passed in the Israeli Knesset'. See the website Black Labour (in Hebrew), www.blacklabor.org, 26 July 2007.

12   Mussawa's annual report on Racism in Israel, 2008.

13   Ibid.

14 Shlomo Hasson and Khaled Abu-Asbah, *Jews and Arabs in Israel Facing a Changing Reality: Dilemmas, Trends, Scenarios and Recommendations*, The Floersheimer Institute for Policy Studies, Jerusalem, 2003, pp. 99–100 (Hebrew).

15 *Haaretz*, 26 September 2010.

16 This transpired when the Israeli army radio station, in cooperation with the Palestinian NGO Mussawa, sent one of its members to try to be hired by the coffee chain, see *Haaretz*, 7 June 2006.

17 *Haaretz*, 4 October 2010.

INTRODUCTION

1 Sammy Smooha and Don Peretz, 'The Arabs in Israel', *Journal of Conflict Resolution*, vol. 26, no. 3 (September 1982), pp. 451–84.

2 Nadim N. Rouhana, 'The Political Transformation of the Palestinians in Israel: From Acquiescence to Challenge', *Journal of Palestine Studies*, vol. 18, no. 3 (Spring 1989), p. 55.

3 Rouhana, ibid., p. 55.

4 Nadim N. Rouhana, *Palestinian Citizens in an Ethnic Jewish State: Identities in Conflict*, Yale University Press, New Haven, 1997 and As'ad Ghanem, *The Palestinian-Arab Minority in Israel, 1948–2000: A Political Study*, SUNY Press, New York, 2001.

5 Ilan Pappé, *The Ethnic Cleansing of Palestine*, Oneworld Publications, New York and London, 2006.

6 Ilan Pappé, *Out of the Frame: The Struggle for Academic Freedom In Israel*, Pluto Press, London, 2010.

CHAPTER 1: OUT OF THE ASHES OF THE *NAKBAH*

1 Ilan Pappé, *The Ethnic Cleansing of Palestine*, Oneworld Publications, New York and London, 2006, pp. 17–22.

2 David Ben-Gurion oral testimony, Report to the General Assembly, vol. 3, annex A, UN Publications, Lake Success, 1941, p. 17.

3 Ilan Pappé, *The Making of the Arab-Israeli Conflict, 1947–51*, I.B. Tauris, London and New York, 1994, pp. 17–25.

4 Two books were published recently with both photos of the period and an analysis of them: Ariela Azouali, *Formative Violence, 1958–1950*, Resling, Tel Aviv, 2008 (Hebrew) and Rona Sella, *For the Public Eye: Photos of the Palestinians in the Israeli Military Archives*, Helena, Tel Aviv, 2009 (Hebrew) – two volumes: one with text and one with photos that came out in a limited edition.

5 Ben-Gurion Archives, Ben-Gurion's Diary.

6 Pappé, *The Ethnic Cleansing*, pp. 179–95.

7 Quoted in Isabelle Humphries, 'A Muted Sort of Grief: Tales of Refuge in Nazareth (1948–2005)' in Nur Masalha (ed.), *Catastrophe Remembered: Palestine, Israel and the Internal Refugees*, Zed Books, London, 2005, p. 150.

8 Her story is recounted in detail in Adri Nieuwhof and Jeff Handmaker, 'Haifa, Peaceful Town with a Silent Pain', *Electronic Intifada*, 21 June 2005.

9 Pappé, *The Making of the Arab-Israeli Conflict*, pp. 228–33.

10 Emil Habibi interview on the website of the Israeli Communist Party, www.maki.org.il. There is now a large section of oral history on the occupation of Haifa and the struggle to keep Abbas Street on that website.

11 In Yaira Ginosar, 'The Red Parcel in Sarya, the Devil's Daughter: A Chapter from a Woman and her Men in Emil Habibi's Work', *Iyunim be-Tekumat Israel* (a journal in Hebrew Studies in the History of Israel), vol. 10 (2000), p. 595.

12 Quoted in Donald Neff, 'Arab Jaffa Seized before Israel's Creation in 1948', *Washington Report*, April–May 1994, p. 75.

13 Bulus Farah, *From Ottoman Rule to a Hebrew State: The Life Story of a Communist and a Palestinian Patriot, 1910–1991*, al-Sawt, Haifa, 1985 and a Hebrew version appeared with a forward by Udi Adiv in 2009, pp. 120–21.

14 The protocol in full is in Tom Segev, *1949: The First Israelis*, Holt and Company, New York, 1986, pp. 68–72.

15 Hanna Nakkarah, *Memoirs*, unpublished manuscript, p. 38.

16 This relationship in the past and in the present is explored in several sources. The most comprehensive ones are Ella Shohat, *Israeli Cinema, East/West and the Politics of Representation*, University of Texas Press, Austin, 1989; Sami Shalom Chetrit, *Intra-Jewish Conflict in Israel: White Jews, Black Jews*, Routledge, Oxford, 2009; and Yehouda Shenhav, *The Arab Jews: A Postcolonial Reading of Nationalism, Religion and Ethnicity*, Stanford University Press, Stanford, 2006.

17 IDF Archives, 49/6127, telegram from Brigade 7, HQ, 17 July 1948 and Ben-Gurion's reply scribbled on it.

18 See the historical background chapter in the Arab Association for Human Rights 2005 report titled 'On the Margins 2005: Annual Review of Human Rights Violations of the Arab Palestinian Minority in Israel 2005', Nazareth, 2005, and available electronically on the Association's website: www.arabhra.org.

19 Muhammad Hasan Amara and Abd el-Rahman Mar'i, *Language Education Policy: The Arab Minority in Israel*, Kluwer Academic Publishers, Boston, 2002 and Muhammad Amara and Sufyan Kabha, *A Divided Identity: Political Division and Social Implications in a Divided Village*, Institute for Peace Studies, Givat Haviva, 1996.

20 Pappé, *The Ethnic Cleansing*, pp. 193–95.

21 Ibid., pp. 91–103.

22 'Wedding at Beit Safafa', *Time* magazine, 3 September 1956.

23 See the interview with survivors quoted in Ilan Pappé, 'The Tantura Case in Israel: The Katz Research and Trial', *Journal of Palestine Studies*, vol. 30, no. 3 (Spring 2001), pp. 19–39.

24 In fact Ben-Gurion already declared many parts of Palestine as purely Jewish for the first time after two thousand years in his speech to the Zionist Executive on 6 April 1948, see David Ben-Gurion, *In the Campaign*, vol. 5, Tel Aviv, Israeli Ministry of Defense, (1952), pp. 288–301 (Hebrew).

25 This is the theory put forward in Yair Bäuml, *A Blue and White Shadow: The Israeli Establishment's Policy and Actions among the Arab Citizens. The Formative Years, 1958–1968*, Pardes, Haifa, 2007.

26 On Palmon's role in the 1948 ethnic cleansing, see Pappé, *The Ethnic Cleansing*, pp. 20–21, 52–3.

27 Benny Morris, *The Birth of the Palestinian Refugee Problem Revisited*, Cambridge University Press, Cambridge, 2003, p. 529.

28 14 January 1953.

29 Moshe Sharett, *Political Diary*, Am Oved, Tel Aviv, 1972, vol. 5, p. 506 (Hebrew).

30 See more on Sharett in Ilan Pappé, 'An Uneasy Coexistence: Arabs and Jews in the First Decade of Statehood' in S. I. Troen and N. Lucas (eds), *Israel: The First Decade of Independence*, SUNY Press, New York, 1995, pp. 633–51.

31 Elie Rekhess, 'Initial Israeli Policy Guidelines towards the Arab Minority, 1948–1949', in L. J. Silberstein (ed.), *New Perspectives on Israeli History: The Early Years of the State*, SUNY Press, New York, 1991, pp. 103–23.

32 Segev, *1949: The First Israelis*, p. 60.

33 Ian Lustick, *Arabs in the Jewish State: Israel's Control of a National Minority*, University of Texas Press, Austin, 1980, p. 78.

34 These ideas were aired in a meeting Ben-Gurion had with his Advisors on Arab Affairs in Tiberias and recorded in his diary. Ben-Gurion Archives, Ben-Gurion's Diary, entry 18 December 1948.

35 These policies of expulsion between 1948 and 1967 are discussed at length by Nur Masalha, in his *A Land Without a People: Israel, Transfer and the Palestinians*, Faber and Faber, London, 1997.

36 Benny Morris, *The Birth of the Palestine Refugee Problem Revisited*, p. 529.

37 *Al-Ittihad*, 2 March 1950.

38 Pappé, *The Ethnic Cleansing*, p. 91.

39 The Knesset Protocols, vol. 6, 10 July 1950, p. 2135.

40 Ibid., vol. 12, 23 July 1950, p. 2702.

41 See his remarks in the Israel State Archives, Foreign Ministry Files, file 2402/29, Director General Remarks on Palmon's views.

42 See Pappé, *The Making of the Arab-Israeli Conflict*, pp. 87–97.

43 Interview with Fred Sahayun carried out in his family home in July 2006.

44 This is discussed extensively in Benny Morris, *Israel's Border Wars, 1949–1956*, Clarendon Press, Oxford, 1993.

45 Ben-Gurion Archives, Ben-Gurion's Diary, entry 4 January 1949.

46 Israel State Archives, Foreign Ministry Files, file 2444/19.

47 This is described in Tom Segev, *1949: The First Israelis*, p. 60. See also Ben-Gurion Archives, Ben-Gurion's Diary, entry 7 June 1948, for a reference to the Safad expulsion. See also the complaints in the Israeli Foreign Ministry about not being told in time about these expulsions in ISA, Walter Eytan to Moshe Sharett, 11 September 1949, doc. 279, pp. 451–2.

48 See comprehensive research on the question in Michael R. Fischbach, *Records of Dispossession: Palestinian Refugee Property and the Arab-Israeli Conflict*, Columbia University Press, New York, 2003.

49 The Knesset Protocols, vol. 6, 10 July 1950, p. 2132.

50 Ibid., vol. 12, 23 July 1952, p. 2701.

51 Ibid., 23 July 1950, p. 2701.

52 Farah, *From Ottoman Rule*, pp. 122–4.

53 Hanna Nakkarah, *Memoirs*.

54 From Amnon Rubinstein, *The Constitutional Law of the State of Israel*, Shoken, Tel Aviv, 1974, p. 410 (Hebrew).

55 Ibid.

56 Ilan Saban, 'Minority Rights in Deeply Divided Societies: A Framework for Analysis and the Case of the Arab-Palestinian Minority in Israel', *International Law and Politics*, vol. 36 (June 2005), pp. 885–1001.

57 Joel S. Migdal, 'State and Society in a Society without State' in Gabriel Ben-Dor (ed.), *The Palestinians and the Middle East Conflict*, Tel Aviv University Publications, Tel Aviv, no date, pp. 396–7.

CHAPTER 2: THE OPEN WOUND: MILITARY RULE AND ITS LASTING IMPACT

1 *The Diary of a Military Governor*, Tel Aviv, 1954.

2 The book came out also in English, Emile Habiby, *The Secret Life of Saeed, the Pessoptimist*, translated from Arabic by Salma Khadra Jay Linn Yusi and Trevor LeGassick, Zed Books, London, 1985.

3 Bäuml, *A Blue and White Shadow: The Israeli Establishment's Policy and Action among the Arab Citizens. The Formative Years, 1958–1968*, Pardes, Haifa, 2007.

4 Dan Rabinowitz and Khawla Abu Bakr, *Coffins on Our Shoulders*, University of California Press, Berkeley, 2005.

5 See in Bäuml, *A Blue and White Shadow* on the special committee.

6 *Haparklit* (the Advocate), February 1946, p. 58 (Hebrew).

7 Ibid., pp. 58–64.

8 The Knesset Protocols, vol. 9, 22 May 1951, pp. 183–4.

9 Ibid.

10 Alina Korn, 'Crime and Law Enforcement in the Israeli Arab Population under the Military Government 1948–1966', in S.I. Troen and N. Lukas (eds), *Israel: The First Decade of Independence*, SUNY Press, New York, 1995, pp. 683–98.

11 See the complaints to Ben-Gurion in Gershon Rivlin and Elhanan Oren (eds), *Ben-Gurion, The War of Independence: Ben-Gurion's Diary*, Ministry of Defense Publication, Tel Aviv, 1982, vol. 3, 9 October 1948, p. 740.

12 Sarah Ozacky-Lazar, 'Israeli Arab Positions towards the State, 1949–1967', MA Haifa University 1990, pp. 37–8.

13 Nur Masalha, *A Land without a People: Israel, Transfer and the Palestinians*, Faber and Faber, London, 1997.

14 *Al-Ittihad*, 6 July 1950.

15 Masalha, *A Land without a People*.

16 Bäuml, *A Blue and White Shadow*.

17 Rivlin and Oren, *Ben-Gurion*, 3 December 1948, p. 863.

18 Sharett's position stemmed from a different perception of the Palestine question, see Ilan Pappé, 'Moshe Sharett, David Ben-Gurion and the "Palestinian Option", 1948–1956', *Studies in Zionism*, vol. 7, no. 1 (1986), pp. 451–60.

19 The Knesset Protocols, vol. 33, 30 June 1962, pp. 1322–3.

20 See his articles in *Beterm* of 15 May 1953 and *Ner* in April–May 1956 (these were very short newsletters).

21 The testimonies are from an article by Gadi al-Gazi, 'The Kafr Qassem Massacre 1956 and operation Mole' in http://www.tarabut.info/he/articles/article/Ben-Gurion-Kufr-Kassem/, 24 October 2009 and from Rubik Rosenthal (ed.), *Kafr Qassem: Events and Myths*, Kibbutz Meuhad, Tel Aviv, 2000 (Hebrew).

22 Ibid.

23 Ibid.

24 Ibid.

25 The Israeli Communist Party, *Kafr Qassem, 1956–2006*, a booklet published on 29 October 2006.

26 Ibid.

27 Ibid.

28 Nur Masalha, 'Operation Hafarferet and the Massacre of Kafr Qassem, October 1956', *The Arab Review* (Summer 1994), pp. 15–21.

29 The Israeli Communist Party, *Kafr Qassem, 1956–2006*.

30 Ibid.

31 Isar Harel, *Security and Democracy*, Am Oved, Tel Aviv, 1989, p. 441 (Hebrew).

32 Hillel Cohen, *Good Arabs: The Israeli Security Agencies and the Israeli Arabs, 1948–1967*, translated by Haim Watzman, University of California Press, Berkeley, 2011.

33 Bakri appears with story in a documentary film *The Milky Way* (Ali Nassar director, Sinbal production, 1997).

34 Salman Natour, *Going on the Wind*, Kibbutz Meuhad, Tel Aviv, 1992 (Hebrew).

35 Kais Firro, *The Druze in the Jewish State: A Brief History*, Brill, Leiden, 1999.

36 Rabah Halabi, *Citizens of Equal Duties, Druze Identity and the Jewish State*, Kibbutz Meudad, Tel Aviv, 2006 (Hebrew).

37 Israel State Archives, Report on the Process of Recruitment of the Arabs in Israel to the IDF, Foreign Ministry Files, 2402/18, 1 October 1954. I wish to thank Mrs Ozacky-Lazar for sharing this document with me.

38 Erez Yaakobi, Amir Paz-Fuchs and Moshe Karif, the Annual Uno Report, Qiryat Uno College, the Faculty of Law, 2009.

39 Muhammad Muslih, *The Origins of Palestinian Nationalism*, Institute of Palestine Studies, Washington DC, 1988.

40 Hanna Nakkarah, *Memoirs*.

41 Amnon Linn, *Before the Tempest: Jews and Arabs between Hope and Despair*, Kineret, Tel Aviv, 1999, p. 241 for a Zionist Perspective, and for a balanced view see

Lawrence Joffe, 'Obituaries: Maximos V: Spiritual leader of Million Christians', *The Guardian*, 28 July 2001.

42 Ibid.

43 Ilana Kaufman, *Arab National Communism in the Jewish State*, University of Florida Press, Miami, 1997 and Elie Rekhess, *The Arab Minority in Israel: Between Communism and Nationalism, 1965–1991*, Dayan Center Publication, Tel Aviv, 1992.

44 *Kol Haam*, 1 July 1953 (this was the Hebrew-language journal of the Israeli Communist Party).

45 Salman Natour, *Going on the Wind*, Kibbutz Meuhad, Tel Aviv, 1992 (Hebrew).

46 Majid al-Haj, *Education Among the Arabs in Israel: Control and Social Change*, Haifa University Press, Haifa, 1996 (Hebrew).

47 Majid al-Haj, *Social Change and Family Processes: Arab Communities in Shefar-'Am*, Westview Press, Boulder, 1997.

48 Shlomo Hasson and Khaled Abu-Asbah, *Jews and Arabs in Israel Facing a Changing Reality: Dilemmas, Trends, Scenarios and Recommendations*, The Floersheimer Institute for Policy Studies, Jerusalem, 2003, p. 98.

49 *Haaretz*, 6 March 1950 – this was raised by Tawfiq Tubi in the Knesset.

50 *Maariv*, 16 September 1950.

51 Ibid.

52 As we learn from the complaints by a Mapam member in the Knesset.

53 Musa Budeiri, *The Palestinian Communist Party: 1919–1948*, Haymarket Books, New York, 2010.

54 Linn, *Before the Tempest*, pp. 100–101.

55 Ian Lustick, *Arabs in the Jewish State: Israel's Control of a National Minority*, University of Texas Press, Austin, 1980, p. 204; Uzi Benziman and Attalah Mansour, *Sub-Tenants: The Arabs of Israel, Their Status and Policies Towards Them*, Keter, Tel Aviv, 1992, p. 66 (Hebrew).

56 From his speech, the 'Meaning of the Negev', 17 January 1955.

57 The citations and documents are from Geremy Forman, 'Military Rule, Political Manipulation, and Jewish Settlment: Israeli Mechanisms for Controlling Nazareth in the 1950s', *The Journal of Israeli History*, vol. 25, no. 2 (September 2006), pp. 335–59.

58 Ibid.

59 I have discussed this at length in Ilan Pappé, *The Modern Middle East*, Routledge, London and New York, 2006, pp. 223–69.

60 Khalil Nakhleh, 'The Direction of Local-level Conflict in Two Arab Villages in Israel', *American Enthnologist*, vol. 2, no. 3 (August 1975), pp. 497–516.

61 Gideon Shilo, *The Arabs of Israel in the Eyes of the PLO and the Arab World*, Magnes, Jerusalem, 1982, pp. 11–19 (Hebrew).

62 *Al-Ittihad*, 12 March 1955.

63 Figures are from Hanna Nakkarah, *Memoirs*.

64 Ghanem, *The Palestinian*, p. 24.

65 Reported both in *Al-Hamishmar* and *Davar*.

66 The paper was almost shut down in November 1956 following the publication of such articles, see *Al-Rabita*, 22 October 1956.

67 *Al-Ittihad*, 6 June 1957.

68 *Maariv*, 17 August 1958.

69 Linn, *Before the Tempest*, pp. 168–169.

70 Hanna Nakkarah, *Memoirs*, p. 49.

71 Ahmad H. Saadi, 'Control and Resistance at Local-level Institutions: A Study of Kafr Yassif's Local Council Under Military Rule', *Arab Studies Quarterly*, vol. 21 (2001), pp. 14–23.

72 A very personal view on al-Ard can be found in Fouzi el-Asmar, *To be an Arab in Israel*, Frances Pinter, London, 1975, pp. 62–94.

73 Ghanem, *The Palestinian-Arab Minority*.

74 Ibid., p. 108.

75 Joel Beinin, *Was the Red Flag Flying There? Marxist Politics and the Arab–Israeli Conflict in Egypt and Israel, 1948–1965*, University of California Press, Berkeley, 1990.

76 He repeated his ideas in the Protocols of the Knesset, vol. 33, 20 February 1962, p. 1319.

77 Lustick, *Arabs in the Jewish State*.

78 Rekhess, *The Arab Minority*.

79 Elia T. Zureik, *The Palestinians in Israel: A Study in Internal Colonialism*, Routledge and Kegan Paul, London, 1979, p. 200.

80 Ibid.

CHAPTER 3: MILITARY RULE BY OTHER MEANS, 1967–1977

1 Yair Bäuml, *A Blue and White Shadow: The Israeli Establishment's Policy and Action among the Arab Citizens. The Formative Years, 1958–1968*, Pardes, Haifa, 2007.

2 Majid al-Haj and Henry Rosenfeld, *Arab Local Government in Israel*, Westview Press, Boulder, 1992.

3 Shlomo Hasson and Khaled Abu-Asbah, *Jews and Arabs in Israel Facing a Changing Reality: Dilemmas, Trends, Scenarios and Recommendations*, The Floersheimer Institute for Policy Studies, Jerusalem, 2003, pp. 99–100 (Hebrew), p. 99.

4 Pappé, *Ethnic Cleansing*, p. 114.

5 Amtanes Shehadeh, *Capping the Development: The Economic Policy towards the Arab Minority in Israel*, Mada Carmel, Haifa, 2006 (Hebrew).

6 Nadim Rouhana, *Palestinian Citizens in an Ethnic Jewish State: Identities in Conflict*, Yale University Press, New Haven, 1997.

7 The history of legislation on the land laws is from the Adalah position paper published on the Israeli land law on 21 July 2009.

8 Ibid.

9 Virginia Tilley, 'Have We Passed the Tipping Point? Querying Sovereignty and Settler Colonialism in Israel-Palestine' in Ilan Pappé (ed.), *Peoples Apart: Israel, South Africa and the Apartheid Question*, forthcoming.

10 'Second Class: Discrimination against Palestinian Arab Children in Israel's Schools' available at www.hrw.org/en/reports/2001/09/30/second-class-0.

11 Khaled Abu-Asbah and Libat Avishai, *Perspectives on the Advancement of Arab Society in Israeli no. 1, Recommendations for the Improvement of the Arab Education System in Israel*, Van Leer, Jerusalem, 2007.

12 The Knesset Protocols, Session 314, from 31 March 1987, had a retrospective discussion on the situation as part of its budgetary discussions for 1987.

13 Alina Korn, 'Crime and Legal Control: The Israeli Arab Population during the Military Government Period, 1948–66' in Ilan Pappé (ed.), *The Israel/Palestine Question*, Routledge, New York and London, 2007, pp. 207–31.

14 Bäuml, *A Blue and White Shadow*, p. 245; see note 34.

15 Ibid., p. 245; see note 37.

16 Ibid.

17 *Haaretz*, 1 December 1969.

18 Fouzi El-Asmar, *To be an Arab in Israel*, Frances Pinter, London, 1975, pp. 153–201.

19 Daniel Bar-Tal and Gavriel Salomon, 'Israeli–Jewish Narratives of the Israeli–Palestinian Conflict: Evolution, Contents, Functions, and Consequences' in R. Rotberg (ed.), *Israeli and Palestinian Narratives of Conflict: History's Double Helix*, Indiana University Press, Bloomington, 2006, pp. 19–46.

20 *Davar*, 20 May 1969.

21 Uzi Benziman and Attalah Mansour, *Sub-Tenants: The Arabs of Israel, Their Status and Policies Towards Them*, Keter, Tel Aviv, 1992 (Hebrew), p. 146 and Majid al-Haj and Henry Rosenfeld, *The Education among the Arabs in Israel*, Kibbutz Mehuhad, Tel Aviv, 1990, p. 96 (Hebrew).

22 A.A. Elrazik, R. Amin and U. Davis, 'Problems of Palestinians in Israel: Land, Work and Education', *Journal of Palestine Studies*, vol. 7, no. 3 (Spring 1978), pp. 31–54.

23 Hatim Kanaaneh, *A Doctor in the Galilee: The Life and Struggle of a Palestinian in Israel*, Pluto, London, 2008, p. 8.

24 Yoram Binur's book *My Enemy, My Self*, appeared in English published by Penguin in 1990.

25 Rebecca B. Kook, *The Logic of Democratic Exclusion: African Americans in the United States and Palestinians Citizens in Israel*, Lexington Books, Boston, 2002.

26 Dan Ben David, Avenr Ahituv, Noah Levi Epstein and Haya Steir, *A Public Blueprint on the Employment Situation in Israel*, University of Tel Aviv Press, Tel Aviv, 2004 (Hebrew).

27 Ibid.

28 Muhand Mustafa and Khaled Arar, 'Access of Minorities to Higher Education: The Case of the Arab Society in Israel' and Qawasi Haj and Khaled Arar, 'The Movement of Arab Students in Israel to Jordanian Universities: Pull and Push Factors' both in Rassem Khamaisi (ed.), *The Third Book on the Arab Society in Israel*, Van Leer, Jerusalem, 2009.

29 Michael Meyer-Brodnitz and Daniel Czamanski, 'The Industrialization of the Arab Settlements in Israel', *The Economic Quarterly*, no. 128 (1986), p. 536 (Hebrew).

30 I. Schnell, I. Benenson, M. Sofer, 'The Spatial Pattern of Arab Industrial Markets in Israel', *Annals of Association of American Geographers*, vol. 89, no. 2 (1999), pp. 331–6.

31 Dan Giladi, *Politics and Economy*, Tel Aviv University, Tel Aviv, 1998 p. 18 (Hebrew).

32 Ghanem, *The Palestinian-Arab Minority*.

33 An overview can be found in As'ad Ghanem and Faisal Azaiza, *Is It Possible to Overcome the Crisis? The Arab Municipalities in Israel in the Beginning of the 21st Century*, Carmel, Jerusalem, 2008 (Hebrew).

34 Henry Rosenfeld, 'The Class Situation of the Arab National Minority in Israel', *Comparative Studies in Society and History*, vol. 20 (1978), pp. 374–407.

35 Ibid, pp. 387–8.

36 Rouhana, *Palestinian Citizens*.

37 *Al-Ittihad*, 1 August 1967.

38 *Haaretz*, 1 April 1969.

39 Amara and Kabha, *Divided Identity*.

40 Rekhess, *The Arab Minority*, pp. 35–45.

41 Yair Ettinger, 'The PLO is his Life's Work', *Haaretz*, 17 November 2004.

42 Dan Rabinowitz, 'The Palestinian Citizens of Israel, the Concept of Trapped Minority and the Discourse of Transnationalism in Anthropology', *Ethnic and Racial Studies*, vol. 24, no. 1 (1 January 2001), pp. 64–85.

43 Nadim Rouhana, 'Accentuated Identities in Protracted Conflicts: The Collective Identity of the Palestinian Citizens in Israel, *Asian and African Studies*, 27 (1993), pp. 97–127.

44 Shual Mihsal, *West Bank/East Bank: The Palestinians in Jordan, 1949–1967*, Yale University Press, New Haven, 1978, Peter Gubser, *Jordan: Crossroads of the Middle Eastern Events*, Westview, Boulder, 1982.

45 Rouhana, *Palestinian Citizens*, p. 217.

46 Ibid, pp. 148–9.

47 Oren Yiftachel, 'Israeli Society and Jewish-Palestinian Reconciliation: "Ethnocracy" and its Territorial Contradictions', *Middle East Journal*, vol. 51, no. 4 (Autumn 1997), pp. 505–19.

48 *Haaretz*, 6 March 1969.

49 *Davar*, 7 March 1968.

50 Azmi Bishara, 'On the Question of the Palestinian Minority in Israel', *Theory and Criticism*, 3 (1993), pp. 7–20 (Hebrew).

51 *Haaretz*, 6 March 1969.

52 *Al-Ittihad*, 2 June 1970.

53 Reported in *al-Ittihad*, 16 March 1970.

54 Hanna Nakkarah, *Memoirs*.

55 See Joel Beinin, *Was the Red Flag Flying There? Marxist Politics and the Arab–Israeli Conflict in Egypt and Israel, 1948–1965*, University of California Press, Berkeley, 1990.

56 *Davar*, 7 March 1968.

57 Adalah on Land Law.

58 Nadim Rouhana, 'The Political Transformation of the Palestinians in Israel: From Acquiescence to Challenge', *Journal of Palestine Studies*, vol. 18, no. 3 (Spring 1989), pp. 38–59.

59 Uri Davis, Antonia Maks and John Richardson, 'Israel's Water Policies', *Journal of Palestine Studies*, vol. 9, no. 2 (1980), pp. 3–32.

60 Ilana Kaufman, *Arab National Communism in the Jewish State*, Miami: University of Florida Press, 1997.

61 Rouhana, 'The Political Transformation of the Palestinians', p. 42.

62 Israeli Arabs, Ghanem calls them in his *The Palestinian-Arab Minority*.

63 Uri Davis, *Apartheid Israel: Possibilities for the Struggle from Within*, Zed Books, London, 2004.

64 I wish to thank Gabi Piterberg for pointing this out to me.

65 *Al-Hamishmar*, 15 September 1976.

66 Ghazi Falah, 'Israel's "Judaization" Policy in the Galilee', *Journal of Palestine Studies*, vol. 20, no. 4 (1991), pp. 69–85.

67 Tawfiq Zayyad, 'The Fate of the Arabs in Israel', *Journal of Palestine Studies*, vol. 6, no. 1 (Autumn 1976), pp. 92–103.

68 Raja Khalidi, 'Sixty Years after the UN Partition Resolution: What Future for the Arab Economy in Israel?', *Journal of Palestine Studies*, vol. 37, no. 2 (Winter 2008), pp. 6–22. The comparison between the Jewish and Arab places was published by the Ministry of Interior and appeared in *al-Ittihad* on 21 November 1989.

69 *Haaretz*, 21 March 1976.

70 *Haaretz*, 30 March 1976,

71 *Yediot Achronot*, 10 March 1976.

72 Interview in Adalah newsletter, vol. 11, March 2005.

73 These quotes are from Oren Yiftachel, 'The Day of the Land' in Adi Ophir (ed.), *Fifty to Forty Eight: Critical Moments in the History of Israel*, Van Leer, Jerusalem, 1999, pp. 279–99, and the interview by Shehadeh Shehadeh in *Zo Haderech*, 31 March 2010 (both in Hebrew).

74 Ibid.

75 31 March 1976.

76 Ahmad Masarwa's testimony was published in *Matzpen*, vols 78–9, September 1976 (Hebrew).

77 Tal Ben Zvi (curator), A special exhibition by Abed Abadi and Gershon Knispel, 'The Story of a Monument: The Land Day Sakhneen: 1976–2000', 2001, Hagar Gallery, Tel Aviv.

78 E. Avraham, G. Wolfsfeld and I. Aburaiya, 'Dynamics in the News Coverage of Minorities: The Case of the Arab Citizens of Israel', *Journal of Communication Inquiry*, vol. 24, no. 2, 2002, pp. 117–33.

CHAPTER 4: BETWEEN THE DAY OF THE LAND AND THE FIRST
INTIFADA, 1976–1987

1 *Maariv*, 20 November 1978.
2 *Maariv*, 7 September 1977.
3 Ghazi Falah, *Judaization*, pp. 69–79.
4 *Haaretz*, 'The Double Test for Masad Barhoum', 8 November 2007.
5 It became such a point of interest that Cambridge University Press decided to publish a whole monograph on the topic: Tamir Sorek, *Arab Soccer in a Jewish State: The Integrative Enclave*, Cambridge University Press, New York, 2007.
6 Nadim Rouhana, 'The Political Transformation of the Palestinians in Israel: From Acquiescence to Challenge', *Journal of Palestine Studies*, vol. 18, no. 3 (Spring 1989), pp. 34–55.
7 Gershon Shafir and Yoav Peled, *Being Israeli: The Dynamics of Multiple Citizenship*, Cambridge University Press, Cambridge, 2002, pp. 94–5.
8 *Haaretz*, 25 February 1977.
9 Edward W. Said, *Culture and Imperialism*, First Vintage Books, London, 1994, pp. 3–15.
10 *Al-Ittihad*, 29 March 1977.
11 Khaled Abu-Asbah, 'The Arab Education in Israel: Dilemmas of a National Minority', The Floersheimer Institute for Policy Studies, Jerusalem, 2007.
12 Ilan Pappé, 'Post-Zionism and its Popular Cultures' in Rebecca Stein and Ted Swedenburg (eds), *Palestine, Israel, and the Politics of Popular of Culture*, Duke University Press, Durham, 2005, pp. 77–98.
13 Quoted in David Grossman, *Sleeping on a Wire: Conversations with Palestinians in Israel*, Vintage Books, London, 2010.
14 Supreme Court Files 2/83, 3/84 Nayman and Avneri against the chair of the central election committee to the 11th Knesset, verdict 39, p. 2.
15 *Maariv*, 3 June 1982.
16 Natan Baron in *Yediot Achronot*, 23 June 1982.
17 Quoted in Salman Natour, *Going on the Wind*, Kibbutz Meuhad, Tel Aviv, 1992 (Hebrew).
18 Nadim Rouhana and As'ad Ghanem, 'The Crisis of the Minorities in Ethnic States: The Case of the Palestinians in Israel', *International Journal of Middle East Studies*, vol. 30, no. 3 (August 1998), pp. 321–46.
19 See a thoughtful reflection on this in Joseph Massad, 'Palestinians and the Limits of Radicalized Discourse', *Social Text*, no. 34 (1993), pp. 94–114.
20 *Haaretz*, 16 May 1979.
21 And even more general is the approach developed by Edward W. Soja, *Thirdspace: Journeys to Los Angeles and Other Real-and-Imagined Places*, Wiley-Blackwell, London, 1996.
22 Sabri Jiryis, 'The Arabs in Israel, 1973–1979', *Journal of Palestine Studies*, vol. 8, no. 4 (Summer 1979), pp. 31–56.
23 Raif Zreik, 'Palestine, Apartheid, and the Rights Discourse', *Journal of Palestine Studies*, vol. 34, no. 1 (Autumn 2004), pp. 68–80.
24 Yoav Peled, 'Meir Khana' in Ophir, *Forty Eight on Fifty*, pp. 321–6.
25 Amendment no. 9 for the 1985 basic law was passed on 31 July 1985.
26 Joseph L. Ryan, 'Refugees within Israel: The Case of the Villages of Kafr Bir'im and Iqrit', *Journal of Palestine Studies*, vol. 2, no. 4 (summer 1973), pp. 55–8.
27 Thomas Meyer, *The Resurgence of the Muslims in Israel*, Institute for Arab Affairs, Givat Haviva, 1988 and Issam Abu Riya, 'The 1996 Split of the Islamic Movement in Israel: Between Holy Text and Israeli Palestinian Context', *International Journal of Politics, Culture, and Society*, vol. 17, no. 3 (Spring 2004), pp. 439–55.
28 Nohad Ali, 'Political Islam in an Ethnic Jewish State: Its Historical Evolution and Contemporary Challenges', *Holy Land Studies Journal*, vol. 2, 2004.

29   As'ad Ghanem, *The Palestinian-Arab Minority in Israel, 1948–2000: A Political Study*, SUNY Press, New York, 2001.

30   Aziz Haidar, *Obstacles for Economic Development in the Arab Sector in Israel*, Arab-Jewish Institute for Development, Tel Aviv, 1994 and Rames Hamaisi, 'The Arab Industry in Israel', MA thesis for the Technion in 1984 (both in Hebrew).

31   Leila Farsakh, *Palestinian Labour Migration to Israel: Labour, Land and Occupation*, Routledge, London and New York, 2005, pp. 80–90.

32   Jonathan Cook, *Blood and Religion: The Unmasking of the Jewish and Democratic State*, Pluto, London, 2004.

33   Rouhana, *The Political Transformation*, p. 41.

34   'The Arabs in the Mixed Towns: Strangers in their own Homes', *Globes*, 13 January 2002.

35   Arnon Soffer, 'The Role of Demography and Territory in Jewish–Arab Relations in Israel', *Horizons in Geography*, nos. 60–61 (2004), pp. 492–515.

36   Penny Maddrell, *The Bedouin of the Negev*, Minority Rights Group, No. 81, London, 1990.

37   *Haaretz*, 6 April 1979.

38   *Al-Ittihad*, 7 September 1978.

39   Hasson and Abu-Asbah, ibid.

40   Sammy Smooha, *The Orientation and Politicization of the Arab Minority in Israel*, Arab Jewish Center, Haifa, 1984.

41   Daphna Birenbaum-Carmeli, 'The Age Quota in the Universities (Ethnic Regulation in the Labour Market)', *Mittam*, 23 (2010), pp. 39–47 (Hebrew).

CHAPTER 5: AFTER THE FIRST *INTIFADA*: BETWEEN PALESTINIAN
ASSERTIVENESS AND JEWISH UNCERTAINTY, 1987–1995

1   Arieh Ratner and Gideon Fishman, *Justice for All? Arabs and Jews in the Israeli Justice System*, Center for Crime Investigation, Haifa University, 2001 (Hebrew).

2   See Joel Beinin and Joe Stork, 'On the Modernity, Historical Specificity, and International Context of Political Islam' in Beinin and Stork (eds), *Political Islam: Essays from Middle East Report*, University of California Press, Berkeley, 1997, pp. 3–28.

3   See note 14 in the Prologue.

4   Manar Hassan, 'The Destruction of the City and the War against Memory: The Victorious and the Defeated', *Theory and Criticism*, 27 (Autumn 2005), pp. 197–207 (Hebrew) and Hanna Herzon, *Gendering Politics, Women in Israel*, University of Michigan Press, Ann Arbor, 1999.

5   Nur Masalha, 'Present Absentees and Indigenous Resistance' in Nur Masalha (ed.), *Catastrophe Remembered*, pp. 23–55.

6   Ibid.

7   *Haaretz*, 25 August 1988.

8   Nadim Rouhana, 'The Intifada and the Palestinians in Israel: Resurrecting the Green Line', *Journal of Palestine Studies*, vol. 19, no. 3 (Spring 1990), pp. 58–75.

9   Avi Shlaim, 'The Oslo Accord', *Journal of Palestine Studies*, vol. 23, no. 4 (Spring 1994), pp. 24–40.

10   *Maariv*, 2 May 1989.

11   *Maariv*, 4 October 1989.

12   Rassem Khamaisi, *The Third Book on the Arab Society in Israel: Population, Society and Economy*, Van Leer Publications, Jerusalem, 2009.

13   Ibid.

14   *Yediot Achronot*, 27 July 1989.

15   Ibid.

16   Yossi Melman, 'So the Secret Service Demanded Equality, so What?', *Haaretz*, 23 May 2004.

17 Ibid.
18 Nadim Rouhana, 'The Political Transformation of the Palestinians in Israel: From Acquiescence to Challenge', *Journal of Palestine Studies*, vol. 18, no. 3 (Spring 1989), pp. 34–55.
19 Edward Said, 'Permission to Narrate', *Journal of Palestine Studies*, vol. 13, no. 3, 1984, pp. 27–48 and *al-Ittihad*, 1 July 1988.
20 Nurith Gertz and George Khleifi, *Palestinian Cinema: Landscape, Trauma and Memory*, Indiana University Press, Bloomington, 2008.
21 The debate took place on the pages of the monthly magazine *Politika* in January 1986.
22 Jonathan Cook, 'In Israel, Intermarriage Viewed as Treason', *The National* (Abu Dhabi), 29 September 2009.
23 Ibid.
24 *Al-Ittihad*, 30 March 1989.
25 *Al-Ittihad*, 4 February 1990
26 *Al-Sirat*, 11 February 1991
27 The position of the Communist Party in the first Gulf War is discussed in detail in Ilan Pappé, 'A Modus Vivendi Challenged, the Arabs in Israel and the Gulf War', in A. Baram and B. Rubin (eds), *Iraq under the Ba'th*, St. Martin's Press, New York, 1993, pp. 163–76.
28 See Muhamad Mia'ri's article in *al-Sunara*, 5 January 1991.
29 A distortion of Hashem Mahamid into *Hashem Tamid* ('Always guilty' in Hebrew) was the headline in *Kol Haemek Ve-Hagalil*, 15 January 1993, pp. 10–12.
30 Yercah Tal, 'Catering for Western Listeners', *Haaretz*, 30 December 1992; for Tibi's words see Shalom Yerushalmi, 'Catering for Western Listeners', *Kol Hair*, 23 November 1990, pp. 34–5.
31 *Davar*, 3 February 1991.
32 *Al-Hamishmar*, 20 January 1991.
33 *Hair*, February 1991; and see a thorough analysis of these positions in As'ad Ghanem and Sarah Ozacky-Lazar, *The Arabs in Israel under the Shadow of the Iraq War*, Institute for Peace Studies, Givat Haviva, 1991 (Hebrew).
34 *Davar*, 23 January 1991.
35 'Bridging the Green Line: The PA, Israel, and the Final Status, an Interview with Azmi Bishara', *Journal of Palestine Studies*, vol. 26, no. 3 (Spring 1997), pp. 67–80.
36 The Galilee Society's website was under construction when this book was written but its newsletters since 2003 are available online.

CHAPTER 6: THE HOPEFUL YEARS AND THEIR DEMISE, 1995–2000

1 *Haaretz*, 1 February 1996.
2 Shlomo Hasson and Khaled Abu-Asbah, *Jews and Arabs in Israel Facing a Changing Reality: Dilemmas, Trends, Scenarios and Recommendations*, The Floersheimer Institute for Policy Studies, Jerusalem, 2003, pp. 99–100 (Hebrew).
3 Nadim Rouhana, 'The Political Transformation of the Palestinians in Israel: From Acquiescence to Challenge', *Journal of Palestine Studies*, vol. 18, no. 3 (Spring 1989), p. 42.
4 *Haaretz*, 2 September 1995
5 Chris McGreal reviewed these laws and compared them to what occurred in South Africa in long review in *The Guardian* under the title 'Worlds Apart', 6 February 2006; see also Ben White, *Israeli Apartheid: A Beginner's Guide*, Pluto, London, 2009.
6 Asher Arian and Michal Shamir, *The Elections in Israel 1996*, SUNY Press, Albany, 1999.
7 Ibid.
8 All Adalah's annual reports are online at www.adalah.org.

9 The Arab Human Rights Association has published a report on the background for these clashes under the title 'Life in the Margins' the third chapter of which deals with land expropriation and house demolitions. See www.arabhra.org/hra.

10 *Haaretz*, 20 May 1996.

11 Andre Elias Mazawi, 'University Education, Credentialism and Social Stratification among Palestinian Arabs in Israel', *Higher Education*, vol. 29, no. 4 (June 1995) pp. 351–68.

12 Ilan Peleg, 'Jewish–Palestinian Relations in Israel: From Hegemony to Equality?', *International Journal of Politics, Culture, and Society*, vol. 17, no. 3 (Spring 2004), pp. 415–37.

13 Manar Hassan, 'The Politics of Honour: Patriarchy the State and the Honour Murders', in D. Izraeli (ed.), *Sex, Gender and Politics*, Hakibbutz Ha-Meuhad, Tel Aviv, 1999, pp. 267–307 (Hebrew) and M. Haj-Yahia, 'Beliefs about Wife Beating among Palestinian Women: The Influence of their Patriarchal Ideology', *Violence Against Women*, vol. 15 no. 5 (1998), pp. 533–58.

14 Nurith Gertz and George Khleifi, *Palestinian Cinema: Cinema: Landscape, Trauma and Memory*, Indiana University Press, Bloomington, 2008, pp. 171–89.

15 Arian and Shamir, *The Elections in Israel 1999*.

16 Ilan Pappé, 'The Post-Zionist Discourse in Israel', *Holy Land Studies*, vol. 1, no. 1 (2002), pp. 3–20.

17 *Haaretz*, 13 June 1996.

18 Ilan Pappé, 'The Square Circle: The Struggle for Survival of Traditional Zionism' in E. Nimni (ed.), *The Challenge of Post-Zionism*, Zed Books, London, 2003, pp. 42–62.

19 *Yediot Achronot*, 6 April 2001.

20 Ilan Gur-Zeev and Ilan Pappé, 'Beyond the Deconstruction of the Other's Collective Memory: Blueprints for Palestinian/Israeli Dialogue', *Theory, Culture & Society*, vol. 20, no. 1 (February 2003), pp. 93–108 and Azmi Bishara, 'The Arabs and the Holocaust', *Zmanim* 53 (Summer 1996), pp. 765–75 (Hebrew).

21 *Al-Ittihad*, 29 October 1997.

22 *Haaretz*, 26 April 1997.

23 Rouhana, 'The Political Transformation', p. 42; and see Mazawi, 'University Education'.

24 Aziz Haidar, *The Book of Arab Society*, Van Leer, Jerusalem, 2005, p. 175 (Hebrew).

25 *Yediot Achronot*, 19 June 2006.

26 *Hair*, September 1993.

CHAPTER 7: THE 2000 EARTHQUAKE AND ITS IMPACT

1 Azmi Bishara, 'Reflections on October 2000: A Landmark in Jewish–Arab Relations in Israel', *Journal of Palestine Studies*, vol. 30, no. 3 (Spring 2001), pp. 54–67.

2 See Nurith Gertz and George Khleifi, *Palestinian Cinema: Cinema: Landscape, Trauma and Memory*, Indiana University Press, Bloomington, 2008.

3 The Orr Commission, vol. 1, pp. 43–4.

4 See Report by the Israeli Association for Civil Rights, prepared by advocate Awni Banna and sent to the chair of the Committee for Internal Affairs in the Knesset, 10 January 2010.

5 Salim Tamari, 'What the Uprising Means', *Middle East Report*, no. 152, 'The Uprising' (May–June 1988), pp. 65–79.

6 Bishara, 'Reflections on October 2000'.

7 Nida Shoughry, ' "Israeli-Arab" Political Mobilization: Between Acquiescence, Participation and Resistance', PhD thesis, Aberystwyth University (2010).

8 As'ad Ghanem, *The Palestinian-Arab Minority in Israel, 1948–2000: A Political Study*, SUNY Press, New York, 2001.

9   Adalah report, 6 September 2006.
10 Interview in *Haaretz*, 6 October 2004.
11 Raef Zreik, 'Palestine, Apartheid, and the Rights Discourse', *Journal of Palestine Studies*, vol. 34, no. 1 (Autumn 2004), pp. 68– 80.
12 Avirama Golan in *Haaretz*, 3 October 2009.
13 Richard Falk, 'Azmi Bishara, the Right of Resistance, and the Palestinian Ordeal', *Journal of Palestine Studies*, vol. 31, no. 2 (Winter 2002), pp. 19–33.
14 For a critical view on the Arab leadership see Amal Jamal, 'The Arab Leadership in Israel: Ascendance and Fragmentation', *Journal of Palestine Studies*, vol. 35, no. 2 (Winter 2006), pp. 6–22.
15 Oren Yiftachel and As'ad Ghanem, 'Towards a Theory of Ethnocratic Regimes: Learning from the Judaization of Israel/Palestine' in Eric P. Kaufman (ed.), *Rethinking Ethnicity: Majority Groups and Dominant Minorities*, Routledge, London and New York, 2004, pp. 177–97.
16 As'ad Ghanem and Faisal Azaiza, *Is It Possible to Overcome the Crisis? The Arab Municipalities in Israel in the Beginning of the 21st Century*, Carmel, Jerusalem, 2008 (Hebrew).
17 *Haaretz*, 19 December 2003.
18 Vered Levi Barzilai, 'In Tiberias We Defined the Jewish State', *Haaretz*, 2 January 2002.
19 Ghanem, *The Palestinian-Arab Minority*.
20 Elia Zureik, 'Demography and Transfer; Israel's Road to Nowhere', *Third World Quarterly*, vol. 23, no. 4 (August 2003), pp. 619–30.
21 Levi Barzilai, 'In Tiberias'.
22 Gidi Wietz and Dror Mishani, 'Friendly Fire' an interview with A.B. Yehoshua, *Haaretz*, 13 February 2002.
23 Yitzhak Laor, 'A.B. Yehoshua and the *"Mizrachi* Animosity to the Arabs" ', *Mittam*, 2 (2005) (Hebrew).
24 The Arab–Jewish relationship Index published by the University of Haifa in 2003 called it the 'Liebermanization' of the Jewish public opinion, namely, a clear support for transfer.
25 *Jewish Week*, 30 July 2001.
26 Amos Oz, *Nomads and a Snake*, Am Oved, Tel Aviv, 1976, p. 28.
27 The Constitution draft can be read on the website of the Israel Democracy Institute in English, www.idi.org.il.
28 Shawqi Khatib, 'The Future Visions of the Palestinian-Arabs in Defining the Conflict', *BADIL's Publications* in Beit Lehem, 8 September 2009.
29 For an excellent evaluation of the vision see Ran Greenstein, 'Israel/Palestine and the Apartheid Analogy: Critics, Apologists and Strategic Lessons', *Monthly Review*, August 2007. For a Zionist perspective see Elie Rekhess, 'The Arab Minority in Israel: The Analysis of the "Future Vision" Documents', *American Jewish Congress*, www.ajc.org (no date); and Yitzhak Reiter, 'Nakba and Revival: A Zionist-Jewish Perspective on the Vision Documents of the Arabs in Israel' in S. Ozacky-Lazar and M. Kabha (eds), *Between Vision and Reality: The Vision Papers of the Arabs in Israel, 2006–2007*, Citizens' Accord Forum, Jerusalem, pp. 140–58 (Hebrew).
30 The Haifa Declaration can be found in full on the website of Mada al-Carmel, at www.mada-research.org/UserFiles/file/haifaenglish.pdf
31 I. Schnell and and M. Sofer, 'Embedding Entrepreneurship in Social Structure: Israeli Arab Entrepreneurship', *Journal of Urban and Regional Research*, 2003.
32 Ghanem, *The Palestinian-Arab Minority*.
33 Mary Totary on the vision documents, a six-page response in Hebrew on the official website of Oranim College, www.oranim.ac.il/sites/heb.
34 Sammy Smooha, 'The Israeli Palestinian-Arab Vision of a Binational Democracy', *Constellations*, vol. 16, no. 3 (September 2009), pp. 509–22.

35 Totary, on the vision documents.
36 Ghazi Falah, Israel's "Judaization" Policy in the Galilee', *Journal of Palestine Studies*, vol. 20, no. 4 (1991), pp. 69–85.
37 Diana Bachor, 'The Government Approved 14 New Settlements', *Yediot Achronot*, 21 July 2002.
38 Quoted in Ahikam Moshe David, *Maariv*, 10 September 2008.
39 *Globes*, 14 November 2004.
40 Ibid.
41 'The Olive Trees in the Land of Zion', *A Diary of Discrimination* published by the Arab Human Rights Committee, diary two published on 12 February 2008 in www.arabhra.org/HRA/Categories/CategoryPage.aspx?Category=66 on the Discrimination Diary page.
42 *Yediot Achronot*, 28 August, 2006.
43 *Haaretz*, 31 May 2005.

EPILOGUE: THE OPPRESSIVE STATE

1 See Ilan Pappé, 'The *Mukhabarat* State of Israel: A State of Oppression is not a State of Exception', in Ronit Lentin (ed.), *Thinking Palestine*, Zed Books, London, 2008, pp. 148–71.
2 Ibid.
3 Pierre van den Berghe (1981) used the term 'Herrenvolk democracy' with reference to apartheid South Africa.
4 Gershon Shafir and Yoav Peled, *Being Israeli: The Dynamics of Multiple Citizenship*, Cambridge University Press, Cambridge, 2002.
5 Pappé in Lentin.
6 Ibid.
7 John P. Entelis is one of the most prolific writers on this issue, see John P. Entelis, 'The Democratic Imperative vs. the Authoritarian Impulse: The Maghreb State between Transition and Terrorism', *Strategic Insights*, vol. 4, no. 6 (June 2005).
8 John P. Entelis, 'The Democratic Imperative vs. the Authoritarian Impulse: The Maghrib State between Transition and Terrorism', *Middle East Journal*, vol. 59, no. 4 (Autumn 2005), p. 537 (full citation pp. 537–58).
9 Pappé in Lentin.
10 Ibid.; see note 37 in the article.
11 Ibid.
12 Ibid.
13 B'tselem report, July 2009.

APPENDIX: NOTE ON THE SCHOLARSHIP

1 The first book seems to be by Walter Schwartz, *The Arabs in Israel*, Faber & Faber, London, 1959.
2 For a complete list of the academic and semi-academic works on the Palestinians in Israel see Sammy Smooha and Ora Cibulski, *Social Research on Arabs in Israel, 1948–1976: Trends and an Annotated Bibliography*, Turtledove Publishing, Ramat Gan, 1978 (Hebrew).
3 Ori Stendel, *The Arabs in Israel: A Political Study*, Sussex Academic Press. Brighton, 1996; it appeared in Hebrew for the first time in 1992.
4 Noam Chomsky, *Hegemony or Survival*, Hamish Hamilton, New York, 2003.
5 For a discussion of the application of the theories of modernization in Middle Eastern studies and the critique of it, see the discussion in Ilan Pappé, *The Modern Middle East*, 2nd edition, Routledge, New York and London, 2006, pp. 2–17; and Ahmad H. Sa'di, 'Modernization as an Explanatory Discourse of Zionist–Palestinian Relations, *British Journal of Middle East Studies*, vol. 24, no. 1 (May 1997), pp. 25–48.

6   Gabriel Piterberg, *The Returns of Zionism: Myths, Politics and Scholarship in Israel*, Verso, London, 2008.

7   Sammy Smooha, *Israel: Pluralism and Conflict*, University of California Press Berkeley, 1978, pp. 14–15.

8   See among his many books S.N. Eisenstadt, *Tradition, Change, and Modernity*, John Wiley and Sons, London, 1983 and the application of his theory for the case study of Israel in S.N. Eisenstadt, *The Transformation of Israeli Society: An Essay in Interpretation*, Westview Press, Boulder, 1986,

9   There are quite a few examples for this legacy. In 1985 his students published a book in his honour that exemplifies this trend. Erik Cohen, Moshe Lissak and Uri Almagor (eds), *Comparative Social Dynamics: Essays in Honor of S.N. Eisenstadt*, Westview Press, Boulder, 1985. See also a special issue of the journal he edited in Israel, the *Jerusalem Quarterly*, vol. 2 (Winter 1977) edited by S.N. Eisenstadt, Dan Horowitz and Moshe Lissak. The latter two were his most faithful disciples.

10 His early work includes Sammy Smooha and Don Peretz, 'The Arabs in Israel', *Journal of Conflict Resolution*, vol. 26, no. 3 (September 1982), pp. 451–84 and a later work is Sammy Smooha, 'Ethnic Democracy: Israel as an Archetype', *Israel Studies*, vol. 2, no. 2 (Fall 1997), pp. 198–241.

11 Paul Ricoeur, *The Conflict of Interpretations*, Northwestern University Press, Chicago, 1974.

12 Hans-Georg Gadamer, *Truth and Method*, Continuum, New York, 2004.

13 Typical research of the kind mentioned was done by Jacob Landau, *The Arab Minority in Israel, 1967–1991: Political Aspects*, Oxford University Press, Oxford, 1993. For a critique of Israeli anthropology, see Smadar Lavie, 'Israeli Anthropology and American Anthropology', *Anthropology News*, vol. 46, no. 1 (January 2005), p. 9.

14 See Dan Rabinowitz, 'Oriental Othering and National Identity: A Review of Early Israeli Anthropological Studies of Palestinians', *Identities: Global Studies in Culture and Power*, 9 (2002), pp. 305–24.

15 Elia Zureik, *Palestinians in Israel: A Study in Internal Colonialism*, Routledge and Kegan Paul, London, 1979.

16 Ian Lustick, *Arabs in the Jewish State: Israel's Control of a National Minority*, University of Texas Press, Austin, 1980.

17 These are just selected single publications out of the many which have been produced by these scholars. Nadim N. Rouhana, *Palestinian Citizens*; As'ad Ghanem, *The Palestinian-Arab Minority*; Majid al-Haj, *Education, Empowerment, and Control: The Case of the Arabs in Israel*, SUNY Press, New York, 1995; Ramzi Suleiman, 'Minority Self-categorization: The Case of Palestinians in Israel', *Peace and Conflict: Journal of Peace and Psychology*, vol. 8, no. 1 (March 2002), pp. 31–46; Adel Manna (ed.), *The Second Yearbook of the Arab Society in Israel*, Van Leer Publications, Jerusalem, 2008 in Hebrew; and Ahmad Sa'di, 'The Incorporation of the Palestinian Minority by the Israeli State, 1948–1970: On the Nature, Transformation and Constraints of Collaboration', *Social Text*, vol. 21, no. 2 (2003), pp. 75–94. As for the double marginality paradigm, see Ramzi Suleiman, 'Minority Self-categorization'; Nadim Rouhana, 'Interactive Conflict Resolution: Issues in Theory, Methodology and Evaluation', *International Conflict Resolutions after the Cold War*, published by the Commission on Behavioral and Social Sciences and Education, 2000, pp. 294–337; and Marwan Darwish and Andrew Rigby, *Palestinians in Israel: Nationality and Citizenship*, Peace Research Report, no. 35, University of Bradford, Bradford, 1995.

18 Adel Manna, *History of Palestine in the Late Ottoman Period, 1700–1918*, Institute of Palestinian Studies, Beirut, 1999 (Arabic).

19 Butrus Abu-Manneh, *Studies on Islam and the Ottoman Empire in the 19th Century, 1826–1876*, Isis, Istanbul, 2001; Adel Manna, *Double Marginality in Jerusalem: Palestinians, Israelis in Jerusalem*, Publication of the Jerusalem Institute, Jerusalem, 2006 (Hebrew); Mustafa Abbasi, 'The Battle for Safad in the War of 1948: A

Revised Study', *International Journal of Middle East Studies*, vol. 36, no. 1 (2004), pp. 21–47; and Mahmoud Yazbak, *Haifa in the Late Ottoman Period, 1864–1914: A Muslim Town in Transition*, Brill, Leiden, 1998.

20 Erez Wise, 'Notebooks on Criticism' in Ophir, *Forty Eight on Fifty*, pp. 301–4.

21 Davis, *Apartheid Israel* and Oren Yiftachel, 'Ethnocracy, Geography and Democracy: Comments on the Politics of the Judaization of the Land', *Alpaiym*, 19 (2000), pp. 78–105 (Hebrew).

22 See Noah Levin-Epstein and Moshe Semyonov, *The Arab Minority in Israel's Economy*; N.S. Eisendstadt, *Israeli Society*, London: Weidenfeld and Nicolson, 1967; and Eliezer Ben-Rafael, *The Emergence of Ethnicity: Cultural Groups and Social Conflict in Israel*, Greenwood, London, 1982.

23 Pappé, *Post-Zionism*.

24 Raja Khalidi, 'Sixty Years after the UN Partition Resolution: What Future for the Arab Economy in Israel?', *Journal of Palestine Studies*, vol. 37, no. 2 (Winter 2008), pp. 6–22.

25 Azmi Bishara, 'On the Question of the Palestinian Minority'.

26 Khalil Rinawai, *The Arab Society in Israel: An Ambivalent Agenda*, The College for Management Publications, Tel Aviv, 2003 (Hebrew).

27 For reference see Aziz Haidar, *The First Book of Arab Society*, pp. 13–16, which includes the main veteran and new researchers on the topic.

28 Davis, *Apartheid Israel*.

29 See Masalha, *A Land without a People*, and Masalha, 'Present Absentees'.

30 Jimmy Carter, *Palestine: Peace not Apartheid*, Simon and Schuster, New York, 2007.

31 Sammy Smooha, 'The Model of Ethnic Democracy: Israel as a Jewish and Democratic State', *Nations and Nationalism*, vol. 8, no. 4 (2002), pp. 475–503.

32 See Yiftachel, 'Ethnocracy'.

33 See the collection of Rassem Khamaisi, *The Third Book on the Arab Society in Israel: Population, Society and Economy*, Van Leer Publications, Jerusalem, 2009 (Hebrew).

34 The work that is being done by Daniel Bar-Tal is typical; see his 'Psychological Obstacles to Peace-making in the Middle East and Proposals to Overcome Them', conflict & communication online, vol. 4, no. 1 (2005), www.cco.regener-online.de

BIBLIOGRAPHY

Primary Sources

Advisor on Arab Affairs and Secret Service Compilations in Givat Haviva, Israel
Annual Reports of B''Tselem, Arab Committee for Human Rights, Adalah, Mussawa, Mada al-Carmel and the Israeli Association for Civil Rights
Ben-Gurion Archives
Communist Party Documentations and *al-Ittihad* Archival material, Emil Touma Institute, Haifa, Israel
Labour Party Archives, The Arab Committee Files, Beit Berl, Israel
Israel State Archives, Foreign Ministry Files
The Knesset Protocols

Newspapers

Davar, Fasl Maqal, Haaretz, Al-Hamishmar, Al-Ittihad, Kol-Ham, Kul-Alarab, Maariv, Sawt al-Haq wal-Huriaya, Sirat, Al-Sunara, Yediot Achronot, Zo Haderech

Secondary Sources

Abbasi, M. 'The Battle for Safad in the War of 1948: A Revised Study', *International Journal of Middle East Studies*, vol. 36, no. 1 (2004), pp. 21–47
Abu-Asbah, K. 'The Arab Education in Israel: Dilemmas of a National Minority', The Floersheimer Institute for Policy Studies, Jerusalem, 2007
Abu-Asbah, K. and Avishai, L. *Perspectives on the Advancement of Arab Society in Israel, No. 1, Recommendations for the Improvement of the Arab Education System in Israel*, Van Leer Institute, Jerusalem, 2007 (Hebrew)
Abu-Manneh, B. *Studies on Islam and the Ottoman Empire in the 19th Century, 1826–1876*, Isis Press, Istanbul, 2001
Abu-Raya, I. 'The 1996 Split of the Islamic Movement in Israel: Between Holy Text and Israeli Palestinian Context', *International Journal of Politics, Culture and Society*, vol. 17, no. 3 (Spring 2004), pp. 439–55
Al-Haj, M. *Education, Empowerment, and Control: The Case of the Arabs in Israel*, SUNY Press, New York, 1995

——, *Education Among the Arabs in Israel: Control and Social Change*, Haifa University Press, Haifa, 1996 (Hebrew)

——, *Social Change and Family Processes: Arab Communities in Shefar-'Am*, Westview Press, Boulder, 1997

Al-Haj, M. and Rosenfeld, H. *Arab Local Government in Israel*, Westview Press, Boulder, 1990

——, *The Education among the Arabs in Israel*, Kibbutz Mehuhad, Tel Aviv, 1990 (Hebrew)

Ali, N. 'Political Islam in an Ethnic Jewish State: Historical Evolution, Contemporary Challenges and Future Prospects', *Holy Land Studies Journal*, vol. 3, no. 1 (2004)

Amara, M.H. and Kabha, S. *A Divided Identity: Political Division and Social Implications in a Divided Village*, Institute for Peace Studies, Givat Haviva, 1996

Amara, M.H. and Mar'i, A. *Language Education Policy: The Arab Minority in Israel*, Kluwer Academic Publishers, Boston, 2002

Arian, A. and Shamir, M. *The Elections in Israel 1996*, SUNY Press, Albany, 1999.

——, *The Elections in Israel 1999*, SUNY Press, Albany, 2002

El-Asmar, F. *To Be an Arab in Israel*, Frances Pinter, London, 1975

Avraham, E., Wolfsfeld, G. and Aburaiya, I. 'Dynamics in the News Coverage of Minorities: The Case of the Arab Citizens of Israel', *Journal of Communication Inquiry*, vol. 24, no. 2 (2000), pp. 117–33

Azouali, A. *Formative Violence, 1958–1950*, Resling, Tel Aviv (Hebrew)

Bar-Tal, D. 'Psychological Obstacles to Peace-making in the Middle East and Proposals to Overcome Them', *conflict & communication online*, vol. 4, no. 1 (2005), www.cco.regener-online.de

Bar-Tal, D. and Salomon, G. 'Israeli–Jewish Narratives of the Israeli–Palestinian Conflict: Evolution, Contents, Functions, and Consequences' in R. Rotberg (ed.), *Israeli and Palestinian Narratives of Conflict: History's Double Helix*, Indiana University Press, Bloomington, 2006, pp. 19–46

Bäuml, Y. *A Blue and White Shadow: The Israeli Establishment's Policy and Action among the Arab Citizens. The Formative Years, 1958–1968*, Pardes, Haifa, 2007

Beinin, J. *Was the Red Flag Flying There? Marxist Politics and the Arab–Israeli Conflict in Egypt and Israel, 1948–1965*, University of California Press, Berkeley, 1990

Beinin, J. and Stork, J. 'On the Modernity, Historical Specificity, and International Context of Political Islam' in J. Beinin and J. Stork (eds), *Political Islam: Essays from Middle East Report*, University of California Press, Berkeley, 1996, pp. 3–31

Ben David, D., Ahituv, A., Levi Epstein, N. and Steir, H. *A Public Blueprint on the Employment Situation in Israel*, University of Tel Aviv Press, Tel Aviv, 2004 (Hebrew)

Ben-Rafael, E. *The Emergence of Ethnicity: Cultural Groups and Social Conflict in Israel*, Greenwood, London, 1982

Ben-Gurion, D. *In the Campaign*, vol. 5, Israeli Ministry of Defense, Tel Aviv (1952) pp. 288–301 (Hebrew)

Benziman, U. and Mansour, A. *Sub-Tenants: The Arabs of Israel, Their Status and Policies Towards Them*, Keter, Tel Aviv, 1992 (Hebrew)

Binur, Y. *My Enemy, My Self*, Penguin, London, 1990

Birenbaum-Carmeli, D. 'The Age Quota in the Universities (Ethnic Regulation in the Labour Market)', *Mittam*, 23 (2010), pp. 39–47 (Hebrew)

Bishara, A. 'On the Question of the Palestinian Minority in Israel', *Theory and Criticism*, vol. 3 (1993), pp. 7–20 (Hebrew)

——, 'The Arabs and the Holocaust', *Zmanim*, vol. 53 (Summer 1995), pp. 765–75, (Hebrew)

—— 'Reflections on October 2000: A Landmark in Jewish–Arab Relations in Israel', *Journal of Palestine Studies*, vol. 30, no. 3 (Spring 2001), pp. 54–67

Meyer-Brodnitz, M. and Czamanski, D. 'The Industrialization of the Arab Settlements in Israel', *The Economic Quarterly*, no. 33 (1986), pp. 533–46 (Hebrew)

Budeiri, M. *The Palestinian Communist Party: 1919–1948*, Haymarket Books, New York, 2010

Carter, J. *Palestine: Peace not Apartheid*, Simon and Schuster, New York, 2007

Chetrit, S.S. *Intra-Jewish Conflict in Israel: White Jews, Black Jews*, Routledge, Oxford, 2009

Chomsky, N. *Hegemony or Survival*, Hamish Hamilton, New York, 2003

Cohen, E., Lissak, M. and Almagor, U. (eds) *Comparative Social Dynamics: Essays in Honor of S.N. Eisenstadt*, Westview Press, Boulder, 1985

Cohen, H. *Good Arabs: The Israeli Security Agencies and the Israeli Arabs, 1948–1967*, trans. by Haim Watzman, University of California Press, Berkeley, 2010

Cook, J. *Blood and Religion: The Unmasking of the Jewish and Democratic State*, Pluto, London, 2004

—— 'In Israel, Intermarriage Viewed as Treason', *The National* (Abu Dhabi), 29 September 2009

Dayif, A. *Palestinian Women under the Yoke of National and Social Occupation*, Pardes, Haifa, 2007 (Hebrew)

Davis, U. *Apartheid Israel: Possibilities for the Struggle Within*, Zed Books, London, 2004

Davis, U., Maks, A. and Richardson, J. 'Israel's Water Policies', *Journal of Palestine Studies*, vol. 9, no. 2 (1980), pp. 3–32

Darwish, M. and Rigby, A. *Palestinians in Israel: Nationality and Citizenship*, Peace Research Report 35, University of Bradford, Bradford (October 1995)

Eisenstadt, S.N. *Tradition, Change, and Modernity*, John Wiley and Sons, London, 1983

——, *The Transformation of Israeli Society: An Essay in Interpretation*, Westview Press, Boulder, 1986

Elrazik, A.A., Amin R. and Davis, U. 'Problems of Palestinians in Israel: Land, Work and Education', *Journal of Palestine Studies*, vol. 7, no. 3 (Spring 1978), pp. 31–54

Entelis, J.P. 'The Democratic Imperative vs. the Authoritarian Impulse: The Maghreb State between Transition and Terrorism', *Strategic Insights*, vol. 4, no. 6 (June 2005)

Falah, G. 'Israel's "Judaization" Policy in the Galilee', *Journal of Palestine Studies*, vol. 20, no. 4 (1991), pp. 69–85

Farah, B. *From Ottoman Rule to a Hebrew State: The Life Story of a Communist and a Palestinian Patriot, 1910–1991*, al-Sawt, Haifa, 1985

Falk, R. 'Azmi Bishara, the Right of Resistance, and the Palestinian Ordeal', *Journal of Palestine Studies*, vol. 31, no. 2 (Winter 2002), pp. 19–33

Farsakh, L. *Palestinian Labour Migration to Israel: Labour, Land and Occupation*, Routledge, London and New York, 2005

Firro, K. *The Druzes in the Jewish State: A Brief History*, Brill, Leiden, 1999

Fischbach, M.R. *Records of Dispossession: Palestinian Refugee Property and the Arab-Israeli Conflict*, Columbia University Press, New York, 2003

Forman, G. 'Military Rule, Political Manipulation, and Jewish Settlment: Israeli Mechanisms for Controlling Nazareth in the 1950s', *Journal of Israeli History*, vol. 25, no. 2 (September 2006), pp. 335–59

Gadamer, H.-G. *Truth and Method*, Continuum, New York, 2004

Gertz, N. and Khleifi, G. *Palestinian Cinema: Landscape, Trauma and Memory*, Indiana University Press, Bloomington, 2008

Ghanem, A. *The Palestinian-Arab Minority in Israel, 1948–2000: A Political Study*, SUNY Press, New York, 2001

Ghanem, A. and Azaiza, F. *Is It Possible to Overcome the Crisis? The Arab Municipalities in Israel at the Beginning of the 21st Century*, Carmel, Jerusalem, 2008 (Hebrew)

Ghanem, A. and Ozacky-Lazar, S. *The Arabs in Israel under the Shadow of the Iraq War*, Institute for Peace Studies, Givat Haviva, 1991 (Hebrew)

Giladi, D. *Politics and Economy*, Tel Aviv University Press, Tel Aviv, 1998 (Hebrew)

Ginosar, Y. 'The Red Parcel in Sarya, the Devil's Daughter: A Chapter from a Woman and her Men in Emil Habibi's Work', *Iyunim be-Tekumat Israel* (a journal in Hebrew Studies in the History of Israel), vol. 10 (2000), pp. 592–9

Golan, A. 'The Settlement in the First Decade' in H. Yablonka and Z. Zameret (eds), *The First Decade, 1948–1958*, Yad Ben Zvi, Jerusalem, 1997, pp. 83–102 (Hebrew)

Greenstein, R. 'Israel/Palestine and the Apartheid Analogy: Critics, Apologists and Strategic Lessons', *Monthly Review* (August 2007)

Grossman, D. *Sleeping on a Wire: Conversations with Palestinians in Israel*, Vintage Books, London, 2010

Gubser, P. *Jordan: Crossroads of the Middle Eastern Events*, Westview Press, Boulder, 1982

Gur-Zeev, I. and Pappé, I. 'Beyond the Deconstruction of the Other's Collective Memory: Blueprints for Palestinian/Israeli Dialogue', *Theory, Culture & Society*, vol. 20, no. 1 (February 2003), pp. 93–108

Habas, B. *The Book of the Second Aliya*, Am Oved, Tel Aviv, 1947 (Hebrew)

Habiby, E. *The Secret Life of Saeed, the Pessoptimist*, trans. Salma Khadra Jayyusi and Trevor LeGassick, Zed Books, London, 1985

Haidar, A. *Obstacles for Economic Development in the Arab Sector in Israel*, The Arab-Jewish Institute for Development, Tel Aviv, 1994 (Hebrew)

—— *The First Book of Arab Society*, Van Leer, Jerusalem, 2005 (Hebrew)

Haj-Yahia, M. 'Beliefs about Wife Beating among Palestinian Women: The Influence of their Patriarchal Ideology', *Violence Against Women*, vol. 15 no. 5 (1998), pp. 533–58

Haj, Q. and Arar, K. 'The Movement of Arab Students in Israel to Jordanian Universities: Pull and Push Factors' in R. Khamaisi (ed.), *The Third Book on the Arab Society in Israel*, Van Leer, Jerusalem, 2009, pp. 227–51

Halabi, R. *Citizens of Equal Duties, Druze Identity and the Jewish State*, Kibbutz Meudad, Tel Aviv, 2006 (Hebrew)

Harel, I. *Security and Democracy*, Am Oved, Tel Aviv, 1989 (Hebrew)

Hassan, M. 'The Destruction of the City and the War against Memory: The Victorious and the Defeated', *Theory and Criticism*, vol. 27 (Autumn 2005), pp. 197–207 (Hebrew)

—— 'The Politics of Honour: Patriarchy, the State and the Honour Murders' in D. Izraeli (ed.), *Sex, Gender and Politics*, Hakibbutz Ha-Meuchad, Tel Aviv, 1999, pp. 267–307 (Hebrew)

Hasson, S. and Abu-Asbah, K. *Jews and Arabs in Israel Facing a Changing Reality: Dilemmas, Trends, Scenarios and Recommendations*, The Floersheimer Institute for Policy Studies, Jerusalem, 2003 (Hebrew)

Humphries, I. ' "A Muted Sort of Grief": Tales of Refuge in Nazareth (1948–2005)' in N. Masalha (ed.), *Catastrophe Remembered: Palestine, Israel and the Internal Refugees*, Zed Books, London, 2005, pp. 145–67

Jamal, A. 'The Arab Leadership in Israel: Ascendance and Fragmentation', *Journal of Palestine Studies*, vol. 35, no. 2 (Winter 2006), pp. 6–22

Jiryis, S. 'The Arabs in Israel, 1973–1979', *Journal of Palestine Studies*, vol. 8, no. 4 (Summer 1979), pp. 31–56

Kanaaneh, H. *A Doctor in the Galilee: The Life and Struggle of a Palestinian in Israel*, Pluto, London, 2008

Kaufman, I. *Arab National Communism in the Jewish State*, Miami, University of Florida Press, 1997

Khalidi, R. 'Sixty Years after the UN Partition Resolution: What Future for the Arab Economy in Israel?', *Journal of Palestine Studies*, vol. 37, no. 2 (Winter 2008), pp. 6–22

Khamaisi, R. 'The Arab Industry in Israel', MA thesis for the Technion in 1984 (Hebrew)

—— , *The Third Book on the Arab Society in Israel: Population, Society and Economy*, Van Leer Publications, Jerusalem, 2009 (Hebrew)

Khatib, S. 'The Future Visions of the Palestinian-Arabs in Defining the Conflict', *BADI's Publications*, Beit Lehem, 8 September 2009

Kook, R.B. *The Logic of Democratic Exclusion: African Americans in the United States and Palestinians Citizens in Israel*, Lexington Books, Boston, 2002

Korn, A. 'Crime and Law Enforcement in the Israeli Arab Population under the Military Government 1948–1966' in S.I. Troen and N. Lucas (eds), *Israel: The First Decade of Independence*, SUNY Press, New York, 1995, pp. 659–78

Laor, Y. 'A.B. Yehoshua and the "*Mizrachi* Animosity to the Arabs" ', *Mittam*, vol. 2 (2005; Hebrew)

Landau, J.M. *The Arab Minority in Israel, 1967–1991: Political Aspects*, Oxford University Press, Oxford, 1993

Lavie, S. 'Israeli Anthropology and American Anthropology', *Anthropology News*, vol. 46, no. 1 (January 2005), pp. 9–15

Levin-Epstein, N. and Semyonov, M. *The Arab Minority in Israel's Economy* and N.S. Eisendstat, *Israeli Society*, Weidenfeld and Nicolson, London, 1967

Linn, A. *Before the Tempest: Jews and Arabs between Hope and Despair*, Kineret, Tel Aviv, 1999 (Hebrew)

Lustick, I. *Arabs in the Jewish State: Israel's Control of a National Minority*, University of Texas Press, Austin, 1980

Manna, A. *History of Palestine in the Late Ottoman Period, 1700–1918*, Institute of Palestinian Studies, Beirut, 1999 (Arabic)

Manna, A. (ed.), *The Second Yearbook of the Arab Society in Israel*, Van Leer Publications, Jerusalem, 2008 (Hebrew)

Massad, J. 'Palestinians and the Limits of Radicalized Discourse', *Social Text*, no. 34 (1993), pp. 94–114

Masalha, N. *Expulsion of the Palestinians: The Concept of 'Transfer' in Zionist Political Thought, 1882–1948*, Institute of Palestine Studies, Washington, 1992

——, 'Operation Hafarferet and the Massacre of Kafr Qassem, October 1956', *The Arab Review* (Summer 1994), pp. 15–21

——, *A Land Without a People: Israel, Transfer and the Palestinians, 1949–96*, Faber and Faber, London, 1997

——, 'Present Absentees and Indigenous Resistance' in N. Masalha (ed.), *Catastrophe Remembered: Palestine, Israel and the Internal Refugees*, Zed Books, London, 2005, pp. 23–55

Mazawi, A.E. 'University Education, Credentialism and Social Stratification among Palestinian Arabs in Israel', *Higher Education*, vol. 29, no. 4 (June 1995), pp. 351–68

Meyer, T. *The Resurgence of the Muslims in Israel*, Institute for Arab Affairs, Givat Haviva, 1988 (Hebrew)

Migdal, J.S. 'State and Society in a Society without State' in G. Ben-Dor (ed.), *The Palestinians and the Middle East Conflict*, Tel Aviv University Publications, Tel Aviv, pp. 396–7

Mihsal, S. *West Bank/East Bank: The Palestinians in Jordan, 1949–1967*, Yale University Press, New Haven, 1978

Morris, B. *Israel's Border Wars, 1949–1956*, Clarendon Press, Oxford, 1993

—— *The Birth of the Palestinian Refugee Problem Revisited*, Cambridge University Press, Cambridge, 2003

Muslih, M. *The Origins of Palestinian Nationalism*, Institute of Palestine Studies, Washington DC, 1988

Mustafa, M. and Arar, K. 'Access of Minorities to Higher Education: The Case of the Arab Society in Israel' in R. Khamaisi (ed.), *The Third Book on the Arab Society in Israel*, Van Leer, Jerusalem, 2009, pp. 204–26 (Hebrew)

Nakhleh, K. 'The Direction of Local-level Conflict in Two Arab Villages in Israel', *American Enthnologist*, vol. 2, no. 3 (August 1975), pp. 497–516

Naqara, H. *Memoires*, unpublished manuscript

Natour, S. *Going on the Wind*, Kibbutz Meuhad, Tel Aviv, 1992 (Hebrew)

Ozacky-Lazar, S. 'Israeli Arab Positions towards the State, 1949–1967', MA Haifa University, 1990

Pappé, I. 'Moshe Sharett, David Ben-Gurion and the "Palestinian Option", 1948–1956', *Studies in Zionism*, vol. 7, no. 1 (1986), pp. 451–60

—— *The Making of the Arab-Israeli Conflict, 1947–51*, I.B. Tauris, London and New York, 1994.

——, 'An Uneasy Coexistence: Arabs and Jews in the First Decade of Statehood' in S.I. Troen and N. Lucas (eds), *Israel: The First Decade of Independence*, SUNY Press, New York, 1995, pp. 633–51

——, 'The Tantura Case in Israel: The Katz Research and Trial', *Journal of Palestine Studies*, vol. 30, no. 3 (Spring 2001), pp. 19–39

——, 'The Post-Zionist Discourse in Israel', *Holy Land Studies*, vol. 1, no. 1 (2002), pp. 3–20

—— 'The Square Circle: The Struggle for Survival of Traditional Zionism' in E. Nimni (ed.), *The Challenge of Post-Zionism: Alternatives to Israeli Fundamentalist Politics*, Zed Books, London, 2003, pp. 42–62

——, *The Modern Middle East*, 2nd edn, Routledge, London and New York, 2006

——, 'Post-Zionism and its Popular Cultures' in R. Stein and T. Swedenburg (eds), *Palestine, Israel, and the Politics of Popular of Culture*, Duke University Press, Durham, 2005, pp. 77–98

—— *The Ethnic Cleansing of Palestine*, Oneworld Publications, New York and London, 2006

—— 'The *Mukhabarat* State of Israel: A State of Oppression is not a State of Exception' in R. Lentin (ed.), *Thinking Palestine*, Zed Books, London, 2008, pp. 148–71

——, *The Modern Middle East*, Routledge, New York and London, 2nd edition, 2010

——, *Out of the Frame: The Struggle for Academic Freedom in Israel*, Pluto Press, London, 2010

Peled, Y. 'Meir Khana' in A. Ophir (ed.), *Fifty to Forty Eight: Critical Moments in the History of Israel*, Van Leer, Jerusalem, 1999, pp. 321–6

Peleg, I. 'Jewish–Palestinian Relations in Israel: From Hegemony to Equality?', *International Journal of Politics, Culture, and Society*, vol. 17, no. 3 (Spring 2004), pp. 415–37

Piterberg, G. *The Returns of Zionism: Myths, Politics and Scholarship in Israel*, Verso, London, 2008

Prior, M. 'Zionism and the Challenge of Historical Truth and Morality' in M. Prior (ed.), *Speaking the Truth about Zionism and Israel*, Melisende, London, 2004, pp. 27–37

Rabinowitz, D. 'The Palestinian Citizens of Israel, the Concept of Trapped Minority and the Discourse of Transnationalism in Anthropology', *Ethnic and Racial Studies*, vol. 24, no. 1 (1 January 2001), pp. 64–85

——, 'Oriental Othering and National Identity: A Review of Early Israeli Anthropological Studies of Palestinians', *Identities: Global Studies in Culture and Power*, vol. 9 (2002), pp. 305–24

Rabinowitz, D. and Abu Bakr, K. *Coffins on Our Shoulders: The Experience of the Palestinian Citizens of Israel*, University of California Press, Berkeley, 2005

Rattner A. and Fishman, G. *Justice for All? Arabs and Jews in the Israeli Justice System*, Center for Crime Investigation, Haifa University, 2001 (Hebrew)

Rekhess, E. *The Arab Minority in Israel: Between Communism and Nationalism 1965–1991*, Dayan Center Publication, Tel Aviv, 1992 (Hebrew)

——, 'Initial Israeli Policy Guidelines towards the Arab Minority, 1948–1949', in L.J. Silberstein, (ed.), *New Perspectives on Israeli History: The Early Years of the State*, New York University Press, New York, 1991, pp. 103–23

Reiter, Y. 'Nakba and Revival: A Zionist-Jewish Perspective on the Vision Documents of the Arabs in Israel' in S. Ozacky-Lazar and M. Kabha (eds), *Between Vision and Reality: The Vision Papers of the Arabs in Israel, 2006–2007*, The Citizens' Accord Forum, Jerusalem, 2008, pp. 140–58 (Hebrew)

Ricoeur, P. *The Conflict of Interpretations*, Northwestern University Press, Chicago, 1974

Rinawai, K. *The Arab Society in Israel: An Ambivalent Agenda*, The College for Management Publications, Tel Aviv, 2003 (Hebrew)

Rivlin G. and Oren E. (eds), *Ben-Gurion, The War of Independence: Ben-Gurion's Diary*, Ministry of Defense Publication: Tel Aviv, 1982

Rosenfeld, H. 'The Class Situation of the Arab National Minority in Israel', *Comparative Studies in Society and History*, vol. 20 (1978), pp. 374–407

Rosenthal, R. (ed.), *Kafr Qassem: Events and Myths*, Kibbutz Meuhad, Tel Aviv, 2000 (Hebrew)

Rouhana, N.N. 'The Political Transformation of the Palestinians in Israel: From Acquiescence to Challenge', *Journal of Palestine Studies*, vol. 18, no. 3 (Spring 1989), pp. 34–55

——, 'The Intifada and the Palestinians in Israel: Resurrecting the Green Line', *Journal of Palestine Studies*, vol. 19, no. 3 (Spring 1990), pp. 58–75

——, 'Accentuated Identities in Protracted Conflicts: The Collective Identity of the Palestinian Citizens in Israel', *Asian and African Studies*, vol. 27 (1993), pp. 97–127

——, *Palestinian Citizens in an Ethnic Jewish State: Identities in Conflict*, Yale University Press, New Haven, 1997

——, 'Interactive Conflict Resolution: Issues in Theory, Methodology and Evaluation', *International Conflict Resolutions after the Cold War*, Commission on Behavioral and Social Sciences and Education, New York (2000), pp. 294–337

Rouhana, N.N. and Ghanem, A. 'The Crisis of the Minorities in Ethnic States: The Case of the Palestinians in Israel', *International Journal of Middle East Studies*, vol. 30, no. 3 (August 1998), pp. 321–46

Rubinstein, A. *The Constitutional Law of the State of Israel*, Shoken, Tel Aviv, 1974 (Hebrew)

Ryan, J.L. 'Refugees within Israel: The Case of the Villages of Kafr Bir'im and Iqrit', *Journal of Palestine Studies*, vol. 2, no. 4 (Summer 1973), pp. 55–8

Sa'di, A.H. 'Modernization as an Explanatory Discourse of Zionist–Palestinian Relations', *British Journal of Middle East Studies*, vol. 24, no. 1 (May 1997), pp. 25–48

——, 'The Incorporation of the Palestinian Minority by the Israeli State, 1948–1970: On the Nature, Transformation and Constraints of Collaboration', *Social Text*, vol. 21, no. 2 (2003), pp. 75–94

Saban, I. 'Minority Rights in Deeply Divided Societies: A Framework for Analysis and the Case of the Arab-Palestinian Minority in Israel', *International Law and Politics*, vol. 36 (June 2005), pp. 885–1001

Said, E.W. 'Permission to Narrate', *Journal of Palestine Studies*, vol. 13, no. 3 (1984), pp. 27–48

——, *Culture and Imperialism*, First Vintage Books, London, 1994

Schnell, I. Benenson, I. and Sofer, M. 'The Spatial Pattern of Arab Industrial Markets in Israel', *Annals of the Association of American Geographers*, vol. 89, no. 2 (1999), pp. 331–6

Schnell, I. and Sofer, M. 'Embedding Entrepreneurship in Social Structure: Israeli Arab Entrepreneurship', *Journal of Urban and Regional Research*, vol. 2 (2003)

Schwartz, W. *The Arabs in Israel*, Faber and Faber, London, 1959

Segev, T. *1949: The First Israelis*, Henry Holt and Company, New York, 1986

Seligson, M.A. and Caspi, D. 'Arabs in Israel: Political Tolerance and Ethnic Conflict', *Journal of Applied Behavioral Science*, vol. 19, no. 1 (1983), pp. 55–66

Sella, R. *For the Public Eye: Photos of the Palestinians in the Israeli military Archives*, Helena, Tel Aviv, 2009 (Hebrew)

Shafir, G. and Peled, Y. *Being Israeli: The Dynamics of Multiple Citizenship*, Cambridge University Press, Cambridge, 2002

Shehadeh, A. *Capping the Development: The Economic Policy towards the Arab Minority in Israel*, Mada Carmel, Haifa, 2006 (Hebrew)

Shenhav, Y. *The Arab Jews: A Postcolonial Reading of Nationalism, Religion, and Ethnicity*, Stanford University Press, Stanford, 2006

Shilo, G. *The Arabs of Israel in the Eyes of the PLO and the Arab World*, Magnes, Jerusalem, 1982 (Hebrew)

Shlaim, A. 'The Oslo Accord', *Journal of Palestine Studies*, vol. 23, no. 3 (Spring 1994), pp. 24–40

Shohat, E. *Israeli Cinema, East/West and the Politics of Representation*, University of Texas Press, Austin, 1989

Shoughry, N. ' "Israeli-Arab" Political Mobilization: Between Acquiescence, Participation, and Resistance', PhD thesis, Aberystwyth University, 2010

Smooha, S. *Israel: Pluralism and Conflict*, University of California Press, Berkeley, 1978

—— , *The Orientation and Politicization of the Arab Minority in Israel*, The Arab Jewish Center, Haifa, 1984

—— , 'Ethnic Democracy: Israel as an Archetype', *Israel Studies*, vol. 2, no. 2 (Fall 1997), pp. 198–241

—— , 'The Model of Ethnic Democracy: Israel as a Jewish and Democratic State', *Nations and Nationalism*, vol. 8, no. 4 (2002), pp. 475–503

—— , 'The Israeli Palestinian-Arab Vision of a Binational Democracy', *Constellations*, vol. 16, no. 3 (September 2009), pp. 509–22

Smooha, S. and Cibulski, O. *Social Research on the Arabs in Israel, 1948–1976: Trends and Annotated Bibliography*, Turtledove Publishing, Ramat Gan, 1978 (Hebrew)

Smooha, S. and Peretz, D. 'The Arabs in Israel', *Journal of Conflict Resolution*, vol. 26, no. 3 (September 1982), pp. 451–84

Soffer, A. 'The Role of Demography and Territory in Jewish–Arab Relations in Israel', *Horizons in Geography*, nos. 60–61 (2004), pp. 492–515

Soja, E.W. *Thirdspace: Journeys to Los Angeles and Other Real-and-Imagined Places*, Wiley-Blackwell, London, 1996

Sorek, T. *Arab Soccer in a Jewish State: The Integrative Enclave*, Cambridge University Press, New York, 2007

Stendel, O. *The Arabs in Israel: A Political Study*, Sussex Academic Press, Brighton, 1996

Suleiman, R. 'Minority Self-categorization: The Case of Palestinians in Israel', *Peace and Conflict: Journal of Peace and Psychology*, vol. 8, no. 1 (March 2002), pp. 31–46

Tamari, S. 'What the Uprising Means', *Middle East Report*, no. 152, 'The Uprising', (May–June 1988), pp. 65–79

Totary, M. on the vision documents, a six-page response in Hebrew on the official website of Oranim College, www.oranim.ac.il/sites/heb

Yazbak, M. *Haifa in the Late Ottoman Period, 1864–1914: A Muslim Town in Transition*, Brill, Leiden, 1998

Yiftachel, O. 'Israeli Society and Jewish–Palestinian Reconciliation: "Ethnocracy" and its Territorial Contradictions', *Middle East Journal*, vol. 51, no. 4 (Autumn 1997), pp. 505–19

—— , 'The Day of the Land' in A. Ophir (ed.), *Fifty to Forty Eight: Critical Moments in the History of Israel*, Van Leer, Jerusalem, 1999, pp. 279–99 (Hebrew)

—— , 'Ethnocracy, Geography and Democracy: Comments on the Politics of the Judaization of the Land', *Alpaiym*, 19 (2000), pp. 78–105 (Hebrew)

Yiftachel, O. and Ghanem, A. 'Towards a Theory of Ethnocratic Regimes: Learning from the Judaization of Israel/Palestine' in E.P. Kaufmann, *Rethinking Ethnicity: Majority Groups and Dominant Minorities*, Routledge, London, 2004, pp. 179–97

Zayyad, T. 'The Fate of the Arabs in Israel', *Journal of Palestine Studies*, vol. 6, no. 1 (Autumn 1976), pp. 92–103

Zreik, R. 'Palestine, Apartheid, and the Rights Discourse', *Journal of Palestine Studies*, vol. 34, no. 1 (Autumn 2004), pp. 68–80

Zureik, E.T. *The Palestinians in Israel: A Study in Internal Colonialism*, Routledge and Kegan Paul, London, 1979

—— 'Demography and Transfer: Israel's Road to Nowhere', *Third World Quarterly*, vol. 24, no. 4 (August 2003), pp. 619–30

INDEX

water quotas 123
Weitz, Yosef 19
Weizman, Ezer 180
West, Cornel 154
West Bank
  administrative arrests 103
  Ariel Sharon 135, 137, 255
  attempts at segregation 28
  Binyamin Zeev Kahana 226
  checkpoints 71
  divided 194
  double pressures in 77
  Emergency Regulations 49, 273
  enlisting Jordanian support 77
  expulsion policy and 4, 5, 6
  first *Intifada* 172, 174
  immigrant workers 161
  Jaljulia siege and 3
  military rule 97
  military takeover contemplated 80
  Palestinian focus in 122
  Palestinian reunion 111–13
  PLO and 115, 134
  refugee camps 176
  segregation wall 245
  subtler approaches 153
  Triangle 27, 33
  Wadi Ara and 37
  Yoram Binur's travelogue 107
West Point 2
White House 170
Wikipedia, Hebrew 244
women
  Bedouin 210
  Coalition of Women for Peace 181
  feminism 75, 143, 180–1, 219–20,
    251–3
  growing employment
    opportunities 165
  Islam 177
  joint groups 180–1
  Nasser's rhetoric 95
  Palestinian women and their
    spouses 203
  post 1967: 100, 109
  post 1982: Lebanon war 151
  spinning mills 161, 252
  traditional Arab society 81
  triple marginality 284
  violence against in Palestinian
    society 199
  working outside the home 75
Workers' Day 80
writers 76–8, 188–9

Yafat al-Naserh 189, 229
Yani, Yani Kustandi 84, 85, 96
Yasin, Khayr Muhammad 132
Yazbak, Mahmoud 229, 285
Yazbak, Wesam 229
Yediot Achronot 130, 150, 228, 275
Yehoshua, A.B. 103, 190, 248
Yehoshua, Zahara 78
Yeruham 128
Yeshua 260
Yiftachel, Oren 285, 289
Yishai, Eli 3, 4, 7, 252
Yizhar, S. 139
Yonay, Yuval 190
Yosef, Rabbi Ovadia 224
Yugoslavia 76

Zahalka, Gamal 86
Zarim 29
Zaydan, Adil 189
Zaydani, Said 196, 284
Zayyad, Tawfiq
  arrested 81, 83
  barred from Hebrew University
    152
  Communist Party leader 68
  Nazareth elections 85, 96, 128
  poem 76
Zeydan, Muhammad 183
Zhubahain, Comrade 89
Zidani, Said 197
Zionists
  anthem at football matches 136
  Azmi Bishara 241
  Brit 72
  Christians and 67
  a colonialist movement 250
  Communist Party and 41, 68
  disregard for Palestinians 2, 11
  Hebrew Wikipedia 244
  Kevuzat 77 141
  land cultivation and 1
  left wing of 36, 217, 248
  naturalization policies 41
  neo-Zionism 223, 224, 226
  no room for minority 28
  non-Jewish citizens 35
  overriding ideological perspective
    13, 30
  peace camp 145
  Poland 32
  post-Zionists 144, 223, 286
  preparations for takeover of
    Zionists (*cont.*)
  Palestine 15

Printed and bound by CPI Group (UK) Ltd, Croydon, CR0 4YY

01/11/2024

14584863-0001